Palmer/Pletsch

COUTURE

TH[illegible] OF FINE SEWING

Roberta C. Carr

Edited by Pati Palmer
Associate Editors: Ann Hesse Price and Barbara Weiland

Book design, production coordination and editorial assistance: Linda Wisner

Technical Advisor: Marla Kazell
Metric Consultant: Nicki Young
Technical illustrations: Kate Pryka
Fashion illustration: Diane Russell Kramer
Fashion photography: Anthony Rush Ledbetter
Photographic stylist: Wendy Dreaney
Cover garment by Vicki Swalko.
Back cover garment by Nedra Michalek

This book is dedicated to my aunt, Mamie Droitcour Morrish, who, when I asked her in 1946 if she would teach me to sew, answered "yes."

To my mother, Helen Droitcour Smith, who tolerated threads on the floor, who expected the dining room table to serve as a cutting board and who encouraged and celebrated sewing as an ideal creative outlet and who probably also thought it an ideal way to get me to sit down for more than five minutes.

To my grandmother, Clara Palmer Carr, who took me to Boston to the "fancy" shops to see how "they" did it and who taught me to memorize color so clearly you could match something miles from the original color.

To my sister, Paula Carr Mitchell (Polly), who as a little girl could stand still while I "fitted" her. And who always loved what I made her and wore it! The ultimate compliment. Thank you.

To Julia Coburn, who at Tobe-Coburn School for Fashion Careers taught me the discipline of fashion; that the study of fashion did not mean "can I wear it?" or "do I like it?" but what is "in fashion"; what direction fashion is taking in color, fabric, silhouette and detail.

To Ann Hyde, who opened my eyes to the Couture, who taught me couture techniques, always insisting on perfection, and who introduced me to the world of fine fabrics.

To my good friend, Rena Shaefer, who said, "Why don't you open a fabric store, start a sewing school, make videos, write a book." "Do it—teach sewing." My grateful thanks for her encouragement, support, her faith, and her belief that I could do it.

These are the people who taught me, supported me, led me and always celebrated my interest in couture fashion and sewing. It is to these special friends and family that I dedicate this book.

And I would like to acknowledge:

Donna Shepard for her color photos of Théâtre de la Mode, and to Maryhill Museum of Art for the black & white images photographed by L. Sully-Jaulmes.
The houses of Christian LaCroix, Yves Saint Laurent and Nina Ricci for photographs and fashion art, and Butterick Company Inc. and Vogue Patterns for archive photos of designs by Dior, Grès and Paquin.
Lenore Hofmann for assistance and a meticulous attitude toward the original manuscript drawings.
Julie Moore for typing the original manuscript—on deadline!
Harrison Typesetting, Inc., for the final typeset pages.
And Cheryl Reed for willing and capable graphic production at all hours of the day and night.

Whenever brand names are mentioned, it is only to indicate to the consumer products which we have personally tested and with which we have been pleased. It is also meant to save our students time. There may be other products that are comparable to aid you in your sewing.

Library of Congress Catalog Card Number:
Published by Palmer/Pletsch Associates, P.O. Box 12046, Portland, OR 97212-0046. U.S.A.
Printed by Craftsman Press, Seattle, Washington. Separations and film work by Wy'East, Portland, OR.

ISBN 0-935278-28-1 softcover ISBN 0-935278-32-X hardcover

Foreword by Pati Palmer

Why would a sewer want to do couture work? Well, all you have to do is to meet Roberta Carr. You'll understand instantly. You'll see that it's pride. It's achievement. It's an attitude that enhances self-esteem. It means you are the best. After all, isn't that why clients of couture pay the price they do?

Today, couture not only exists in The Couture Houses in Paris, London, Milan, or New York; it also exists in **your home.**

There's a new breed of women sewing couture for themselves or their private clientele. Roberta C. Carr (Bobbie to her friends) has been a role model and teacher to many of them.

One of Bobbie's students, Marla Kazell, has spent several sessions studying under her. She now excels in sewing and fitting skills.

Marla is the "New Couturier," making a living doing quality sewing for those who appreciate and can afford excellence. Marla's couture clothes have been worn at the Multnomah Athletic Club Christmas Ball, a major social event in Portland.

I often thank Bobbie myself, because when I am too busy to get myself ready for a trade show or to fashion a wardrobe for a seminar, I can call on Marla for help, confident that she can handle **any** fabric or technique I may want her to use.

Sewing can be an isolated sport. There you are alone in your sewing room. But you are not alone. For the New Couturier, there is a worldwide organization for networking called The Professional Association of Custom Clothiers (PACC). To find out where there are chapters in the United States, Canada, and Australia or to form a chapter, write Kathleen Spike, National Chairperson, 1880 S.W. Heiney Rd., Gresham, OR 97080.

Also, the American Home Sewing and Craft Association (AHSCA), a trade organization of fabric, pattern, notions, and craft companies has added a new membership category for those teaching sewing. For information, write AHSCA, 1375 Broadway, New York, NY 10018.

Enjoy this book and join the "couture attitude" of which Bobbie speaks. This book will change your level of appreciation for the fine **art** of sewing and spending extra time to achieve perfection and special details. has for me.

Happy Sewing!

Pati Palmer

Pati Palmer, President
Palmer/Pletsch Publishing

About the Author

Roberta "Bobbie" Carr brings a fashion approach to home sewing. Since opening her store, The Fabric Carr, in Los Altos, California, in 1980, Bobbie has specialized in teaching the art of fine sewing in her design studio; in intensive, themed Sew Weeks; in seminars throughout the United States; and on video in her "Couture Techniques" series of six titles.

Bobbie began teaching these techniques after discovering that her customers were interested in creating unique designs with the fine fabrics they found at her shop. Her work with museum pieces had enabled her to learn original techniques of high-fashion designers, and she incorporated these into her classes. Soon after, she expanded her store to include a sewing school, and she began to offer fine sewing tools and books, a service which has grown into a mail-order catalog that is distributed internationally.

When she is not teaching in her own school, Bobbie may be heard lecturing in colleges and universities throughout the United States or presenting couture-sewing seminars in retail stores and to sewing guilds and Extension groups. She also has written articles for **Sew News**, **Vogue Patterns** magazine, the Singer Sewing Reference Library and **Threads** magazine.

Before starting her own business, Bobbie spent 15 years with the Girl Scouts of the United States of America, eventually rising to director of sales and marketing. But she also has an extensive background in fashion, sewing and retailing. She gained early experience at Saks Fifth Avenue and Macy's New York and San Francisco. She holds a home economics degree from the University of Rhode Island and studied at New York's Tobe-Coburn School. And Bobbie has been sewing since she was 8 years old, when she was taught by her aunt Mamie Droitcour Morrish, to whom this book is dedicated.

"Couture is like having a closet full of Rolls Royces. It's the height of one-up-manship. Where you go when you no longer need a label. What you wear when someone else's signature no longer suits you. It's the ultimate statement of "I can do it myself..." and better.

Paula Carr Mitchell
Glendale, California

About This Book...

Couture is an attitude. It's a way of thinking about sewing. As I write this book, I am thinking about you—the home sewer, the dressmaker, the teacher in locations around the world—Tucumcari, New Mexico; Lumpkin, Georgia; Quonochontaug, Rhode Island; Hollywood, California; Chicago, Illinois; Dallas, Texas; Sydney, Australia; Victoria, Canada; or right where you are.

Sit for a moment and peruse, or, in the middle of a sewing project, get this book out as a reference.

The subject is couture—not complex. It's about concepts—how to approach a technique, or a way of accomplishing a particular look. Yes, it's a "how-to" book, but I hope it's a "how-to-think" book as well.

Following a week-long couture sewing class, I asked Vicki Swalko, a student from Portland, Oregon, what she liked best about the class. She said, "You taught me how to think." I was astounded. What did she mean? She went on to explain that with each technique, I had given students the reasons why, the alternatives, when to use each one and the results to expect.

My philosophy is that there is no one way to do anything in couture sewing. Seamstresses create beautiful clothing by analyzing problems and choosing from alternative techniques, and then selecting the best solutions to create their version of perfection.

In preparing to write this book I labored over outlines and lists of couture techniques. They're all here, along with narrative, illustrations and photos.

When you have finished reading this book, I hope you, too, will "think" couture sewing and join me in thanking Vicki Swalko for her insight.

As you come upon something new, please read through it first. You see, I'm asking you to do this because I know how I look at the pictures. Take the bellows pocket (page 180) for instance. All those diagrams must mean bellows pockets take hours! Not true; 20 minutes of sewing time and you'll be a "couturier." And it will be fun, too. It's **never difficult** once you learn how to do it.

And then, I ask you to experiment. Let this book be a catalyst—a jumping-off point. Use any of the techniques and expand on them. You become the designer. The **couture concept** is a step that takes you beyond technique.

A final note: There may also be new words to learn with new pronunciations. To make it easier for you, we've added a chapter called "The Vocabulary of the Couture" beginning on page 34. Refer to it whenever you need to!

Roberta C. Carr

Roberta C. Carr

"Couture sewing for the home sewer means being able to build into wonderful fashions comfort and fit, bringing with it confidence, self-assurance and security in self."

Patricia Hauser
Bloomfield Hills, Michigan

Table of Contents

Christian Lacroix Haute Couture printemps Eté 1992
CX

CHAPTER 1

The Fantasy of The Couture

Couture! Just the sound of the word conjures up glamour—the finest—the best—fantasy. Yes! Couture is fantasy in so many ways. It's a dream, a vision, all those beautiful people in exotic places celebrating the happiness of life. Or is couture me or you or the lady next door? What is couture?

In its simplest form couture means to sew. **Haute couture**, or "high sewing" in French, means aura around the sewing—the fashion, the people, the designers, the artisans and craftspeople—who make **The Couture** more than an event. It's a way of life, an industry, a global affair.

Charles Worth is called the father of Couture, the originator of beautiful, custom-made dresses for the grand ladies of Paris. It is said there was a time when he made 1,000 dresses a week for women who wore a dress only once. It was the custom. It sounds extravagant today, but I'm glad those women didn't wear their clothes until they fell apart. Now we are able to see the **real** thing in museums around the world—laces and ruffles and petticoats—miles of chiffon with little hand stitches—beads—tucks—each so even and meticulous. The seamstresses must have been very disciplined. Work of such precision can only come from peace of mind.

I am reminded of a student who, when asked, "Have you taken any sewing classes?" answered, "No, I **only** learned from my grandmother." Oh, how lucky! Without realizing it, she had also learned from her grandmother's grandmother and her great-grandmother's grandmother, all the way back to the peace of mind of those tiny stitches. That's the essence of couture.

Mystery and intrigue—"**secrets**"—surround "**The Couture**." What goes on behind the closed doors of a couture house? Maybe volumes of precious fabric, a couturier dashing about, designs flowing from the mind and hand of this larger-than-life person, never ending creativity?

I know one thing for sure. Designers have a passion, a burning desire to create, to experiment, to try. In my study of The Couture and of specific designers, a common thread emerges. They wanted to design no matter what. Their families thought they should be doctors or lawyers or in the diplomatic corps—and some tried, but sooner or later, one way or another, they pursued their passion.

I know another thing for sure: home sewers, women of the 21st century also have a passion. Those who love to sew feel it deeply. Yes, there are other responsibilities, a complexity to our lives, time rushing on at breakneck speed, but the passion to sew is relentless.

Designs from Christian LaCroix

The couture house of Yves Saint Laurent, l'Avenue Marceau.

The couture house has as its leader the couturier. Then there are the patternmakers, seamstresses, tailors and fitters, each skilled in a particular aspect of sewing—beading, tailoring, hand finishing, working on chiffon or sculpting gazar (see page 34, Vocabulary of the Couture).

I'm always fascinated with the young girls just starting to work in a couture house who rush around Paris all day looking for ribbon or a flower in just the "right" color. The inventiveness of someone creating just the perfect accessory, the total look, that's couture.

Unlike the couturier who draws on the skills and talents of so many skilled assistants and artisans, the home sewer wears many hats; she does it all!! She's the couturier, the seamstress, the tailor, the hand finisher **and** the "little girl" that rushes about to find the perfect ribbon or lining or accessory.

As seamstresses, we look for direction, inspiration, and ideas from The Couture. As a child I always thought designers made some wonderful drawing on a piece of paper (always in sparkling color) and poof; like magic it became a dress. It never dawned on me that lines and designs might be tried over and over until they really worked or that the most fabulous fabric might not be suitable for a particular design.

I never realized that the support system, the underpinnings, were such an integral part of the beauty of the final costume. This was **not** done according to any standard, any textbook; it was inventive, the designer's solution to a problem.

If you ask contemporary designers to explain "The Couture," you will most likely hear things like it's a laboratory, a place for experimentation, an arena for the unique, an avenue for expression. The Couture is a world without restriction, no boundaries. There's no checkbook! Everything is possible in The Couture. Isn't that fantasy?

Sometimes I become a purist and am disturbed at the liberal use of the word couture. The media seems to think couture, when used as an adjective, automatically makes something greater—"better than." But no, haute couture is custom. It is handmade especially for only one person.

Who is the woman who "shops couture?" She is wealthy. (Having a couture dress made costs money—lots of it!) She lives all over the world. She's a princess; she's prominent; her lifestyle affords her the luxury of wearing couture clothes; she's seen in the right places; she **is**.

For a moment, let's follow this woman through the couture. She arrives in Paris with an entourage and stays at the Maurice, the Ritz or the Bristol Hotel. With her are maids, hairdressers, a secretary and whomever she needs to assist her in putting together her wardrobe, arranging the social aspects of her life, or simply taking care of her while in Paris.

Her first visit to the couture house is to view the current collection and plan her wardrobe selections. As a regular customer, her mannequin is there—a dress form exactly like her body, updated from time to time. If a dress she selects is close fitting, such as a strapless ball gown, the dress form will be compressed to reflect her body shape in such a costume. A piece of muslin is shaped and attached tightly to the dress form to simulate the effect of a strapless dress. (The original dress form is made to exactly imitate the client's shape.)

With her wardrobe selected from the current collection, the client will discuss colors, accessories, and how and where it will be worn.

While the couture house is making a toile—a muslin of the garment in her size—our "madame" is entertaining and being entertained in the social whirl of Parisian life.

The toile is sewn, shaped, tailored, molded and finished to look like the real thing. It is perfect and ready for a fitting.

Madame returns for the fitting. Every nuance is checked. The line, design, drape, fit, flare, and proportion. Adjustments are indicated—a nip here, a release there. It may take a few moments or a few hours.

Once the toile is fitted and marked, it is returned to flat (taken apart) and all corrections are meticulously made. Here's where the home sewer and The Couture part ways, having different priorities and allegiances. For the most part, I suspect the home sewer does not return a garment to flat every time a correction is made—and surely I do not recommend it. But I find it absolutely fascinating that such loyalty to perfection perseveres in The Couture.

At the couture house, the patternmaker, seamstresses, directress, and fitter are all involved. The couture dress is an evolution; it's theater with a cast of characters; it is an orchestrated production. In Paris, if the couture garment requires beading, it is sent to LeSage—the house famous for beading. They can create any motif—any illusion. LeSage is a womb; skilled seamstresses are sheltered in an old building in Paris—a hide-away..

Who could imagine that at the top of those worn stairs, alighting from an open elevator, one would find a giant part of the magic of couture. History is there, too! Monsieur LeSage, and his father before him, have kept a sample of every beading motif ever done by the house of LeSage.

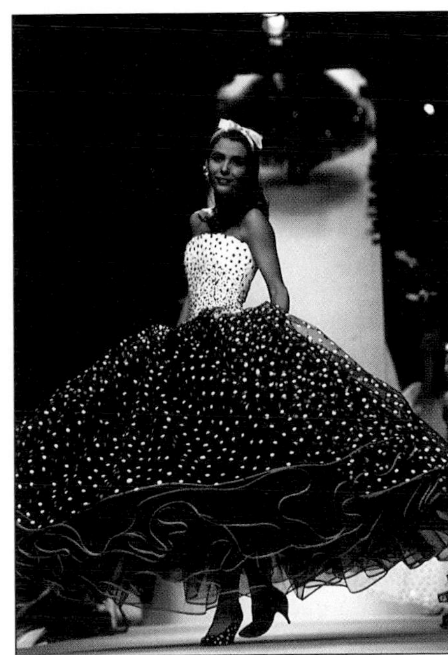

Designers on the runway...a coat and dress from the Christian LaCroix Winter 1987/88 collection above, and gown from Nina Ricci's Spring 1992 collection at right.

Once I asked M. LeSage if he had any of the pewter beading of Madame Vionnet. Well of course, there it was in the box marked 1937. And Chanel and LaCroix and Dior and—and—and—they were all represented in the "archives" of LeSage. There would be the real thing—not a photograph or a memory—but the actual piece to touch and feel and inspire contemporary designers. Talk about a kid in a candy shop! And I saw the beads! There are rooms full of them, and braid, and tassels and passementerie. Remember—nothing is impossible in The Couture.

While our "Madame Couture" is enjoying the palette of Paris—the museums, the shops, the restaurants, the aura, The Couture is working for her. Meanwhile, a shoemaker, an artisan with as much passion and skill in his hands as any couturier, is molding the perfect shoes—soft supple leather dyed-to-match a special dress— piped in gold—lined in satin.

At Hermes, a piece of luggage is being made to house her newest hat or shoes or handbag, perhaps in yellow leather to match "Madame's" trunks and suitcases.

Madame returns to the couture house for fittings and sees this beautiful creation emerge from a flat piece of fabric. It's a grey day in Paris. The sky and air and buildings are all one color—grey! Light, bright, grey—a oneness, a sameness. But, in the fitting room there is an excitement, color, a swish of taffeta to break the calmness, anticipation of the festivities to come.

"Couture sewing means creating with the best of fabrics, using the techniques of the Paris designers, outstanding workmanship, fine details inside and out, all combined with care, patience and time."

Nelda Jones
Campbell, California

CHAPTER 2

Couture Makes History

Artists of the cloth—that's how designers of couture shall be remembered. Charles Worth, as father of The Couture, took sewing, dressmaking—call it what you will—to a new height in the late 1860's. Clients of Worth were women of prominence. Their lifestyle was one of prestige and sometimes royalty. No matter who they were, they desired beautiful clothes.

The Couture has changed over the years. The lifestyles of the women who shop The Couture changed. Fashion has moved in many directions, but Couture is still Couture.

Couture is: creativity; freedom versus control; cut or shape; complex yet simple in appearance; evidence of effort; permanent; evolutionary; never ending; expression of a designer; detail; finishing; and who wears it. Couture has historical significance.

Yet The Couture of then and The Couture of now is vastly different. Years ago, the customer of the couture was an older woman whose prominence had been achieved. Today, the woman is of any age. Previously the couture client came mainly from Europe, but today she comes from every place in the world.

The Couture in the 21st century is truly global. In the early days of The Couture, there was great loyalty to one designer. Today, the woman shops with many different designers to create a wardrobe that serves the various aspects of her life. Secrecy was once the chosen attitude. Today, the press is welcomed. But the study of The Couture means understanding the history makers. Here is a synopsis of designers who in one way or another influenced other designers around the world, hence ALL of fashion.

Dior

Chanel had one of the longest reigns as a couturier. She was born in 1886 and died in 1971. By the time she was 20 years old, she had a hat shop in Paris and with time out during two world wars, she continued to influence fashion with her designs. Her influence is felt, even today.

Chanel was a feisty sort who loved to compete. She loved bright people and her intellectual thirst was satisfied by artists, writers who frequently "sat with her" on Sunday afternoons in her apartment. All entrepreneurs can take a lesson from Coco Chanel that the well of creativity needs to be filled on a regular basis.

Chanel had an inborn mental gift of knowing what women wanted. While realizing that women should always look elegant, she was part of a group of designers who pushed fashion into the 20th century.

Today we talk about having the sleeve touch the top of the wristbone to elongate the hand. It was Chanel who introduced this. She also thought pockets and buttons and buttonholes as a method of closure should be used.

Chanel created perfection with proportion. She will forever be remembered for the clean lines of the "Chanel jacket/suit," and its gold chain that weighted the back hem; the combination of fabrics, tweeds and wool jersey; horn-rimmed sunglasses and fake jewelry; and softness created by big bias bows at the neck.

To talk about The Couture is to talk about economics. A laboratory with no bottom line and a limitless checkbook is a concept in theory only. Someone has to pay the bills. There is no free lunch.

In the late 1920's, Chanel introduced Chanel #5 (her lucky number), a perfume that swept the globe. It was the perfume that made her and her company rich. It rapidly became a status symbol.

A friend of mine told me a wonderful story about when she arrived at college and her roommate's father sent her a huge bottle of Chanel #5. So large was this bottle that all the girls liberally used it for years. Decades later, when meeting for a reunion, it was not a surprise that they were all wearing Chanel #5. That is called "lasting quality." A compliment to Chanel and thank you to the dear father that sent it.

While Chanel had one of the longest careers, **Dior** had one of the shortest. Dior was born in1905 when Chanel was opening her millinery shop. Interestingly, the first designs Dior sold were hats. The House of Dior opened in 1947. Dior knew proportion, the lines of a seam, and most of all, the shape of a silhouette. He knew nothing about cutting or sewing which he left to his technical director, Mme. Marguerite Carré. She is a woman I have admired over the years. She was not introduced to the public until after Dior's death.

Dior's greatest success came immediately after World War II with the introduction of The New Look—a mid-calf pleated skirt, topped with a fitted jacket shown in a variety of designs. The skirts often had 220 yards of fabric, 350" (890 cm) at the hem and an inner structure to hold such a weighty garment. Often the fabric was completely underlined with tulle.

Dior loved ball gowns made of tulle, organza and alaskine. Custom-made corsets gave the foundation shape. For Dior, shape came first, fabric and color later. It has been said that muslins (toile) were stiffened before they were shown to Dior so the effect would be perfectly perceived.

Dior gave letter names to specific designs and subsequent collections. The "A-line", a chemise narrow at the shoulders and full at the hem, continues today as a classic term. The "H-line" was first introduced with the crossbar low on the body at the hip. This silhouette minimized the bust and elongated the body. The "Y" silhouette with slim hips was created with wide collars and low V-necklines.

Dior was one of the designers offering perfume (Miss Dior) as an adjunct to beautiful clothes. And, to add to the financial success of the House of Dior, the Dior name was licensed to companies making fur coats, hosiery and ready-to-wear.

Dior was a serious businessman who liked simple things and became one of the most famous designers of all time. Now, nearly 35 years after his death, The House of Dior continues to have global impact.

Upon Dior's death, a 21-year-old designer who had been an assistant was named the Head Designer, House of Dior. His name was **Yves Saint Laurent**.

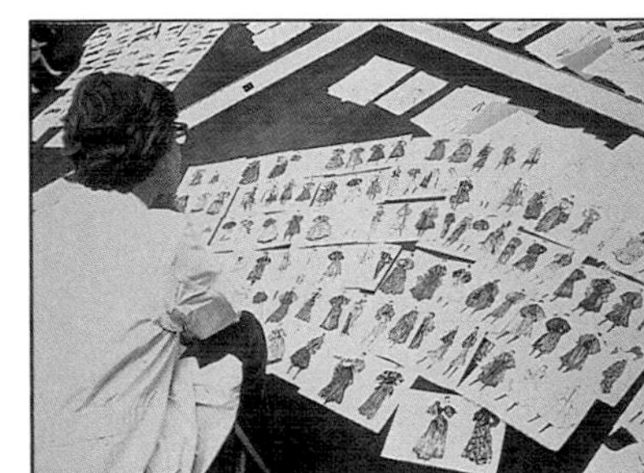

After several noticeable collections, and a stint in the French army, St. Laurent opened his own House in 1962. To this day it flourishes.

St. Laurent realized early on that the work of Haute Couture could not be duplicated in ready-to-wear. Thus he creates a special collection of prêt-à-porter designs that can be successfully made on machines and in quantity. But his Haute Couture collections continue the elegance, precision and timelessness of the passing face of fashion.

St. Laurent is a man of all seasons, a designer for all hours of a woman's life. St. Laurent has moved through the times of our lives and has transformed fashion.

A Picasso-inspired evening dress by St. Laurent gives us enthusiasm for art-to-wear. Beading of crystal or wood is a clear St. Laurent signature from the most extravagant dinner suits to an African summer dress with a bare midriff. A St. Laurent pant will surely make you a full 10' (3 meters) tall and look close to it. Elongated proportion often emerges in each collection in the form of a tuxedo shirt or variation thereof. Oh, yes, you'll find a circular ruffle here and there. Imagine white taffeta circular ruffles, bound with black satin—DRAMA! Ostrich feathers flutter, cotton pique is embroidered with crusty flowers. Bows are used on the shoulder of an evening dress in lieu of shoulder pads, Mondrian-inspired color blocking, leather applique, wedding dresses of silk ottoman, backless dresses, organza capes, St. Laurent is Couture...
Couture is St. Laurent.

"Robe Picasso" from Yves Saint Laurent Winter Collection, 1979-80.

At left, Saint Laurent "devant ses croquis".

Théâtre de la Mode

In May 1990, I had the great privilege of joining the Board of Trustees of Maryhill Museum of Art on a trip to Paris. It was a historic moment in the world of fashion and a great moment of reflection on times past. We were there to review the opening of Théâtre de la Mode.

Théâtre (tay-ah'-tra) *de la Mode* is an exhibit of couture clothes shown on miniature mannequins in a theater setting.

Imagine walking into the Louvre in darkened rooms, hushed silence and seeing the spotlights shining on 174 mannequins, each 27½" tall, dressed in the finest clothes that The Couture could produce in 1945. It was as if these slender people had come alive to tell us a story about World War II and what it did to the French fashion industry.

During World War II in Paris, the bitter cold, lack of food, the sadness of death that overshadowed everyone's life made existence more important than fashion in this world's fashion capital.

The German occupation of Paris and the persistence of their desire to move The Couture to Berlin was an ever present threat. The women of the resistance created "hats" and wore them around Paris to remind everyone of the fashion industry.

After Paris had been liberated with the war still going on, it was the concern for women and children that took priority. They needed relief. The organization *L'Entraide Francaise* was responsible for providing for those in need. The *Chambre Syndicale de la Couture Parisienne*, the organization that represents and markets the entire couture industry in France, was asked to help in hopes it would rekindle the fashion industry. (There was also concern that New York would become the fashion capital.)

In a remarkable cooperative effort, it was decided to combine art, theatre and haute couture in an exhibit of "dolls" dressed by the couture houses, put them in a theater setting and exhibit them to raise money for the relief.

Due to the shortage of fabric, it made sense for the clothes to be miniature versions of a full-size collection.

It was a magical evening on March 27, 1945, when in the Grand Gallery of the Louvre's Pavillon Marsan *Théâtre de la Mode* opened. Fifty-three designers contributed 150 costumes. They were displayed in 13 original sets complete with music.

At right, A Balenciaga evening dress in miniature.

Below, two of the incredible sets created for the exhibit.

Far right, a Lucile Manguin dinner dress.

Reports of the day told of a hushed silence as people, deprived for so long of glamour, beauty and joyful emotion gazed at these perfectly beautiful mannequins.

I had a similar sense of awe for both the mannequins and the people who came in 1990 to re-enact this historic event. The part that brought tears to my eyes was the old women in 21st century clothes wearing a hat of vintage fluff-feathers, a ribbon, a silk flower, that they saved all these years. A symbol so full of sentiment and hope, it could never be discarded.

In a much abbreviated version, I will tell you that the success of *Théâtre de la Mode* in Paris, grew to a world tour. It went to London, Leeds, Barcelona, Copenhagen, Stockholm, and Vienna. In the spring of 1946, the Chambre Syndicale updated the *Théâtre de la Mode* in the latest 1946 fashions, then sent them on tour of the United States. While admissions from both the European and U.S. tour generated funds for French war relief, the impact of the clothes, accessories, and sets firmly re-established the French as the fashion industry leaders.

The last venue for the exhibition was the De Young Museum in San Francisco. It was there that the exhibit closed and the mannequins were stored in a department store. The exhibit having served its purpose, the French sponsors saw no further reason to have it returned. Subsequently through a benefactor of both museums, the exhibit was donated to its current owners, Maryhill Museum of Art, Goldendale, Washington.

In 1983, Stanley Garfinkle of Kent State University "came upon" the mannequins in his quest to produce a documentary on Dior. What followed would take volumes to tell. A masterful plan with many people in the United States and France cooperating to return the mannequins to France for restoration, recreation of the lost sets, a world opening at the Louvre, Paris and a world tour.

Théâtre de la Mode is one of the greatest sources of inspiration for students, designers and for home sewers to see the **real** thing, the glory of The Couture: magnificent miniature buttons; hats; platform shoes; tiny gold buckles (all functional); the drape of a skirt; the roll of a collar; the match of a plaid; beaded fabrics; furs; jewels.

I couldn't take my eyes off the heads of these delicate mannequins. They are like petite sculptures with hair in every imaginable coiffure. I loved hearing the stories of the girls and women who were seamstresses for these fine clothes. One woman told us of the bias slip she put under one of the dresses. Another told us of a compact (with powder) she put into one of the handbags.

As I watched Elaine Bonabel put last-minute touches on these mannequins that she had sketched over 35 years ago, I saw the sentiment and the passion of couture. Her hand twisted and coaxed these little people as if they were all her own children.

As a student of fashion, I would direct you to the book **Théâtre de la Mode** published by Rizzoli International Publications, Inc., New York City, available from:

Maryhill Museum
35 Maryhill Museum Dr.
Goldendale, WA 98620
(509) 773-3733.

CHAPTER 3

The New Couturier

Couture is custom. Couture is giving a unique treatment to traditional details. Couture is creating an illusion. Couture is perfection in sewing.

A couturier is a designer in Paris whose atelier is a laboratory of experimentation **or** it is the home sewer or dressmaker in Palo Alto, California, or Portland, Oregon, from whose sewing room beautiful clothes emerge. The New Couturiers are just like you and me...students of sewing, designing and executing details with a fine hand.

I always get a little sad when someone says, "I don't sew because I don't have time." The people you see here are some of the busiest people I know.

Among them you will find mothers of new babies, entrepreneurs, managers, teachers, master volunteers, computer consultants, custom dressmakers, a geophysicist, a college professor and an author. All couturiers.

For example, there is Karen Dutch, member of a senior management team by day, new mother and wife all of the time, and she sews. She takes great pride in sewing and wearing her own couture clothing. Her husband is her main fan. Friends are in awe of her abilities and adore the results. She gets as many accolades from her sewing as her corporate expertise. Although it may sound like a cliche, sewing is Karen's creative outlet, her stress reliever, her way to keep reality in focus.

Ronda Chaney is currently the administrator/ chairman of the Fashion and Consumer Arts Department at Canada College, Redwood City, California. Ronda sews for herself. She epitomizes my belief that a teacher of sewing should always wear clothes she has made. By her presence, she is an inspiration to her students. Samples of techniques for classes, as labor intensive as they can be, keep Ronda's fervor for sewing alive. She, too, is a New Couturier.

Read about each of the contributors to the fashion section in this book on page 198. I have featured each one, giving you a little background. I am sure you will relate and become inspired never to say, "I don't have time to sew."

Cynthia Berry

Roberta Carr

Luanne Carson

Ronda Chaney

Karen Dutch

Barbara Frohman

Janet Ghilarducci

Patricia Hagen

Lenore Hofmann

Nelda Jones

Marla Kazell

Joy Lempert

Ruth Ann Loney

Paula Marineau

Mary Margaret

Carolyn Meyerhoffer

Nedra Michalek

Marcia Noulles

Mary Oliveri

Mary Ann Speith, PhD

Jean Sutherland

Vicki Swalko

Joan Venturi

Beaded appliques form a border down the front of this silk velvet jacket...and a pheasant flies across the shoulder. The skirt fabric is an unusual combination of silk taffeta interwoven with chenille. The ruffle at the hem is held out by tulle ruffles on a petticoat. The red of the silk jacquard blouse pulls the whole costume together, with bias ruffles framing the face and wrists.

The silk matelassé jacket was inspired by Christian LaCroix. A combination of flat and gathered ribbons (12 different kinds) were stitched to front and sleeve pieces prior to construction. The jacket closes with covered snaps that do not disturb symmetrical ribbon pattern. The wool crepe dress at right is yet another unique use of ribbon. *See page 110 for a close-up.*

The dress above is a mastery of design—10 yards of silk chiffon with satin and metallic stripes. It hangs straight in the front. The unlined (for "weightlessness") back is a series of quarter circles sewn together to chevron in the stripe and swing gently. To go under the back, a special slip was constructed to hang from a backless bra, adding form to the back of the dress.

At right, a silk velvet bodice sets off the unusual bubble skirt made from 6" squares of taffeta, sewn together to form fabric. Gathering stitches on all sides of each square are drawn up to form poufs.

I wore gown at left on New Year's Eve to The Hapsburg Ball in Vienna. The metallic gold crinkle fabric provides a high contrast to the black silk velvet bodice. Elastic in the sleeves hold them securely over the shoulders. My "couture secret"—shocking pink silk charmeuse lining! The ball gown at right is of a cranberry silk taffeta interwoven with velvet stripes and miniature black beads. Sleeves are on the bias.

The illusion of wide braided trim is created by wrapping Chanel lining to right side. Two thin braids are stitched down to form a frame.

Unique dimensional fabric—lace with ribbon inserted. Serge seams and outside edges for an easy finish—no interfacing, no facings, no major construction!

Another couture secret shocking pink tulle and double silk taffeta under a navy Alaskine dress. The beautiful ruffles are structural, holding garment away from body.

This shawl of silk brocade with silk charmeuse lining is finished with custom beaded tassels. Rectangle of fabric gathers into tassels at each end.

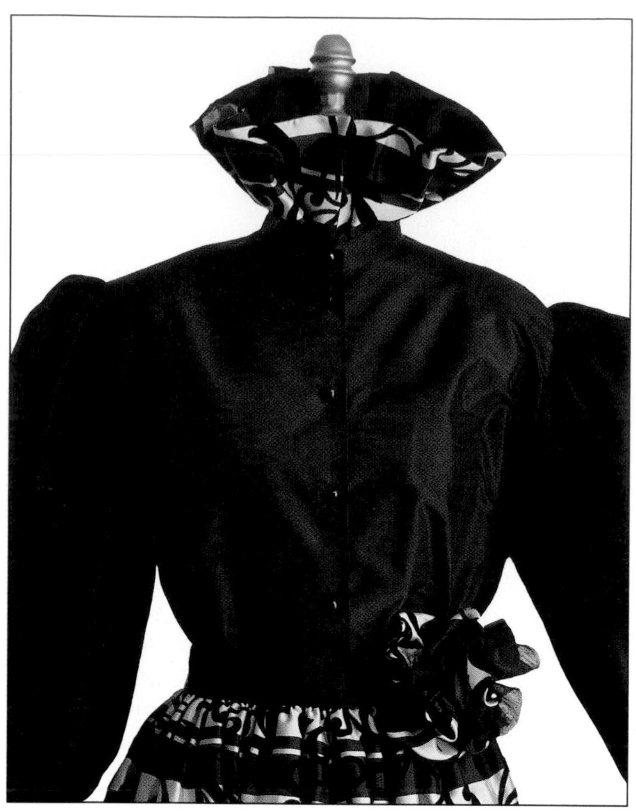

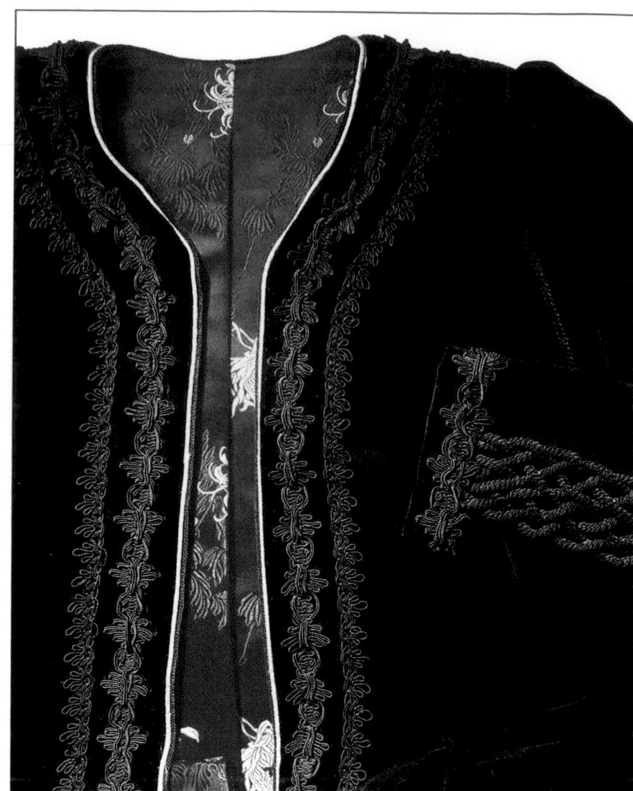

The dress of a Renaissance woman—with leg-o-mutton sleeves, a ruffled collar gathered in front and pleated in back and a fabric flower at the waist. Two-piece dress is of black taffeta combined with stripe with velvet "flocking." The dress below has a whole bouquet of Dior roses forming the bouffant sleeve.

Black braid, plaited and hand sewn into design drawn first on tracing paper, was inspired by a Japanese wedding sleeve. Double piping finishes edges.

More couture secrets—striped pantaloons under these wool crepe culottes. Gold ribbon hides outside seam. Inside is smooth against skin.

Here the theme is sewn-on "jewelry." The casually couture military dress is decorated with metal studs, braid, chains and coins. It is really a to-the-floor sweatshirt. Its channel stitched hem is double braided for weight.

Below, a simple top in wool doubleknit has ivory and bone trinkets sewn at the neckline. Rows of channel stitching stabilize the area.

The wool crepe jacket is given a military attitude with an assortment of ribbons layered on each other to form stripes. Eagle applique and crest complete the look. The Hong Kong bias finish on neck facing is of same fabric as lining. This jacket is worn with the culottes and pantaloons on page 22.

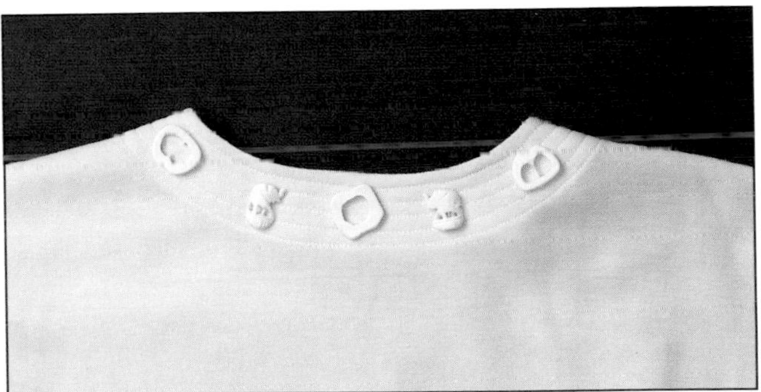

Piecing four colors of wool crepe creates striped effect on yoke and sleeves of the dress at left. Folded rectangles ("jaws") inserted in a piecing seam on the yoke form a foundation for the pin. Seminole patchwork was made for the cuffs.

The dress at right is of 100% Italian cotton jacquard. The dress hem and double sleeve hems are bias bound with self-fabric. Single fold bias is hand-stitched above the hem to create a double effect. The flower can be seen close-up on page 108.

Color blocking is the story here...asymmetrically in the dolman wool crepe tunic. Lapis buttons and coordinating silk charmeuse jacquard lining complete the look. Slot buttonholes are an unusual detail. In the pants a side seam insert incorporates a vertical slash pocket. At right, a totally different look is created using the same fabrics. Seams curving into the side seams provide fit for the bust without a dart. Bias cut sleeves hang perfectly. To complete the outfit—shoes dyed to a perfect match make the couture attitude come alive.

These two pages tell a story of coordinating fabrics. The 100% cotton plaid and rose print from Switzerland receives very different treatment from three different designers. At left the detail is at the neck—with a fabric rose and tiny tubes highlighting the plaid stand-up collar. Above left, bias binding of the print gives definition to the plaid bodice hem, and plaid binding gives contrast at sleeve hem. At right, the same fabric is used in an elongated bomber jacket. Bias ruffle in center seam of sleeve extends into shoulder and around the neck. Skirt is a ¾ circle, chevroned in front and finished with bias binding at the hem. An overlay of black ribbon enhances the plaid.

Sewing with leather, once you know the techniques, is not hard, and the couture result is worth it. At left, a tweed trench coat is given a classic touch with leather at cuffs, back, and a leather belt. At right, on the yoke of the Cabretta suit, tiny tucks are sewn with a double needle. Bound buttonholes are a finishing touch. Remember to save the scraps to make accessories. You'll need a special leather needle for your machine, a single hole throat plate, and a stitch length of 8-12 stitch per inch. Cotton thread is best. And don't pin into the garment area!

The look of the couture—a swing coat in a large hounds tooth check. The edges are bound in double bias self-fabric binding, giving a clean look inside and out, without lining. The cowl throw is attached at the center front seam. Coordinating culottes and silk blouse complete the outfit.

A beautiful couture detail, the heavy tassel adds weight to the tail of the cowl throw.

The flowing sleeves of soft silk crepe de chine drape beautifully, complimented by a series of tiny bias tubes and satin cord in random profusion. Slipstitch tubing in place to hold firm. Below, handwoven mohair gives this swing coat its couture attitude. The flange at the shoulder serves as shoulder pads.

Anytime you use a check, plaid or stripe, the edges need definition. Here self-fabric piping gives a clean edge, without contrast, to the silk & wool jacket. The Chinese ball button, made from tiny tubes of fabric, needs no buttonhole. A covered snap is the closure here. Below, ostrich feathers are the ultimate feminine touch on a wool crepe shawl.

Ten rows of topstitching create the couture detail on the flange of the wool doubleknit dolman dress at left. Topstitching rows are close together along the edge, further apart into the garment. The flange curves to form a pocket. At right, the unlined coat shows off a big plaid. The edges are bound with double bias binding cut six times the finished width.

In this dress a "new" fabric has been created. By layering two semi-sheer stripes at right angles, one pink & white, one lavender & white, a mauve plaid emerges, shifting as it is viewed from different angles.

The fantasy "boa" is a circular ruffle (page 117) with the same perpendicular layering of fabrics and horse hair in the outside edge for structure.

CHAPTER 4

The "Rules" of Couture

In the couture houses of Paris, seamstresses have historically been sworn to secrecy. It is said that if a seamstress ever divulged a design or method, she would not only be fired, she would never be hired by any other couture house. The loyalty of these seamstresses often meant they went to their grave with this secret knowledge intact.

How then does the world at large discover "how it's done"? Today we are fortunate that the masterpieces of the couture are in museums and schools for teachers and students to see, feel, and examine in order to learn how to execute couture techniques.

A study of the couture is not a lesson in how to sew—but how to think. It goes beyond how it's done, to when, where, under which circumstances and why. I often tell my students that The Couture is alternatives—choices, knowing many different ways to do the same thing. It's understanding fabric, letting it talk to you. It's visualization, knowing in your mind what something will look like before it's ever sewn. Couture is experience. After making something once, you know how it will work. Being skilled at constructing many kinds of buttonholes or pockets or seam finishes allows you to choose the perfect application for the design at hand. Couture is freedom. Couture is an art.

Couture is the "ultimate" in quality sewing. Couture techniques are the formal elements of the art of sewing. Couture techniques may sound cut and dried, but they do require judgment. Within every couture technique there are the variables of fabric, size, support, and who will wear it. Thus, there are very few "always" or "never" couture rules.

Somehow, we all want rules, standards to judge success, benchmarks. Here are a few that never change.

The Rules of Couture

1. **Sew with your head.**
2. **Maintain accuracy.**
3. **Let grain be paramount in all decisions.**
4. **Talk to the fabric and listen to the fabric talking to you.**
5. **Reduce bulk wherever possible.**
6. **Understand that couture requires judgment.**
7. **Know that your hands are your best sewing tools.**
8. **Accept the fact that pressing and sewing are synonymous.**
9. **Anticipate that the final garment will show "evidence of effort."**
10. **Enjoy the process as well as the result.**

"Couture is almost a way of life: paying attention to detail, but in an elegant, almost relaxed manner. It means using the finest materials, especially in 'hidden' areas, combined with flawless technique into a perfectly fitting garment..."

Mary Ann Speith, Altadena, California

CHAPTER 5

The Vocabulary of The Couture

Sometimes it seems The Couture has a language all its own. I have created here a glossary of the words you will find sprinkled throughout this book. Some will be familiar to you, others new and exotic!

Atelier—Workroom; the place where seamstresses and tailors work to produce couture clothes.

Bellows Pocket—A form of a patch pocket which has concealed pleats on two sides and the bottom which expand when used, but lie flat when not in use. Commonly seen on "safari" type garments.

Bias—A grain of fabric 45° between the lengthwise and cross grains. In Australia bias is often called "The Cross".

Bias Maker—a device that channels bias fabric strips entering flat and exiting folded; fold is made permanent by simultaneously pressing with heat and steam of an iron as fabric exits the device.

Boa—A long scarf-like garment; can be made of fabric cut in circles.

Couture—To sew; The arena of fashion in Paris, France.

Bound Buttonhole—A buttonhole made of fabric which can take a variety of shapes.

Catch Stitch—A series of stitches that look like a series of X's; can have narrow width at top of X, wider at the bottom, or even as if filling a square.

Channel Stitching—multiple rows of machine stitching with or without a batting type filling to create a quilted effect.

Circular Buttonhole—A form of a bound buttonhole made in the shape of a circle.

Circular Ruffle—A ruffle or flounce made from a series of circles thus utilizing all grains of the fabric.

Clapper—An oblong piece of wood with one end narrower than the other. The hollow sides allow for a firm grip. Top and bottom are perfectly flat. Used to flatten seams, pleats or permanent creases.

Clip—A process of cutting into a seam (usually on a curve) to allow the seam to lie flat for pressing.

Cowl—An extended neckline cut in one with the garment so that the bias grain is directly on the center front and on the neckline which is at right angles to the center front; fabric drapes in soft folds appearing as a scarf. Can also be achieved in the back of a garment.

Cross Baste—A method of basting in both horizontal and vertical directions to hold fabric flat for intricate stitching.

Crosswise Grain—The grain perpendicular to the lengthwise grain.

Dart—A pointed end, shaped tuck, often originating in a seam, used to provide fullness in the body of a garment.

Diagonal Basting—Rows of basting that appear in a diagonal design.

Dior Rose—Fabric flower made of bias-cut football shapes in matching or contrasting fabric.

Dolman Sleeve—A sleeve cut in one with the garment; the shoulder seam continues down the center of the sleeve to the wrist.

Double Needle—A sewing machine needle with one shank and two needles extending from it; requires two spools of thread on the top of the machine and one bobbin thread. Sole plate of machine must have oval opening. Double-needle tucking (pg. 67).

Ease Stitches—Multiple rows of machine stitches (6 stitches per inch) placed within the seam allowance. The process of putting the fabric through the machine usually draws up the fabric enough that excess fabric in the seam allowance can be shrunk out with steam, allowing the piece to be sewn without evidence of gathers. Easing allows one garment piece to be slightly fuller than the other to follow body contours (as in back shoulder seam eased onto smaller front shoulder seam). Sleeve cap easing requires that stitches be drawn up slightly to match garment measurement before permanent stitching.

Fashion Ruler—A form of a french curve invented by Leona Rochas, USA, which duplicates all curves and lines needed in flat pattern development or alteration.

Float Stitch—Attaches two pieces of fabric in such a way that one floats against the other; used to attach interfacing to a garment, and hem to interfacing or garment. A float stitch guarantees no show through. A continuous forward moving stitch is taken with a pick of a fiber on one side (garment) and another pick on the hem (about $^3/_8$"-$^1/_2$" apart).

Flounce—Decoration used at neck, wrist or hem; fabric is cut in circles and is sometimes called circular ruffles.

French Chain—A chain made of hand sewing thread; can be used instead of a metal eye (hook & eye); one end can be attached to hem of garment, the other to lining to prevent separation.

French Curve—A sewing tool that duplicates body curves; used in flat pattern and design adjustments in fabric.

French Dart—A dart of significant length originating on the side seam just above, at, or below the waist. A French dart can be straight or curved to produce a unique design line.

French Seam—An enclosed seam which is sewn to the outside first, seam allowance removed and resewn to the inside. The width of a French seam can be as narrow as the fabric will allow.

Gathering—The process of condensing fabric to achieve fullness by machine stitching multiple rows with the seam allowance (usually at 6 stitches per inch) and then pulling up bobbin threads to desired fullness.

Gazar—100% silk; wirelike stiff fabric with a crisp hand that lends itself to fullness.

Godet—A triangular piece of fabric (a section of a circle) inserted into fabric or a seam to add fullness to a hem, usually put in skirts and sleeves.

Grade—The art of making multiple seams different widths so that no excessive bulk or ridge is evident from the outside of the garment.

Grainboard—A padded wooden surface of significant size (usually 36″ × 54″) used as a cutting and pressing surface. A grainboard cover—printed with 1″ grid marks—can be used as a final surface.

Ham—An oval padded shape (actually resembles a ham roast) that can be turned to re-create curves on the human body. Used as a pressing surface it creates and retains prescribed shape as with darts, sleeve caps, collar rolls, and all curved seams. One side wool, the other cotton.

Ham Holder—A molded plastic shape that holds a ham in any position, leaving both hands free to do the necessary work.

Haute Couture—The best of Couture; the finest sewing; custom made.

Hong Kong Seam—Bias bound seam edge with double-fold bias strips.

Mock Hong Kong Seam—Bias bound seam edge with only one edge folded and machine stitched; seam is wrapped with back side flat.

Interfacing—A fabric specially designed to give a degree of stability or stiffness. Interfacing can be of woven or non-woven material and sew-in or fusible. Commonly used interfacings in the Couture:

Armo Weft—Fusible, knit, 60% polyester, 40% Rayon—This fusible interfacing can give you the look of custom tailoring. Especially designed for medium weight fabrics, choose Armo Weft for suit jackets and coats as a substitute for hair canvas as when you are using speed tailoring methods. Pre-shrink by dip method.

Armo Wool—100% wool, woven, pre-shrink by steam pressing. This gauze-like wool's loosely woven form is perfect for sleeve heads in tailored garments.

Batiste—100% cotton, woven. Cotton batiste can be imported or domestic, and comes sheer (almost like chiffon) to opaque, which can be used for blouses/dresses. Batiste also makes a wonderful soft interfacing. Use with silk crepe de Chine for front facings. It holds a buttonhole perfectly. Use on the bias for a soft rolled collar. Use as a foundation for a fusible interfacing when you can't fuse directly to your fabric. Pre-shrink by machine wash method.

Elephant Flannel—100% cotton, woven. An often neglected fabulous interfacing. Can be used to pad shoulder area of tailored garments; particularly good to add density to an area without bulk such as in yokes. Takes well to channel stitching-can be used to pad armscye edge of shoulder pads for the new soft, rounded look. Pre-shrink by machine wash method.

Hair Canvas—Custom tailoring interfacing, usually a blend of wool, rabbit hair, goat hair and maybe a little linen or rayon. The advantages of these types of interfacings are:

- woven on grain
- can be shaped with steam and it will stay
- can be effectively used on the bias
- are long lasting

Use hand method of applying. Steam press to pre-shrink using a very damp press cloth and lots of steam.

Knit Fuze—Knit construction, fusible, 100% nylon Tricot. This is a luxuriously soft fusible for both knits and wovens. It will add soft support for all light and medium weight fabrics. When used on knit fabrics, it allows you to maintain crosswise stretch while retaining lengthwise stability. Knit Fuze is particularly good to use when you want to fuse interfacing to a whole garment piece such as a jacket front. It will stabilize an otherwise soft fabric. Pre-shrink by dip method.

Kuffner—100% cotton, woven, fusible. While all other interfacings are of themselves the stiffening agent, Kuffner takes its direction from the fabric. In other words, it makes a fabric "more so". Therefore, on cotton, it makes it a little stiffer, on linen it makes linen stiffer. It might be called the universal interfacing. Works wonderfully used on the bias. Takes channel stitching without puckering. It's terrific for waistbands. For an even stiffer waistband, apply to fashion fabric, then apply a second layer of Kuffner over the first, making it $^{1}/_{8}$" smaller on all edges. Kuffner is an exception to other fusibles as it does not need to be included in the seam allowance. Use dip method of pre-shrinking.

Silk Organza—100% silk, woven, sew-in. An excellent interfacing for silk and silk-like fabrics; stable, closely woven. Can also be used as an underlining for wool, linen, silk. Machine wash to pre-shrink (will get very soft) or steam press (will stay stiff).

Silk Weight Interfacing—Fusible, woven, 100% cotton. Very sheer! Woven 100% cotton allows you to cut on grain or use bias. It is so sheer the fusing beads are hard to see (use your fingers to feel the beds). Can be used on silks and sheers to give just a hint of body. Pre-shrink by dip method.

Sof Shape—Non-woven, fusible, 100% nylon. The unique quality of Sof-Shape is that it is all bias. No matter how you cut your pieces, you will automatically get bias. It is particularly good to use on light weight fabrics where you want soft rolls and gentle stability without stiffness (light weight wood, challis, cotton). Pre-shrink by dip method.

Touch of Gold—100% rayon, fusible, extremely light weight; can be fused at low temperatures; can be re-fused after washing or dry cleaning; suitable for very light weight fabrics.

Whisper Weft—Fusible, knit, 60% polyester, 40% rayon. The unique knit construction of this interfacing gives you the ability to shape, roll a lapel and get good stability all at the same time. The soft flexibility allows you to achieve the couture look. Whisper Weft works well on a variety of fabrics: light weight wool, dress linen, silk suiting. Whisper Weft is lighter weight than Armo Weft. Pre-shrink by dip method.

June Tailor Board—Odd-shaped wooden pressing tool has five balanced positions and 12 different shapes.

Kimono Sleeve—Similar to dolman, except that shoulder and sleeve are at right angles to the center front of the garment.

Lapel Roll—A padded tube which, when inserted under a rolled collar or lapel, provides shape for final pressing.

Lengthwise Grain—That grain, commonly called straight grain, parallel to the selvage of the fabric.

Loft—The amount the sleeve cap rises and extends past the natural shoulder line. Loft requires support of a sleeve head, specific to the sleeve design, which is added during construction.

Mannequin—Dress form custom made for a private client.

Meld—Pressing machine stitched threads, both upper and bobbin thread, immediately after stitching. This process imbeds the threads into the fabric and allows seam to be pressed open with no bulk.

Mitering—Joining two pieces of fabric at a corner to produce a sharp, non-bulky point or corner. Mitered corners can be executed in seams as on a pocket or in facings as on a sleeve vent.

Off-Grain—Those outside edges of garments (front edges, slits or pleat edges) that are purposely cut off the exact lengthwise grain while the garment itself maintains the original straight grain.

Overcast Stitch—Hand stitch used to finish raw edges (usually seams) to prevent raveling.

Piping—A bias fabric strip wrapped around a cord, machine stitched, usually with a zipper foot, close to the cord, leaving raw edges free to be stitched between two pieces of fabric; commercial piping (ready-made) is often braid or cord with pre-attached seam allowance.

Pocket—A piece of fabric applied to the right side of a garment (called patch) or to the wrong side of a garment with constructed opening (side seam, welt).

Pocket Pouch—The portion of a pocket, not visible from the outside that holds items.

Point Presser/Pounding Block—A pointed piece of wood on top of wooden clapper. Used to open seams when a crisp flat seam is desired (eliminates seams showing through to right side). The lower edge is used as a pounding block to "hit" in a rhythmic motion thick fabric which requires pressure to flatten bulk—as on a tailored lapel, hem edge or collar.

Pre-Shrinking—The process of preparing fabric by washing or steam pressing to remove residual shrinkage prior to cutting out a garment; applies to fabric interfacing and underlining materials.

Pressing Mitt—A padded pot holder with inside pocket for hand to prevent burning. Can be inserted under fabric as in a sleeve to allow steaming from the right side of a garment. A pressing mitt can be slipped over a sleeve board to recreate the shape of a ham.

Press Cloth—A layer of protective fabric placed between the garment (fabric) and an iron. The thickness, fiber content and ability to absorb moisture is chosen in relation to the desired result.

Prêt-à-Porter—Ready-to wear; clothes designed by a Couturier and mass distributed to high fashion retail stores and boutiques all over the world.

Princess Line—A seam originating in either the shoulder or armhole crossing the apex of the bust (bust point) and extending to waist or hem of a garment.

Raglan Sleeve—A sleeve which extends into the neckline from a straight line originating in the armhole curve.

Ruffle—A piece of fabric, single or double, gathered on one edge, finished on the other, which when gathered is inserted or attached to any edge of a garment.

Saddle Stitching—Hand topstitching of considerable length in even in/out rhythm

Seam Roll—Oblong padded cylinder, one half covered in wool, the second half covered in cotton. Used for pressing seams open with the advantage of preventing seam ridges from showing through to the right side.

Seminole Patchwork—A method of piecing multi-colored fabrics to form a geometric design; originally developed by the Seminole Indians, Florida; more recently introduced to Art/Clothing enthusiasts by Cheryl Grieder Bradkin.

Shoulder Pad—Wadding or premolded material shaped to follow the shoulder contour. Size and thickness is relative to garment design and body of wearer. The purpose of a shoulder pad is to smooth, enhance, support and sustain the intended line of a shoulder in a specific design.

Single-Thread Dart—A dart sewn from the point after the bobbin thread has been wound onto the top spool, thus no loose threads appear at the point.

Sleeveboard—A small firm and lightly padded board narrow enough to slip into a sleeve, can also be used with pant leg; the pressing surface can also be used for necklines, shoulder seams and hard to reach areas.

Sleeve Head—A piece of fabric or interfacing attached to the cap of a sleeve to give support or maintain smoothness.

Slipstitch Baste—The recommended method for couture basting; seams are folded one over the other from the right side. Needle is inserted into one seam and immediately into the fold for $^3/_8$"-$^1/_2$". Basting stitches form a line on the wrong side of the fabric to be used as a guide for machine stitching. Using contrasting colored thread makes it easy to see.

Slipstitch—(See slipstitch baste) A hand stitch exactly like slipstitch baste but used for permanence to hold two pieces of fabric together.

Slot Seam—A seam which is basted, pressed open, a separate piece of fabric is laid behind seam, topstitched from right side before basting is removed (see welt seam).

Spanish Snap Buttonhole—A tiny, thin bound buttonhole made with a single piece of bias fabric.

Stab Stitch—A hand stitch that permanently attaches two seams together so they are perfectly matched and "wedded" together. Needle is inserted straight down between machine stitches so that it penetrates both seams exactly in the well of the seam (the stitching line). The second stitch reverses coming back in opposite direction.

Strapped-Cap Sleeve—Cut in one piece for short sleeves, two pieces for long sleeves, it gives the appearance of a strap or band across the cap of the sleeve.

Taut—The process of holding work (fabric) flat without stretching as it passes through the feed dog of a sewing machine; a method of preventing puckers on machine sewn seams.

Thread Tracing—A method of tracing stitching lines and construction marks using hand needle and thread.

Toile—A muslin of a specific garment finished as it will be worn.

Triangular Buttonhole—A form of a bound buttonhole made in the shape of a triangle.

Trim—Removing a portion of a seam by cutting off (usually where two seams cross).

Tulip Sleeve—A short sleeve with wrapped cap; looks like a tulip.

Underlining—A lightweight fabric such as silk organza, silk chiffon or sheer cotton batiste which is cut exactly like garment pieces, hand basted to the fashion fabric and thus treated as one throughout construction; underlining can be left in or removed from seam allowances depending on desired result or technique being used.

Velvaboard—A pressing surface designed to return rather than absorb moisture while pressing. Especially effective when used with napped fabrics such as velvet and corduroy.

Welt Pocket—A pocket using a separate piece of fabric inserted in a garment similar to a bound buttonhole opening.

Welt Seam—A traditional seam pressed open or to one side and topstitched from the right side in one or more parallel rows.

Whip Stitch—Very small diagonal basting.

Zipper Foot—A machine foot with one side only allowing needle to stitch close to zipper teeth.

CHAPTER 6

The Anatomy of a Couture Garment

Often, the structure of a couture garment goes beyond the obvious, beyond fabulous fabrics, beyond the beautiful finishing touches. The whole structure becomes couture.

The designer takes into account the shape of the person who will wear the garment, the curves over which it will be flowing, and the shape of the design itself. This dress and jacket was inspired by Dior. Worn by my friend Rena Shaefer to the Hapsburg Ball in Vienna Austria on New Year's Eve, it evolved beyond the original Vogue pattern it was based on.

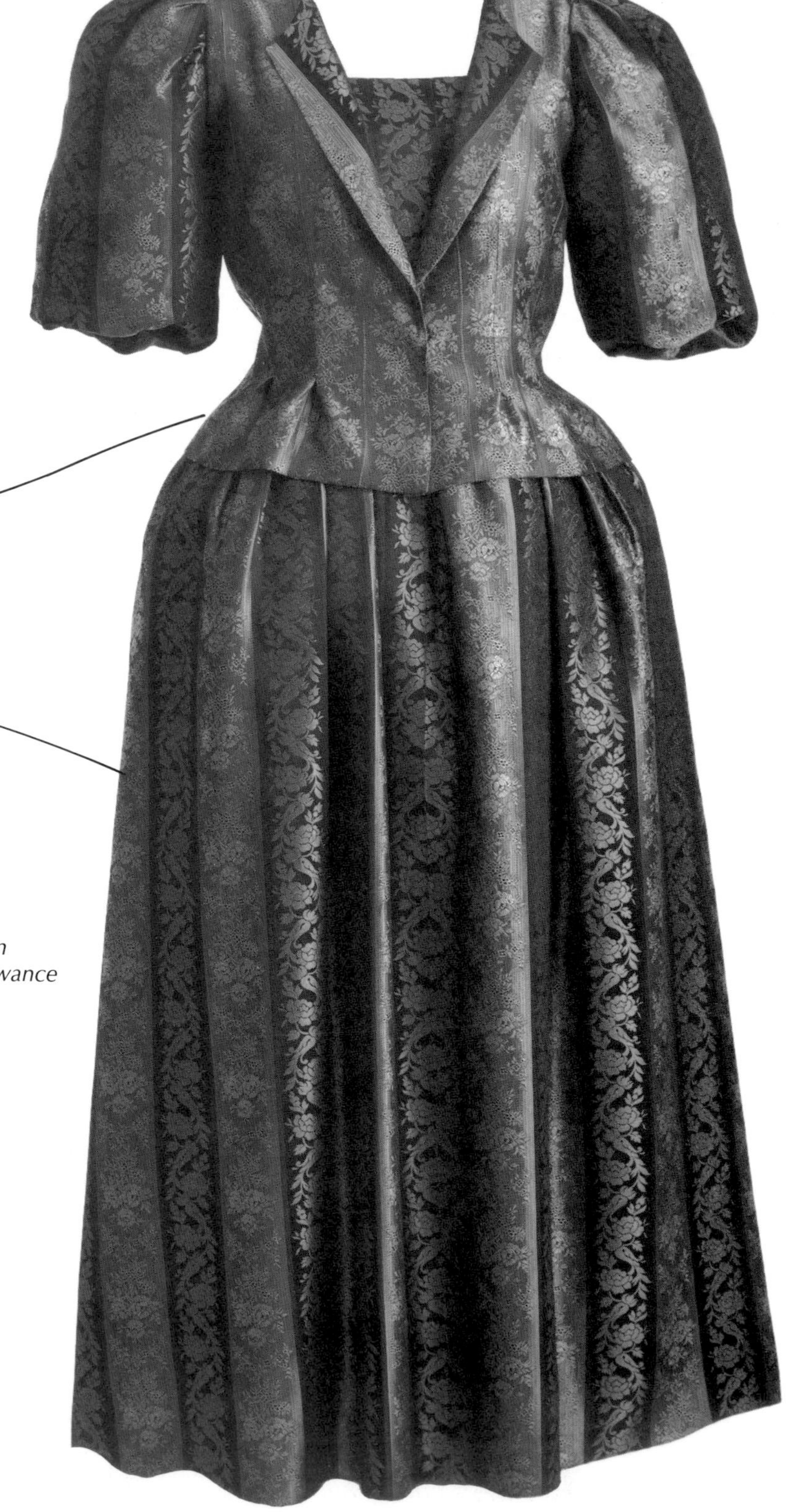

The rayon and silk jacquard stripe fabric became an inspiration. Pleating out stripes and colors creates whole new fabrics. All the black stripes have been pleated out of the jacket fabric. In the bodice of the dress the reverse was done, creating a dark contrast to the rest of the garment. The skirt reveals the original fabric. You can see other examples of this in the color section of this book on pages 102, 103 and 111.

skirt

seam allowance

attached here

silk organza

sewn to garment edge here

No hem stitches show on this garment, hampering the flow of the skirt. Instead, a floating hem has been used. Silk organza sewn to bottom raw edge of the garment creates an underskirt that is attached only to the seam allowances of the skirt, up near the hips, where the weight will not affect the drape of the fabric.

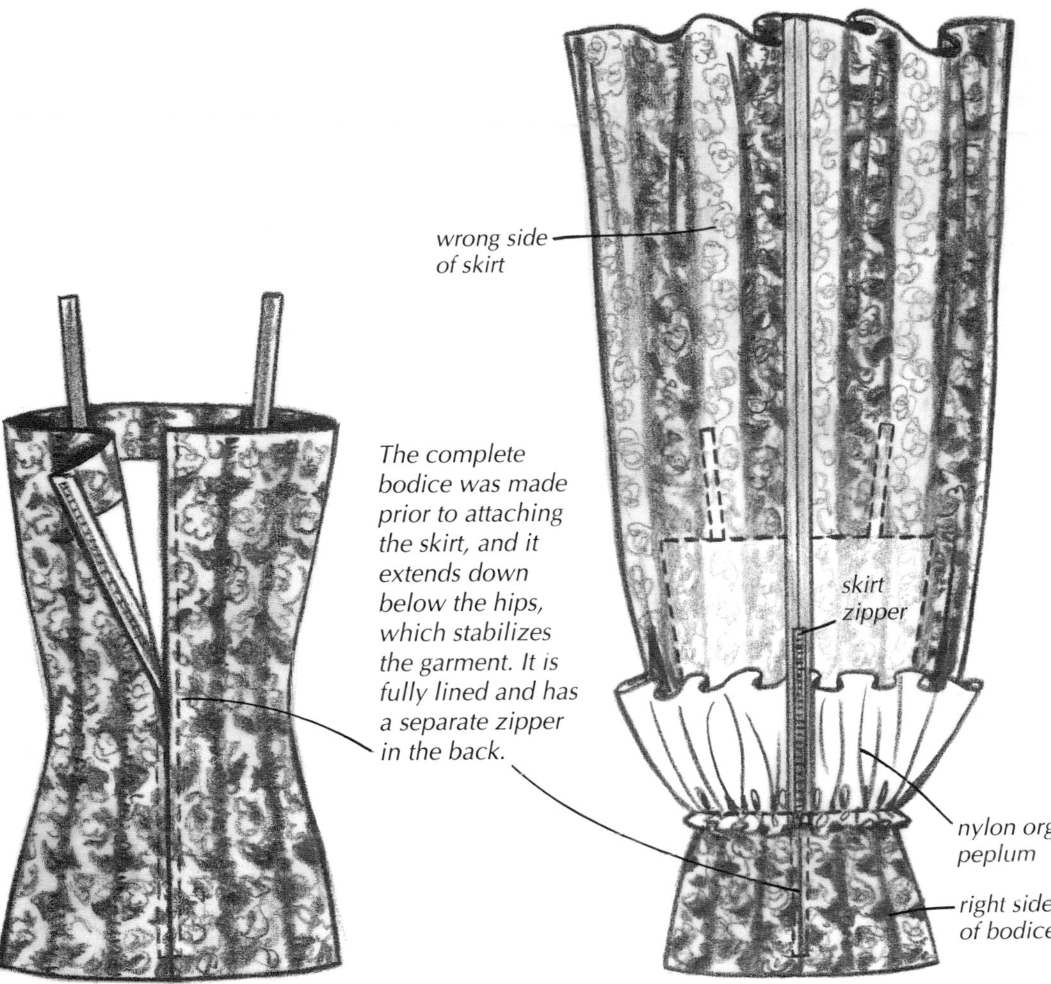

The complete bodice was made prior to attaching the skirt, and it extends down below the hips, which stabilizes the garment. It is fully lined and has a separate zipper in the back.

The skirt is sewn on to the completed bodice, and has a second, separate zipper at the center back. To attach the skirt to the bodice, put right sides together, with waistline of skirt aligned with waistline on bodice and with skirt extending upside down over the top of the bodice. The skirt, and a separate nylon organza peplum/ruffle are then sewn to the bodice along the slightly dropped waistline. Pull down the skirt. Voilà.

The jacket is designed to fit closely at the waist, then fall out over the pleats of the skirt.

*The silhouette of this outfit is one of its primary couture features. The form-fitting dropped waist is contrasted by the curves of the pleats in the skirt, which are designed to stand away from the hips to give the effect of a pannier. And those pleats are no ordinary pleats! The structure of them changes over different parts of the body. Some are box pleats, some tuck to the left, some tuck to the right. Some are larger than others. In each case, a decision was made based on what the designer wanted the fabric to do at that point on the body. As the designer, YOU are in control. Make **your** garments do what **you** want them to!*

Garment constructed by Carolyn Meyerhoffer.

Checklist for Tissue Fitting and Fit-As-You-Sew™

Wearing proper undergarments and the type of clothing you plan to wear under the garment, try on and fit, checking the following:

☐ Shoulder seam goes from bone behind ear straight out center of shoulder. Make a straight line on crease where back of arm and body connect. Where these two lines cross is natural cap point.

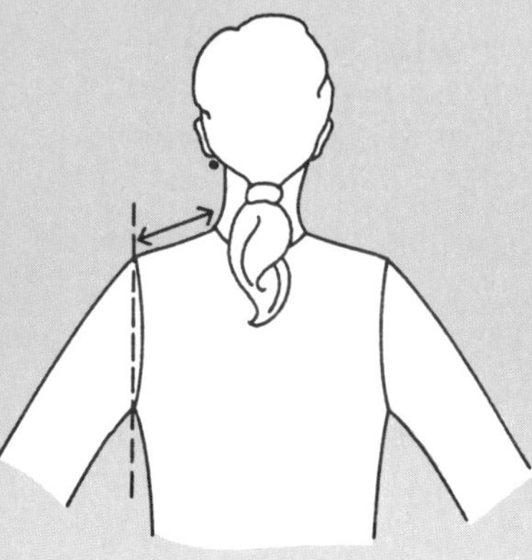

☐ Side seam is perpendicular to floor and, if two-piece, top lines up with skirt or pant side seam.

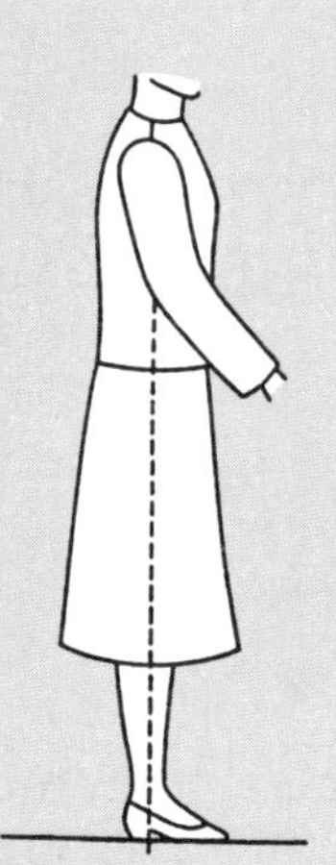

☐ Sleeve should hang as if there is an arm in it, no strain or wrinkles with crosswise grain parallel to floor. The lengthwise grain goes from cap to wrist bone, perpendicular to the floor.

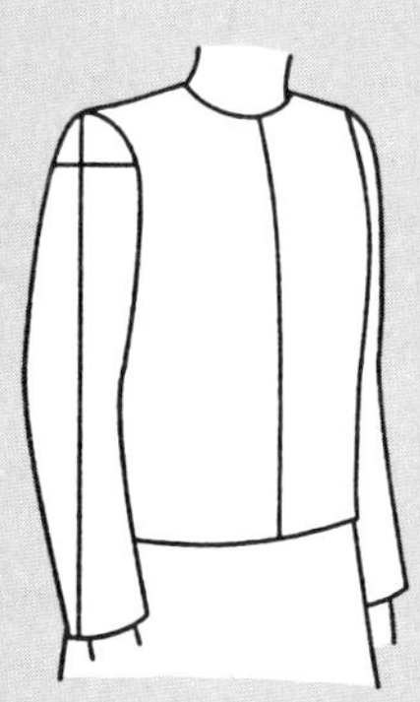

☐ Roll of collar. Collar stands away from neck so it doesn't break with movement of head and is comfortable.

☐ Back of collar covers neckline seam.

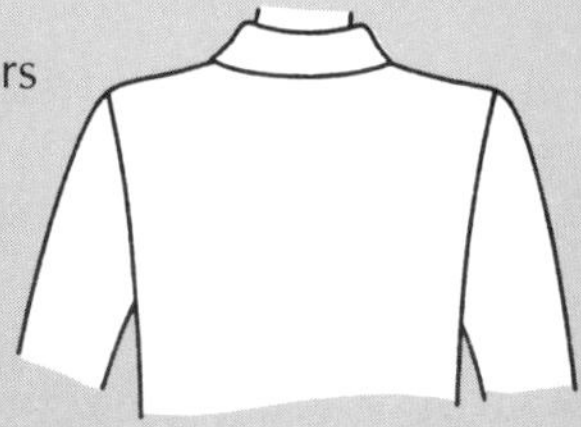

☐ Buttonhole placement. See Chapter 23 on Buttonholes for buttonhole placement (page 187).

☐ Proportion. Sleeve should not end exactly at hem edge of jacket or top. Depending on figure type (length of arms) sleeve hem should be slightly above or below hem.

☐ Never line up short sleeves with bust point.

Make necessary changes and try on again. Re-pin or re-baste if necessary.

CHAPTER 7

Absolutely Fundamental

Sewing is an art. It is a creative process with very few rules. There are concepts and methods with as many ways to approach a subject as there are people who sew. However, couture sewing, that pure, fine, masterful execution of ideas in fabric, has at its base techniques and methods that form a foundation of knowledge. It's a resource, a security base from which one can soar and sew beautiful clothes.

Included here are all the procedures that I feel are absolutely fundamental in fine couture sewing—the attitudes, techniques, and approaches that are themselves the essence of couture.

Fit

Alteration vs. Adjustment

I would like to clarify the distinction between the terms "alteration" and "adjustment" as used in this book. Whether applied to a paper pattern or fabric, an **alteration** is a change made for an individual and is unique to that one person.

An **adjustment** is a couture attitude, making the pattern "better." For example, an adjustment to curve the back shoulder seam would apply to everyone and make the finished garment better.

Try on the Paper Pattern

This may seem elementary to some and revolutionary to others, but in any case, it may be the most important part in the preparation of any garment.

Draw grainlines on the paper using red so you can see them, since you may be drawing over preprinted markings. Draw crosswise grainlines perpendicular to the lengthwise using a T- or L- square. On most garments, these cross grain lines should be parallel to the floor. Being able to see them clearly assists you in the fitting process.

After alterations and adjustments have been made, pin the pattern pieces together. On sleeves, pin the underarm seam, but do not pin it to the garment tissue yet.

With proper undergarments, shoes and shoulder pads in place, try on the paper pattern. Pin the center front (CF) and center back (CB) to your undergarment or, if a jacket, to whatever you plan to wear under the jacket. If making a two-piece garment (skirt and top), try both pieces on at the same time.

How does it fit? Is the shoulder seam directly across **your** shoulder? Are side seams straight? Is there enough ease? Is the length correct? Are you happy with the pocket placement?

Pin sleeve to bodice at underarm and cap. Try on. Is there enough cap height to keep cross grainlines parallel to the floor? Is there equal fullness in front and back no matter what the design? Is the length correct with the arm bent?

Do you like it? Imagine this design in the fabric you've selected; feel it, visualize yourself wearing it; where will you be, what will you be doing? Do you **like** it? Do you **LOVE** it?

Make necessary alterations or adjustments and try on the paper pattern again. Not to be funny, but from experience I ask you again, do you like it? The answer should be a resounding yes before you cut it out of fabric!

If you are not happy, remember, the garment will not miraculously turn into something different. "What you see is what you get." Working long hard hours on something that is a "maybe" may not be so wonderful in the end. Trust the paper; trust yourself in what you see and feel. Love this beautiful garment right from the start and know it will be perfect.

NOTE: There are many good books on fitting, flat pattern alterations and adjusting patterns for a particular body type. It is assumed that skilled seamstresses have become proficient in this important part of fine sewing.

Preshrinking

Everything involved in the construction of a garment must be preshrunk. In the course of developing a couture garment, pressing, shaping, shrinking and stretching are used to permanently shape the finished garment. You must be assured that further shrinkage will not occur after the garment is complete.

Preshrink fabric, lining, zipper, interfacing, linen or rayon stabilizing tape, and underlining. Preshrink everything except thread. Use the same method you intend to use in the care of the finished garment.

- **Wash**—If the garment is to be washed, wash fabric in washing machine with a detergent to remove any surface-finish residues. Dry in dryer on appropriate temperature. Do not overdry. Press as necessary.

- **Dry-Clean**—If you intend to have the finished garment dry cleaned, have the dry cleaner **steam press** the fashion fabric (drycleaning does not shrink the fabric). This also is suitable for linings in garments to be dry cleaned.

- **"London Shrinking"**—considered the ultimate for preshrinking wools. This takes time and requires a large pressing surface. This method is particularly recommended for pants where perfect grain is essential for the permanent hang of the pant.

To London Shrink:

Open out a damp bed sheet and lay wool fabric in a single thickness on top. Fold the four outside edges to the center as many times as necessary to end up with a bundle approximately 18″ × 24″ (45 × 60cm).

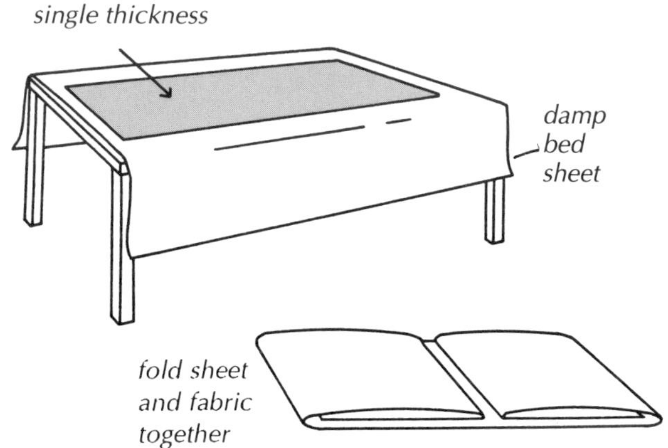

Put in a plastic bag, close tightly and leave eight hours or overnight.

Remove the wool (very damp now) and place it on a grain board (page 54) making sure the cross grain and lengthwise grain (selvage) are at perfect right angles to each other. Using a dry press cloth and dry iron, press until the fabric is dry. In any place the fabric has dried prematurely, a little steam can be applied or a damp press cloth used to produce moisture. Be sure fabric and board are completely dry before cutting out garment.

Thoughts on Grain

In all of couture sewing there is nothing without grain. The grain of the fabric is the dictator, the leader, the part of the fabric that speaks to you. Listen carefully to the whispers of the grain. You cannot expect the final garment to hang perfectly if the grain of the fabric has not been established at the beginning.

Couture relies on the bias to create softness, or fullness or to follow a curve. The fabric must be on the grain, with adherence to a perfect bias. This book is about grain—how to manipulate it, what to expect from it, and when to use which grain— lengthwise, crosswise or bias. Respect for grain ensures success. Grain becomes an asset rather than a liability.

Graining Up

Garments cut from fabric that is on grain will hang properly throughout their lifetimes. Putting fabric on grain is an important step that should be taken seriously when making beautiful garments.

NOTE: Preshrinking is not graining up.

To prepare fabric, either tear on the cross grain or pull a thread and cut across the open space left by the missing thread. (Most fabrics tear easily; test first.)

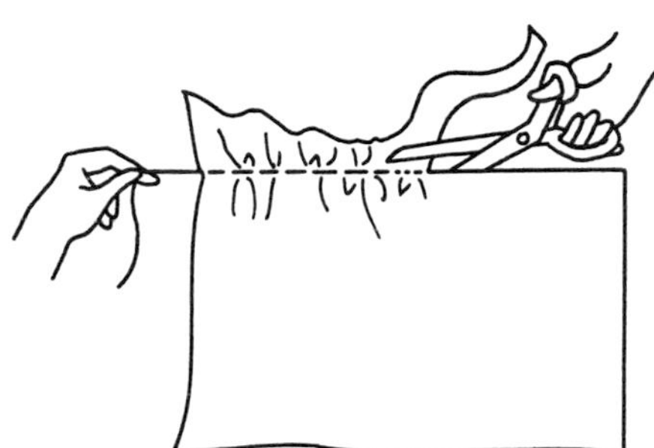

A necessary tool in couture sewing is a grain board. (See Pressing Tools, page 54.) Place the fabric on the grain board so the crosswise and lengthwise grains are at **perfect** right angles.

When we speak of pure couture, garment pieces are cut from a single thickness of fabric and marked before lifting from the board.

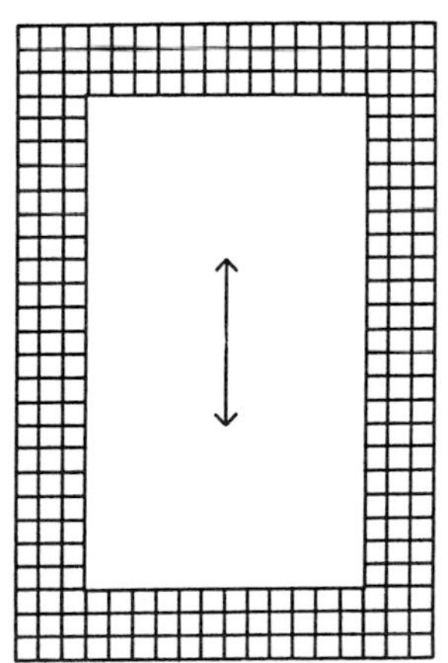

There will be times when you will want to cut double for speed—but I hope that your knowledge of couture and respect for grain will be an ever-present thought, and that your adherence to accuracy will prevail.

Before beginning the graining up process, quickly lay out all pattern pieces to see where they will be placed on the fabric. Then pre-cut the fabric into sections with all cuts either on the crosswise or lengthwise grain. Smaller sections make it easier to achieve perfect graining up.

COUTURE Tip Work in the smallest unit possible to achieve maximum accuracy.

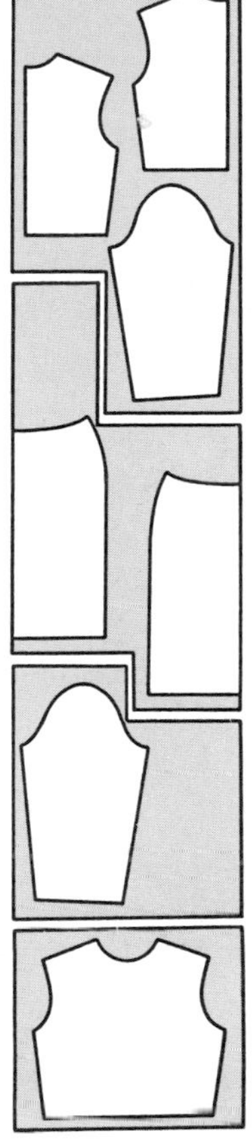

Set one section of fabric on the grainboard, making sure the crosswise grain and lengthwise grain (parallel to the selvage) are at right angles to each other. Pin fabric onto board. It should be perfectly flat.

Do not become disturbed if you have a few wrinkles. **Do not** shove the wrinkles out to edges. The most perfect, beautiful fabric can be slightly off-grain in any given spot. It is your job as a sewer to get the piece on-grain before cutting.

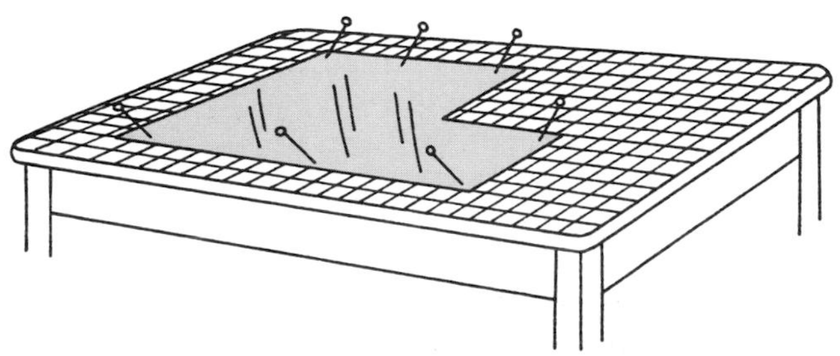

Using a damp press cloth and dry iron, press, watching the straightening process occur. A heavy-duty press cloth with wool back (see page 57) can be used with a dry iron to speed up the drying process.

Remove pins and let stand. Removing the pins should not change the fabric's alignment at perfect right angles.

I am sure that as you read this you are saying, "How much work?" "Who's kidding whom?" "This will take forever!" Well, keep this in mind. Couture lasts a long time; garments are made for permanence.

Learning a new skill takes time. But I promise you the effort is worth the result. Speed is not the goal but you will become faster as you become more proficient. Getting the fabric perfectly on grain, combined with meticulous marking, will bring rewards.

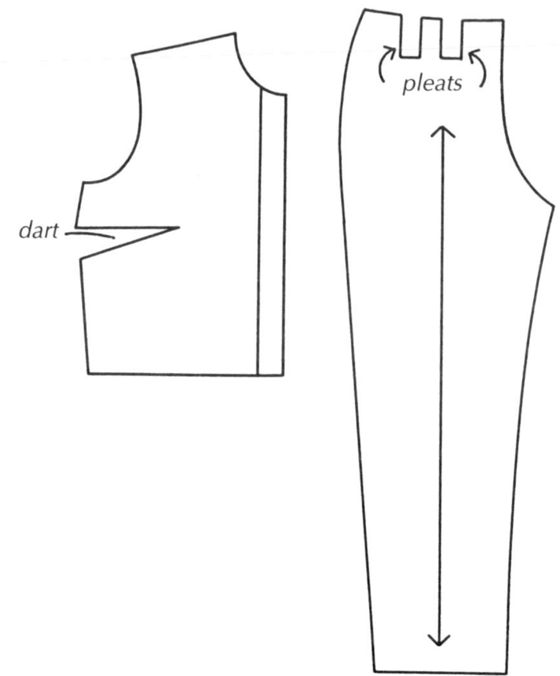

When you are ready to pin pattern to fabric, remember, always pin at right angles to the stitching line. You won't believe how this will help you!! If you have a grainboard you can pin straight into the board.

Marking

After carefully cutting out your pattern, accurate marking is crucial. Whether you are using a commercial pattern (with or without seam allowances included on the tissue) or one you have drafted, all construction marks relate to the stitching line. That's where garment pieces are sewn together, **not on the cut edges**.

Life is easier if there are no seam allowances on the pattern pieces. This means if your pattern comes with seam allowances, **cut them off!** I recommend this because all markings are made at the stitching line for accurate matching. It's easier to mark if there is no paper there. Also, you can then use any size seam allowance you wish. The Couture often uses 1"-wide seam allowances. Also, cut darts and pleats out of paper pattern for more accurate marking.

Choose from the following marking tools and methods:

Chalk
Use flat, hand-held chalk or chalk marking pencils for temporary marks or any mark that will be thread traced.

Dressmakers carbon tracing paper and tracing wheel
Tracing paper or carbon made especially for sewing comes in a variety of colors. Use on the wrong side of the fabric only and make sure you don't see the tracings through to the right side of the finished garment. Choose a single or double tracing wheel. A single wheel traces one line at a time, for example, the stitching line. A double tracing wheel can be adjusted to outline cutting line at the same time as it marks the stitching line.

Thread tracing
Thread tracing means that all marks previously mentioned are thread basted. To thread trace, take a long stitch, then short, then another long.

—— – —— – —— –

This ensures that the fabric will remain flat. Thread tracing is ideal for light-colored fabric or garments that require a long time period for sewing, such as jackets or coats. Short, **even** stitches, in-out-in-out, similar to gathering should not be used for basting or thread tracing.

Transfer the following points/marks from the paper pattern to the cloth:

1. All stitching lines
2. Notches
3. Dots, circles, squares (match points)
4. Gathering marks
5. Any place two seams cross (seam intersections).
6. Darts and pleats
7. Grainlines
8. Center front
9. Buttonhole and button placement
10. Pocket placement
11. Hemlines

It may be necessary to change either buttonhole spacing or pocket placement later, but at the beginning, mark them following the pattern. It is very important to mark the buttonholes so you can always pin the garment together exactly the same way every time you try it on for a fitting.

Purist Theory

In the purist form of couture, stitching lines are indicated on the **right side** of the fabric. This allows you to fold one seam over the other and slip baste from the right side for maximum accuracy.

You may chalk stitching lines, notches, circles, gathering marks, darts and pleats on the **right side**.

To protect the fabric and the final garment, grainlines, center front lines, buttonhole and button placement and hemlines should be chalked on the **wrong** side of the garment and thread traced to the **right** side so they can be clearly seen throughout construction.

Hints for Thread Tracing

- Sometimes it is faster to chalk first, then thread trace over the chalk line.
- Mark on the wrong side and thread trace to the right side for any mark not incorporated in a seam.
- Use silk thread for thread tracing to prevent permanent indentations when the garment is pressed during construction and for easy removal.
- When thread tracing stitching lines, be sure there is one small stitch **exactly** where one seam crosses another so that point is precise.
- Thread marks for notches and dots should begin in the seam allowance, cross the stitching line and continue into the garment. A knot at each end with a tail will prevent it from slipping out. This also allows you to see the mark from the right side of the fabric as well as in the seam allowance. No knots are needed when thread tracing stitching lines.

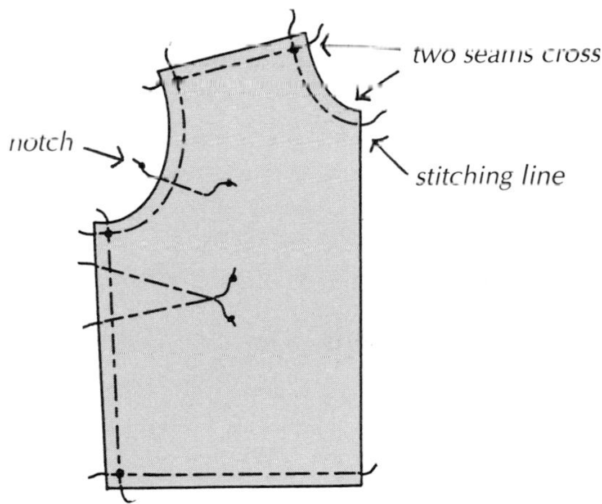

- On complicated designs, marks can be color coded. For example, in a gathered sleeve mark the gathering points on sleeve and garment in red; mark the notches in green.

Basting Is Not the Enemy!

Somehow, in our early days of sewing, basting became an enemy, a punishment. It stood in the way of getting to the machine to do the good stuff. If couture is perfection, basting is simply a means to that end, to accuracy. Basting is not the enemy! It's like having an assistant in your sewing room.

Pin-basting is better than not basting at all. In couture, however, thread basting is preferred to get the garment as close to finished as possible. You can use thread basting as a guide for permanent stitching!

Baste major seams for the first fitting. That means no guessing, no surprises, and most of all, no ripping later. Baste sleeves for control and baste zippers to eliminate the need for pins. Couture techniques are precise, and some are quite intricate.

Baste with a single thread and no knots. On long seams, tie off loosely at the beginning and end to secure basting, especially for fitting.

Baste with silk thread on grainlines or any place where it will remain during construction. Baste with cotton thread in places where it will be removed immediately after machine stitching. Cotton thread must be removed before pressing. Remove basting by clipping the thread every 5″ (13cm). Pulling on long basting threads distorts the fabric.

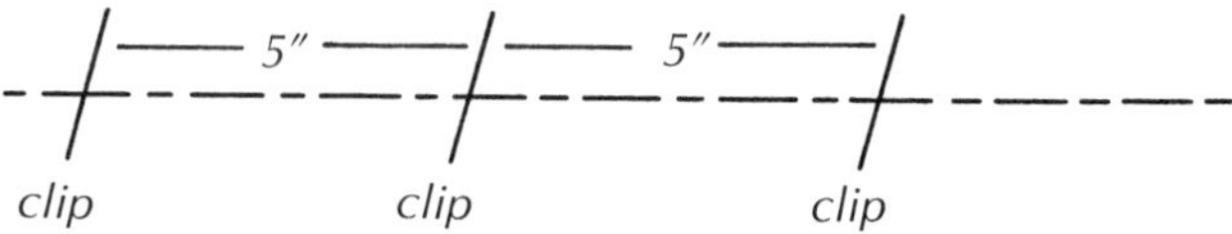

Cross-basting

Cross-basting holds two fabrics together. It will prevent slippage caused by repeated machine stitching. It's a form of control. Basted lines are 2″ to 3″ (5-8cm) apart with stitches 1″ (2.5cm) or more in length. Silk thread is essential in cross-basting.

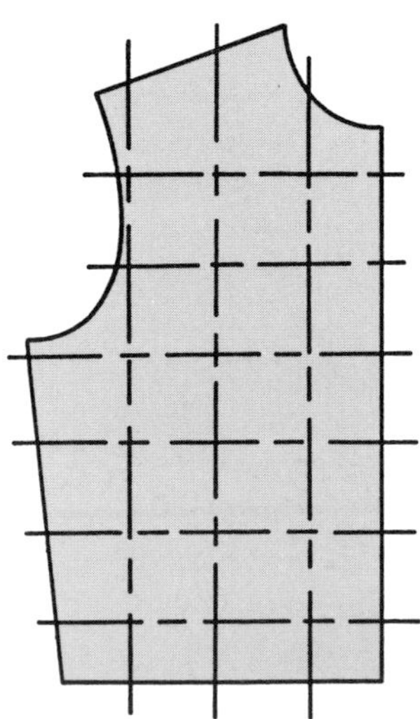

Cross-baste anytime two layers of fabric need to be held together throughout construction, such as:

- when lining to the edge of a garment that will have a bound edge
- when creating any form of channel stitching through two or more layers.
- when you have large garment pieces that will be self-lined, such as a full sleeve or a full skirt.

Sewing Couture Seams

Do not backstitch!

Start and stop each seam by starting at 20 stitches per inch (2.5cm) until you stitch past a crossing seam.

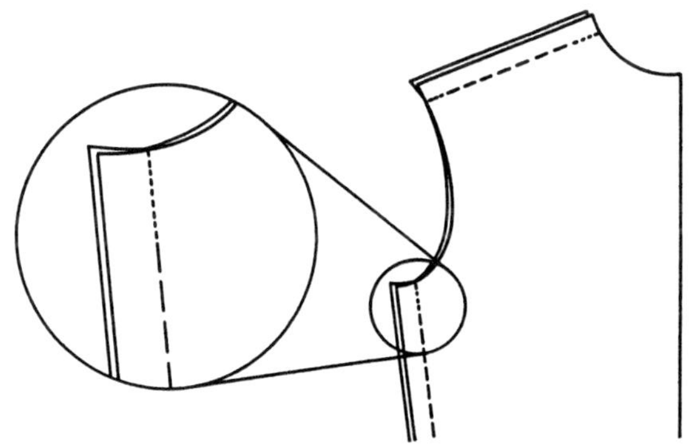

This method allows for only a single row of stitches at the beginning and end of each seam, yet it is secure. Seams will press open perfectly flat.

Stitching Seams of Mixed Grains

When the grain of one seam is being attached to another seam of a different grain, the couture rule is to stitch with the weakest grain on top. The weakest grain is bias, then crossgrain; lengthwise grain is strongest.

When you sew a curved seam line to a straighter seam line, as in princess seams, you are sewing mixed grains together.

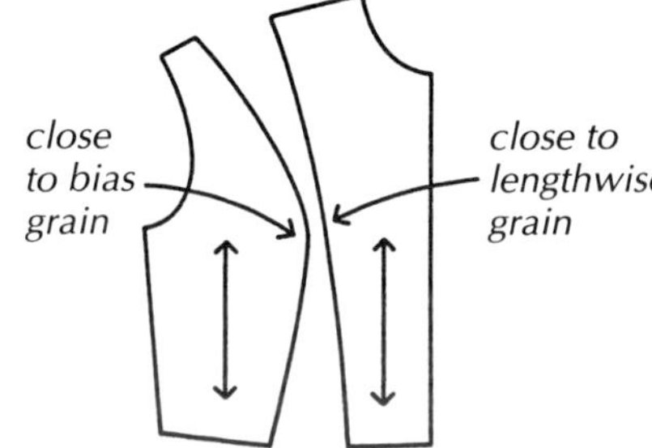

On the princess seam, therefore, you'll sew from the waist to the shoulder on one side and from shoulder to waist on the other side.

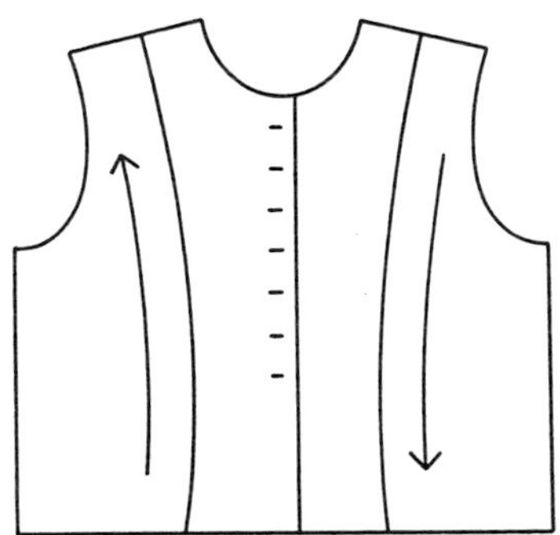

Sewing any seam with the weaker grain on top enables you to keep as much control as possible and prevents slippage.

In couture, hand basting the seam first enhances the control and guarantees a perfectly matched stitching line.

Directional **staystitching** is **rarely** used in couture, and never on necklines as so often recommended nor on armholes. If you are concerned about stretch, fold a bias strip of silk organza over the edge and hand baste. The thread itself will prevent stretch.

As to directional **stitching**, if a seam is hand basted, as it is assumed to be in couture, you can sew it in any direction and retain control if the seams are of like grain. If they are of mixed grain, follow the weakest grain on top rule and hand-baste, then machine baste.

Fitted Side Seam

Seams give stability to a garment. A full 1″-1 1/2″ (2.5 - 4cm) seam allowance in a side seam not only **stabilizes** but gives a smooth, clean line to a garment.

When a side seam is curved (very fitted) it certainly needs clipping, but this will likely result in loss of stability. In couture clothes this "problem" is solved by using a scalloped seam with seam allowances 1″-1 1/2″ (2.5 - 4cm) wide. Meld stitching (page 52) and press seam open.

waist

Cut a series of scallops with the deepest part of the scallop 1/4″ (.6cm) from the stitching line, the widest 1″ (2.5cm) away. Hand overcast, or cut scallops with pinking shears.

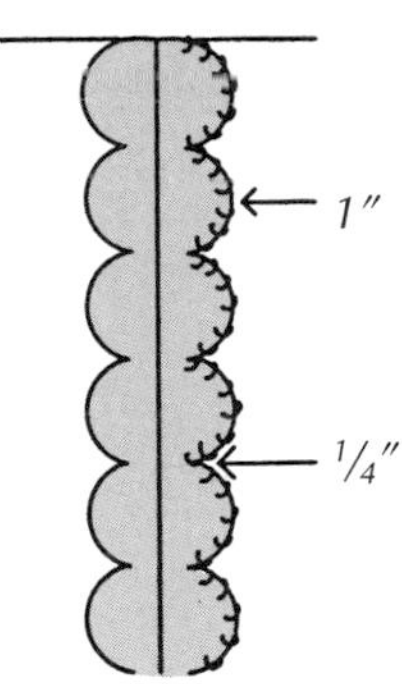

Seams That Cross

The place where two seams cross is always a thick spot that can be bulky if not trimmed.

Reduce bulk wherever possible.

First stitch, press, trim and grade seam allowances. Then, remove excess bulk by trimming at an angle from stitching line to stitching line as shown.

You'll encounter crossed seams on:

1. Sleeve or armhole seams where they cross shoulder seams.

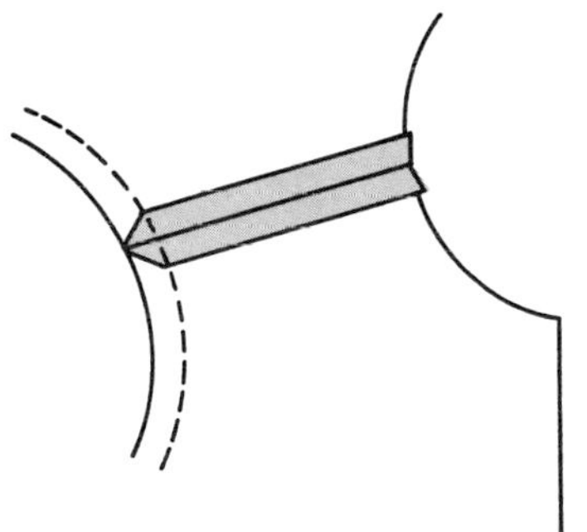

2. Waistlines on skirts or pants.

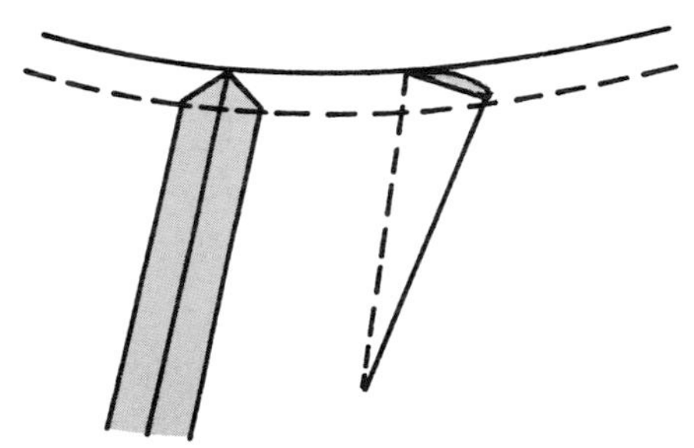

3. Underarm seams.

4. Darts in any seam.

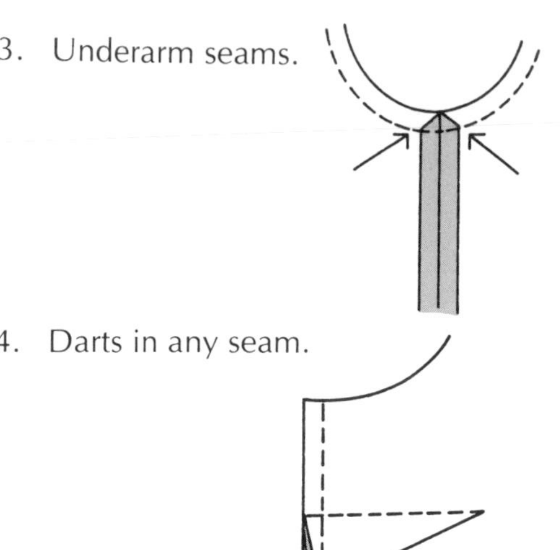

5. Faced necklines with shoulder or other seams coming into them.

Stabilizing

Sometimes an area needs stabilizing to prevent stretching, such as a shoulder seam or neckline, the crotch in pants, or other seams specific to an intricate design.

In Couture, reducing bulk wherever possible is the overriding rule. The stabilizing tapes include:

- **Silk organza**—½″-wide (1.3cm) strips torn from the crosswise grain which tears more easily than lengthwise grain. The edges will be frayed, while the center threads remain intact and strong. It's the thinnest yet strongest stabilizing tape.
- **Rayon hem tape**—a soft, almost flimsy tape that stabilizes and does not form a ridge in a seam.
- **Linen tape**—its narrowest form (⅛″ .3cm) can be caught discreetly in a seam.
- Thin strips of fusible interfacing stabilizes as well. Try ½″ (1.3cm) strips of Knit Fuze™, WhisperWeft, Silk Weight (100% cotton) or Touch of Gold (100% rayon).

I am opposed to cotton and polyester twill tapes and using fabric selvages for seam stability. They are too heavy and not supple enough.

NOTE: Save your selvages to tie up tomato plants; or cut them in pieces in the spring, throw them in your yard, and you'll find them in birds' nests throughout the neighborhood.

Clipping

Curved seams must be clipped in order to lie flat, but as little as is necessary to achieve a flat seam. The great exception is the slightly curved inseam in pants—no clipping there.

In a simple curved seam such as a waistline or the side seam in the hip area of a pant or skirt, clip at an angle to within ⅛″ (3mm) of the stitching line. Stagger so clips are not opposite each other. Clip at an angle so it's on the bias and will not ravel.

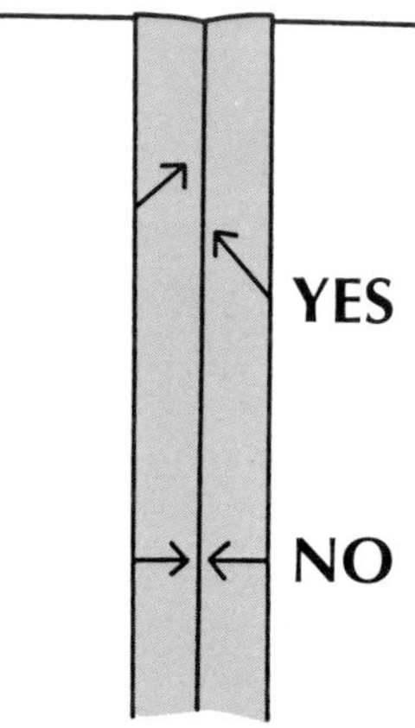

For a neckline with facing, first clip at an angle through **garment seam allowance only**. Then clip into facing seam allowance, alternating the location so no facing clip falls exactly where the clips in garment were made.

Remember, clip only as needed making as few clips as possible. This method provides for some seam allowance to remain everywhere along the curved edge and no flat spots or ripples will result. This is particularly important when topstitching will be added.

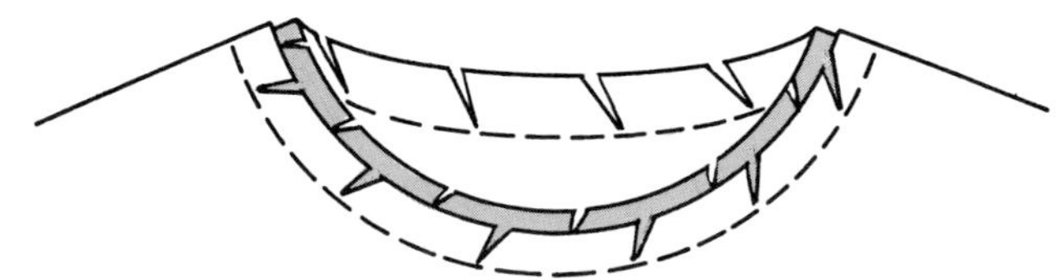

Off-Grain Openings

How many times have you seen a jacket that is buttoned, but separates at the bottom; a slit in a skirt that looks like a wedge has been cut out when it should hang straight and closed?

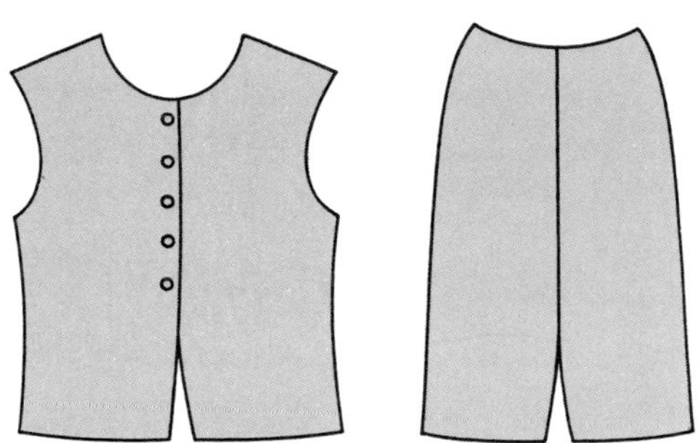

This happens because the edge of the opening is cut on the straight of grain. Students often ask me, "Then why don't pattern companies automatically design the pattern pieces off grain at opening edges?"

The answer is simple. Off graining is a judgment call; couture is full of judgment calls. The amount that a specific garment needs to be adjusted off grain is dependent on **weight**—the weight of the fabric (heavy or light), of interfacing, buttons and buttonholes, and on the **length** of the garment (short jacket vs. full length coat). So, in defense of the major pattern companies, they cannot anticipate what fabric you will use, the kind of buttonhole or interfacing, or how tall you are or what length garment will be right for you.

How to "Off Grain" a Dress, Coat, or Jacket

1. At the waist make a mark $^1/_2$" (1.3cm) out from the front edge of the pattern.

2. Draw a straight line from the highest point of the opening (near neckline), passing through the $^1/_2$" (1.3cm) point at the waist.

3. This now becomes the new finished edge.

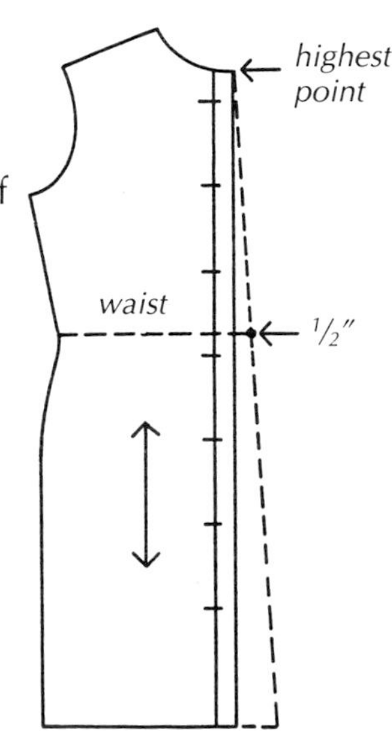

4. Draw a new center front line in from edge the same amount as original pattern.

5. Move button and buttonhole placement marks.

6. Off grain both sides of a garment (left and right).

Never change the grain of the garment itself.

7. Off grain the facing exactly the same as the garment.

8. Re-draw the facing so the new facing piece is same **width** as the original was.

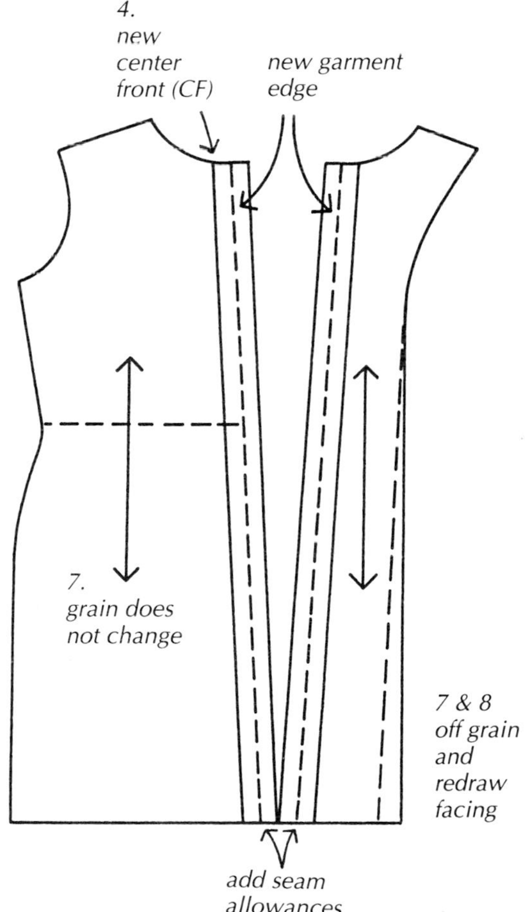

NOTE: If the original pattern has a self facing—it will be necessary to cut it off and treat it as a separate pattern piece. Don't forget to add seam allowances.

9. In lined garments, **off grain the lining also**.

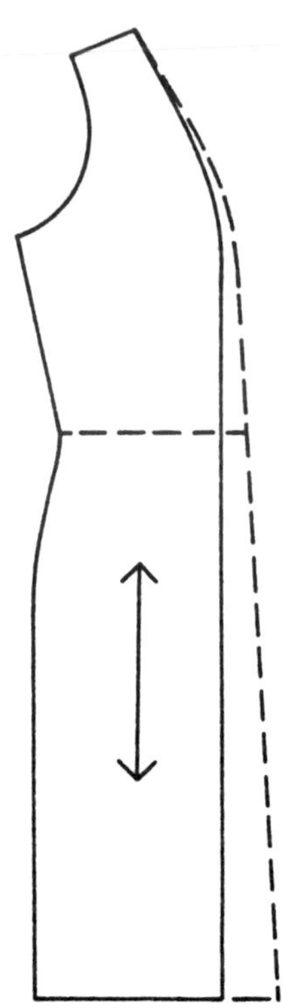

10. Using the 1/2″ (1cm) measurement at the waist is the **minimum**. It allows the amount to increase in relation to the length of the garment.

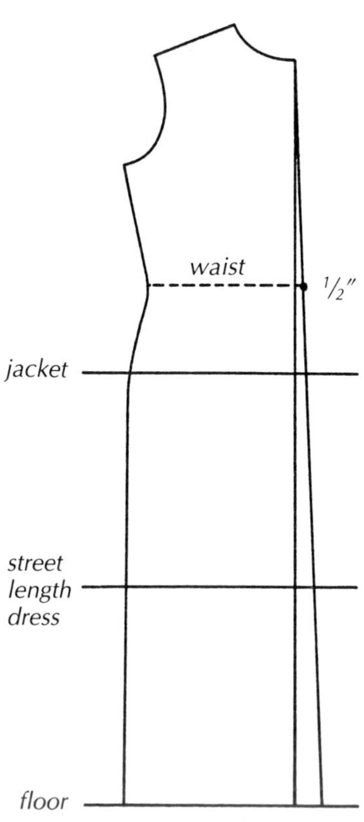

Couture Judgment Off Graining

Off graining 1/2″ (1.3cm) at the waist is the minimum. When that amount is insufficient, use the following hints to help you "judge" how much more off graining is necessary. Additional off graining is done at the hem.

- **Weight of fabric**—gabardine weighs more than flannel; add an additional 1/8″-1/4″ (.3cm-.5cm).
- **Buttons**—heavy metal buttons weigh more than plastic; add an additional 1/8″-1/4″ (.3cm-.5cm).
- **Interfacing**—hair canvas weighs more than organza; pad stitching adds weight; add an additional 1/8″-1/4″ (.3cm-.5cm)

Your job is to calculate the additional amount of off graining needed for a particular garment for a specific person.

Gabardine	1/8″ (.3cm)
Metal buttons	1/8″ (.3cm)
Hair canvas	1/8″ (.3cm)
Pad stitching	1/8″ (.3cm)
Total	1/2″ (1.3cm)

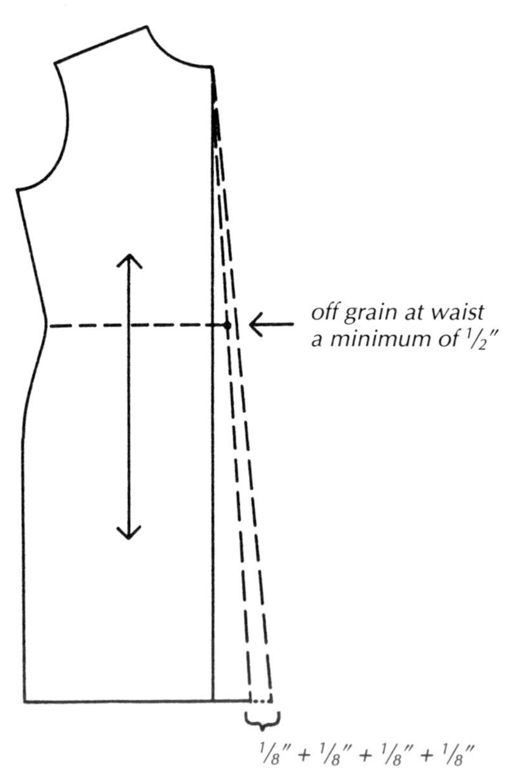

It is impossible for me to offer you all the possible combinations of fabric, interfacing, and other factors that make off graining a necessity. Your judgement and accumulated skill and experience will gradually help you to calculate the right amount of off graining every time. Don't worry if you overestimate as you can always cut off the excess.

> **NOTE:** When using a stripe or plaid and when it is important to have a specific color or plaid on the center front, you may choose not to off-grain.

Slits in Skirts

Off graining for a slit in a skirt must start at the waist and end at the bottom edge, even though the center back seam will be sewn only to the slit mark. Consider off graining 1/2″ (1cm) at the hem to "0" at the waist as the minimum standard.

1. Cut off vent.

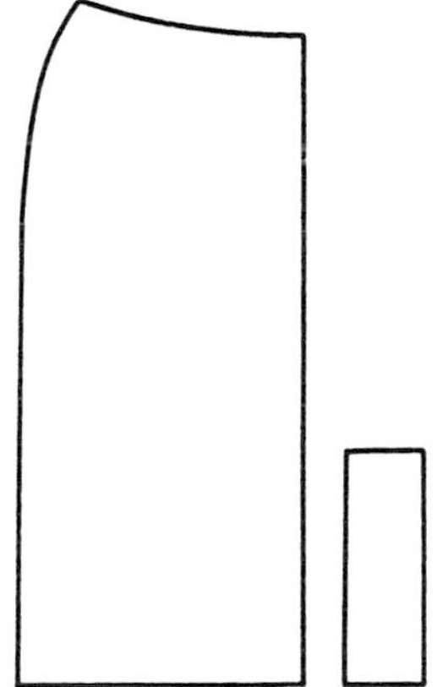

2. Off grain center back.

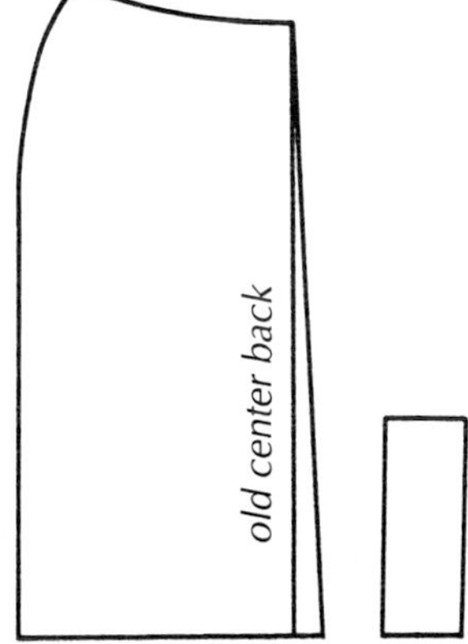

3. Tape vent next to new center back line.

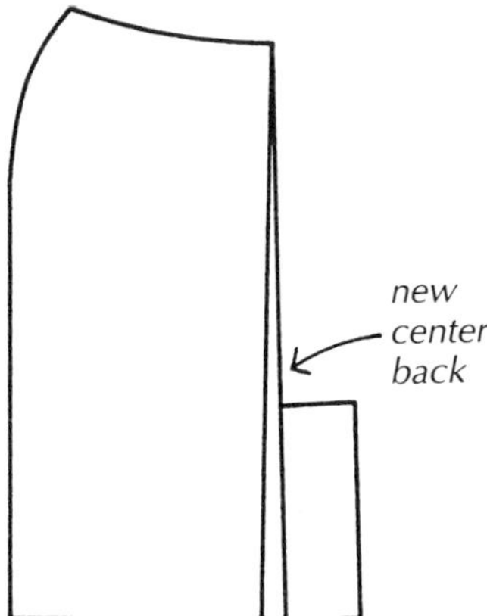

4. To prevent the seam from ripping or splitting just above the slit, use 20 stitches per inch (8 stitches per centimeter) where the slit begins.

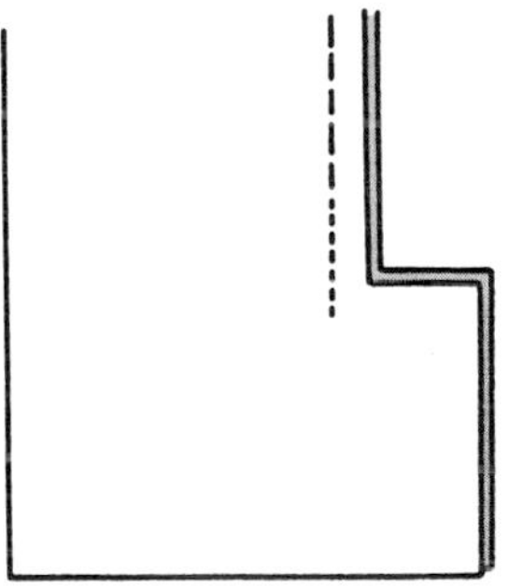

5. When the slit is complete, sew the eye of a hook and eye across the seam just above the opening. You'll never rip this seam when walking.

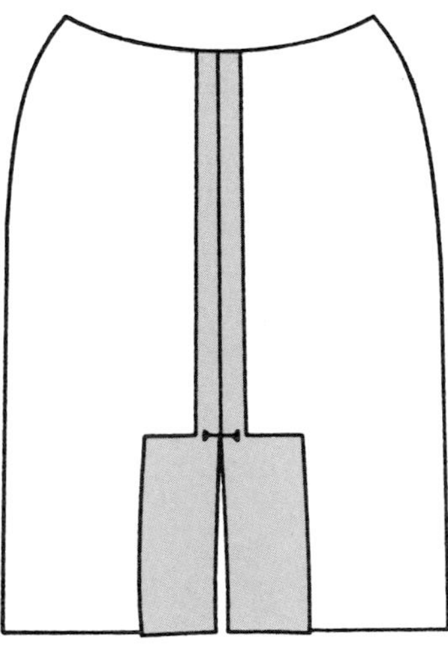

CHAPTER 8

Pressing

Pressing is Couture

The difference between a home-made looking garment and one with a couture attitude is good pressing. This means being patient and careful and using the proper equipment. Here are a few couture pressing techniques followed by proper pressing equipment.

Melding Threads

After machine stitching a seam, meld the top thread and bobbin thread into the fabric. Press the stitching line flat—first on one side, then on the other, then press the seam open.

If you are wondering how important this really is, run your fingers over a row of stitches right out of the machine. You will feel a ridge. Now, meld the threads and feel the stitching line again. You can hardly distinguish the row of stitches from the fabric itself.

Pressing the Seam Open

Pressing during the construction of a garment means lowering and lifting the iron. It is quite different from ironing a finished garment with a gliding motion.

In couture, moisture is usually provided by a press cloth used with a dry iron. Indiscriminate steam from a steam iron might permeate more of the garment than that which requires pressing. When pressing a seam open, for example, only the stitching line needs to pressed. The seam will then lie flat.

When pressing a seam open, choose the correctly shaped pressing surface to get the desired results. (See Pressing Tools, page 53.)

Pressing Rules:

1. Pressing means to raise and lower the iron, not glide it along the fabric, which could cause distortion.

2. Meld both top thread and bobbin thread immediately after taking work from the machine.

3. Press in the same direction as you stitched.

4. Press enclosed seams open before pressing them closed, for example, in a collar.

5. Press on a surface shaped like the garment.

6. For enclosed seams, press before trimming, then grade, clip, trim and re-press, as necessary.

7. On curved edges such as a faced neckline, press perpendicular to the stitching line.

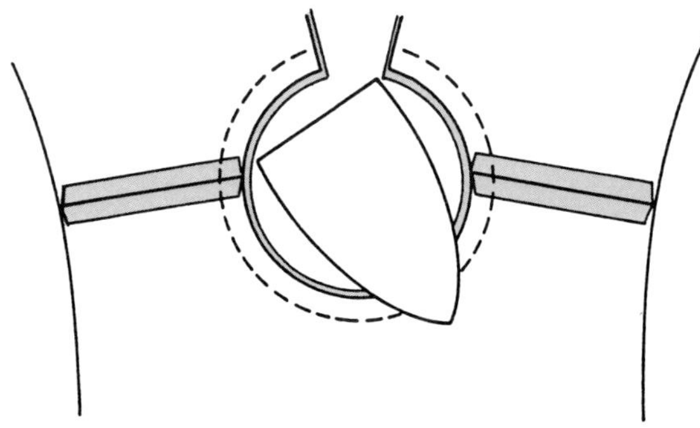

8. Think through whether you need moisture from a press cloth or steam from an iron. Steam goes everywhere. A dry iron with a damp press cloth concentrates moisture where you want it to be.

9. **ALWAYS** let your work cool **BEFORE** you move it from the pressing surface.

Pressing Tools

The following are common pressing tools that are required in couture sewing. Each has a specific purpose: to support the fabric, protect it or enhance the shape. And, some make your work easier.

Pressing, as it applies to sewing, is lifting the iron in an up-and-down motion. Ironing is what you do to laundry—push the iron back and forth across a finished garment.

Pressing equipment generally falls into three categories of tools: wooden, padded and moisture-producing.

Wooden Surfaces

Clapper

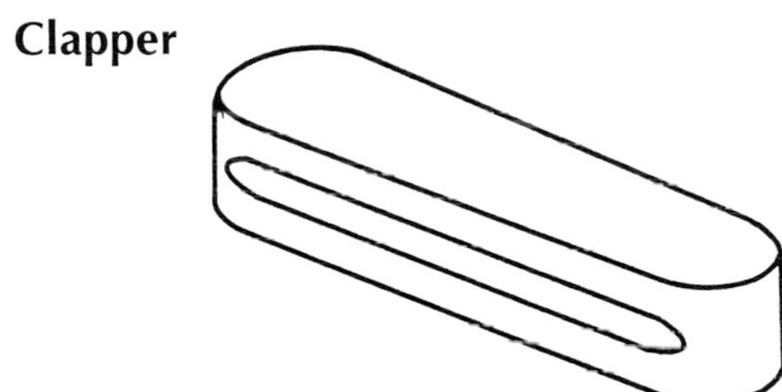

A clapper is an oblong piece of wood with one end narrower than the other and usually with a hollow on each side. These hollows allow you to grasp the clapper comfortably at the wide or narrow end. The top and bottom of the clapper are perfectly flat.

A clapper is a flattening device. Even after a seam, hem, lapel, collar, buttonhole, pleat or crease has been pressed, the fabric may remain resilient and need further flattening. Dampen the fabric slightly by pressing over a damp press cloth with a dry iron, using a lift-and-lower motion. Remove the press cloth, and while the work is still damp and warm, hold the clapper firmly on the seam or edge to be flattened and apply pressure for several seconds. Allow the fabric to dry thoroughly before handling again.

Because the wood of the clapper absorbs the warm moisture, turn it over constantly to use the "cool" side. If the area to be flattened is small, use the clapper on its end and gently rock while applying pressure.

Use caution to avoid a mark (indentation) on the garment itself. The first choice is to use the clapper directly on the work, but fragile, soft fabrics may need the protection of a dry press cloth.

Wooden Point Presser/Pounding Block

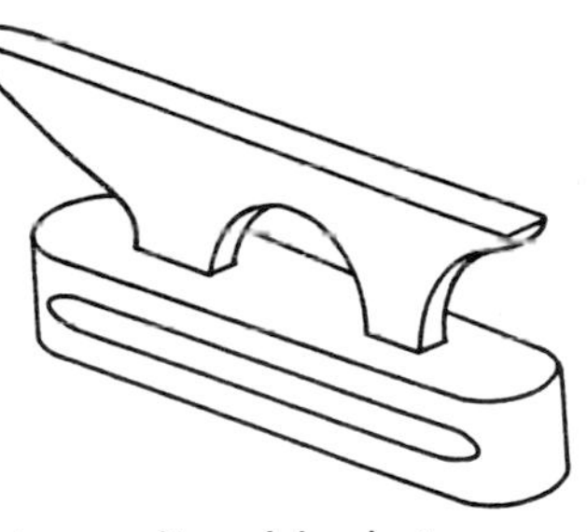

The point presser/pounding block is a pointed piece of wood attached to a wooden clapper. The pointed end allows you to get into points, as in the point of a collar.

Use the point presser to press open any seam where a crisp, flat seam is desired. It gives a sharp press, while a seam roll gives you a soft edge.

Also, use the point presser to press open **enclosed** seams before turning them to the right side for a final press, such as a facing seam.

The flat bottom of a point presser can be used as a clapper or pounding block. What is "pounding?" Pounding is a rhythmic movement. The point presser is held 12"-24" (30-60cm) above the work and dropped with force, then raised rapidly and dropped again. Each drop overlaps the previous one. Pounding is most frequently used in tailoring or to flatten bulky edges. Pounding should be done with the work on a padded surface, either a grainboard or an ironing board.

The pointer becomes a handle so you can get a good grip on this tool. To get a good rhythm, sing "Hail to the Chief" slowly!

The June Tailor® Board

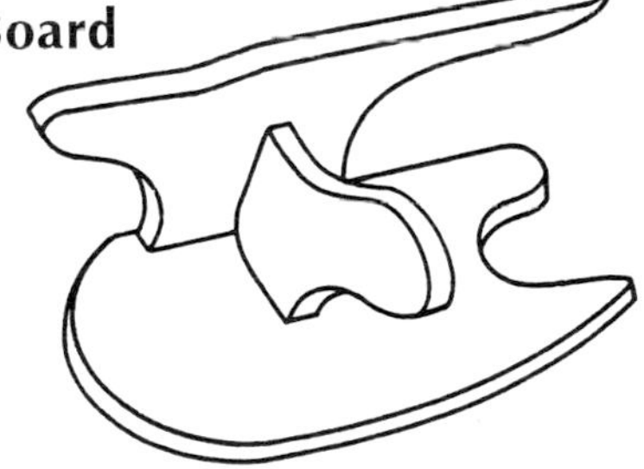

This odd-shaped, wooden pressing tool expands pressing possibilities beyond those of the traditional point presser. The June Tailor Board has many different curved edges, so that no matter what the design, which curve or how small a seam to press open, there is a curve to match.

Because the Tailor Board is wooden, the seam to be opened will be pressed crisp/sharp. For a soft press, place a piece of bias-cut wool over the wooden curve before placing the garment on the Tailor Board.

Padded Surfaces

Sometimes a soft edge or a rounded seam or shaping are desired. Thus, a padded surface or a sewing tool is needed. Depending on the tool, the surface may be wool flannel or a smooth cotton fabric. Wool absorbs moisture faster than cotton. Specific techniques throughout this book will identify which surface is better.

Grainboard

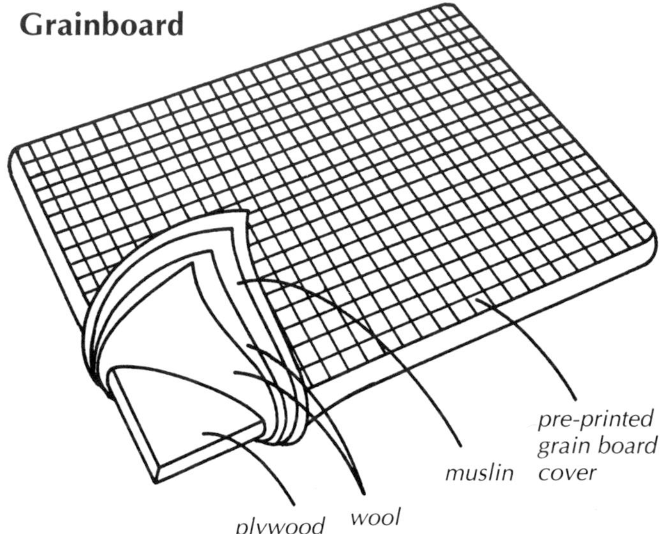

A grainboard is a large pressing surface you can make yourself to dimensions best suited to your space and kind of sewing. The standard grainboard is 36″ wide by 54″ (90 × 135cm) long. Use plywood, $^{1}/_{2}$″ (1cm) thick for a board that is easy to move. If you have a permanent location, use $^{3}/_{4}$″ (2cm) thick plywood.

Why do I need a grainboard? A grainboard is the best surface for graining-up fabric (see page 43), for cutting-out a garment, and for fusing interfacing. It also provides a large pressing surface to support your work throughout construction, so it doesn't drag or hang when other pressing tools are being used.

To make a grainboard:

1. Cover the grainboard with two layers of wool for a minimum depth of $^{1}/_{2}$″ (1cm). Old wool blankets are perfect. Army/Navy surplus stores are a good source.

   Cut one blanket to the board's exact size. Cut the other so you can wrap about 4″ (10cm) of fabric to the underside of the board. Place the larger layer over the smaller one and use tacks or a staple gun to secure tightly, cutting away excess at corners on the underside.

2. Cover with a piece of good-quality, smooth-surfaced, 100% cotton muslin. Do not preshrink the muslin. Pin the muslin to the top side of the board following the order in the chart below, being absolutely sure both crossgrain and lengthwise grain are kept taut and **at perfect right angles**.

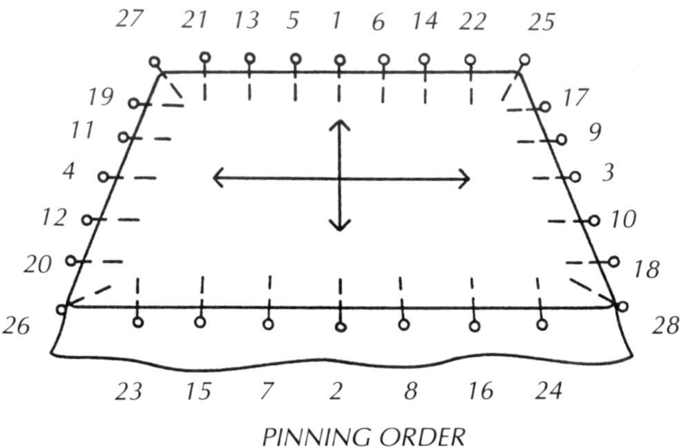

PINNING ORDER

3. Turn board over and tack or staple muslin in place. Remove pins.

4. Steam press from the right side to slightly shrink muslin.

Fabric stores and mail-order catalogs offer heavy cotton covers pre-printed with a 1″ (2.5cm) grid to mark grain lines. Such a grainboard cover should be applied to ensure perfect grain **over** the muslin, not instead of it, as an additional cushion to smooth out the old wool blankets. To ensure perfect grain, apply grainboard cover as you did the muslin, following the pinning order above.

Ironing Board

The perfect ironing board for **sewing** is made of wood and is relatively narrow with a narrow nose. Like the grainboard, it is covered first with wool padding and then muslin. It should be perfectly flat with no dip in the middle.

A sewing ironing board may need to be recovered more frequently than a family ironing board. If a hollow develops, seams cannot be pressed open evenly and fusing will become impossible.

Ironing Board Cover

An ironing board cover should be 100% cotton lightweight canvas. There are several ironing board covers available that have grid lines which help establish grain when pressing small pieces. Avoid Teflon covers as they return too much heat to your work and can cause shine. Besides, they do not absorb moisture.

COUTURE Tip Make an investment in yourself and your sewing by providing your family with their own personal ironing board, iron and scissors with a love note that says, "Don't you dare touch my sewing tools."

Sleeve Board

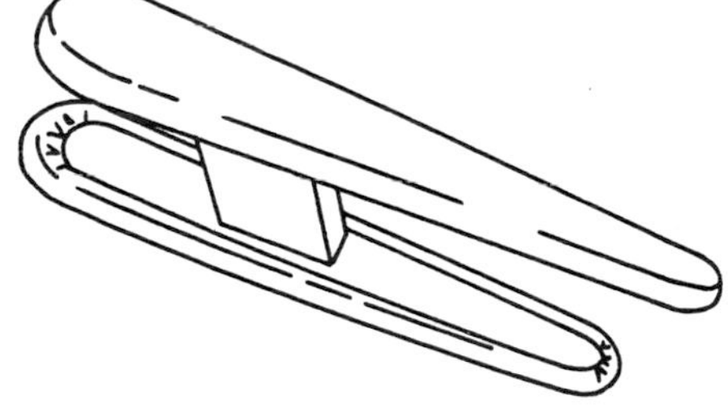

A sleeve board is a small ironing board, narrow enough to slip into a sleeve. The ideal sleeve board is strong and stable (will not fall over or collapse during use) and has sufficient space between the board and base so work doesn't wrinkle. A sleeveboard also serves as an excellent pressing surface for necklines, shoulder seams, and small or hard-to-reach areas.

A sleeve board should be firm, smooth and padded, but not over-padded. Use only one layer of wool and a 100% cotton cover.

Seam Roll

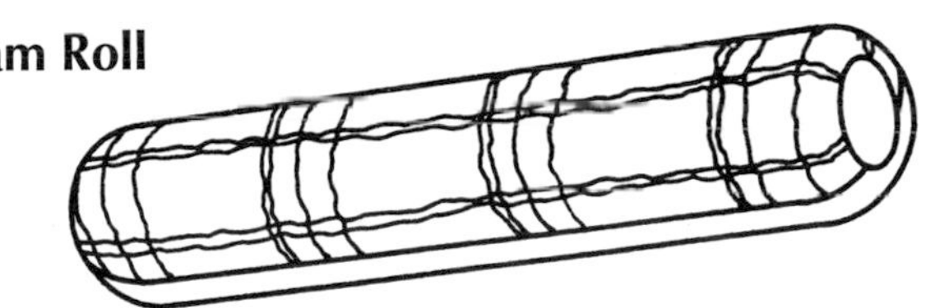

A seam roll is an oblong, padded cylinder with a cotton cover on one half and wool on the other. The wool absorbs moisture rapidly, preventing it from returning to the work. The soft rounded surface prevents a ridge from forming when you press seams open. It is also small enough to fit into sleeves and pant legs.

Ham

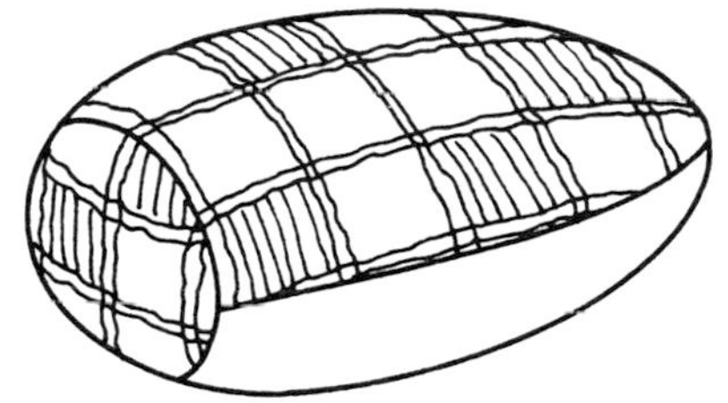

Similar to the seam roll, a ham is padded and covered in wool on one side and cotton on the other. It is a firmly packed oval, wider at one end than the other, and corresponds to body curves. Use it to retain a curve when basting, pressing, or shaping any curved garment section, such as darts, curved shoulder seams, princess seams over the bust, and the hip area of side seams. The ham also is useful when shaping the cap of a sleeve and setting the roll of a collar.

Because of its rounded edges, a ham tends to wobble around when in use. To stabilize it, pin it to a grainboard or ironing board or put it into the June Tailor Hamholder. Eventually, you will want two hams—one to use and one to hold work that must dry.

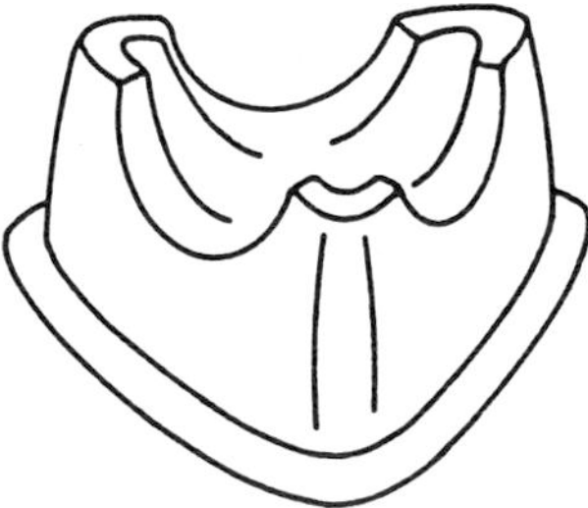

Hamholder

A unique invention by June Tailor, this molded plastic container holds a ham in any position. A hole in the outer rim allows you to pin it securely to a grainboard or hang it on a hook for storage. Using a hamholder is like having two free hands!

Pressing Mitt

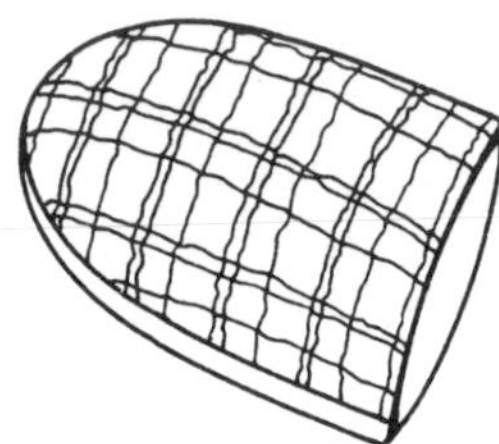

A pressing mitt has an inside pocket so you can tuck your hand inside and support an area from the inside while steaming from the outside. The pocket also enables the mitt to be slipped over a sleeve-board to simulate a ham. Consider the pressing mitt as a small ham to be used where a traditional ham is too big or bulky.

The June Tailor Press Mitt is covered with wool. If you have an old one covered with a Teflon coating, you may want to replace it.

How to Make a Lapel Roll

When rolling a lapel just after taping the roll line and again during the final pressing, you need something under the lapel to maintain the shape. A seam roll is usually too large. You need a lapel roll instead.

You can make a lapel roll using "fat" cording (cotton cord #7) and Armo Wool or hair canvas.

1. Start with a 36" (90cm) length of cording and a 4" × 14" (10 × 35cm) bias piece of Armo wool or hair canvas. Place the wool over the cording.
2. At the halfway point, stitch across cording to anchor.
3. Stitch close to the cording with a zipper foot. Trim away excess fabric, leaving a 1/4"-wide (.5cm) seam allowance.

4. Turn wool over cord by pulling it onto the remaining cord.

5. Cut off excess cord including the stitching across the end. Insert a piece of string or rayon tape in each end, then whipstitch ends closed.

Tuck a lapel roll under the lapel when steaming to shape it. This lapel roll can also be tied around a ham and used to steam press the roll of the collar.

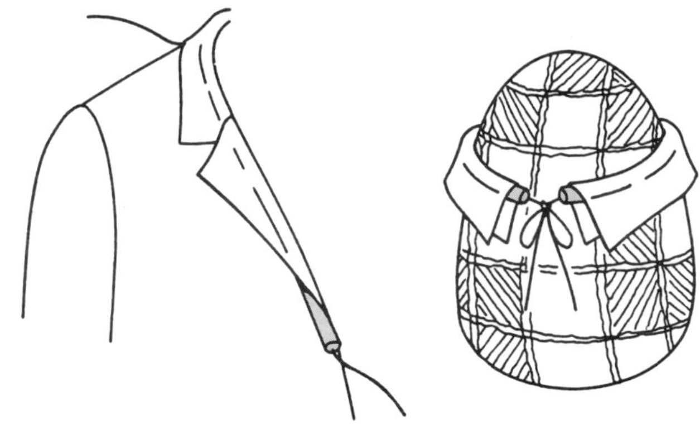

Moisture-Producing Sewing Tools

Steam Iron

Today's irons fall into two categories: "home use" and "professional use." A sewer needs an iron that has adequate weight and that produces plenty of steam but also can be used as a dry iron. A burst of steam is a very helpful option.

If you sew a lot or are a professional dressmaker, you might want to research professional irons with either gravity-feed or siphon steam.

Steamer

A hand-held instrument with or without a brush is a necessity in fine sewing. When you need to steam the garment in an upright position from the right side without the heat of an iron's soleplate, a steamer enables you to do this without damaging the fabric. Some professional irons can steam upright like a steamer, but the sole plate is hot.

Press Cloths

A press cloth is a layer of protective fabric placed between your work and an iron, but it serves other functions, too. It can provide moisture or assist in drying. It can allow you to apply pressure without leaving marks or creating undesirable shine. A well-equipped sewing room has several different types of press cloths:

Heavy-Duty Wool-back Press Cloth

This cloth is heavy cotton duck on one side with wool flannel on the other. It allows you to use either side and protects fabric while allowing steam to penetrate the work. Make one by purchasing a heavy-duty cotton duck press cloth and adding 100% wool flannel to one side. Stitch and pink or serge around all edges to hold the fabrics together.

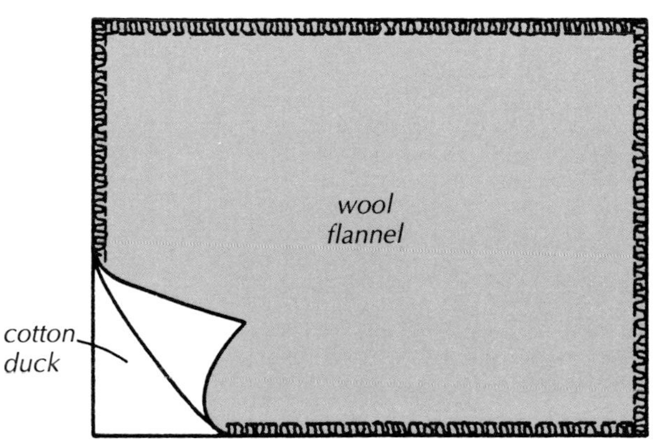

The wool allows moisture to go through gradually. Because the wool is spongy compared to the cotton, it protects work where there are multiple thicknesses (such as bound buttonholes).

This press cloth can also be used to dry fabric after intensive steam pressing. Use a dry iron and place the cloth with the wool side against the fabric. The heavy cotton side can be used to provide a firm surface so the weight of the iron does not make a ridge in your work.

Sheer Press Cloth

Made of cotton batiste, voile or lawn (usually white), this cloth simply protects the fabric from an iron. Because it is sheer, you can see through it to determine exactly where to place the iron.

A sheer press cloth can be used with steam from an iron but because it will not hold moisture, it should not be dampened.

Moisture Press Cloth

The best moisture cloths are flat 100% cotton diapers (not bird's-eye or waffle) or 100% linen towels, preferably old and limp. These fabrics hold moisture and can be used with a dry iron to control the amount of moisture being put into the work.

Fashion Fabric as a Press Cloth

Sometimes the press cloth nearest the garment should be the garment fabric itself. Textured surfaces such as tweeds, raised designs or fabrics with exceptionally soft surfaces will lose their appeal and elegance if flattened by the iron. For these fabrics, make a self-fabric press cloth, then use any other press cloth over it to avoid burning or damaging the self-fabric.

Bristled Press Cloth/Velvaboard

A bristled press cloth prevents napped fabrics from being crushed, while allowing steam to pass through. Use on velvet, velveteen, corduroy, and synthetic suedes.

Another unique pressing surface used with napped fabrics is called the June Tailor Velvaboard. Press napped fabrics from the wrong side with the nap facing the board. It prevents matting, flattening or crushing. Using this surface removes the possibility of ridges from hem edges, darts or seams. In other words, they won't show through to the outside. A velvaboard can be used flat but is also soft enough to wrap around a ham or seam roll as well.

Brown Paper Strips

No matter which pressing tool and press cloth you use, some fashion fabrics can cause seams to show through to the right side. Have 2"-wide (5cm) pre-cut strips from a clean grocery bag ready to slip under each seam allowance as it is being pressed. Brown paper is more desirable than white typing paper because it absorbs more moisture.

CHAPTER 9

Couture Details

To become a master of anything, one needs to be skilled at many levels and have a wide variety of experiences within a field.

In couture, becoming a master means knowing many different ways to do the same thing. It's having alternatives—choices. It's being able to consider many factors such as fabric, design, wearability, and the human form and then come up with exactly the right solution or execution of a detail. It's knowing how to make several types of buttonholes, not just one. It's practicing and perfecting so that no matter what technique you choose, you can do it with meticulous perfection every time. It is judgment.

Couture techniques include being able to do something in its smallest form such as **tiny** loops or expanding a concept such as the bellows pocket. It's taking what has gone before us—designers' solutions over hundreds of years—and adapting them to today, right here in your sewing room.

I am always fascinated by the person who says "I don't need to take a sewing class, I know how to sew." It's so sad.

I am equally fascinated by those who continue to take classes, read, and learn. To them the thought of just one more new way to approach sewing brings joy and anticipation. The fact that you have bought this book and are reading it makes me say congratulations! It is to **YOU** I dedicate my work!

Dior Rose

Dior used fabric roses as decoration. He used them at the hemline, as a single flower on a lapel and to completely cover a sleeve. Making the rose is very easy. It's the choice of fabrics that can take the rose from casual to evening wear. It can be small or large. For ideas, see the cover and pages 22 and 99.

Fabrics

Try silk organza for an airy appearance or taffeta for a bold, stiff rose. Silk crepe de Chine is soft, but holds its shape well. Combine colors, stripes, and prints.

Steps

The purist form of a Dior Rose has three petals with each petal having three pieces.

1. To make a pattern or template, cut three football shapes each 1/2" (1cm) smaller on all edges out of a hard paper (file folder). For example, the largest shape could measure 8" × 5" (20 × 13cm).

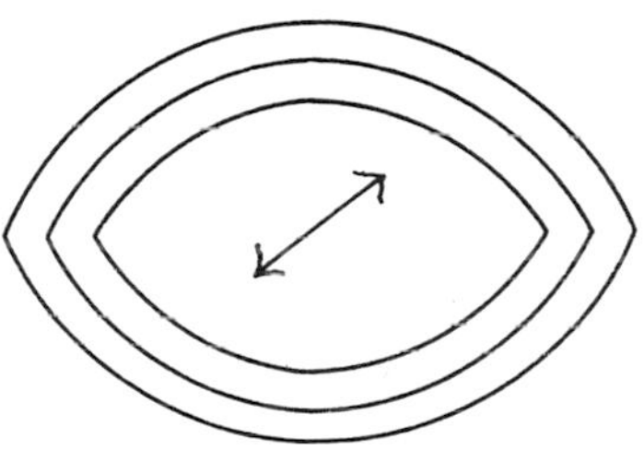

2. Place the center of the shape on the true bias of the fabric. Cut three small, three medium, and three large pieces.

3. Fold each piece on the center line. DO NOT PRESS FOLD.

4. Run two rows of gathering stitches (6 stitches per inch) 1/4" (.6cm), then 1/8" (.3cm) from raw edge.

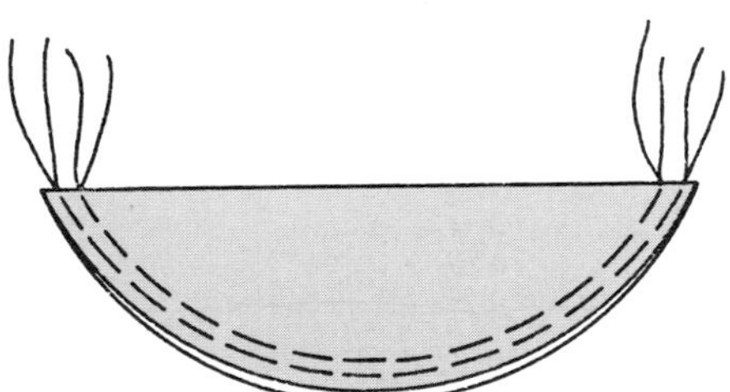

5. Starting with the smallest shape, pull up gathering thread and gently roll to create a "bud."

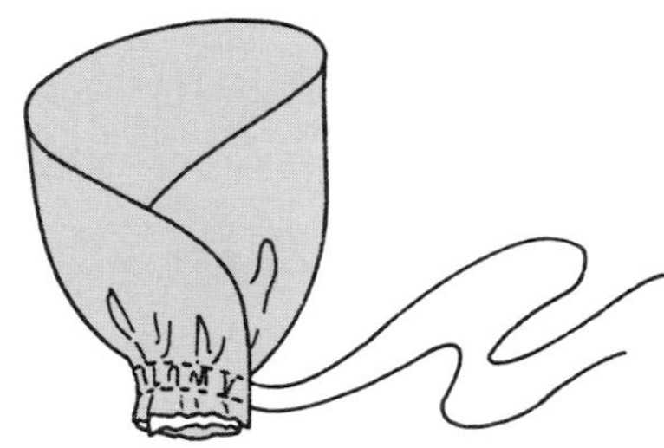

6. Thread a needle with double thread about 8-10″ (20 to 26cm) long. Knot the thread. Holding the center of the small bud, pull up gathers on medium size shape around first bud.

7. Insert hand needle and quickly stab through raw edges to hold in place while you prepare the large shape. (This is when you wish you had three hands.)

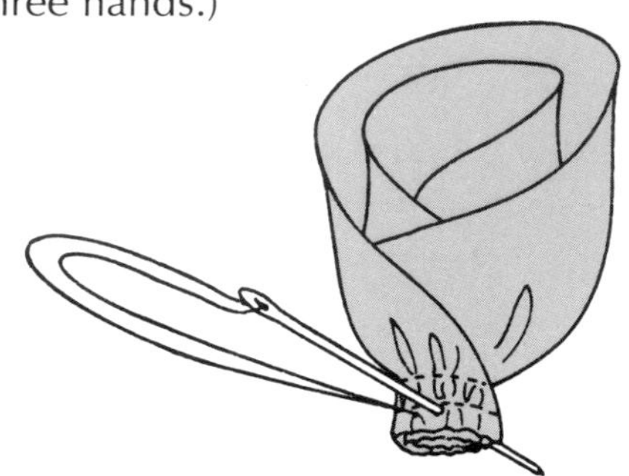

8. Pull up gathers on large shape and wrap around first two buds. Whipstitch over raw edges. You now have one petal. Make three of these.

9. Attach three petals together with a few stitches to form one rose. Spread petals apart gently.

If many roses are to be permanently slipstitched all over a garment, the raw edges will never show.

If the Dior Rose is to be temporarily attached to a lapel, a small silk circle can be slipstitched to the bottom of the rose, covering all raw edges.

Cut a circle the desired size with $^1/_4$″ (.6cm) seam allowances. **Hand** gather around the outside edge $^1/_4$″ (.6cm) from cut edge. Pull up gently so seam curves to wrong side. Press to flatten circle. Lay on bottom of rose and slipstitch around circle.

For excitement and vitality, use a spray of pearls in the center. To achieve a subtle color, silk organza and taffeta can be used together by making a seam at the fold line. Simply cut the football-shaped template in half and add a $^1/_4$″ (.6cm) seam allowance. Because this seam is bias, stretch as you sew. Turn and press edge hard. Trim seam to a scant $^1/_8$″ (.3cm).

Tiny Loops

Sometimes small or tiny indicates perfection. Tiny loops to replace buttonholes are a good example. Loops as thin as a needle are easily done in silk crepe de Chine or charmeuse.

To make loops:

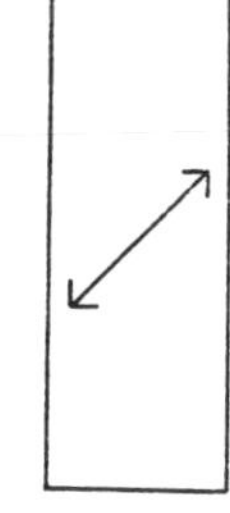

1. Cut a 1″ (2.5cm) wide bias strip of fabric as long as required for the number of loops needed, plus a little extra.

2. Fold in half, right sides together, using just one pin at the beginning.

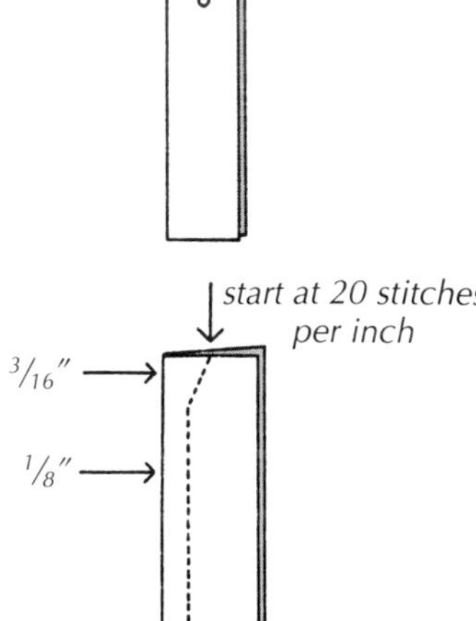

3. With the machine set for 20 stitches per inch (8 stitches per centimeter), stitch $^3/_{16}$″ (.5cm) away from fold to start, quickly tapering to within $^1/_8$″ (.3cm) of fold. Use tiny stitches and stretch fabric as you sew to prevent stitches from breaking when turning or wearing. End the stitching by tapering out again so stitches are $^3/_{16}$″ (.5cm) away from fold.

4. Trim as close as possible to stitching line.

5. Thread a needle with a double piece of thread.

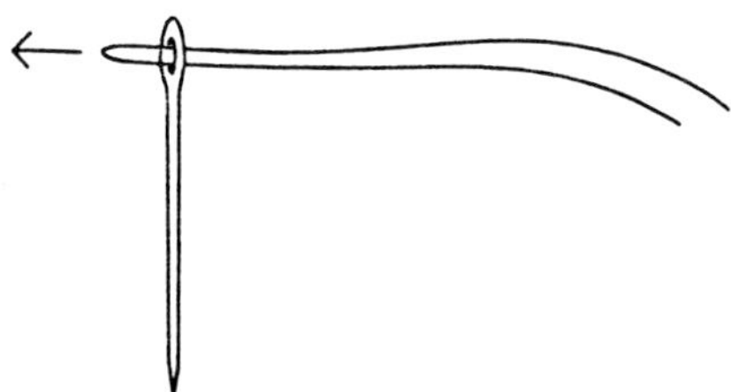

Put the point of the needle through the loop to secure the thread at the eye.

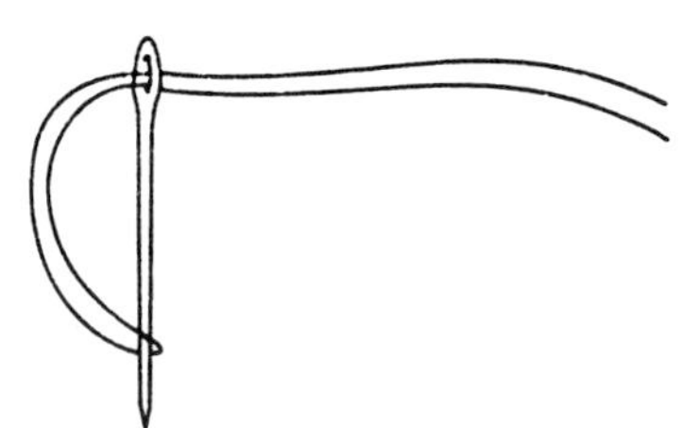

Knot end of thread.

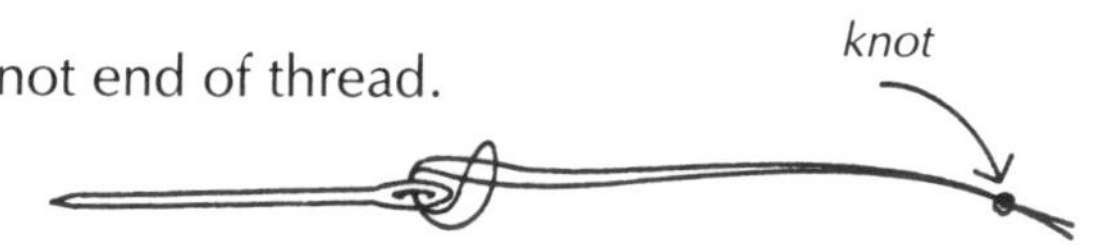

6. Anchor thread by inserting needle through machine stitching, and then through the two strands of thread.

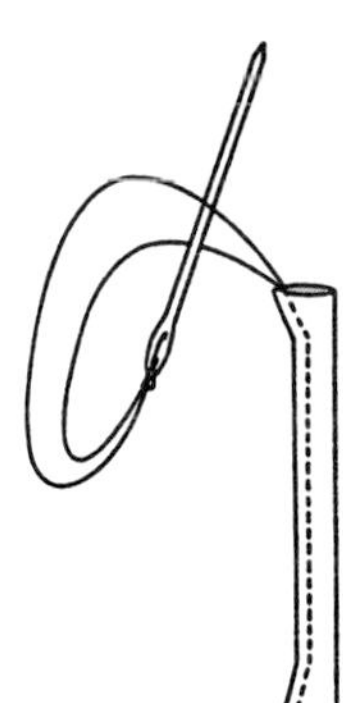

7. Then, insert needle into the loop, **eye first**. Work it through the loop until eye comes out bottom. (The fabric will crush up a little which is fine. It is easier than trying to work with TOO long of a thread.)

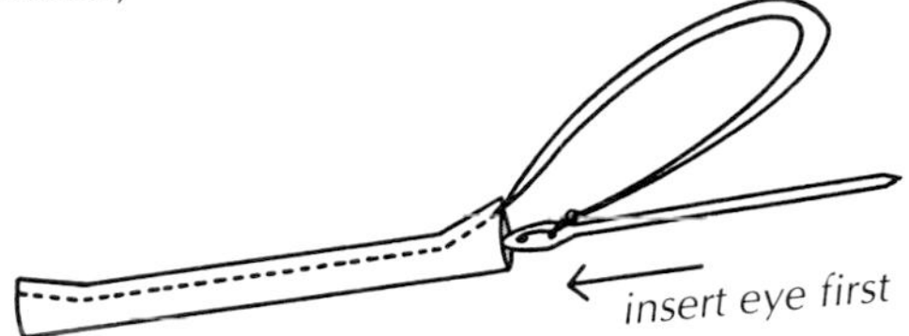

8. Gently work fabric over thread until loop is turned.

9. Cut thread and remove needle.

10. Pin loop to ironing board, stretching as much as possible in order to achieve a fine, narrow tube. Be sure seam is in a straight line.

11. Shoot loop with steam from your iron, Then unpin and roll it in the palm of your hand. Then stretch it, re-pin to board and steam. **Repeat until there is no more stretch left.**

12. Let dry completely before removing from board.

The technique of "steam, stretch, roll" is also very effective for spaghetti straps to prevent further stretching when the garment is worn.

French Seam

A French seam is an enclosed seam that can be made as narrow as the fabric will allow. It prevents raveling and is pretty in sheer fabrics.

I am reminded of one of my students, Christine Tharmstrom, who decided to try her hand at French hand sewing. She made silk charmeuse lingerie and sheer cotton batiste christening dresses. She mastered a French seam $^1/_{32}$" (.1cm) wide. I have never seen anything tinier. It was perfection—couture.

When making a French seam it is imperative that you make a test sample first. It is difficult to estimate how narrow it can be made without trying it first. To make a French seam:

1. Hand baste seam **wrong** sides together on marked stitching line.

2. Machine stitch in seam allowance the same distance from your hand basting as the estimated finished width of the French seam.

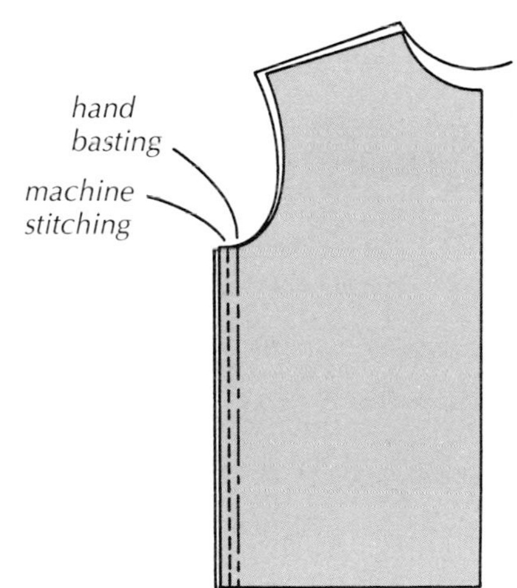

3. Remove basting.

4. Press to meld threads, then press seam open on a hard surface (point presser). Press hard, almost digging the point of the iron into the seam.

5. Leaving full seam allowance intact (very important as the seam allowance itself will provide stability and ultimately prevent rippling), turn garment right sides together and press seam closed. Press hard on the stitched edge.

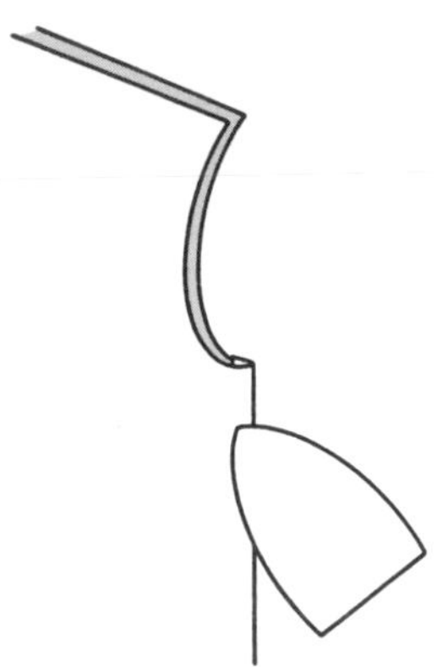

6. Using very sharp scissors, trim seam allowance close to first row of stitching. The seam allowance left will be the final width of the French seam.

7. Pin at right angles to the stitching line, putting the pins into the fabric **exactly** where the seam has been trimmed.

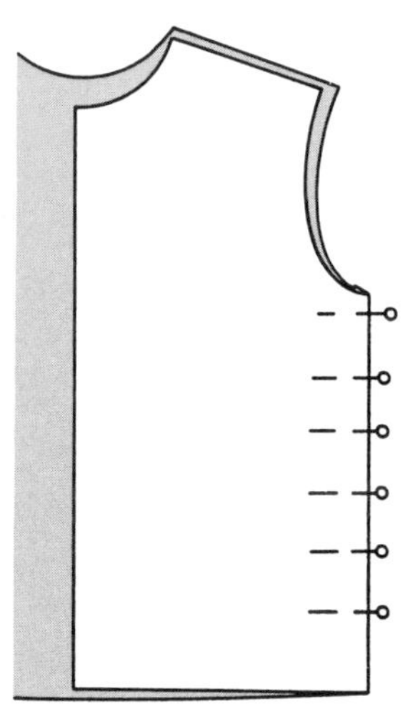

COUTURE Tip You can feel the edge of the seam with your fingers or hold it up to the light and see the shadow line.

8. Machine stitch from pin to pin where they penetrate fabric so no little fabric threads will show through to the right side.

9. Meld threads and press seam in one direction (toward back for side and shoulder seams).

Hong Kong Seam Finish

The Hong Kong seam finish is an elegant finish created by binding the seam or hem allowance with a piece of bias fabric. It is a smooth finish that eliminates all possibility of raveling. In an unlined jacket, use contrasting binding for a decorative Hong Kong seam finish.

Fabrics suitable to use as the binding are silk organza, silk crepe de Chine, silk charmeuse, silk chiffon, any lining fabric or even fashion fabric if it is extremely lightweight.

Apply a Hong Kong seam finish just like you would bias binding (page 85). Cut bias strips 1″ wide and use the small bias tape maker.

Mock Hong Kong Seam Finish

There are times when a full Hong Kong seam edge may be too bulky due to the extra fold where the bias strip is turned under on the wrong side of the seam allowance. A ridge may show through to the right side of the garment in some fabrics such as wool crepe or wool gabardine.

In this case a *mock* Hong Kong is appropriate using the following steps:

1. Cut true bias strips 1″ (2.5cm) wide.
2. Run through small bias maker and press fold on **one** edge only.

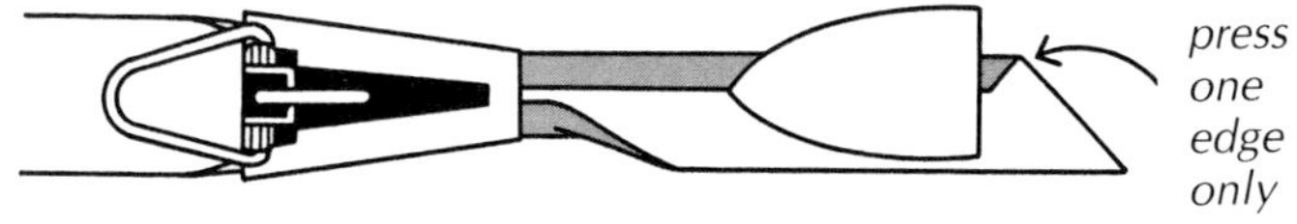

3. Pin bias to seam allowance right sides together and stitch along pressed-in crease.
4. Press seam to meld stitches.

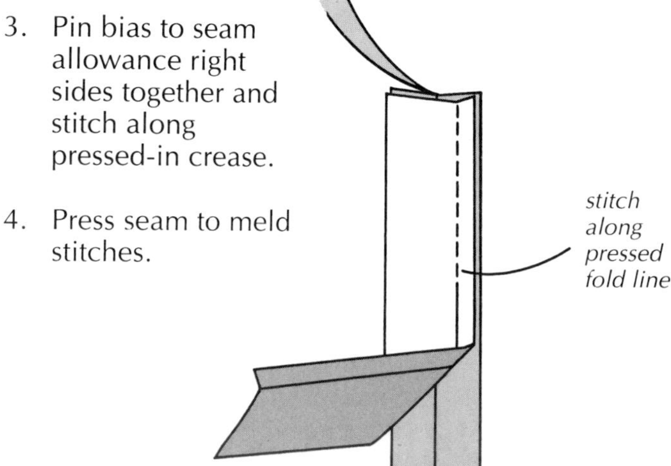

5. Fold bias to wrong side of seam. Pin, keeping pins at right angles to stitching line. The bias fabric on the back of the seam must be absolutely flat.

6. From the right side of the seam, stitch in the ditch (well of seam) to permanently hold the underside of the bias in place. Use thread color to match garment.

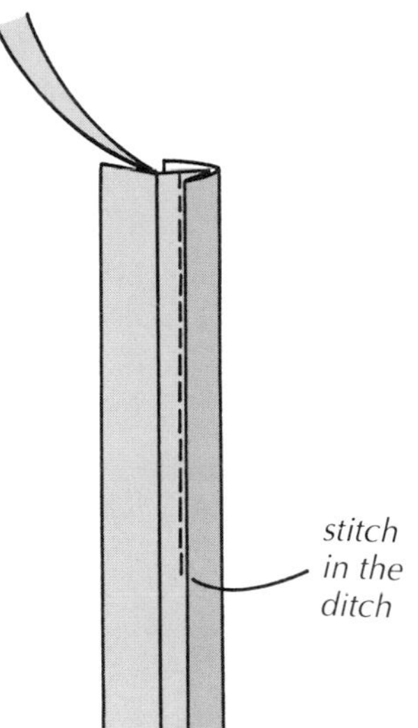

This can be hand stitched or machine stitched, whichever gives you more control.

7. Press at right angles to stitching line.

8. Excess bias on underside of seam can be trimmed to within 1/8" (.3cm) of stitching if desired.

A Very Narrow Hem

In fine sewing, it's sometimes desirable to finish an edge without a traditional hem. Ruffle edges, hem or armhole edges on a lining and the hem of a full or sheer dress are all good examples. The "very narrow hem" is the answer.

1. Add 5/8" (1.5cm) to finished length.

2. Turn up 1/2" (1.3cm) and press with iron perpendicular to hem.

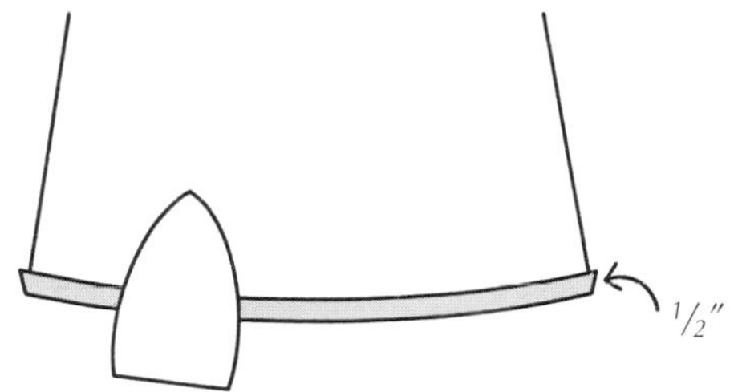

3. From **right side**, machine stitch 1/16" - 1/8" (.15-.3cm) from edge.

4. Press to meld stitches. Always press at right angles to the stitching line.

5. With very sharp scissors (pelican work well), cut away the seam allowance as close to stitches as possible.

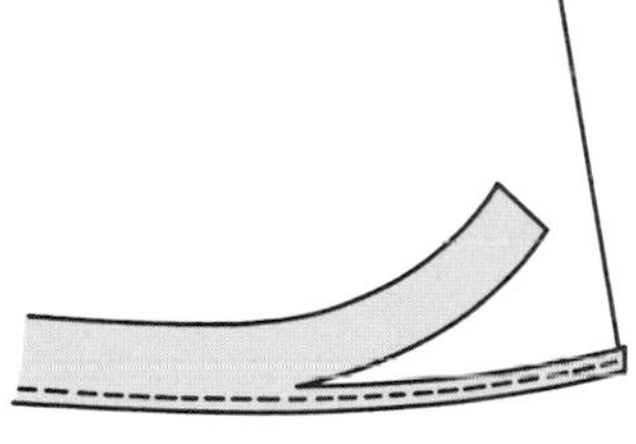

6. Press up stitched edge so original stitches are centered in what you've turned up.

7. From wrong side, slowly machine stitch directly over the first stitches holding fabric taut.

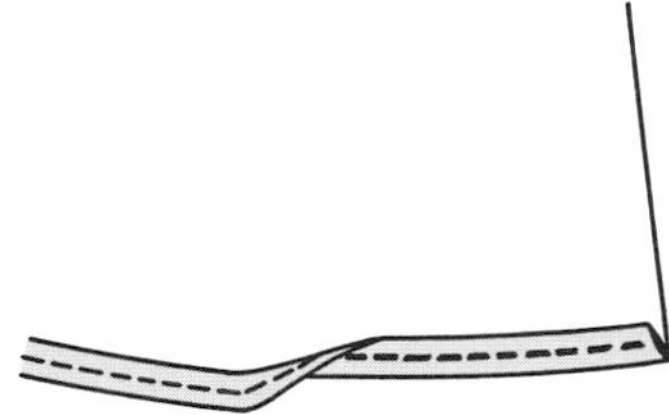

8. Press again to meld stitches.

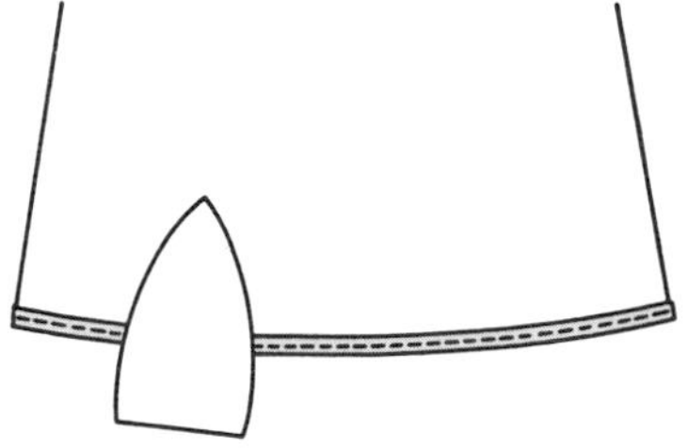

Designer Hems

A truly beautiful hem is one that doesn't show. The "float" stitch is an essential couture technique.

A float stitch attaches two pieces of fabric in such a way that one floats against the other. It moves forward along a single line. It is the "stitch of choice" for a hem. It is also used to attach hem interfacing to the garment and to attach the hem edge to the interfacing.

With a fine needle and single thread take a shallow pick in the hem, then the garment, catching one fiber or, if hem is interfaced, the interfacing, always moving forward and keeping the line of stitches as straight as possible.

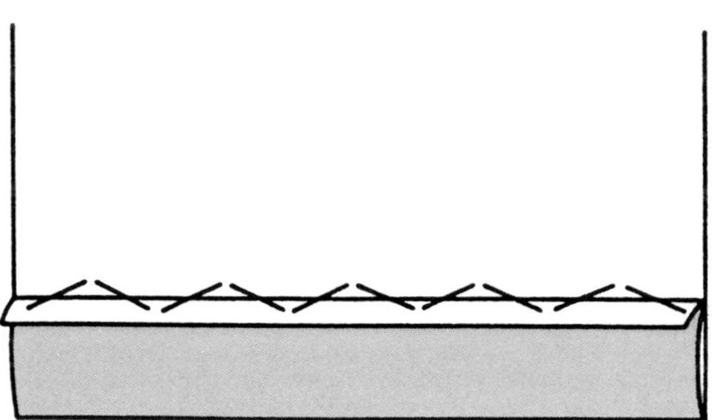

On wide hems, or hems on bias garments, one row may not be sufficient. In that case, peel hem back to within 3/4" (2cm) of hem fold. Float stitch around hem. Add another row of float stitches 1/2" - 3/4" (1.3 - 2cm) from first row. Repeat as necessary to within 1/2" (1.3cm) of hem edge.

Interfaced Hems

Interfacing the hem of a garment IS couture. Whether it be a dress, a skirt, or a pant, a tailored jacket or a coat, an interfaced hem adds weight, thus improving and enhancing the way the garment hangs. An interfaced hem prevents the hem edge from showing through to the right side of the garment and prevents any ridge from occurring during repeated dry-cleanings and/or pressings. An interfaced hem provides a soft, rounded lower edge.

In a coat, the lining hem is interfaced too, to add weight and prevent a fly-away lining. It also adds durability to the lining hem.

The type of interfacing used in an interfaced hem needs to relate to the fashion fabric as well as to the needed weight. The distance around should also be considered. A very full skirt might need a lighter weight interfacing than a straight skirt. On the other hand, a trouser or traditional pant may require a heavier interfacing, even though the leg is slim, to give it a cylindrical effect.

Tailored jackets or coats usually require a hair canvas or another interfacing that is similar to the interfacing used throughout the garment. However, the choice of interfacing should enhance the **hem** independent of other areas of the garment.

The Couture method of interfacing a hem requires sew-in interfacing. Possible materials include silk organza, 100% cotton or rayon/polyester woven interfacing, or a hair canvas.

The concept of an interfaced hem relates to circles. The garment, the interfacing, and the hem are all circles and each needs to be slightly smaller than the other. How much depends on the thickness of the fabric and the thickness of the interfacing. In order to maintain the correct ratio within these concentric circles, it is imperative to work from the right side of the garment as much as possible.

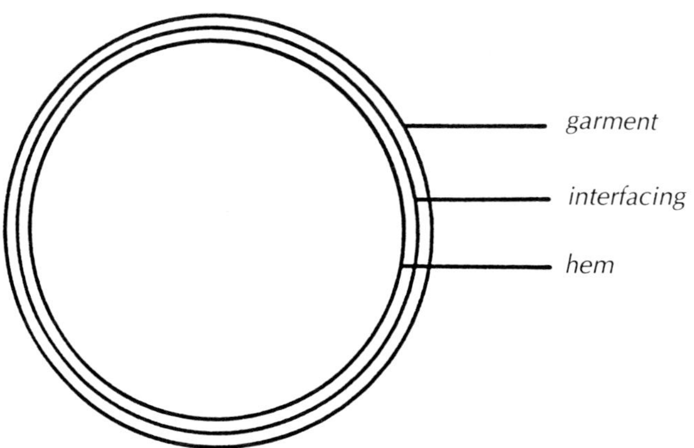

How to Interface a Hem

1. Thread trace the hem foldline with silk thread so it can be seen on the right **and** wrong side of garment.

2. Cut interfacing on the bias, making it the finished width of the hem, plus 1 1/4" (3.2cm).

3. Place interfacing on wrong side of garment with $\frac{5}{8}$" (1.5cm) extending past foldline.

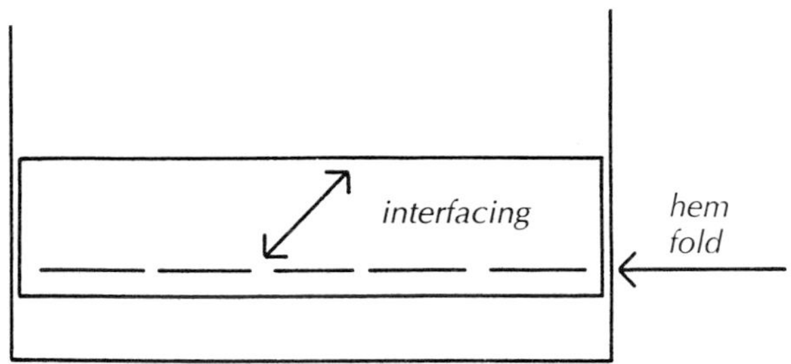

4. Pin interfacing to garment from the **right side** to ensure there is no excess interfacing. Pins should be perpendicular to hem edge.

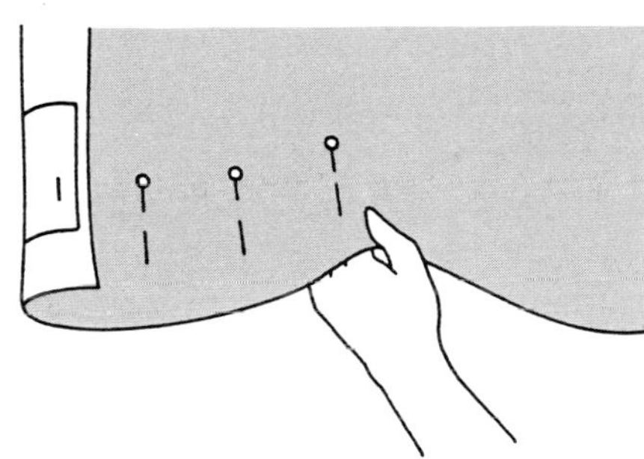

5. Working from the **wrong side**, slip stitch interfacing to fold line.

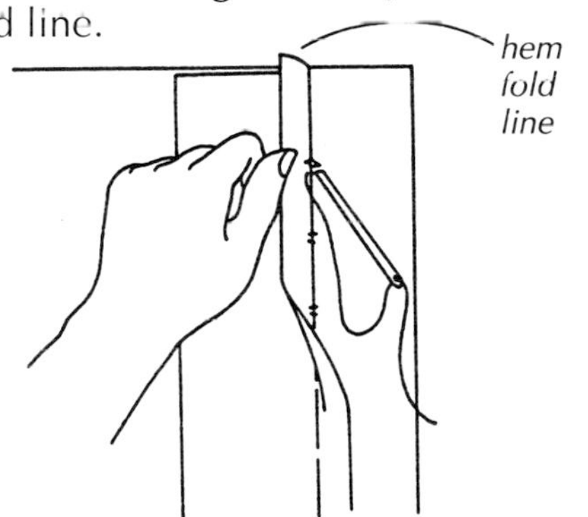

6. Turn up hem and pin in place; pin from **right side** over your hand.

7. Turn back **interfacing edge** and float stitch (see page 64) to garment about $\frac{1}{2}$" (1.3cm) from raw edge; remove pins.

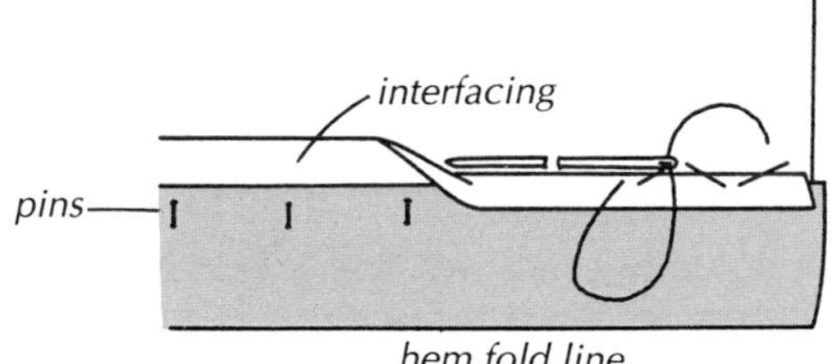

8. Sandwich hem between wool side of heavy duty press cloth. From the right side, **lightly** press hem.

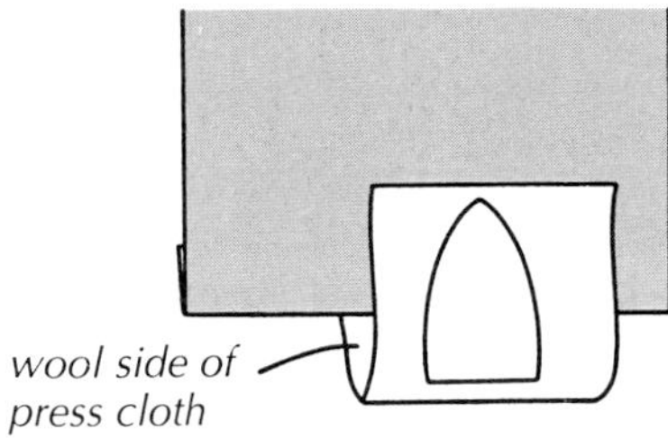

9. Check raw edge of hem to be sure it lies flat against interfacing. Steam shrink hem edge if ripples appear or run two rows of machine ease stitching and pull up bobbin threads to ease in fullness if excess is severe. Don't pull up too tightly.

10. When hem edge lies flat, finish the raw edge of hem with your choice of the following hem finishes:

    a. *Hong Kong (page 62)*
    b. *mock Hong Kong (page 62)*
    c. *serge*
    d. *hand overcast*
    e. *bind with Seams Great or Seam Saver*

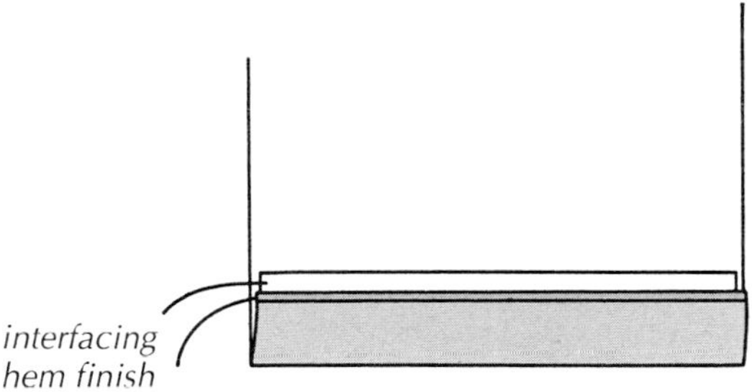

11. Pin hem in place from **right side**.

12. Turn back **hem edge** $\frac{1}{4}$" to $\frac{1}{2}$" (.6 to 1.3 cm) and float stitch hem allowance to interfacing. Be sure needle does not pick up garment fabric. To prevent hem from pulling out, pass needle through loop of thread on every third stitch as if to tie it off.

Mitering

Simply defined, mitering is a way to join two pieces of fabric at a corner to produce a sharp, non-bulky point or corner. Carpenters use mitering when installing molding at the corner of a counter top.

Any corner can be mitered by folding in the seam allowances. For example, on a square-cornered pocket:

1. Fold under seam allowances on the sides.
2. Fold up the bottom edge.
3. Clip diagonally where raw edges of the seam allowances intersect.
4. Pin or mark the corner.

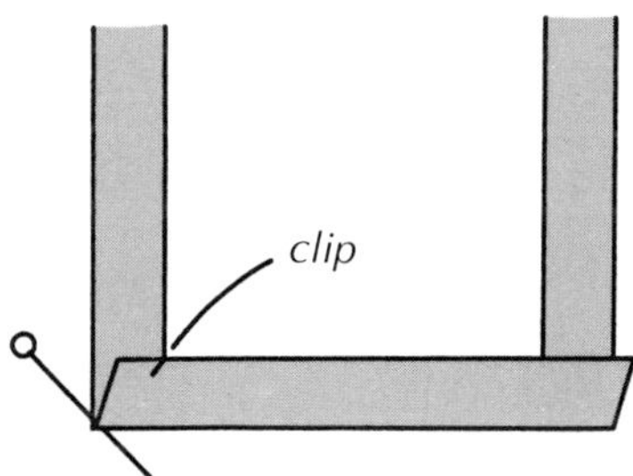

5. Unfold side and bottom edges, then fold right sides together, at corner.
6. Stitch from clips to corner point using 20 stitches per inch (8 stitches per centimeter). Do not backstitch.

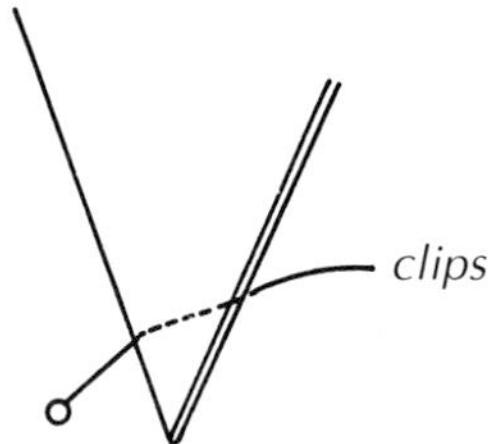

7. Trim the corner to 3/8" (1cm). Trim diagonally to the point. Press seam open over a point presser.

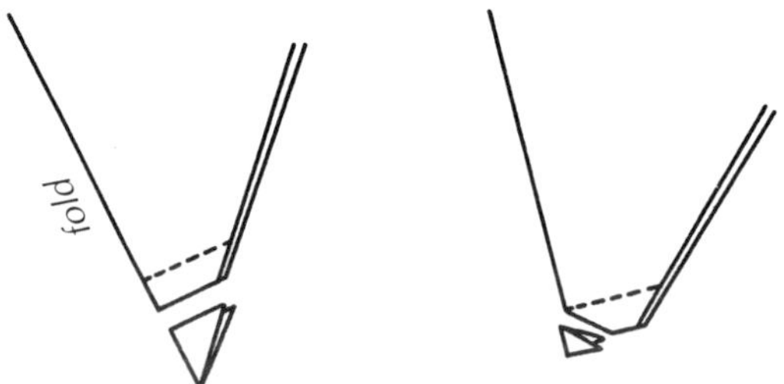

8. Turn seam allowances to wrong side and press corner again.

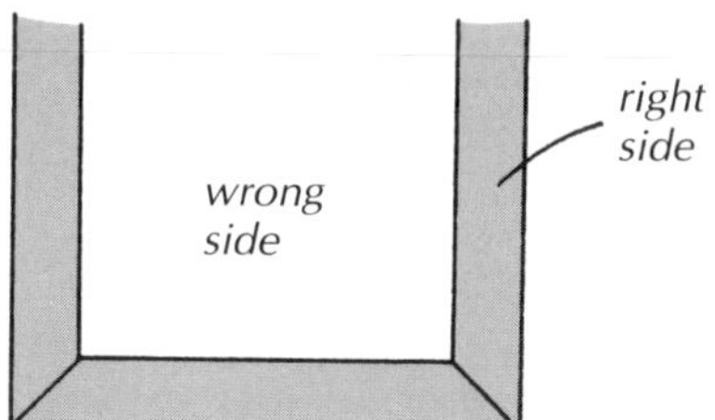

9. **Gently** press from the right side, using a press cloth.

I particularly like this method because it's foolproof. It works even if you have two seams that are not of similar width and when the angle you're trying to miter is not a perfect right angle as in a pointed collar.

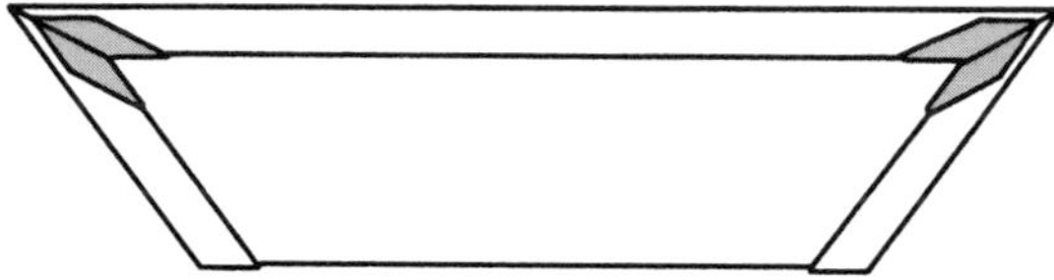

Mitering takes only a minute, and saves time later by eliminating the need to deal with a bulky and often unsightly point.

Double-Needle Stitching

A double needle is just that—two needles on one shank. The distance between the needles and the size of the needles varies. A double needle requires two spools of thread on the top of the machine and one bobbin thread.

To prevent twisting, a common occurrence with double-needle stitching, thread three bobbins. Place two on the top of the machine and one in the bobbin case. This means that all three sources of thread were wound off the original spool in the same direction and they won't twist against each other.

Stitching with a double needle creates two rows of stitching on the right side of the fabric with only one bobbin thread on the wrong side floating between the two rows. The bobbin thread looks like zigzagging.

COUTURE Tip Using a double needle for top stitching, such as on the collars and lapels of a jacket, may not be appropriate because the single bobbin thread underneath will pull up rather than keep the work absolutely flat.

Double-Needle Stitching on the Bias

Double-needle stitching on the bias is not impossible, but skill is required. Here are some tips:

1. Fabric must be **PERFECTLY AND PRECISELY** on grain and bias lines marked accurately.

2. Gently stretch the bias as you sew. Every row **must** be held with the **same** amount of stretch as it goes through the machine.

Double-Needle Tucking

The bobbin thread can be used to advantage in making tiny tucks. By tightening or loosening the bobbin tension, you can adjust the amount of tuck. The tighter the bobbin tension, the greater the tuck.

Rather than adjusting tension, you can also pull up on the bobbin thread and the two rows of stitching will come together, forming a little tuck.

Caution: On some fabrics it is very difficult to pull up the bobbin thread for more than a few inches. Test first and if this happens, tighten the bobbin tension for a deeper tuck instead.

Always test double-needle tucking on a small piece of fabric first. Determine what bobbin tension is necessary. Also, generally, the heavier the fabric, the longer the stitch length should be when double-needle tucking. Test stitch length to find what looks best.

It is difficult to estimate the amount of take-up when tucking; therefore it is advisable to tuck a piece of fabric first, then cut out the pattern piece. Tuck on the straight or cross grain for your first try. After that, the sky's the limit to design or expand on this concept.

Design Ideas with Double-Needle Tucking

- ◆ Tuck a yoke.
- ◆ Tuck a bib front.
- ◆ Tuck short sleeves.
- ◆ Tuck a pocket.

Couture Alternatives for Double-Needle Tucking

Use normal tension in the bobbin or loosen slightly. Sew row of stitches. Thread a blunt hand needle (tapestry needle) with pearl cotton and run it under the bobbin stitches on the wrong side of the fabric. This will make corded tucks. It is a labor of love, requiring time and patience.

Double rows of stitches can be placed evenly (one after the other) or spaced varying distances apart for unique patterns.

CHAPTER 10

Darts

Understanding darts—what they do, where they go, and how you can use darts for fit is foundation knowledge in Couture. That simple "tuck" in the fabric, pointed at one end and called a dart, is a miracle worker.

Darts are devices for shaping and fitting. Darts are not as glamorous or as beautiful as perfect bias ruffles; but you must know where they are or should be, and learn how to manipulate or move them.

Anatomy of a Dart

A dart has two legs (sides), a point and depth called take-up.

- Legs—The two legs of a dart must be the same length.
- Point—The point of a dart must point to the place on the body where fullness is required.
- Take-up—The take-up is relative to the size of the body.

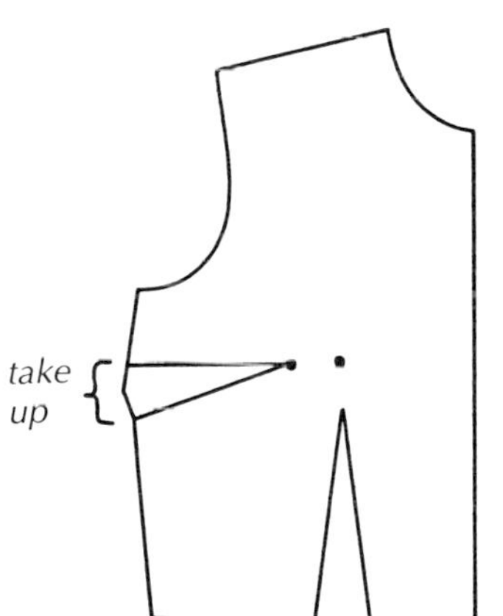

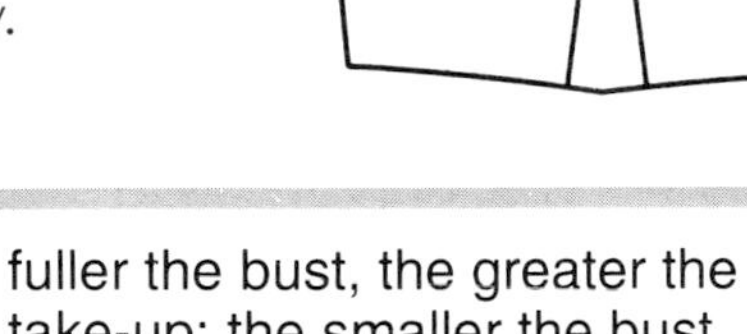

COUTURE Rule The fuller the bust, the greater the dart take-up; the smaller the bust, the less the dart take-up.

Dart legs need not be perfectly straight even if they are that way on the pattern tissue. They can be curved to conform to the body for better fit. For example, in a skirt front, the stitching can be curved into the dart to provide more ease over a body curve.

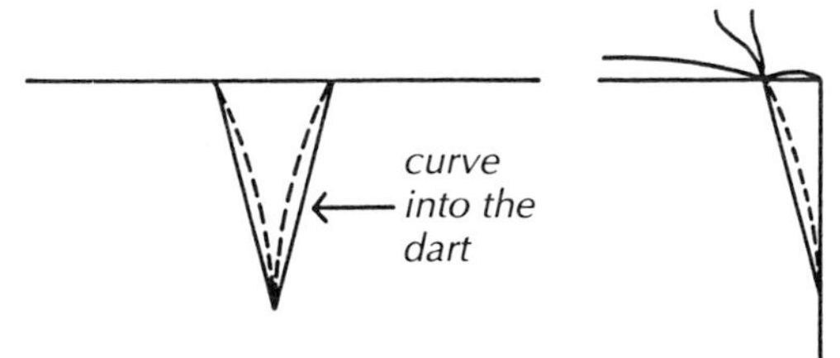

Or, the stitching can be **curved toward the garment** for a closer fit.

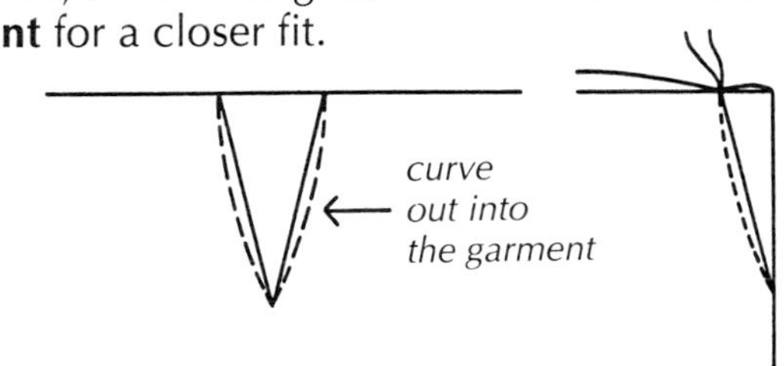

In either case, the take-up and point location remain the same. The curve is very shallow, about $^1/_{16}$″ (3mm) at the midpoint of the dart leg (half way between cut edge and point).

When curving a dart, baste it together on its straight legs for all fittings. Just before stitching, place a French curve on the fashion fabric; chalk a new line. Stitch on the chalked line.

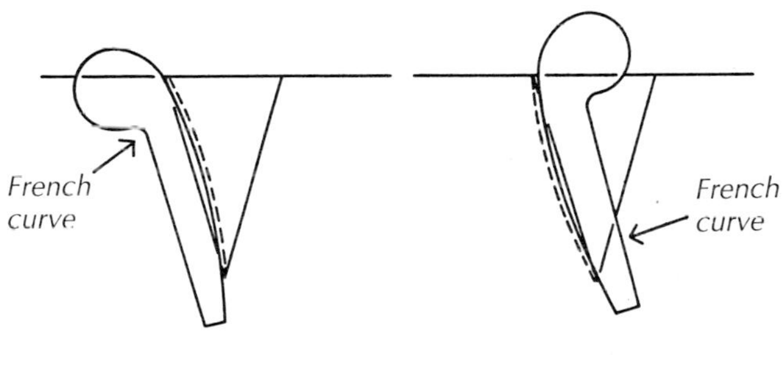

Darts can be lengthened or shortened. When this is done, the take-up remains the same. Only the location of the point changes.

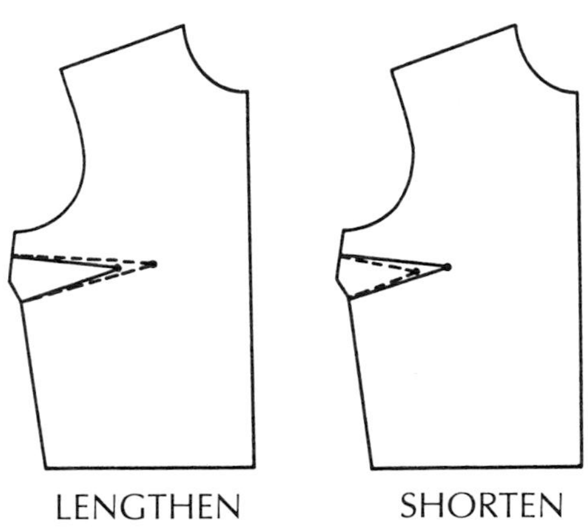

Dart Types

Bust Darts

The area around the bust point (apex) is called the bust circle. It is usually 2″ to 3″ (5 to 7.5cm) in diameter.

COUTURE Tip The bust circle increases in size as the size of the bust increases. The RULES for dart placement are the same for everyone, no matter what size.

Darts for bust fullness, called fitting darts, must point to the apex and come within the bust circle.

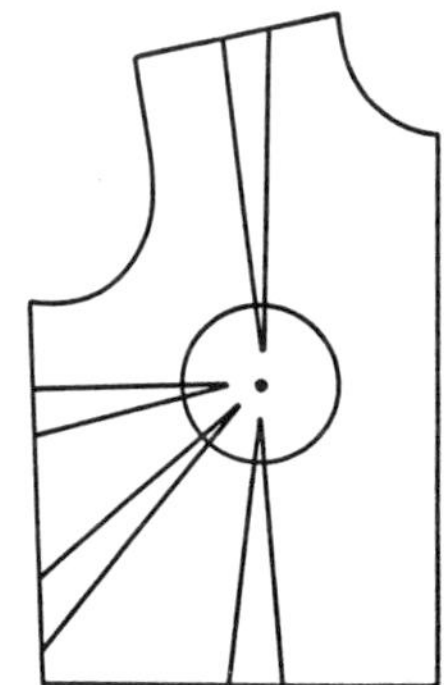

Decorative or design darts can be placed anywhere as long as you know they do not provide fit or shaping. To prevent excess fullness, design darts are usually shallow (not much take up).

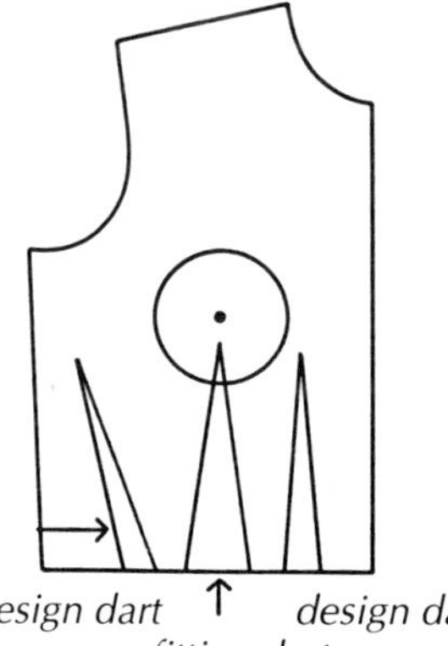

Whether a dart comes to the bust circle or is closer to the apex depends on the number of darts and their placement on a garment.

Understand these rules about darts:

1. If there are two darts, each with similar take-up amounts but coming from different seams, they should end at or just inside the bust circle.

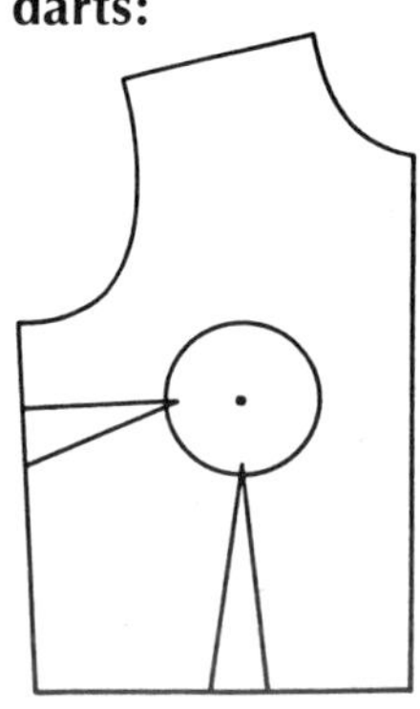

2. If two darts come from the same seam, they should extend almost to the apex and be equally distant from it.

3. If there are two darts coming from two different seams, the dart with the greater angle should end closer to bust point.

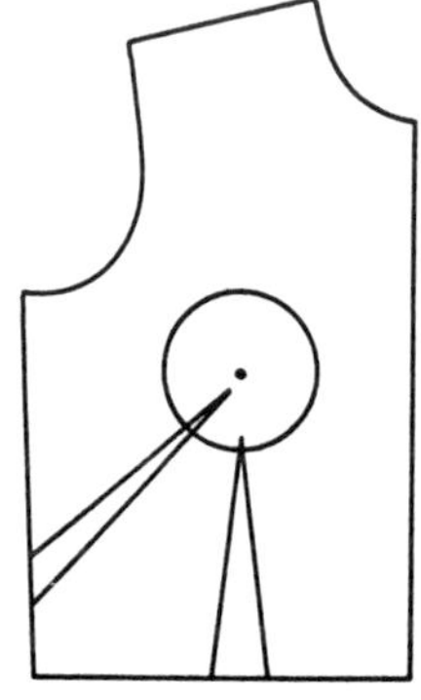

4. A large dart, created by combining two darts, should come almost to the apex to achieve a smooth look.

5. Darts that end right at the apex remove intended fullness and ease.

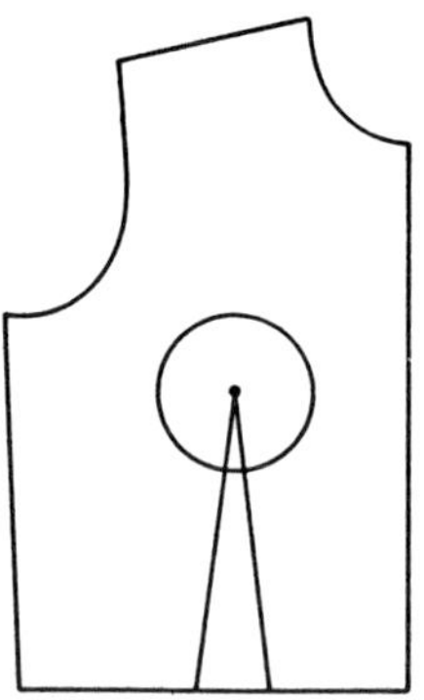

French Darts

A French dart angles toward the bust from the side seam. It can be directed from slightly above the waist, the waist, the high hip, the full hip, or anywhere between. A French dart gives a slimming effect to a one-piece garment (dress, jacket or coat).

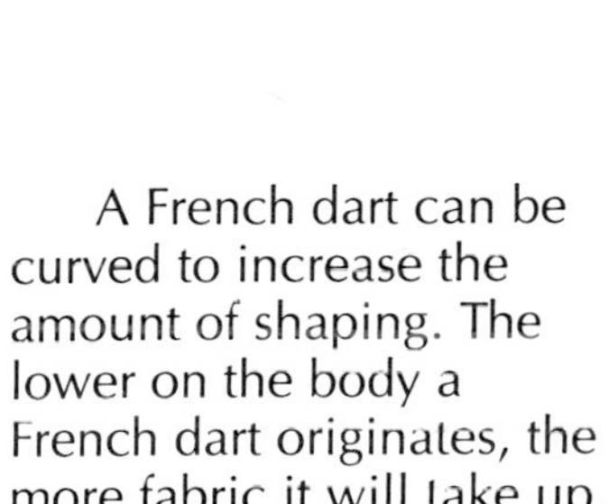

A French dart can be curved to increase the amount of shaping. The lower on the body a French dart originates, the more fabric it will take up.

When pressing a French dart, it may be necessary to slash it along the fold and press it open, trimming seam allowance to 5/8″ (1.5cm).

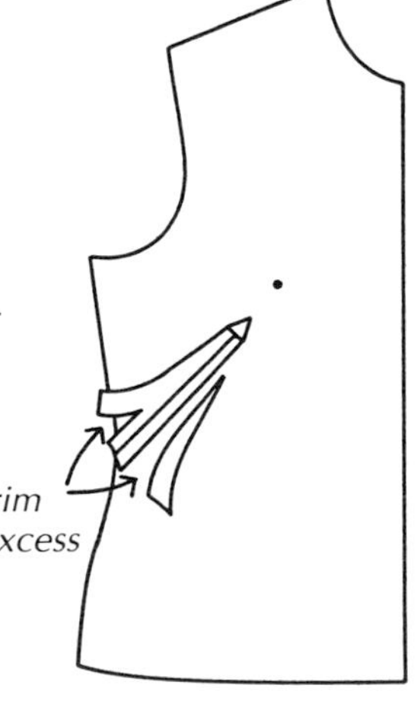

Reduce bulk wherever possible.

If the angle of a dart on a commercial pattern is not pleasing for your body, you can change it to create a French dart.

1. Mark bust point on pattern.
2. Draw a new French dart location line from bust point to side seam; make a couple of marks across the line to serve as notches.

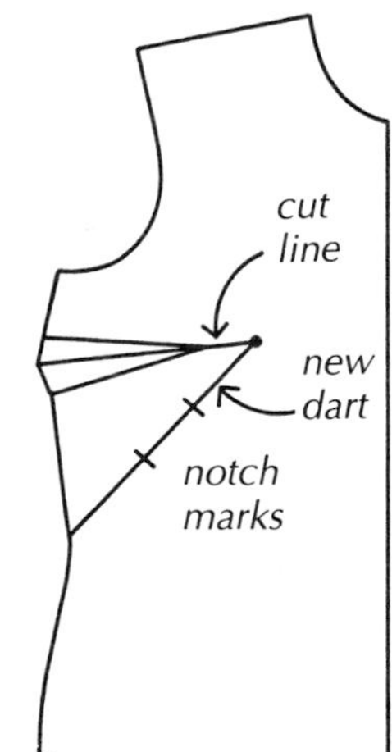

3. Cut through center of the original dart to the bust point. Cut on new dart line.
4. Close original dart by lapping stitching lines and taping in place.
5. Pattern will spread, creating a new dart opening.

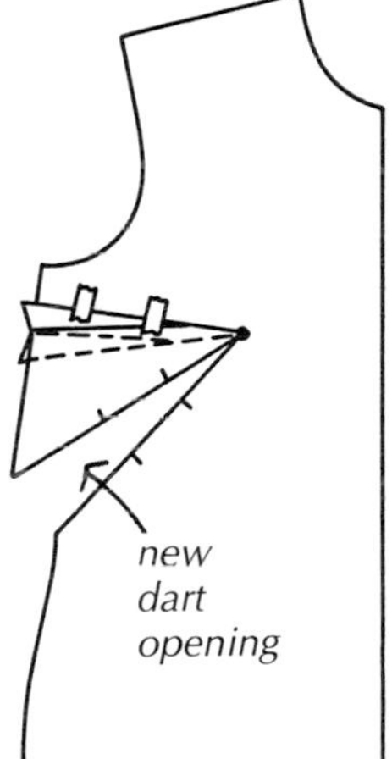

6. Draw new dart with the point the same distance from the apex as the original dart.

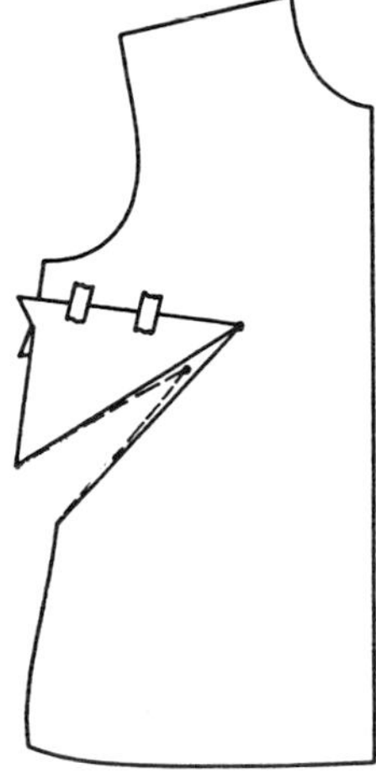

Mark a French dart carefully. Slip-baste together from the right side of the fabric matching notch marks exactly. (See Slip-Basting, page 39.) Machine stitch according to traditional method (page 73) or single thread method (page 74). Meld and press over a ham.

Shoulder Darts

The original sloper used as the foundation for all designs has a dart in the back shoulder to provide fullness for the shoulder blade. In many designs this dart has been converted to ease. You can do this, too, if you wish.

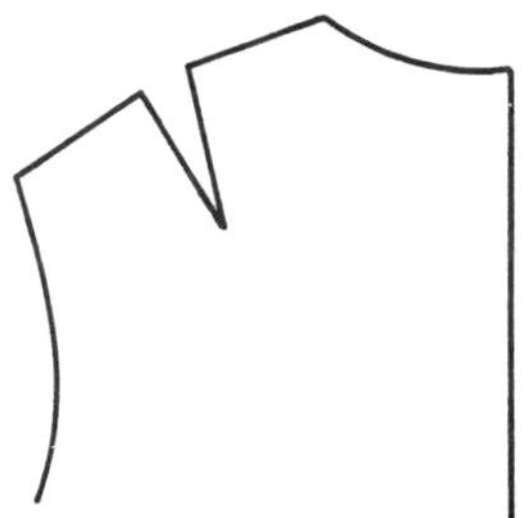

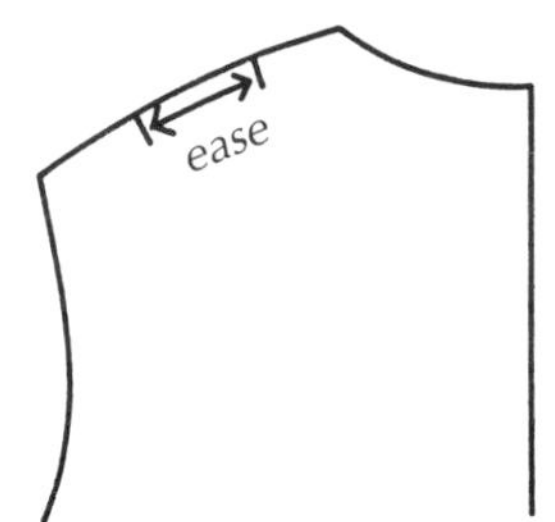

1. Cut dart out of paper pattern.

2. Draw four lines from shoulder seam to dart point, two on each side of the dart, 1/8" (.3cm) apart.

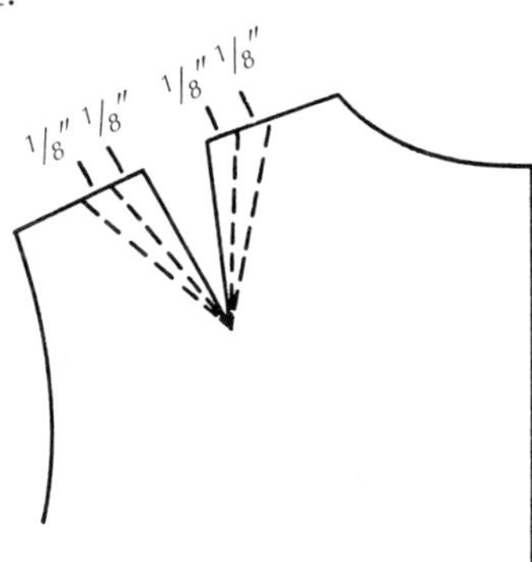

3. Cut on each line stopping at dart point.

4. Spread pie-shaped pieces evenly.

5. With French curve, connect points from shoulder point to neck edge in a slightly curved line. Be sure each wedge is contained within the curve.

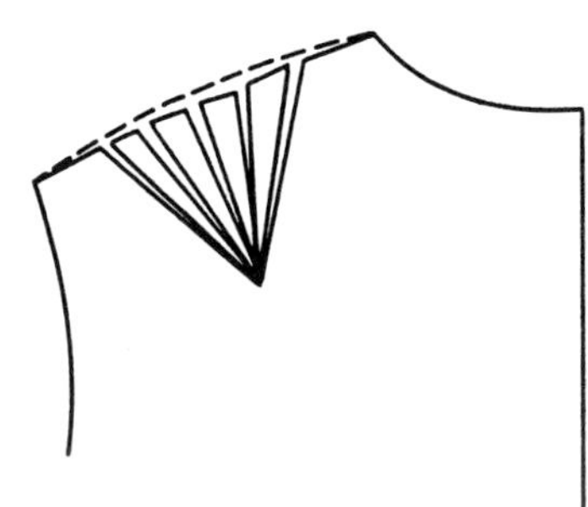

6. Indicate ease between slashes.

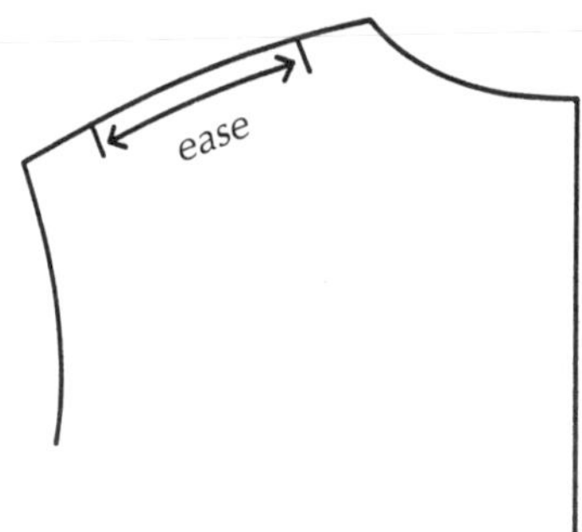

Occasionally, a commercial pattern has a straight back shoulder seam even though there is no dart. For the shoulder seam to lie flat and the garment to fall smoothly over the shoulder down the back, you may want to add a little ease, especially if the garment is a more fitted silhouette.

Measure the shoulder stitching line. At the halfway point, make a dot 1/8" (.3cm) above it. Using the French curve, connect shoulder, new halfway point and neck with a slight curve. Ease back shoulder to fit front shoulder and slip-baste (page 39) from the right side over a ham, folding the back shoulder over the front to retain the curve.

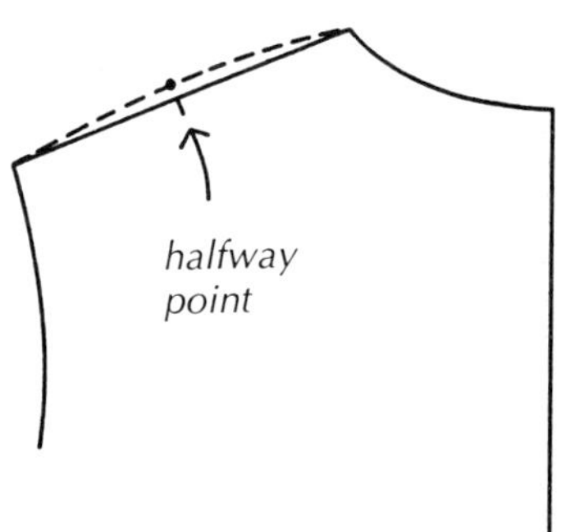

Darts in Pant Back

The two traditional darts in the back of pants serve different purposes. The longer dart nearer the center back provides fullness for the derriere. The shorter dart, nearer the side seam, provides fullness for the flesh that pads the hip.

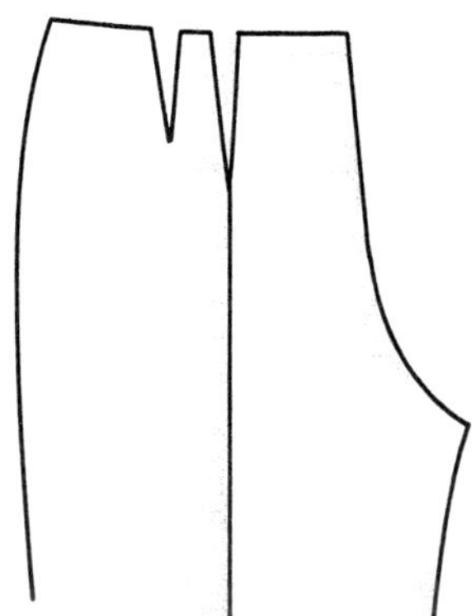

The plumper (fuller) the derriere, or the more padded the hip, the greater the dart take-up.

COUTURE Tip This concept relates to fullness, not size. For example, a size 6 person might have a plump derriere; a size 16 person might have a flat derriere.

For a full derriere, increase the dart take-up nearer the center back. For a flat derriere, release some of the take-up.

For more padded hips, greater take-up is needed on the dart nearer the side seam; for less padding, a narrower dart is needed.

You also may need to curve either dart to follow the body contour.

Angle of Darts in Pant Back

The center back seam is the primary fitting point for pants. The general rule calls for the darts to be parallel to the center back seam. If you change the angle of the center back seam during fitting, you may need to change the angle of the darts.

1. Darts parallel to the center back seam create a long lean line.

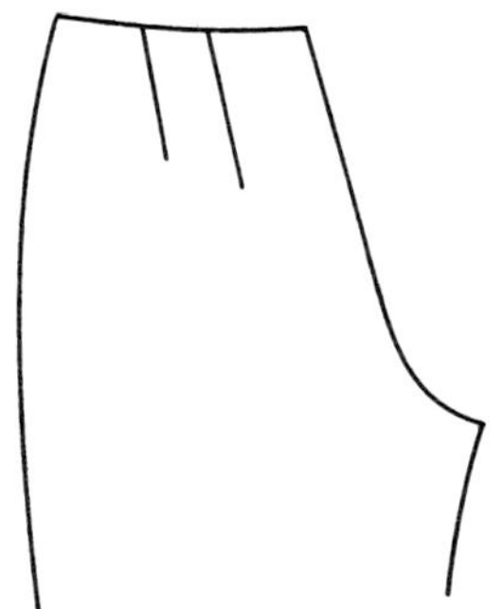

2. To emphasize a small waist, both darts can be angled as shown below. But the darts still must point to the place on the body where fullness is required.

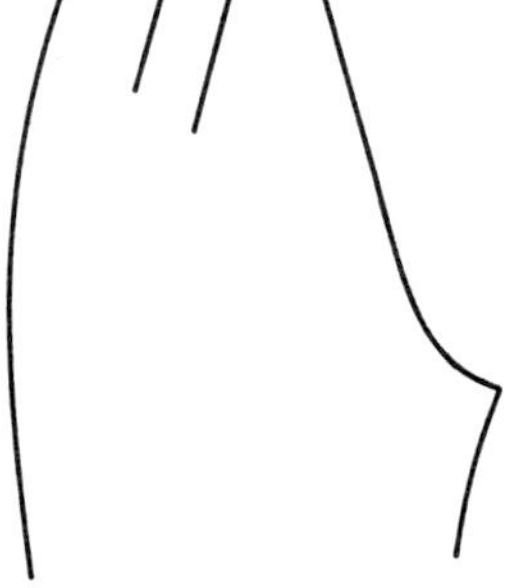

3. If the side seam is very curved in the hip area, it is more appealing to angle the hip dart parallel to the side seam and the dart nearer the center back parallel to the center back.

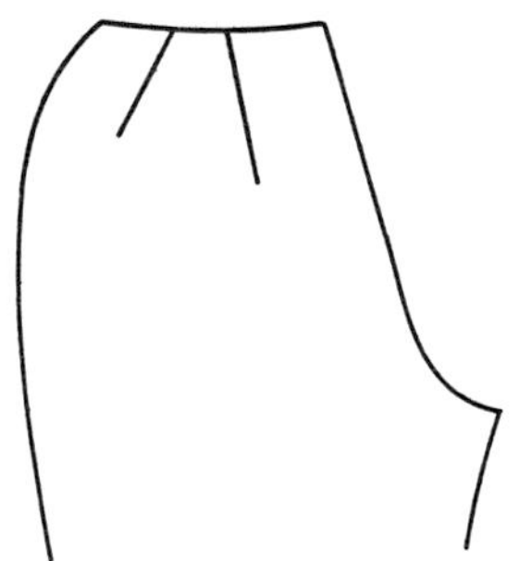

To change the angle of a dart, retain the point but move the legs, measuring the take-up to ensure the amount is not changed.

Sewing a Dart–From Seam to Point!

1. Set the machine at 20 stitches per inch (8 stitches per centimeter) and stitch beginning at the seam edge.
2. After stitching for $1/2''$ (1cm), return machine to regular stitch length and continue to within $1/2''$ (1cm) of the point.

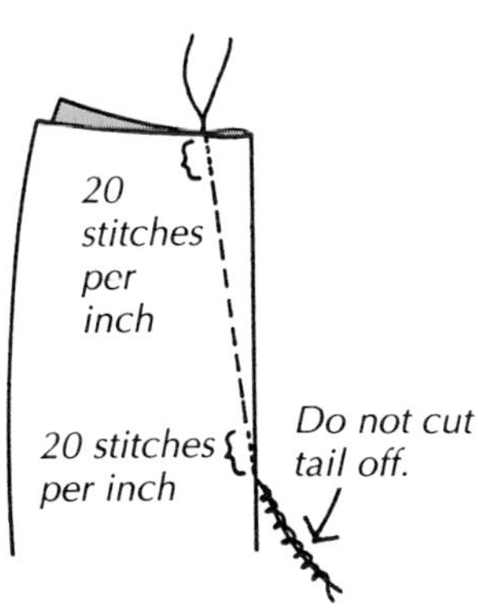

3. Return to 20 stitches per inch and stitch past the point with the last few stitches riding right on the edge of the fold.
4. When the presser foot leaves the fabric, continue stitching 2"-3" (5-8cm) and cut the thread, leaving a tail. This secures the dart without backstitching or tying off with knots.

Single-thread Dart

A single-thread dart has no thread tail at the point. The advantages of a single-thread dart far outweigh the extra time required.

Where to Use a Single-thread Dart:

- On sheer fabrics where shadow-through is expected.
- On short darts ($1\frac{1}{2}$" (4cm) or less), as in the cap of a sleeve.
- On fabric that is difficult to press such as gabardine.
- On darts that extend almost to the bust point.
- In very fitted garments.
- In tailored garments.

Once you make a single-thread dart with its smooth, pucker-free point, and experience the ease of pressing it, you'll probably prefer it. Great! You've just accepted the Couture "attitude." But remember, **practice makes perfect**.

How to Stitch a Single-thread Dart

Test with two different colors of thread to understand this technique.

1. Thread machine as usual, except stop just before threading the needle.
2. Using a needle threader, pull **bobbin** thread backwards through needle eye and tie bobbin thread to needle thread with a tiny square knot.

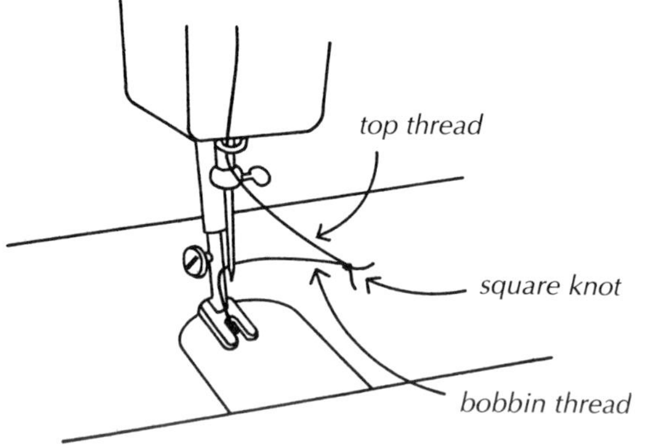

3. Gently re-wind needle thread until bobbin thread comes up to the spool and wraps around several times. You'll need enough thread to sew one dart. Do not skimp. Now only one thread, with no slack, should be at the needle point.
4. **Sew from dart point to seam edge**, the opposite direction from the traditional dart stitching method.

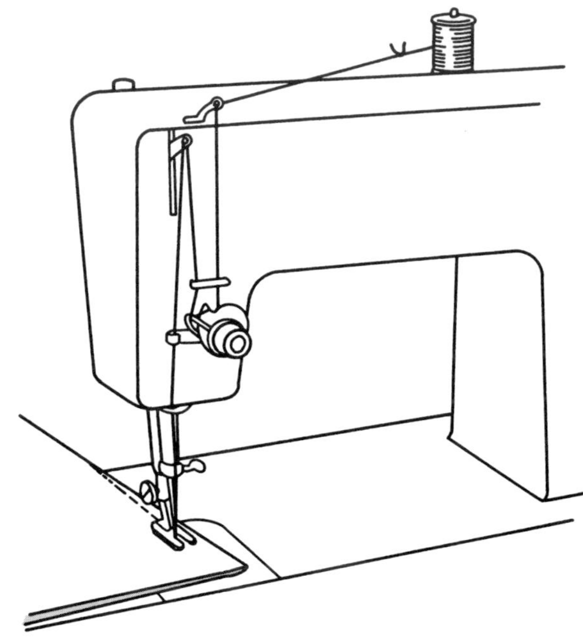

Place the dart point under the needle so first stitch is **exactly** on the fabric fold. Stitch $\frac{1}{2}$" (1cm) at 20 stitches per inch (8 stitches per centimeter), then change to regular stitch length, changing back to 20 stitches per inch $\frac{1}{2}$" before reaching cut edge. Cut threads. To sew the next dart, rethread the machine in the same manner.

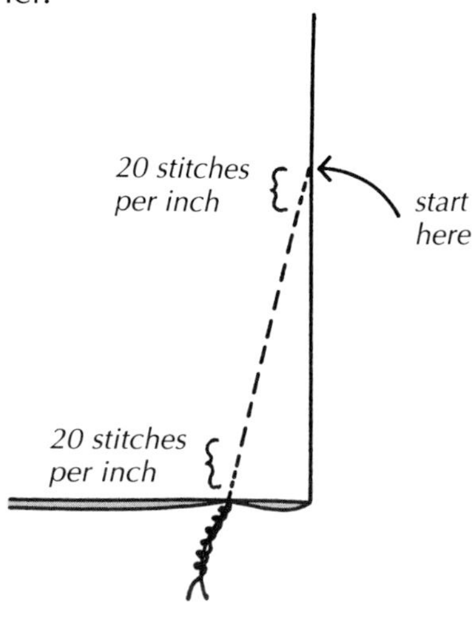

Trimming a Dart

A dart in a seam creates bulk. After sewing a seam over a dart, remove bulk by cutting off the dart seam allowance from seamline to dart stitching line. When pressing, apply a little moisture if necessary, and use a clapper to flatten the dart **in the seam allowance only**.

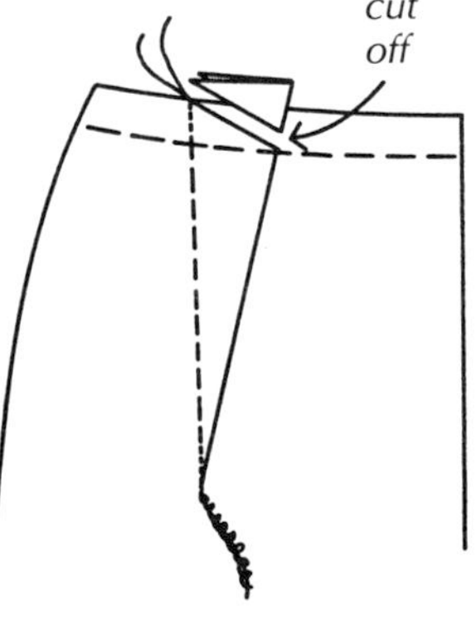

Pressing Darts

1. Press dart flat first on both sides to meld the stitches and permanently crease and flatten the dart fold.
2. Press vertical darts toward the center front or center back; press horizontal darts downward.
3. Because darts are double thickness, they could create a ridge on the right side of the garment, so tuck a piece of brown paper under the dart to protect the garment.

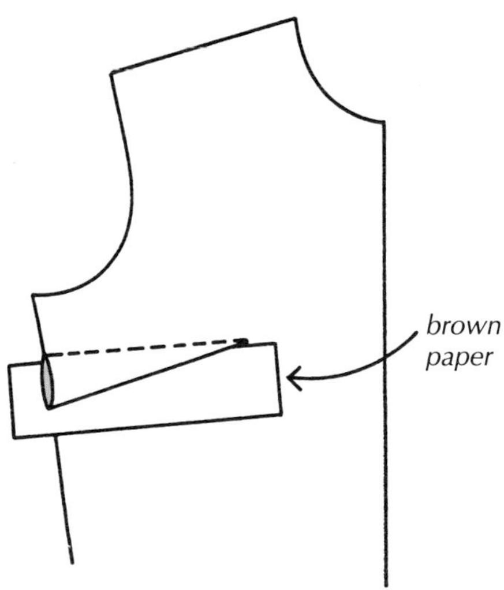

4. Press darts over a ham to retain the intended fullness and curve. The area around the dart point should never be pressed flat; that would defeat the purpose.

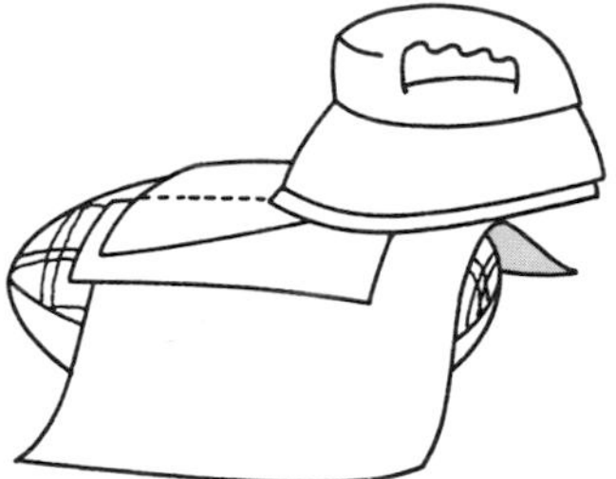

5. Slash deep darts on the fold stopping 1″-1½″ (2.5-4cm) from the point. Press open. Trim seam allowances to ⅝″ (1.5cm) to reduce bulk.

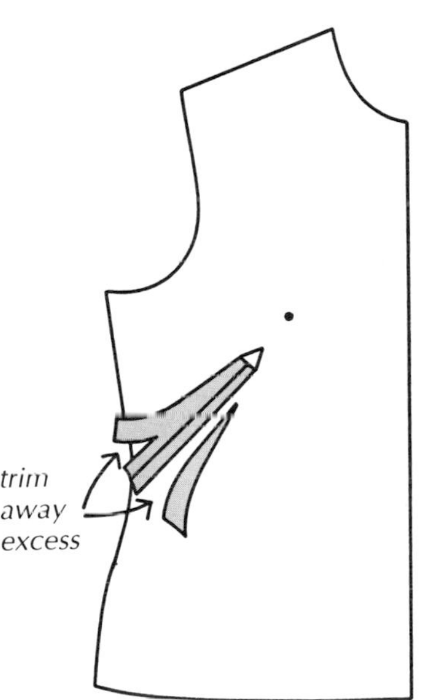

CHAPTER 11

The Bias

Ode to Madame Madeleine Vionnet

Ann Jacobi, a student from Albuquerque, New Mexico, asked me one day who my mentor was. I mentioned a few designers, quite off the top of my head and then spent a week really thinking about this question.

I believe we must understand and study those who have gone before us. No matter what field we're in, those who walked the path first have a lot to tell us. This is especially true with fashion and subsequently sewing. One person I have taken counsel from through books and clothes is Madame Vionnet. Alas, I never sat at her side; she closed her couture house the year I was born. But a mentor from afar, yes.

Let me tell you about her. She was a woman ahead of her time, but in touch with the reality of the day. She ridded fashion of corsets. Oh, if Paul Poiret were here today, he might say he did, but then this is not a contest.

Madame Vionnet freed women by unleashing their beautiful bodies and adorning them with fluid fabrics, the bias cut with very little decoration or ornamentation to clutter the beauty of the woman.

As most couturiers have done, Madame Vionnet worked for others before she opened her own couture house. It is always fascinating to me that the previous experience and exposure of those who are "great" always is reflected in some way in their work.

About 1902, Madame Vionnet worked for Callot Soeurs. The Callot Sisters were a remarkable trio of young women of Russian ancestry, born in France, who designed lingerie as well as beautiful dresses. Their desire for perfection, sense of color, draped lingerie, one-of-a-kind embroideries and exotic details surrounded Madame Vionnet. I like to think of it as 20th century art-to-wear.

By 1907, Madame Vionnet was a designer at the House of Doucet. Jacques Doucet had a heritage from family businesses of lingerie and lace. He loved elegance and was often mentioned in the same breath as Charles Worth. Today it is with envy that we see the interaction and influence of these couturiers on each other.

In 1912, Madame Vionnet opened her own couture house at 222 Rue de Rivoli. In 1922, she moved to 50 Avenue Montaigne. It is said that Vionnet designs were the most original, so different that they could not be copied, even today. She was a technician as well as a designer. As a child, she loved mathematics and those around her thought she should enter that field of endeavor. It translated to cloth instead.

Her fabrics were heavy weight silk crepe, chiffon, silk lame', velvet, crepe-back satin and others, all with a fluid drape as their major characteristic. She felt that drawing designs or working on paper (as in paper patterns) was very restricting and limited innovation. Thus she draped on a $^1/_2$-scale mannequin. I can imagine this little, frail woman sitting in her studio, letting her hands follow the language of the fabric. Her own freedom of expression shouts from her clothes. She was the creator of the art of couture.

It has been said she was an architect and to implement her radical designs cut on the bias, she had special fabric woven 78" (198cm) wide. Aha! There's part of the answer to why there were so few seams in Vionnet designs.

She had, at the root of her being, a natural sense of proportion, rhythm, balance and harmony. She often joined seams with fagoting for greater fluidity and contouring the body. She added godets for extra fullness, still retaining the bias quality. She edged chiffon with rhinestones to give weight.

In looking at the life of Madame Vionnet, one should not go away with the notion that everything she ever designed was fluid as a peignoir. Her collections from the mid-'20s to the late-'30s included suits, dresses and coats. Her cloth coats (velvet) with fur were heralded around the globe. Whether a ball gown with tiers of ruffles or a summer day dress, one could always see the influence of the bias. Madame Vionnet's work possessed her. It was a passion. There are those who consider Madame Vionnet the greatest couturier of all time. When the vote is taken, count me in.

The Bias Grain

You can take advantage of the bias grain in couture garments in two ways.

1. Garment sections or entire garments can be cut on the bias grain to create interesting effects in the drape, fit and visual design of the garment.

2. Bias-cut fabric strips can be used to bind edges and to create piping for both decorative and functional purposes.

The **fear** of working on "**the bias**" was ingrained in many of us at an early age. Some sewing teachers spoke of it as "the enemy," never to be understood and to be kept at a distance. The bias is **not a disease**—it is a **grain** of cloth that when respected, can be used to advantage to produce remarkable results.

Madame Vionnet said, "There are three grains: lengthwise, crosswise, and bias. We must understand them all."

The bias does, at times, have a mind of its own, but with understanding comes control. Couture is control. Couture is about bias. When you can handle bias, you are couture!

- Bias hangs "thinner" than both straight and crossgrain.
- Bias doesn't ravel.
- Bias doesn't wrinkle.
- Bias is soft and rounded.
- True bias is the grain that runs at a 45-degree angle to the lengthwise and crosswise grains.

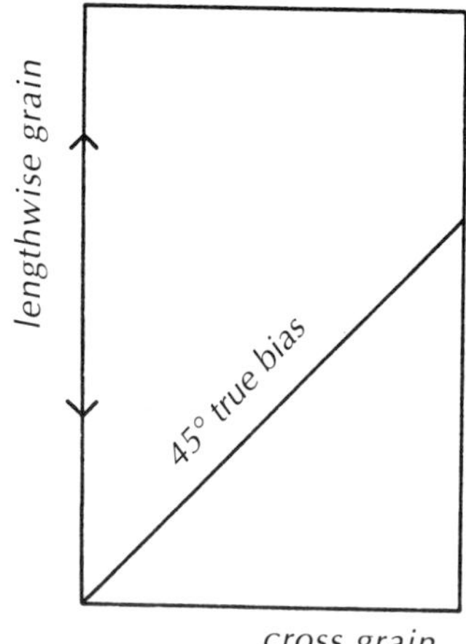

When working on the bias, the fabric must be perfectly grained up and the bias line established. (See Graining Up, page 43.)

Bias-Cut Skirts

It is rare to find a fabric in which exactly the same number of threads are in the crosswise and lengthwise grains. Because of this, an A-line skirt cut on the bias in one piece almost always results in its hanging heavier on one side than the other.

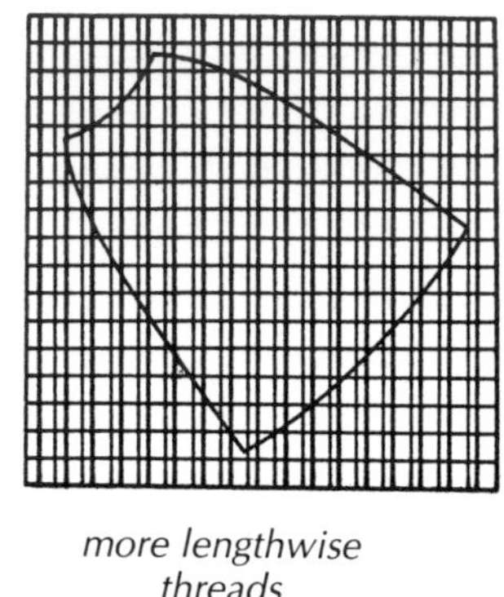
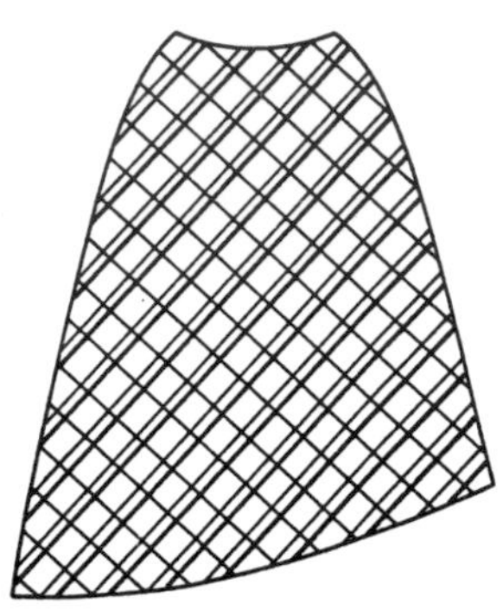

more lengthwise threads

If you cut the same skirt from the same fabric, but in two pieces at right angles to each other, the skirt will be balanced and hang evenly. **No matter how many pieces, each should be at right angles to the other going around the body.** Use this placement whether the fabric is solid, striped or plaid. When it is a stripe or plaid, a beautiful chevron will emerge.

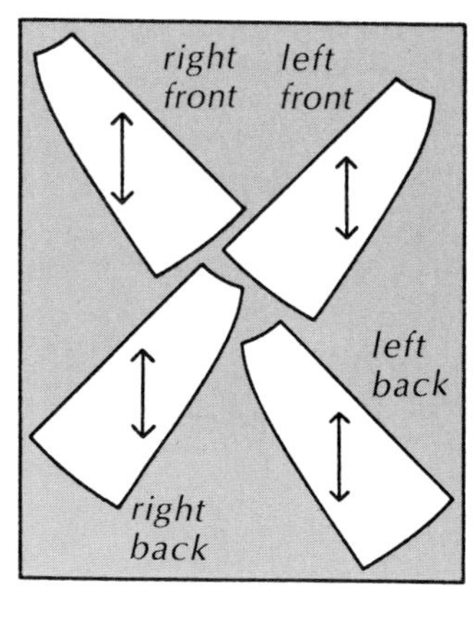

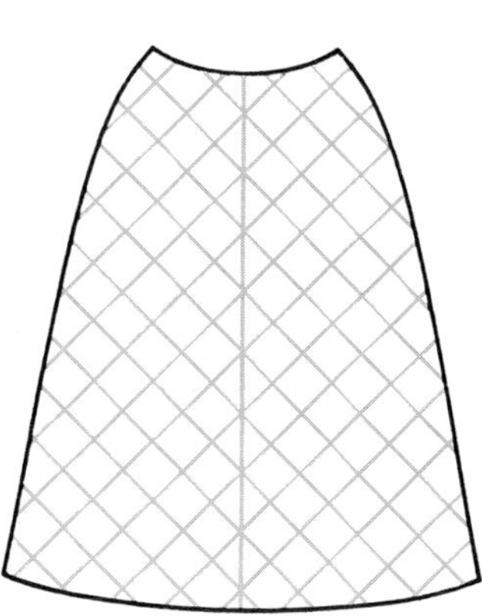

FIBERS IN A SOLID

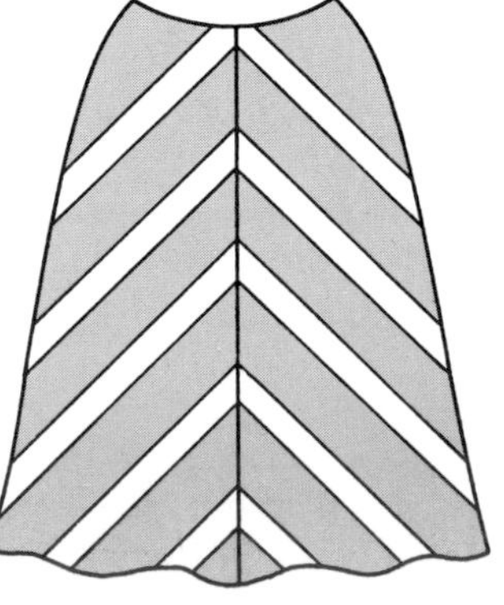

STRIPE

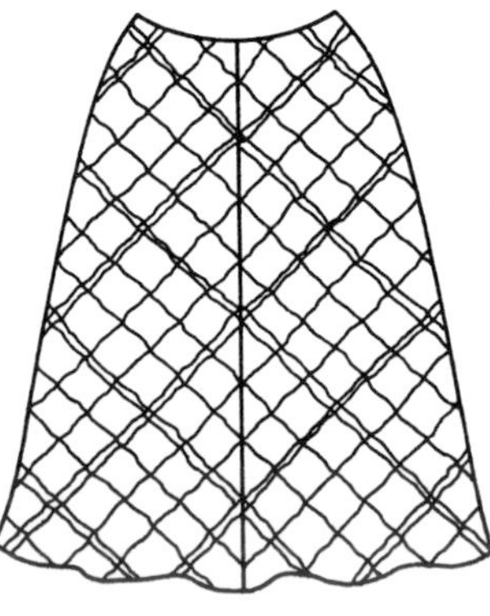

PLAID

Try a 16-gore bias skirt and you'll master this concept and can surely be called a "couturier."

Godets

A godet is used to give extra fullness to a garment. It can be inserted into a seam, dart, or slash. Madame Vionnet used godets to add fullness at the hem without sacrificing the slimness of the garment.

Godets can be as long and as wide as you choose to achieve a look. A fishtail back used frequently in couture is nothing more than a godet that starts as the waist in the center back and continues to the floor.

A godet is a section of a circle. The radius is the length and the circumference the width. No matter how long or wide, the straight grain should always be in the center of the godet.

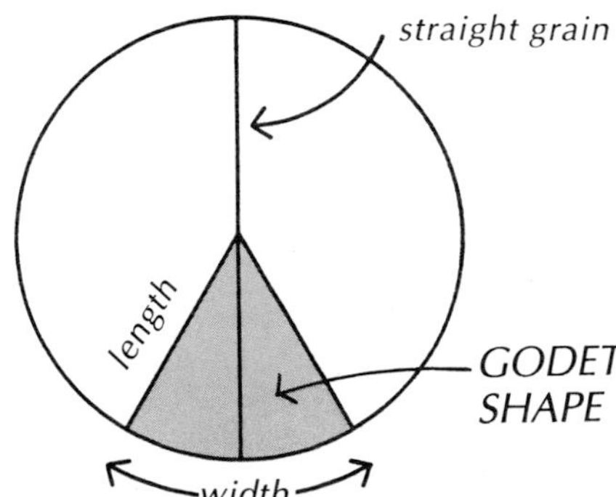

Add 1/4" (6mm) seam allowances to each "leg" of godet plus hem allowance.

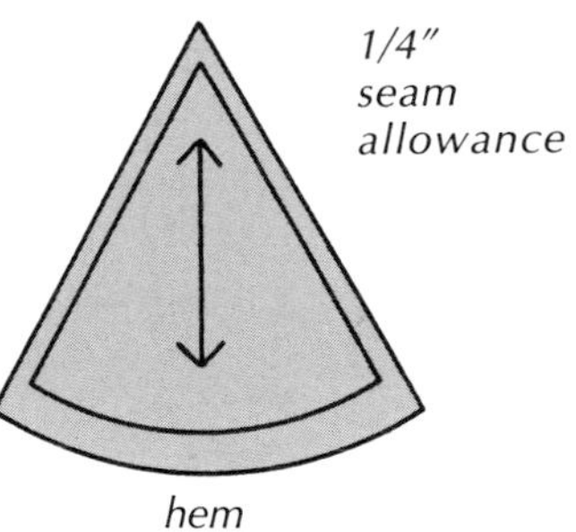

Inserting a Godet

1. Mark the desired location on the garment section with chalk.
2. Place a square of silk organza over what is to become the point and staystitch 1/8" (3mm) around the chalk line.

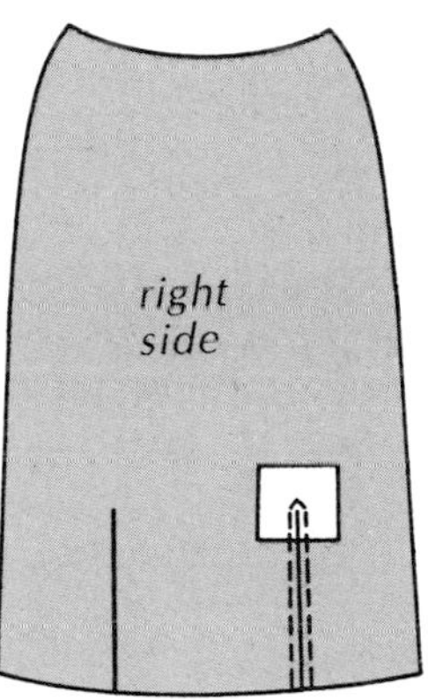

3. Cut on chalk line to point.
4. Turn organza to wrong side of garment and press point area only.

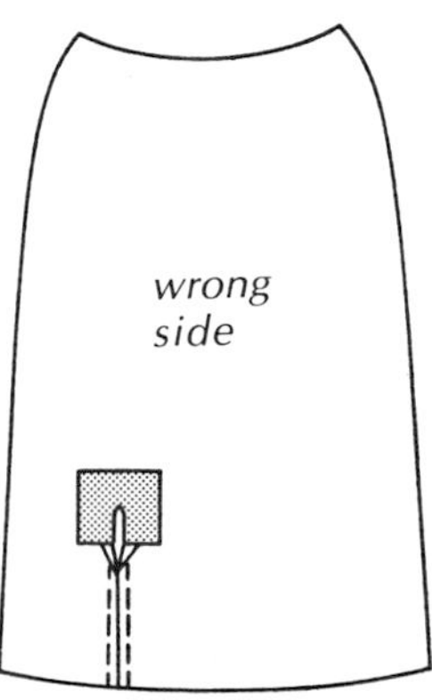

5. Pin godet to cut edges of opening, right sides together.

6. Machine stitch from hem toward point. Change to 20 stitches per inch (8 stitches per centimeter) $^1/_2$" (1 cm) from point. Stitch past stitching line intersection into godet seam allowance, tapering to almost nothing at the point. To stitch down the second side, begin stitching in the seam allowance, crossing the point and continuing to hem.

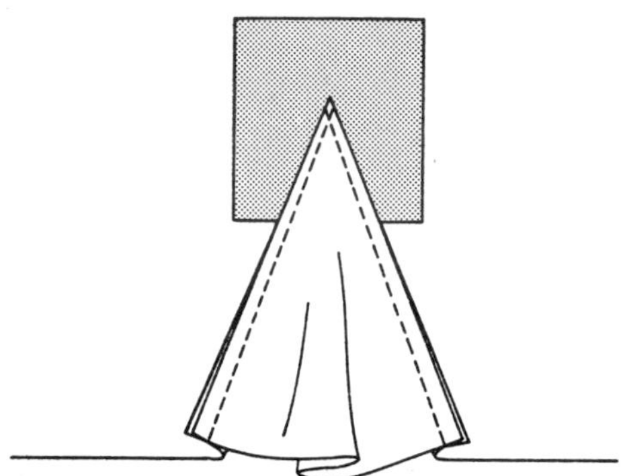

7. Press seams toward garment, away from godet.

NOTE: Organza used to stabilize the point remains in the garment.

Bias-Cut Sleeves

Bias-cut sleeves have many advantages over sleeves cut on the straight of grain.

- Bias sleeves hang thinner and longer, giving a slimmer look.
- The drape in a gathered sleeve cap is softer and more beautiful when cut on the bias.
- Bias can be gathered fuller than any other grain.
- Bias has the most give, making a close-fitting sleeve more comfortable.
- Bias doesn't wrinkle as much, so creases at the elbow line are almost nonexistent.

Bias sleeves should be cut at right angles to each other so a mirror image occurs in the fabric design, hang and drape.

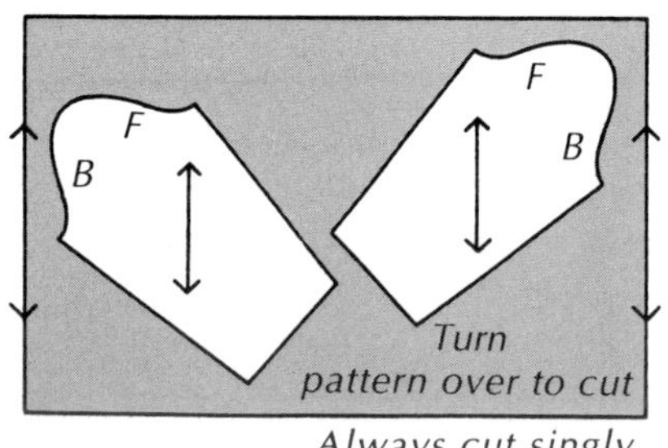

Always cut singly

yes

no

It is often said that bias takes more fabric but hangs so slim it looks like less.

If you are fortunate enough to find an **even plaid** you can take inspiration from Balenciaga and add a seam down the center of the sleeve. Place the pieces at right angles. When sewn together, you will produce a diamond design down the center of the sleeve.

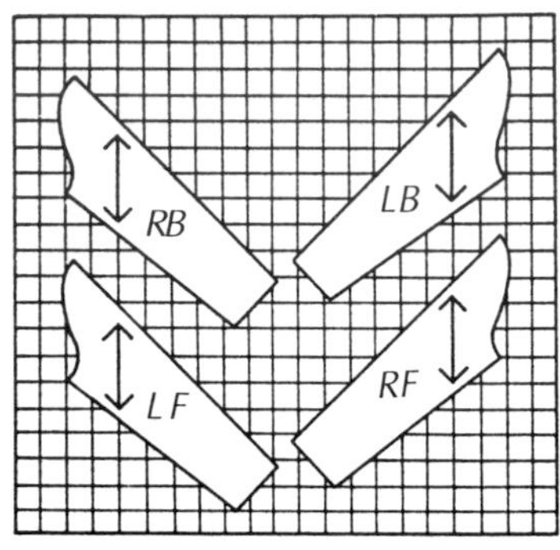

Bias sleeves are often used when working in plaid to avoid the necessity of matching to the garment at the armhole. They also prevent a broadening effect on the body.

Cutting the Bias

When the scissors cut into bias, an explosion of fibers occurs. They are set free. Bias doesn't ravel but the cut edge is far longer than the intended stitching line of the garment.

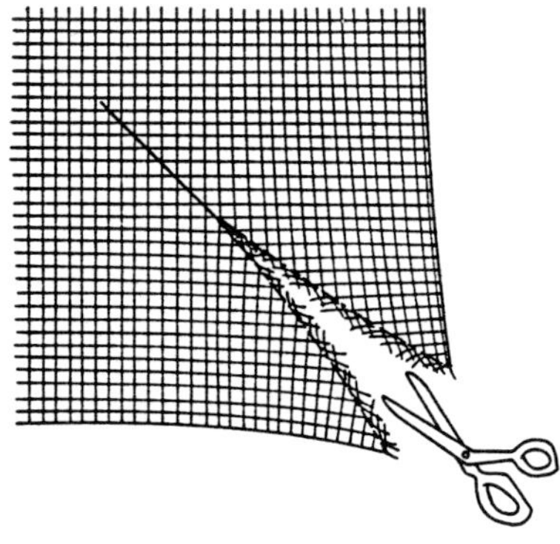

If the seam allowance is too narrow on major pattern pieces and the cut edge is used as the stitching guide for sewing seams, the stitching line becomes elongated and a ripple effect occurs in the seam. I hope you're saying, "Oh, if I had only known this before." Now you do.

I am pointing out what **not** to do because my experience tells me that understanding why this happens and how to correct it will increase your success rate tremendously when working on the bias.

Cut all bias seam allowances 1½" (3.8cm). Then even though the cutting "explosion" occurs, the stitching line is far enough into the fabric so the seams can be sewn accurately.

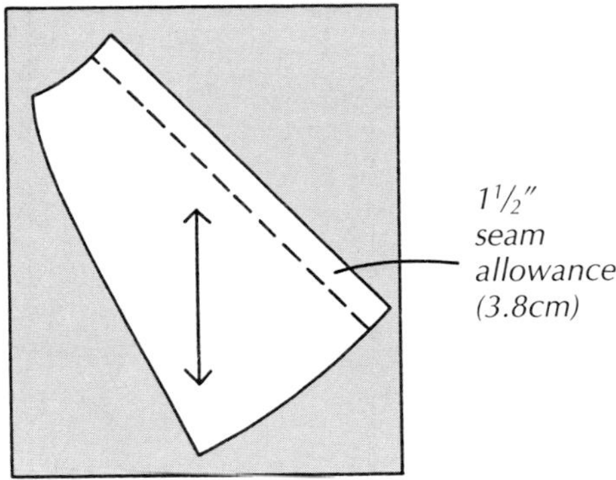

All stitching lines, notches, and construction marks should be clearly marked.

Fitting Bias Seams by Basting

Fitting bias garments can be done effectively only from the right side, so baste bias seams wrong sides together (seam allowances on the outside), following these steps:

1. Thread trace all stitching lines (see page 44).
2. Pin seams **wrong** sides together so seams are on the **outside** of the garment.
3. Hand baste seams together. Baste in sections 5"-10" (13-26cm) long with **no** knots. Breaking the thread at the 5"-10" (13-26cm) point prevents the seam from pulling up or shortening.
4. Fit. Pin changes by placing pins parallel to the stitching lines.
5. Re-mark stitching lines by thread tracing from the wrong side through a **single** layer, or chalk the stitching line on both front and back, making sure to chalk directly over any pin which has been used to alter the original stitching line.

COUTURE Tip To avoid confusion, use two colors of thread for basting—one for basting the seam and another for re-marking after fitting.

6. Remove original hand basting. From the right side, fold the front seam over the back seam, matching stitching lines, and slip-stitch together, breaking thread every 5"-10" (13-26cm).

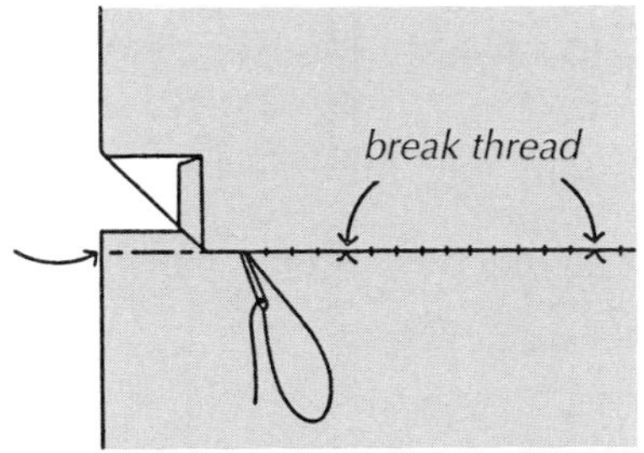

7. Try on again and do a final fit check.
8. Machine stitch seams.

Machine Stitching a Bias Seam

Stretch as you sew! Bias is not fragile; it will not break.

1. Lower the presser foot, then the needle.
2. Stretch the fabric as much as possible without using force. Let the fabric speak to you. Stretching while stitching anticipates the hang of the garment in its most extended form.
3. Be sure to follow the marked stitching line because the seam allowance will appear narrower than it really is because of the nature of bias. This way you won't have to worry about seam width—the only way to sew bias!
4. Stitch 5"-10" (13-26cm), then STOP with needle down. Lift the presser foot and let the fabric settle to help maintain the grain, so crosswise and lengthwise grains are always perpendicular at the stitching line.
5. Stitch the next 5"-10" (13-26cm) section as in step 4.
6. Repeat to the end of the seam.

Completed bias garments should be hung 24 hours before hemming. This applies to skirt hems, sleeve hems, or garments with godets.

Bias garments should **NOT** be hung during construction. Keep them **flat**.

When machine stitching bias seams, the surface around the machine should be as flat and as large as possible. If the garment hangs over the edge, it can distort the grain. To prevent slippage, cover the surface with an old sheet or a piece of muslin.

Cutting Bias Strips

Cutting bias strips for binding, ruffles and couture touches must be done with great care. Never short-cut the process. Always cut more than you think you'll need, because some will be lost in piecing or you may need a certain color in a print or striped fabric in a specific place.

1. Grain up fabric for strips. (See Graining Up, page 43.)
2. Pin fabric to the grainboard.
3. Using a ruler with a 45-degree bias line, establish the first true bias line.
4. Continue to chalk-mark parallel cutting lines the desired width.
5. As each line is drawn, pin the previous strip straight down into the grainboard, staggering pins from one strip to another.

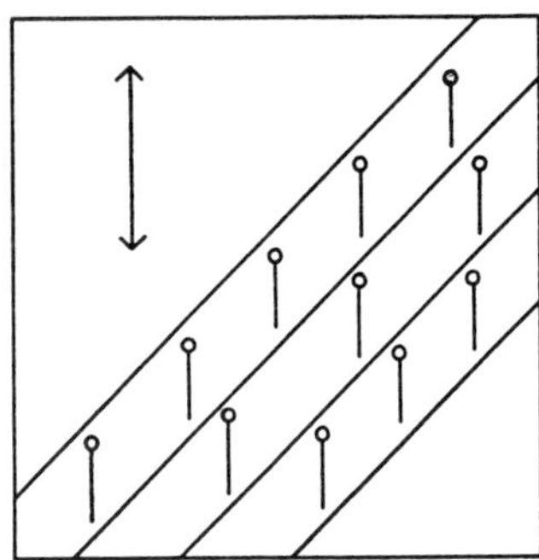

6. Cut all strips.
7. Remove pins.
8. Let the fabric rest a minute. You will see a small separation develop between the strips.

Piecing Bias Strips

The less piecing the better, but sometimes piecing is necessary. Perfect piecing means joining **exactly** on the straight grain.

1. Cut the ends of the strips at right angles.

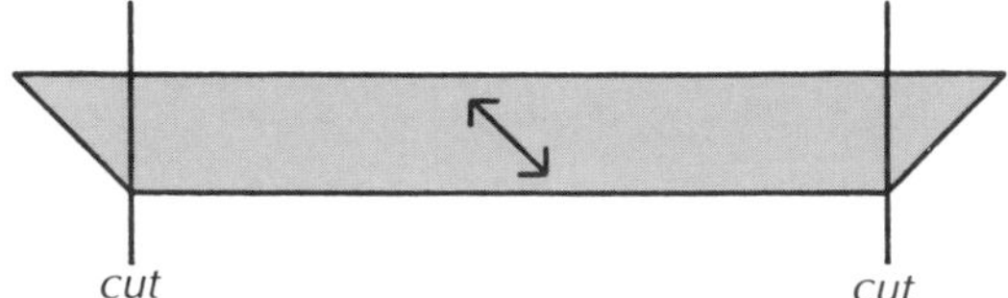

2. Place right sides together at a right angle.

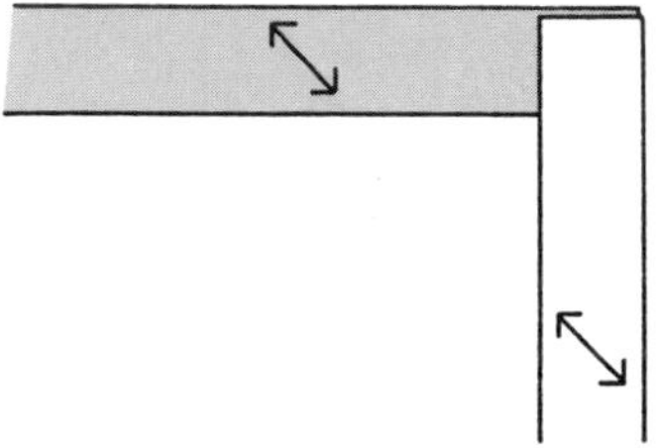

3. Stitch as shown on the straight of grain.

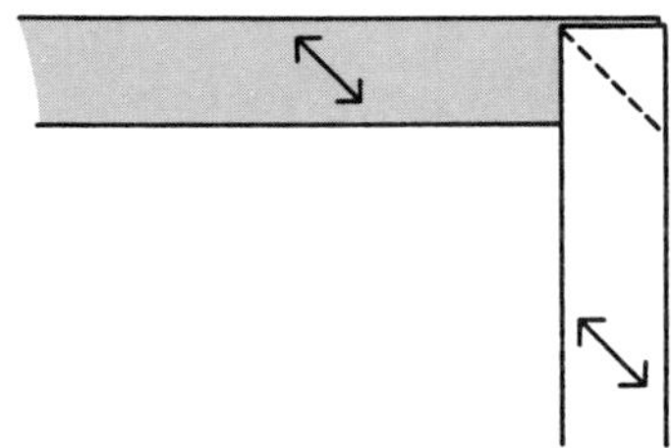

4. Meld the stitches (page 52), press open and trim seams to 1/4″ (6mm).

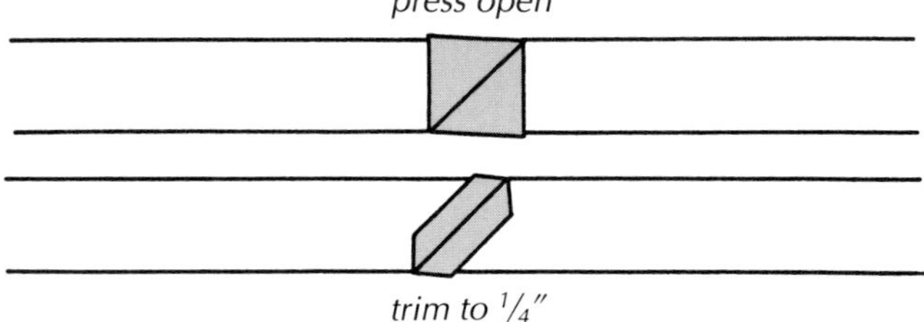

If you are working with a **striped** fabric or an obvious **directional print**, match the design when piecing the bias strips so the pattern appears continuous.

Bias Ruffles

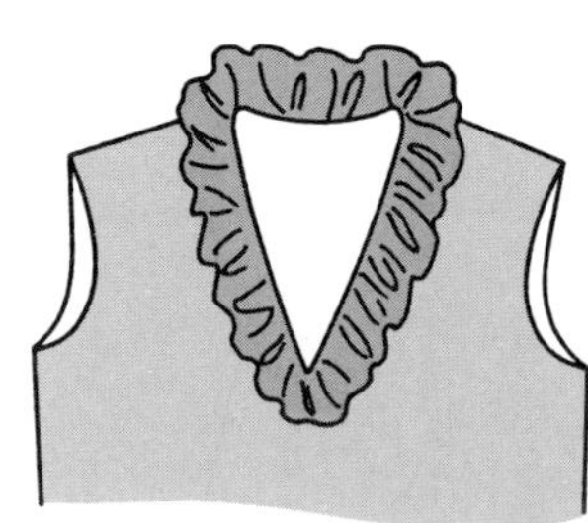

Bias is the perfect grain for ruffles because it can be gathered more fully than any other grain, and bias ruffles have a soft, rounded edge. They do take plenty of fabric, so be sure to buy enough extra if you're adding them to a design.

Bias ruffles can be cut double width, then folded in half lengthwise, then gathered and inserted into a seam. This makes the folded edge soft and rounded.

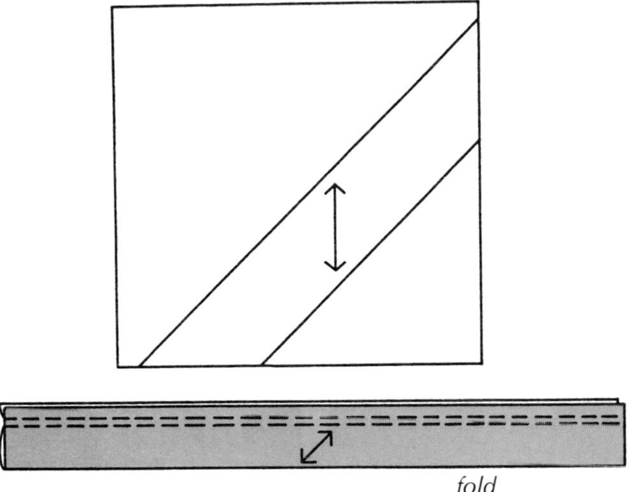

Couture Bias Double Ruffle

This is a bias ruffle inserted into a V-neckline. It is wider at the center back and quite narrow at the "V".

1. Make a paper pattern twice the length needed to go around the neckline. (See Gathers, page 113 for ratios.)

2. Mark the center back on the pattern piece.

3. At each end of the pattern, mark the **finished** width of the ruffle desired at the V.

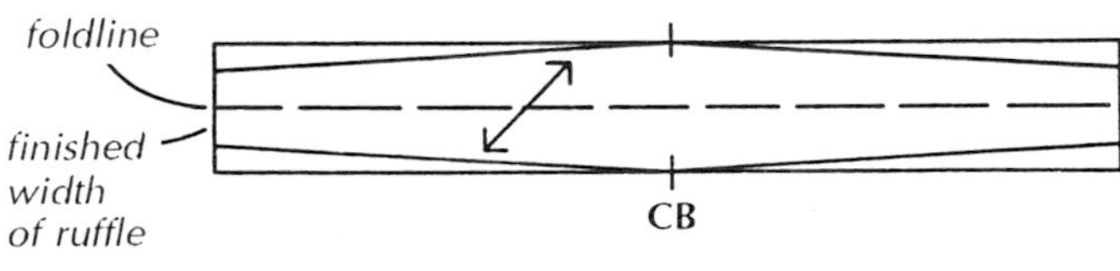

COUTURE Tip Depending on the angle, there may be very little space right at the V. The finished width of the double ruffle could be as narrow as $^1/_4$" (.6cm).

4. Draw a straight line from the center back to the mark you made at the end. Cut pattern on these lines and add seam allowances.

5. Cut on the bias, fold in half lengthwise, gather raw edges and insert between garment and facing.

Haute Couture Bias Ruffle

The wider a ruffle, the fuller it must be to appear as full as a narrower ruffle, so the ratio of gathers may change within the same strip. In the V-neck ruffle, for example, the ratio from center back to shoulder might be 3-to-1, $2^1/_2$-to-1 from shoulder to halfway in front, and 2-to-1 from that point to center front.

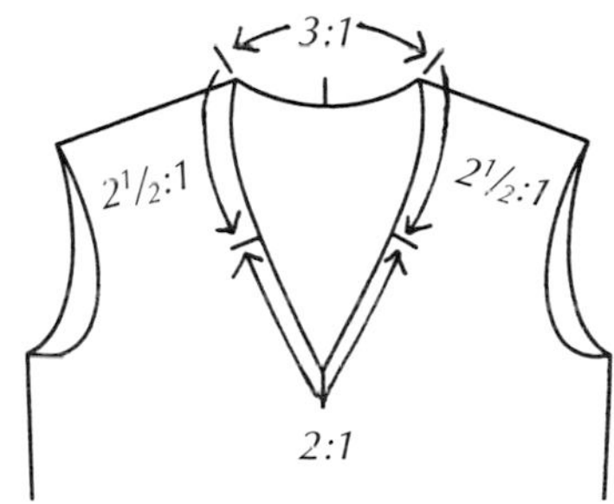

An Example:

Measure the garment where the ruffle will be applied.

	garment	ratio	fabric needed
CB to Shoulder	4" (10cm)	3:1	12" (30cm)
Shoulder to half CF	5" (12.5cm)	$2^1/_2$:1	$12^1/_2$" (32cm)
half CF to CF	5" (12.5cm)	2:1	10" (25cm)
		TOTAL per side	$34^1/_2$" (87cm)
		two sides = 69" (174cm)	

Fabric can be pieced to get the total length. Mark the garment and ruffle accurately. Gather and match marks, and the planned fullness will appear in the right places.

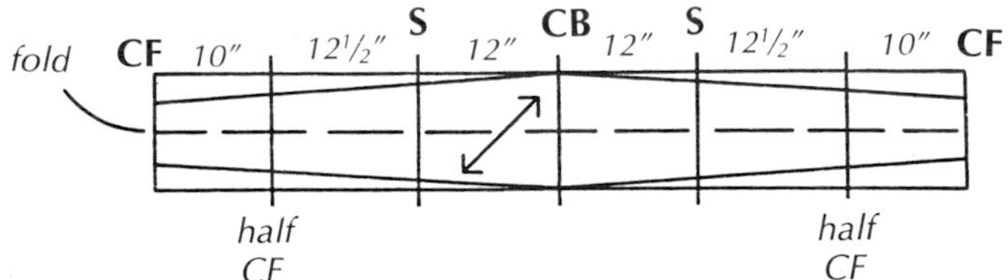

CHAPTER 12

Bias Binding...A Couture Finish

Understanding and respecting bias binding and following a few application rules give you the freedom to create endless variations, designs and treatments.

Bias binding is a strip of fabric, folded and stitched to a garment's raw edge as a finish.

Bias binding can:

- ◆ eliminate the need for a facing on sheer, white or light-colored fabrics where you do not want show-through and choose not to underline
- ◆ serve as a hem finish
- ◆ stabilize and take the place of interfacing
- ◆ be decorative
- ◆ be combined with piping
- ◆ be shaped to go around curves, so it's an ideal finish for a severe curve that you don't want to face.

Bias binding is easy to apply once you learn the sequence of cutting, piecing, stitching and finishing. The rationale is defined in each step so you will understand the process and can decide how to use it most effectively.

1. For **traditional** bias binding, cut bias strips four times the finished width.

2. For **single-fold bias**, fold the two outside edges to the center, leaving a small space for the turn of the cloth; press. A bias tape maker simplifies this step.

3. For **double-fold bias**, fold on the center line and press with raw edges inside. This is used for bias binding.

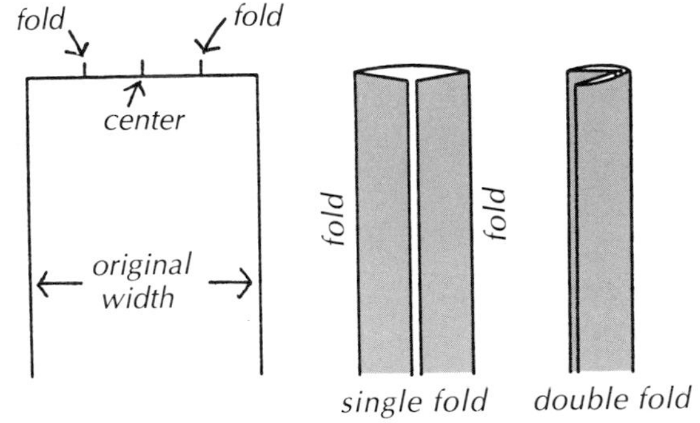

COUTURE Tip

The bias tape maker is a remarkable, readily available sewing tool. It comes in three sizes:

- ◆ 2″-wide (5cm) single fold; 1″-wide (2.5cm) double fold. Cut bias strips 4" (10cm) wide.
- ◆ 1″-wide (2.5cm) single fold; 1/4″-wide (1.3cm) double fold. Cut bias strips 2″ (5cm) wide.
- ◆ 1/2″ (1.3cm) single fold; 1/2″ (1.3cm) double fold. Cut bias strips 1″ (2.5cm) wide.

The tool does the folding, you press and—voila! bias binding!

To use a bias tape maker:

Use a pin to start fabric through the tool.

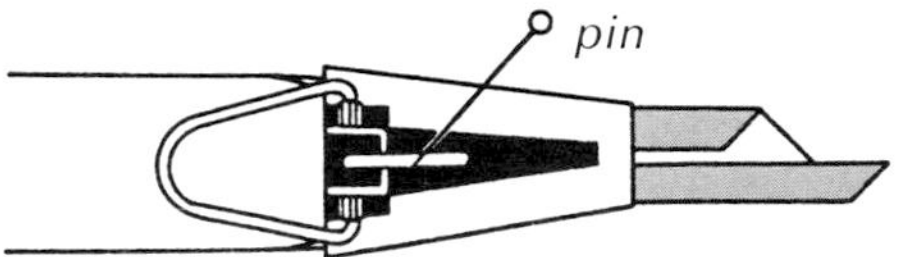

Carefully pull the bias tape maker along the bias strip. Press with the point of the iron touching the center of the bias tape maker.

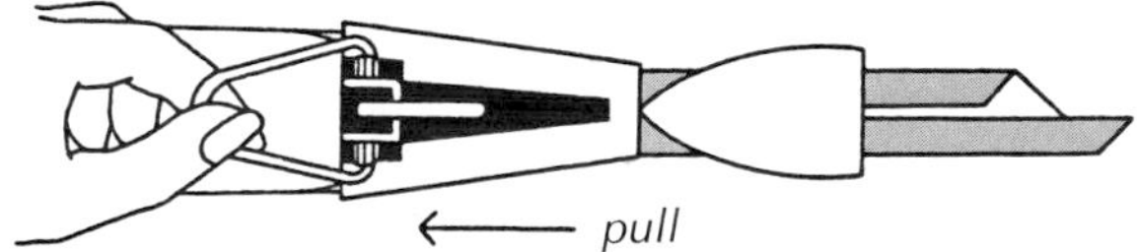

Do not anchor the pressed end with a pin as you continue, or the bias will stretch and become narrower!

Applying Bias Binding

When applying bias binding as a finish to the garment neckline or hem edge, trim away the garment seam or hem allowance first, so the finished garment line becomes the new cut edge. This will ensure the garment will fit as intended.

Shaping Bias Binding to a Curved Edge

Bias is pliable and goes around curves. A deep curve, however, may require pre-shaping with steam.

1. First create a double-fold bias strip as previously shown.
2. Using the garment or the paper pattern as a guide, apply light pressure with a steam iron while shaping the bias with your other hand. Do not stretch bias binding as it becomes narrower where stretched.

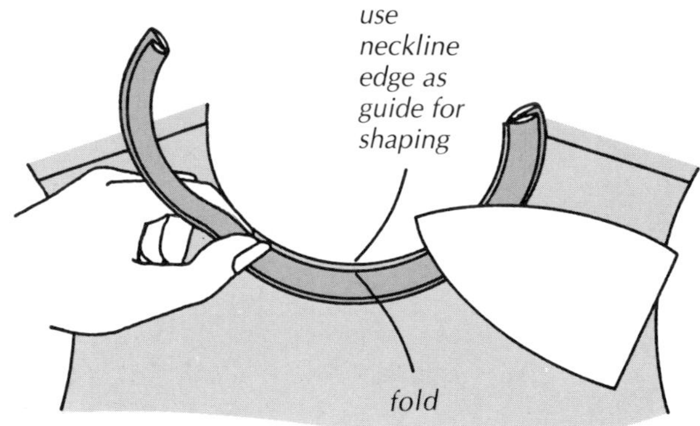

3. Compare bias to garment edge and continue shaping as needed until the bias conforms to it perfectly.

COUTURE Tip Remember, it is the **folded center** edge of the bias that must be shaped to match the cut edge of the garment.

Attaching Bias Binding

Bias binding is applied in a 1-to-1 ratio with no stretching or easing.

1. Open out the bias strip and match the cut edge of bias to the garment cut edge, right sides together.
2. Pin from the bias side with pins perpendicular to the edge. Pin into first fold and out through the center fold to hold the binding flat for stitching.

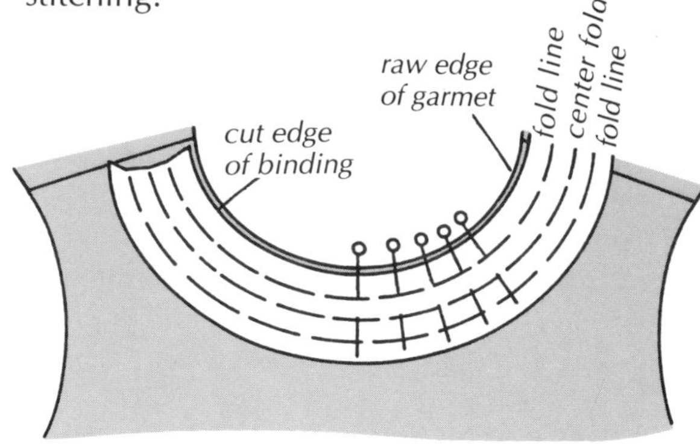

3. To prevent rippling, pin in segments in the order shown rather than from one end to the other.

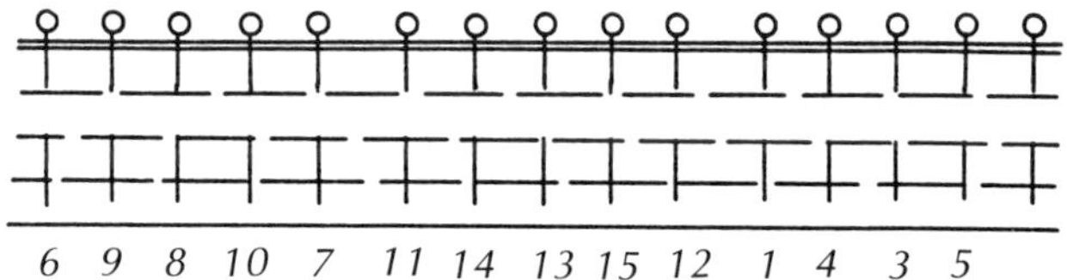

COUTURE Tip If you are applying bias binding to a circle, you will need to join the ends. See "Joining Bias Binding," page 87.

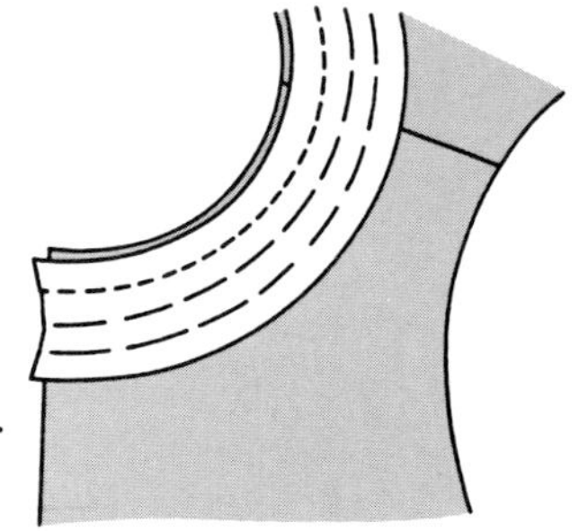

5. Machine stitch bias in place **exactly** along the fold line nearest the cut edge.
6. Meld stitches, using the tip of the iron so it just covers the stitches. Be sure the iron stays in the seam allowance and **does not touch the bias binding**.

7. **Do not trim seam.**

8. Fold bias over and around raw edge; pin from wrong side of garment so folded edge just barely covers stitching line. Pin in segments as in step 3.

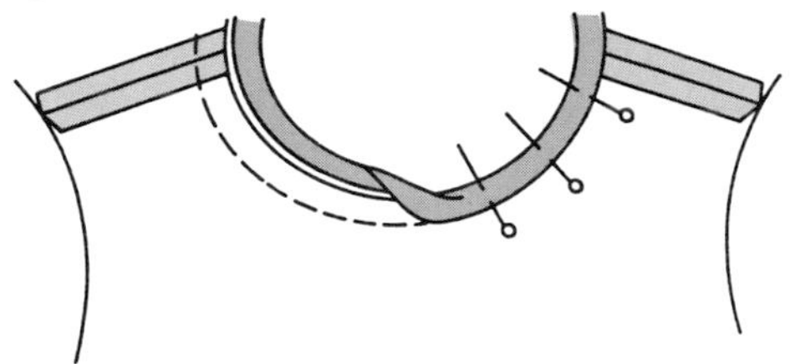

9. Slipstitch the binding to the garment by inserting the needle under one machine stitch, then into the binding fold for 1/4"-3/8" (.6cm-1cm) and again immediately under a machine stitch; repeat to the end. The binding floats against the garment.

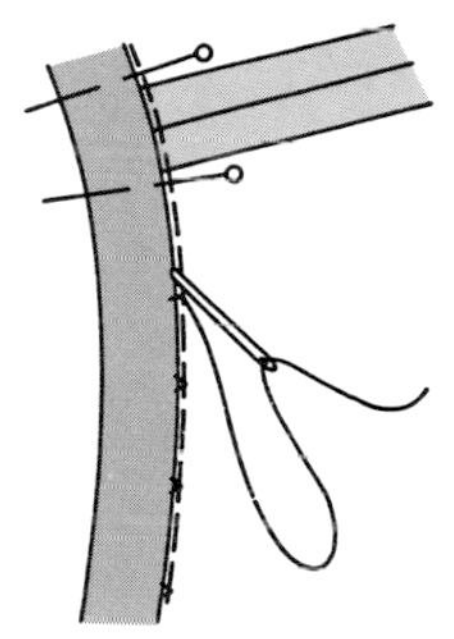

10. Steam gently as shown in step 6; do not hard press.

Joining Bias Binding

On hems or other circular edges, it is usually necessary to join the ends of the binding where they meet.

1. Pin binding to edge to within 3" (7.5cm) of where it is to be pieced.

2. Working from the wrong side, fold under the left end on the straight grain.

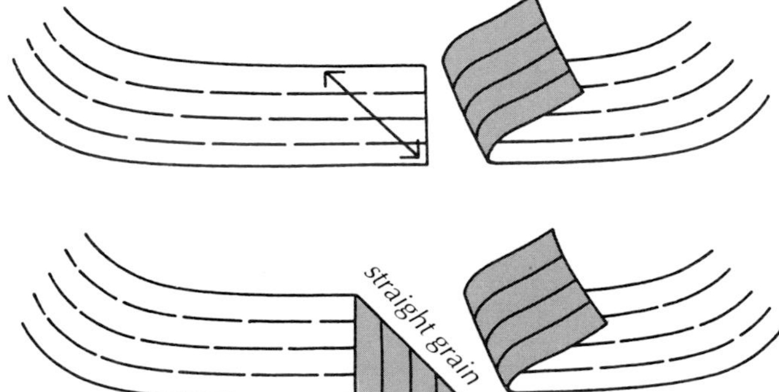

3. Lap the right end over the folded one and cut it even with the cut edge of the left end.

4. Remove a few pins to loosen the binding enough so you can machine stitch bias ends together.

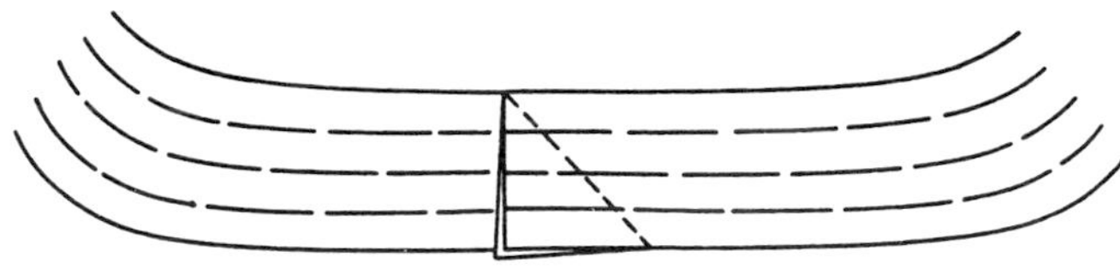

5. Meld stitches and press seam open; trim to 1/4" (.6cm).

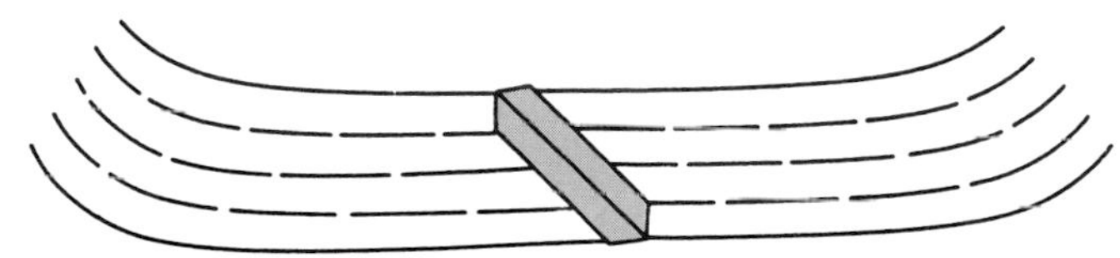

6. Pin joined bias binding to edge and machine stitch.

Couture Touches With Bias Binding

When binding a neckline, at the back zipper:

1. Fold under the left side even with the center back. On the right side, leave a 4"-long (10cm) tail.

2. After the binding has been hand stitched, fold under the "tail" to create a small bow. Whip stitch the raw end of the 4" (10cm) tail to the binding at the center back. With the same thread, run a few gathering stitches at the center of the bow, pull up and secure.

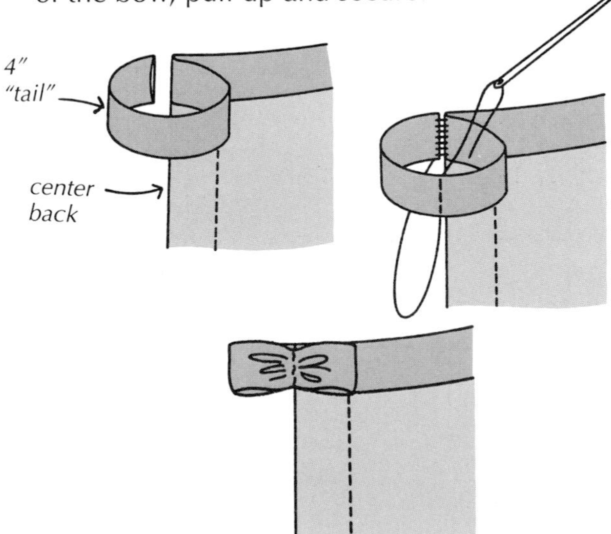

3. Attach a small hook and eye under the bow.

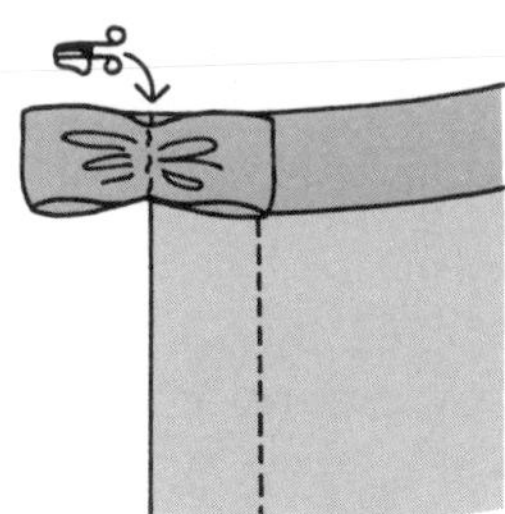

Sleeve "Cuff" Finish

A bias binding applied to the wrist of a traditionally gathered dress or blouse sleeve is particularly appropriate for sheer or silky fabrics. It is the ideal substitute for a standard buttoned cuff—a very feminine couture detail.

Before substituting bias binding, lengthen the sleeve by adding on the finished width of the original cuff. Remember, always trim off the seam allowance on a bound edge first.

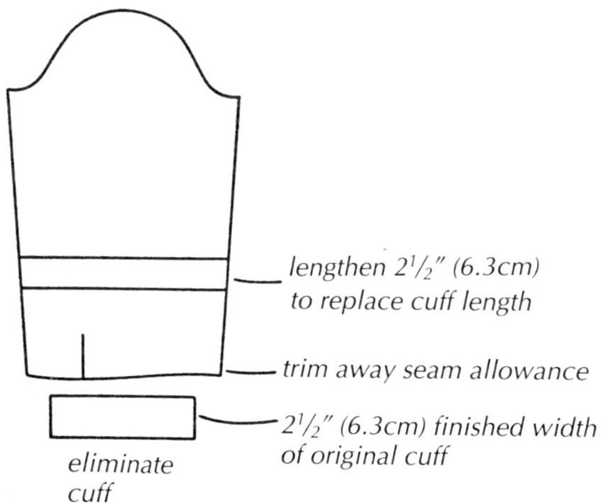

Stitch three gathering rows on the sleeve edge in a space equal to the finished width of the binding.

Method I: Apply bias binding to the gathered edge of the sleeve, leaving a 4"-6" (10cm-15cm) long "tail" on each side of the placket opening. After slipstitching the binding in place, continue to slipstitch the "tails," folding in the ends. Add a small crystal bead or pearl at the ends as an elegant touch. To close the cuff, tie a small bow.

Method II: Apply bias binding to the gathered edge, folding in each end even with the placket opening just before machine stitching. Make a tiny bias loop for each sleeve (see page 60), and insert into the end of the binding as the last step. Secure with hand stitches. Apply a small round or dome button for a beautiful finish.

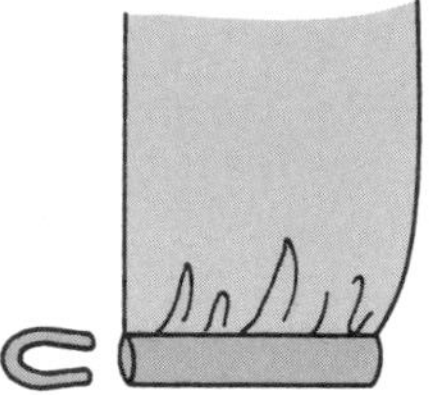

loop into opening at end of bias binding

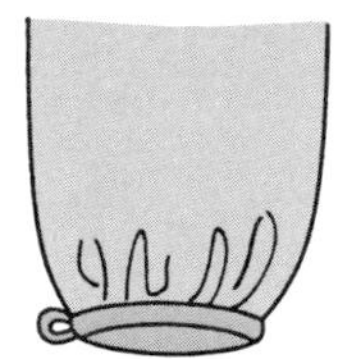

hand stitch in place

Double Bias Binding

Double bias binding, distinguished from traditional double-fold bias binding, creates a beautifully rounded edge that appears corded. It is a perfect finish for outside edges (such as neckline and front) of unlined coats, or jackets without facing, where lining comes right up to the finished edge.

1. Grain up fabric. (See page 43.)

2. Cut strips six times the desired finished width. For example, for a finished width of 1/2" (1.25cm), cut strips 3" (7.5cm) wide.

3. Measure the stitching line on the garment edge where binding will be applied.

4. Piece strips to make enough length for the measurement from step 3 plus seam allowances. For a wrist finish, use the exact measurement of the finished sleeve edge. Using the joining technique shown on page 87, sew strips into a circle.

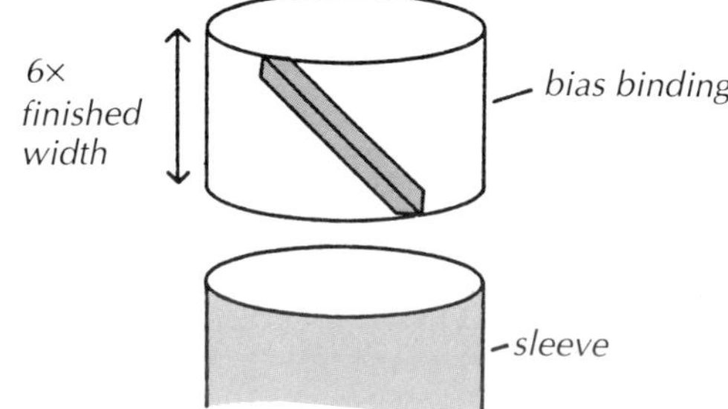

5. Fold bias strip in half, wrong sides together.

6. Hand baste raw edges together.

7. Cut off seam or hem allowance at the stitching line or finished length of garment.

8. Pin raw edges of binding to garment with pins perpendicular to the cut edge.

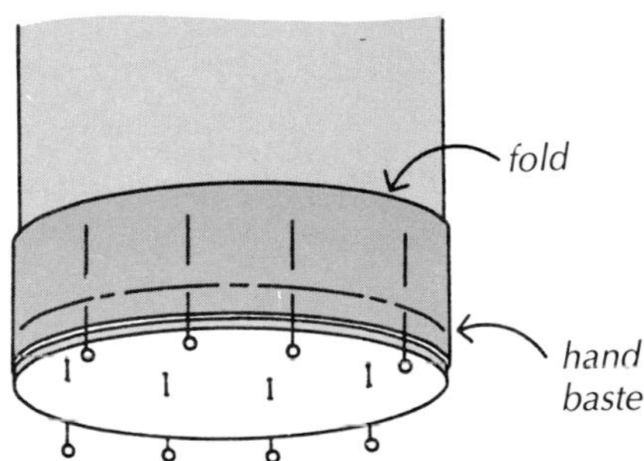

COUTURE Tip Thick fabrics may require hand basting so pins can be removed before machine stitching.

9. Machine stitch bias to garment, using a seam allowance equal to the planned finished width.

10. Remove hand basting and meld stitches, keeping the iron on the seam allowance only.

11. Wrap folded edge of binding over the cut edge so the fold is directly over the machine stitching line on the inside of the garment.

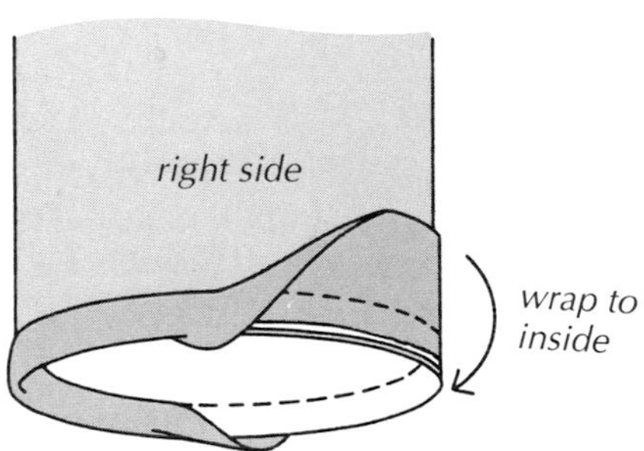

12. Slipstitch by hand, inserting the needle under one machine stitch, then through the fold to the binding, spacing stitches $^1/_4$"-$^3/_8$" (.6cm-1cm) apart. (See page 87, step 9.) Repeat to the end.

13. Steam gently, holding iron above work.

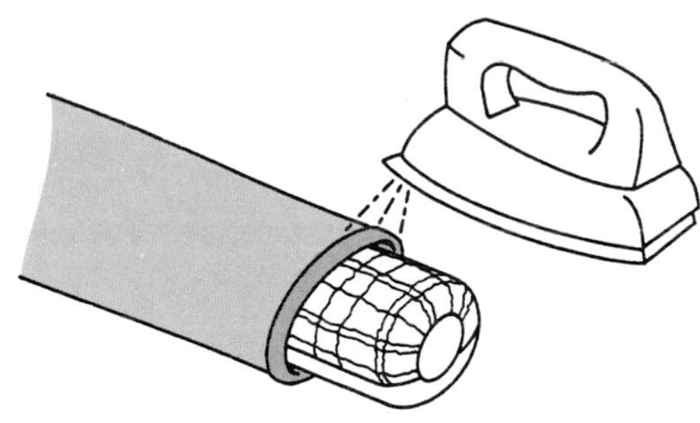

14. Holding the binding between the palms of your hands, move your hands forward and backward to create a rolled edge.

Mystery Binding

Coco Chanel was a master at binding edges. She had one technique that I call "mystery binding." Always done in high-contrast colors—a white suit with navy binding, for example—it looks like the undercollar wraps around the upper collar.

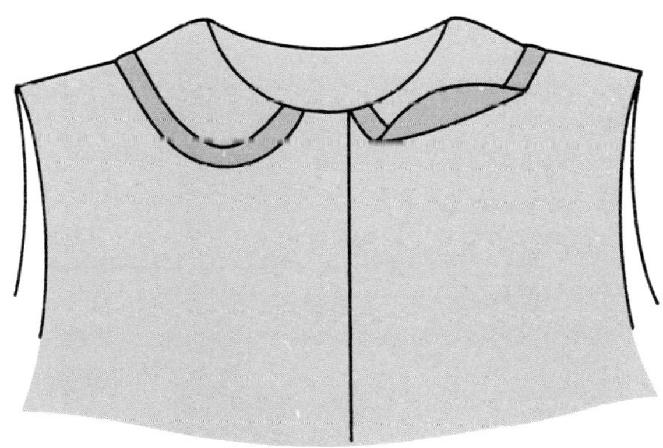

Actually, it's simpler than that! The **upper** collar is **bound** in the contrasting color and the **under**collar is **cut** in the same contrasting color.

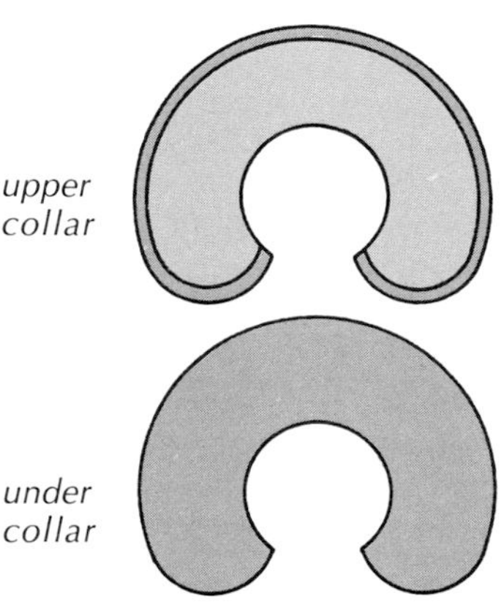

1. Cut bias binding twice the desired finished width plus a 5/8" (1.5cm) seam allowance.

   For example, for a 1/2"-wide (1.3cm) finished binding, cut strips (2 × 1/2") + 5/8" = 1 5/8". Metric: (2cm × 1.3cm) + 1.5cm = 4.1cm.

2. Turn under the finished width on one raw edge; press.

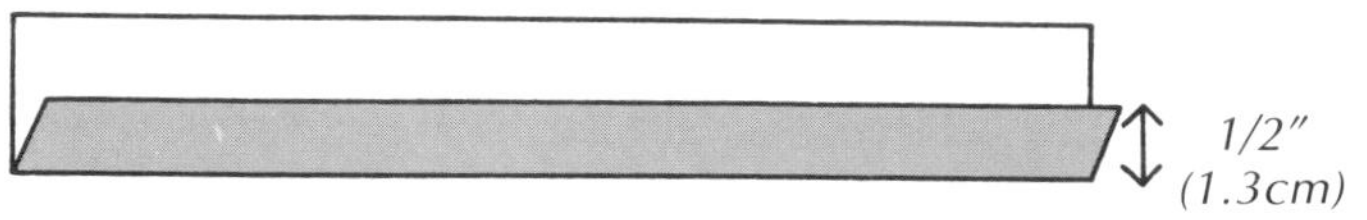

3. For full round curves, shape the binding with steam before stitching. (See page 86.)

4. Place bias binding on the upper collar in the finished position. The binding cut edge will match the collar cut edge.

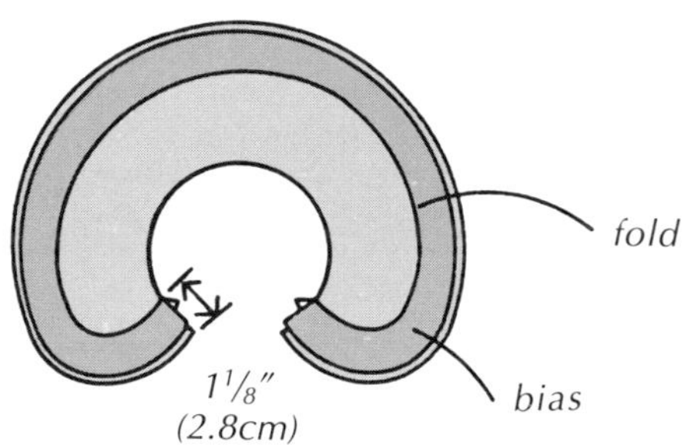

5. Slipstitch along the fold from the right side.

COUTURE Tip If binding can be controlled with no slippage, pinning may be adequate. Open out binding and pin perpendicular to edge.

6. Open out binding and stitch on fold line.

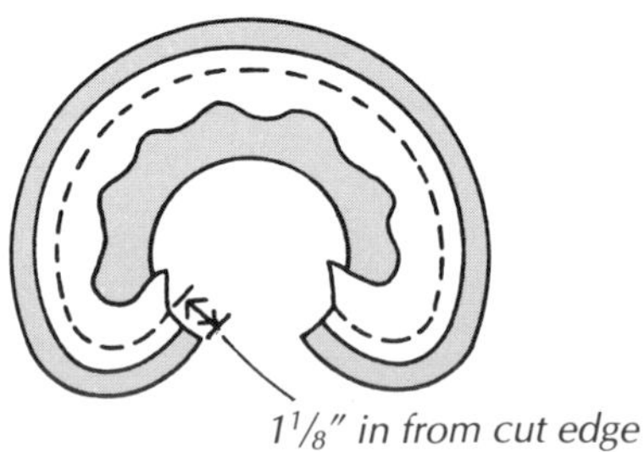

7. Fold binding back to finished position and press. Again, binding cut edge will match collar cut edge.

8. Pin binding to collar to hold in place and hand baste binding to collar using stitching line on wrong side of collar as a guide.

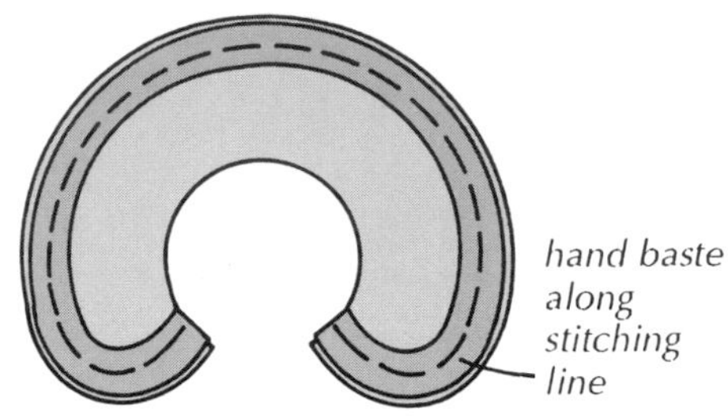

9. Cut undercollar of contrasting color and stitch collars together in traditional manner.

Mitered "Mystery Binding"

On a pointed collar, miter the corners before applying the binding to the upper collar. (See Mitering, page 66.)

An easier method than mitering is to cut the binding on the same grain as the collar.

1. Cut binding twice the desired finished width plus 5/8" (1.5cm) seam allowance on the same grain as the collar. Mark the fold line.

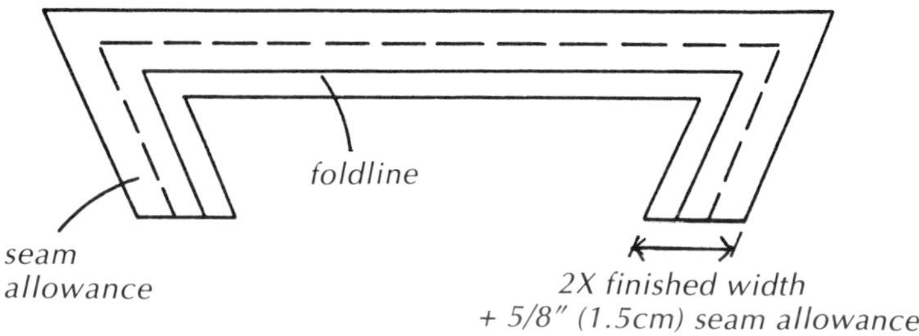

2. Staystitch 20 stitches per inch (8 stitches per centimeter) on the foldline ½″ (1.3cm) on each side of inner corner. Clip to the corner.

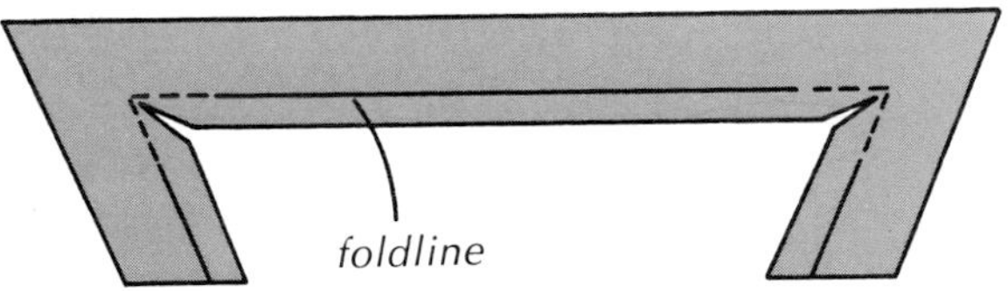

3. Press under along foldline.

4. Place binding on collar in the finished position. Cut edges of binding should match the collar cut edges. Slipstitch along the fold from the right side.

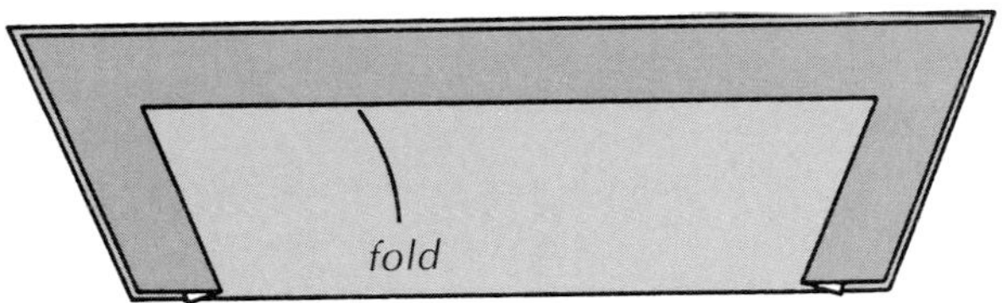

5. Open out binding along one end of collar and stitch on fold line. For 1/2″ (1.3cm) on each side of corner, use 20 stitches per inch.

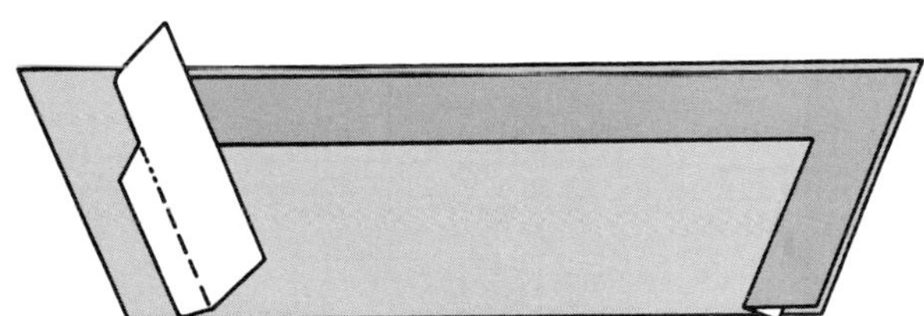

6. Open out binding along long edge of collar and stitch on fold line. Again, use short stitches at corners.

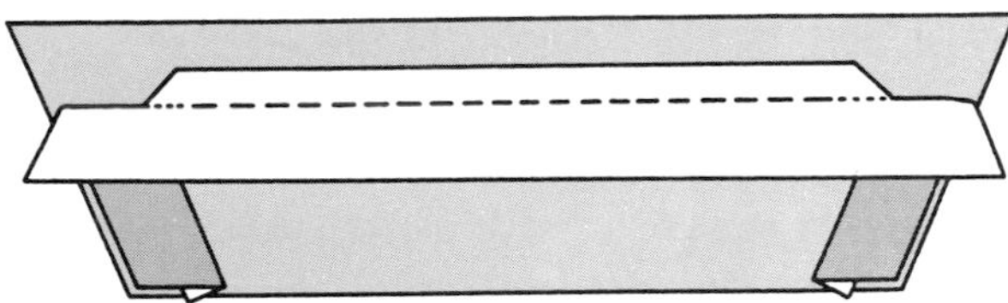

7. Open out binding at other end. Stitch on fold line, switching to short stitches at corner.

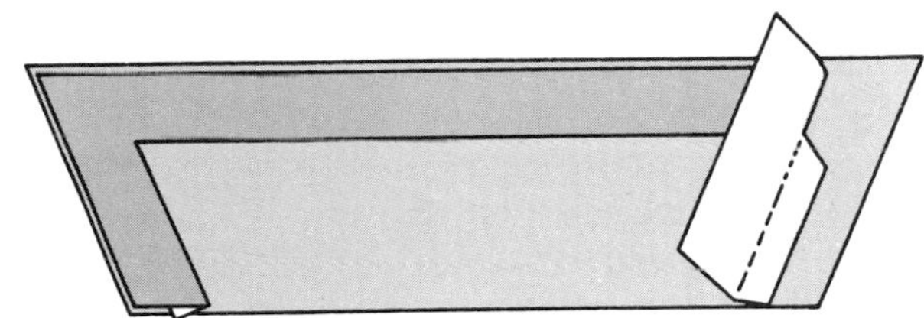

8. Fold binding to finished position and press. Use wool side of press cloth. (See page 57.)

9. Pin binding to collar to hold in place. Hand baste binding to collar, using stitching line on wrong side of collar as a guide.

10. Cut undercollar of contrasting color and stitch collars together in traditional manner.

CHAPTER 13

Piping

Piping is simply a bias fabric strip wrapped around a cord, then inserted into a seam. Piping can be functional or decorative; it can be single or double; it can be fat or thin.

Piping can be purchased or custom-made. Ready-made piping is often a braid with a seam allowance that can be inserted into a seam.

Making piping and applying it require meticulous adherence to the "rules": **precision**, **patience** and **accuracy**. Piping is Couture.

- **Piping is a filler** when two thick fabrics are sewn together, such as a facing onto a coat front edge. The piping fills in and gives the appearance of a hard edge. Without the piping, this edge might be very difficult to press flat.
- **Piping is an equalizer** when sewing two unlike fabrics together, as when applying a silk lining to a wool facing. It makes an effective grade to the lighter weight.
- **Piping is a balancer**, where two unlike fabrics are sewn together within a garment piece, as in wearable art.
- **Piping is a stabilizer** to maintain an edge on a soft or fragile fabric, such as the neckline edge of a silk blouse or the slash-pocket edge in pants.
- **Piping controls gathers** by **forcing** them to lie in one direction when caught in the seamline between a flat and a gathered layer. Examples include a blouse gathered to a yoke or a sleeve to a cuff.

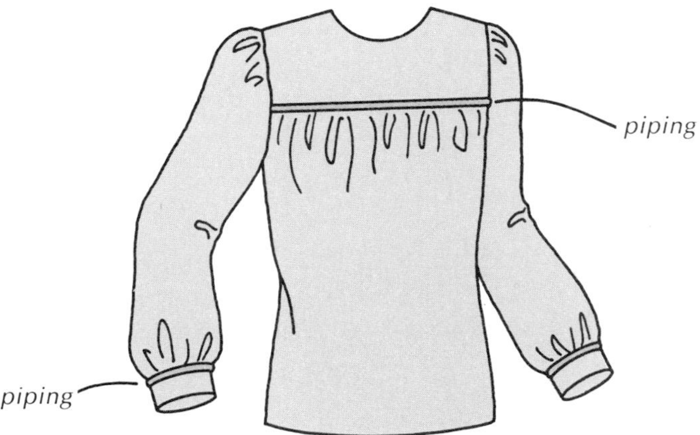

- **Piping is decorative** when used in a contrasting color or fabric to edge collars or cuffs.
- **Piping is subtle** when inserted in the side seam of a pant or in a princess seam to add a clean line and create a slimming effect. Black satin piping on black wool is subtle and Couture!
- **Piping is dramatic** when a stripe is used. The angle created by stripes on the bias makes an elegant edge on a striped garment.

- **Piping adds width** to an edge—an asset or a problem? For example, if a neckline is meant to be a 16" (40.5cm) opening when finished and you insert a $^1/_4$" (.6cm) piping on the original stitching line, the neckline opening will be 14$^1/_2$" (36.8cm). That could be too small!

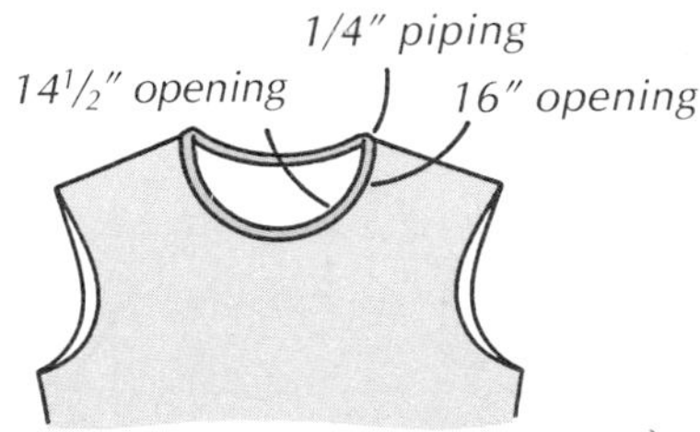

Rule I: When applying piping to a garment edge, increase the seam allowance width by the piping width. For example, when applying a 1/4"-wide (.6cm) piping, sew the neckline seam 1/4" (.6cm) deeper.

Rule II: When inserting piping between two seams, stitch on the original marked stitching line. Width appears to be added, yet nothing has changed.

How to Make Piping

Cut fabric for custom-made piping on the bias following general bias rules:

1. Grain up fabric. (See page 43.)
2. Cut strips with a width equal to the amount needed to wrap around the filler cord plus 3/4" (two 3/8" (1cm) seam allowances).

The most accurate way to determine the strip width is to wrap a piece of fabric around the cord; mark and measure the amount of fabric required.

3. Piece strips (page 82) allowing 6"-8" (15-20.5cm) extra length.
4. Wrap fabric around cord and pin parallel to cord (just two pins).

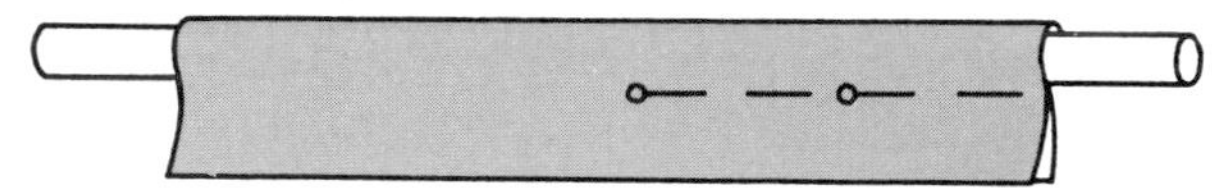

5. Using a zipper foot, stitch as close to cord as possible.
6. Stretch as you sew, stretching fabric as much as you can while stitching and at the same time keeping cut edges together. The seam allowance will appear to become smaller, but will return to 3/8" (1cm) after stitching.

When making piping, use a contrasting color thread in the bobbin to make stitching easy to see when applying the piping to the garment. (It will never be seen in the finished garment.)

7. Press seam allowance only, letting edge of iron barely pass over stitches; the corded portion should never be pressed.

Applying Piping

1. Align the piping stitching line with the marked stitching line of garment. Pin or hand baste in place if the fabric is slippery or the seamline is intricate.
2. Stitch with a zipper foot one thread inside the original piping stitching.

Once you are experienced with piping and understand both the concept and application technique, pin at the beginning only, then guide the work by hand while following the line to be stitched.

Rules for Handling Piping

1. When piping an edge which will be faced, stitch the piping to the garment, not the facing. Apply the piping to the facing when a "piped" lining is desired.
2. Always apply piping to the garment in a 1-to-1 ratio; that is, do not stretch the garment or the piping.
3. When inserting piping into a seam, apply piping to the straighter edge if one is more curved than the other, as in a princess seam.
4. When grading a seam, ignore the piping seam. Do not grade or trim.
5. **Do not clip piping seam allowance unless you must.**

Turning a Pointed Corner with Piping

1. Stitch piping to the exact point where the turn will occur. Shorten stitches to 20 stitches per inch (8 stitches per centimeter) for 1/2" (1.3cm) on either side of the point.
2. Once the needle reaches the point, with the needle in the fabric, lift presser foot. Clip piping seam allowances only from the point to the stitching.

3. Turn the work, lower the presser foot and continue stitching.

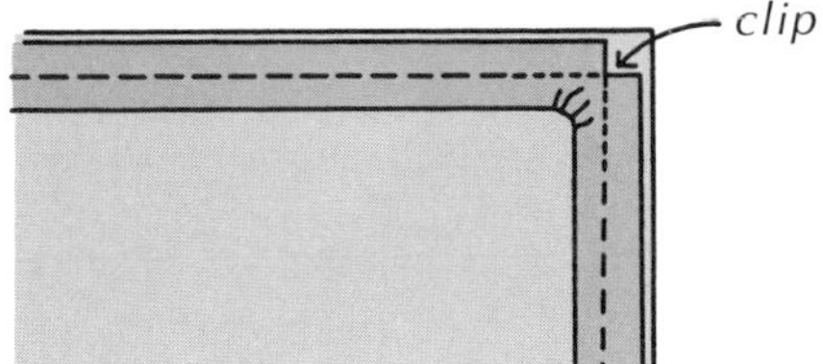

Double Piping

Double piping is ideal on a lined edge with no facing. On necklines, at center front opening edges or at hems, you can line to the piped edge, hand stitching it in place to the piping. The lining will not show on the right side of the garment.

Use double piping as a design detail on patch pockets or where you need a contrasting or decorative line.

Double piping applied between the lining and facing of a tailored jacket or coat is a couture detail; prints and striped fabrics—or one piping of each—add an elegant touch here.

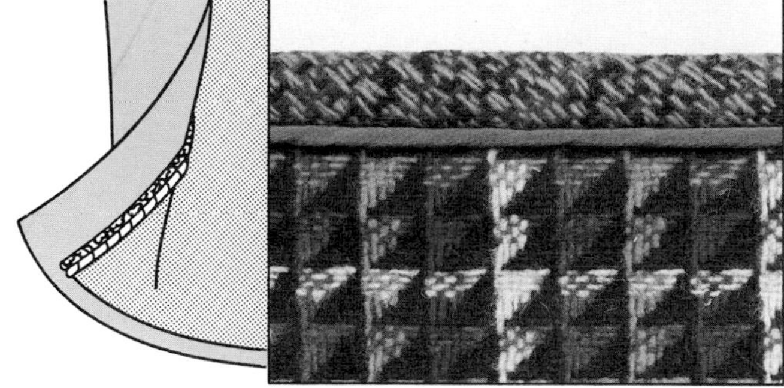

How to Make Double Piping

Make two separate pieces of piping.

1. For piece A that will be nearer the garment edge, cut the bias the determined finished width, plus ½″ (1.3cm) (for two ¼″ (.6cm) seam allowances).

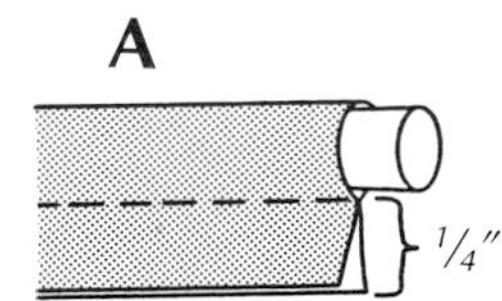

2. For piece B that will be at the outer edge, cut the bias strip the determined width, plus 1″ (2.5cm) (for two ½″ (1.3cm) seam allowances).

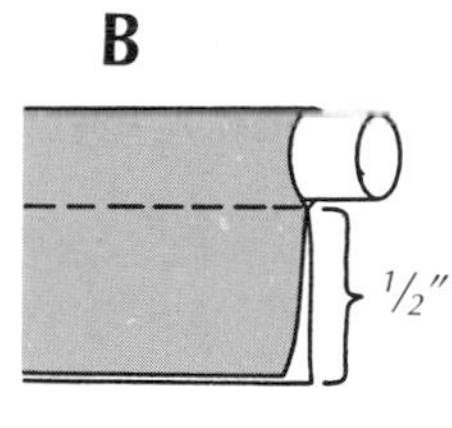

3. Place A on top of B and stitch, using a zipper foot and contrasting thread in the bobbin, following the stitching line of A.

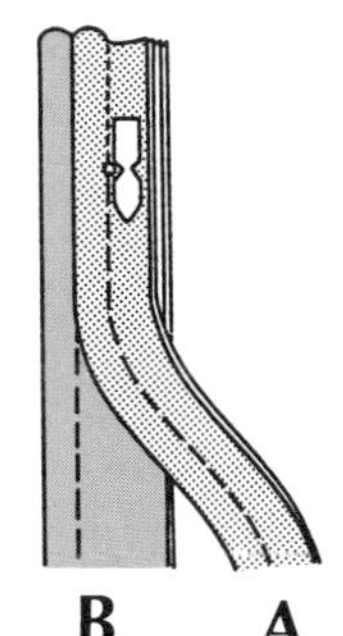

4. Position double piping on the garment with A nearer the garment edge. Use the stitching line of A as a guide, matching it to the marked stitching line on the garment. Stitch using the zipper foot.

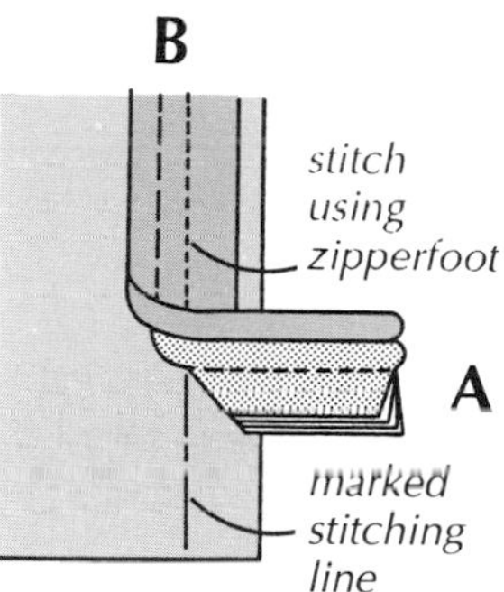

NOTE: Remember, when measuring for placement of garment stitching line, be sure to allow for the width of double piping. For example, if each piping is ¼″-wide (.6cm), increase the seam allowance ½″ (1.3cm) to allow for the added width.

5. Apply facing or lining.

Variation—Piping Plus Binding

Traditional bias binding can be used with piping. First apply the piping to the garment along the stitching line for the binding. Then apply the binding as previously described (see page 86).

When piping is used with bias binding, all stitching is done with a zipper foot.

The Designers

Whole books have been written about the designers of The Couture. Here's a brief synopsis of the leaders:

Cristobal Balenciaga (1895-1972) A student of art, used color and luxurious fabrics from tailored jackets to extravagant evening gowns; frequently used embroidery, ornamentation, fringe, passementerie, ruffles and bows.

Callot Soeurs (1895-1953) French Couture House established by three sisters.

Marie Callot Gerber
Marthe Callot Bertrand
Regina Callot Chantrelle

Masters of femininity using lace, organza, chiffon; also famous for embroidery and fabric embellishment; inspired by their love of the Orient.

Pierre Cardin (1922—) Worked for Paquin, Dior prior to opening his own house in 1950. Innovative, avant-garde, a master of architecture in fabric. A champion of licensing agreements using his name.

Gabrielle "Coco" Chanel (1883-1971) Fashion, perfume, jewelry; the liberator of structure; Chanel Suit, quilted handbags, beige/black sling back pumps.

Christian Dior (1905-1957) The new look, fabric flowers, A-H-Y design lines; absolutely beautiful clothes.

Hubert de Givenchy (1927—) Worked for Fath, Piguet, Lelong and Schiaparelli before opening his own house in 1952, a close friend of Balenciaga whom he considered a "mentor." Designs for internationally elegant women, most notably Audrey Hepburn. Simple elegance is reflected in all Givenchy designs.

Alix Grés (1910—) Original salon opened under name Alix, changed to Gres after World War II. Remarkably talented using draping to mold silk jersey, cowl necklines and dolman sleeves in the manner of a sculptor, her first love.

Valentino Garavani (1932—) Apprenticed with Dessés, Laroche; Couture House in Milan, shows collection in Paris. Opulent fabrics, streamlined designs, clothes to make women beautiful.

Christian La Croix (1951—) First as designer for Patou, then in his own house, La Croix shook the couture world. His clothes spoof, are full of creative humor; daring, bold, lavish color and flourish.

Paquin—The House of Paquin was founded in 1892, closed 1956. Mme. Paquin was first woman to achieve prestige in Haute Couture. Fur trimmed tailored suits, lingerie and custom accessories highlighted each collection. It is said that no two dresses were ever made exactly alike at the House of Paquin.

Jean Patou (1887-1936) Made fashion history introducing couture sportswear, lowering waistlines, shortening skirts and then lowering them in following seasons. A master of geometric design.

Elsa Schiaparelli (1890-1973) Innovative, unconventional, great use of shocking pink; used clever buttons, fantasy accessories and made sweaters fashion.

Yves St. Laurent (1936—) Trained by Dior. A designer of inspiration; tailoring; magnificent pants; experimental designs using beads, wood.

Madame Madeleine Vionnet (1876-1975) Modern inventor of the bias; designed/draped on half scale mannequins; proponent of crepe de chine, wool crepe.

Charles Worth (1826-1895) Father of the Couture. Opulence, elegance; gowns of such extravagance they needed crinoline, support and intense inner structure.

Grés

DIOR

Fashion illustration and fashion photography have, throughout history, communicated not only the details of The Couture, but also its essence. When you turn the page, you'll turn to the present ...another color section of beautiful clothes made by the New Couturiers.

Paquin—1949

The jacquard silk organza was the starting point for this cocktail blouse with ten yards of circular ruffles in the sleeves. Ruffles are each single thickness with a narrow hem. Worn with a narrow silk charmeuse skirt, the effect is of a fluttery butterfly.

This unusual dress has bodice and sleeves of body-hugging Lycra®. The neckline treatment on the lace yoke picks up the colors of the silk satin in skirt and hand-fringed sash. Satin and velvet bows, tulle tufts, silk roses and net bring the focus to the face.

At left the story is one of collars and contrast. The wool crepe dinner suit has a chiffon draped collar that allows the jacket to be worn without a blouse. The wool crepe cocktail dress with large satin Bertha collar has curved side seams that help to create the side drape. The summery yellow linen dress uses a dramatic single black lapel to provide contrast. The red wool gabardine is accented with black velvet collar and belt. Brass buttons add to its classic look.

On this page the story is coordinating fabrics...this time in a sheer wool. The 54″ square shawl folded on the diagonal adds drama to the dress on the right.

Pleating out plaids and stripes can create beautifully dramatic effects. In this wool plaid only one color is seen when standing still. Movement reveals the plaid. The checkerboard effect at right is created by cutting and piecing one stripe off in yoke and hem insert. At the waist the white is pleated out of the skirt to accentuate and feature a small waist.

This beautiful wool of deep, rich colors was 54" scarf squares, cut and pieced to form a border, yoke and v cap sleeve. The three-tiered skirt shows the wonderful paisley. Scarf borders were used at the hem.

The yellow jacket and coordinating blouse, above, is couture art clothing...with banding, binding, piping, welts, coordinating fabrics, and a beautiful Dior rose at the lapel, ornamented with tiny loop tubing.

At left is beautiful casual couture in the spirit of art clothing. Wool crepe pants have a wool & silk check insert. Pocket is bound with a bias silk print. The side panel of the sweatshirt is wool ribbing for give and comfort, with sleeves of wool double knit (a tip: when combining very different fabrics, bind the edge of one, lay over the next fabric piece, and stitch in the ditch). The coordinating bomber jacket uses a multitude of couture techniques—piping around the neck; an outside neck facing with a mock Hong Kong bias binding of sheer wool; wool braid on raglan shoulder and pocket welt; a contrasting silk lining, and a Dior rose on the lapel! *See page 108 for a close-up.*

This art jacket was designed with strong inspiration from Koos van den Akker. Wool is pieced on wool double knit. Silk bias strips are shaped, topstitched with military braid. Batting is stitched into the shoulders eliminates the need for shoulder pads.

Beautiful couture clothes deserve an equally beautiful hanger—here made of matching fabric (see Chapter 24, page 194),

Yes, bomber jackets can be couture. The top one is of silk crepe de Chine (scarf fabric!). Piping at the neck gives definition. Buttons and buttonholes replace exposed zippers for an elegant look. Multiple rows of elastic substitute for ribbing. The silk charmeuse lining, which picks up the outside colors, is quilted to very thin batting for warmth and body.

The lower two jackets are similar designs, but in two totally different fabrics.

More casual couture...a silk crepe-de-chine T-shirt combined with silk sweat pants, above, sports stripes of color inset into left yoke, and, for balance, the right sleeve. The back even has a loop like real T-shirts (see inset at right). Pink jacket has a lining of the same stripe. The color blocking of the bomber jacket at right, above, gives an art clothing attitude. The blouse is a T-shirt design with ribbing at hem and cuffs. Bias bow tie at neckline eliminates need for ribbing at neck.

Hand beading enhances the brocade to give a three-dimensional look to waist insert and cuffs in silk-more dress.

Here a polka dot silk crepe-de-chine is back-to-back with sheer wool in a smaller dot. Ten inch silk fringe dramatically finishes the 45″ scarf.

Below, two very different flowers: Held securely by an antique hat pin, the traditional Dior rose mixes several different silk prints. In the center is a passementerie button. At right, the flower is made up of twenty individually sewn petals.

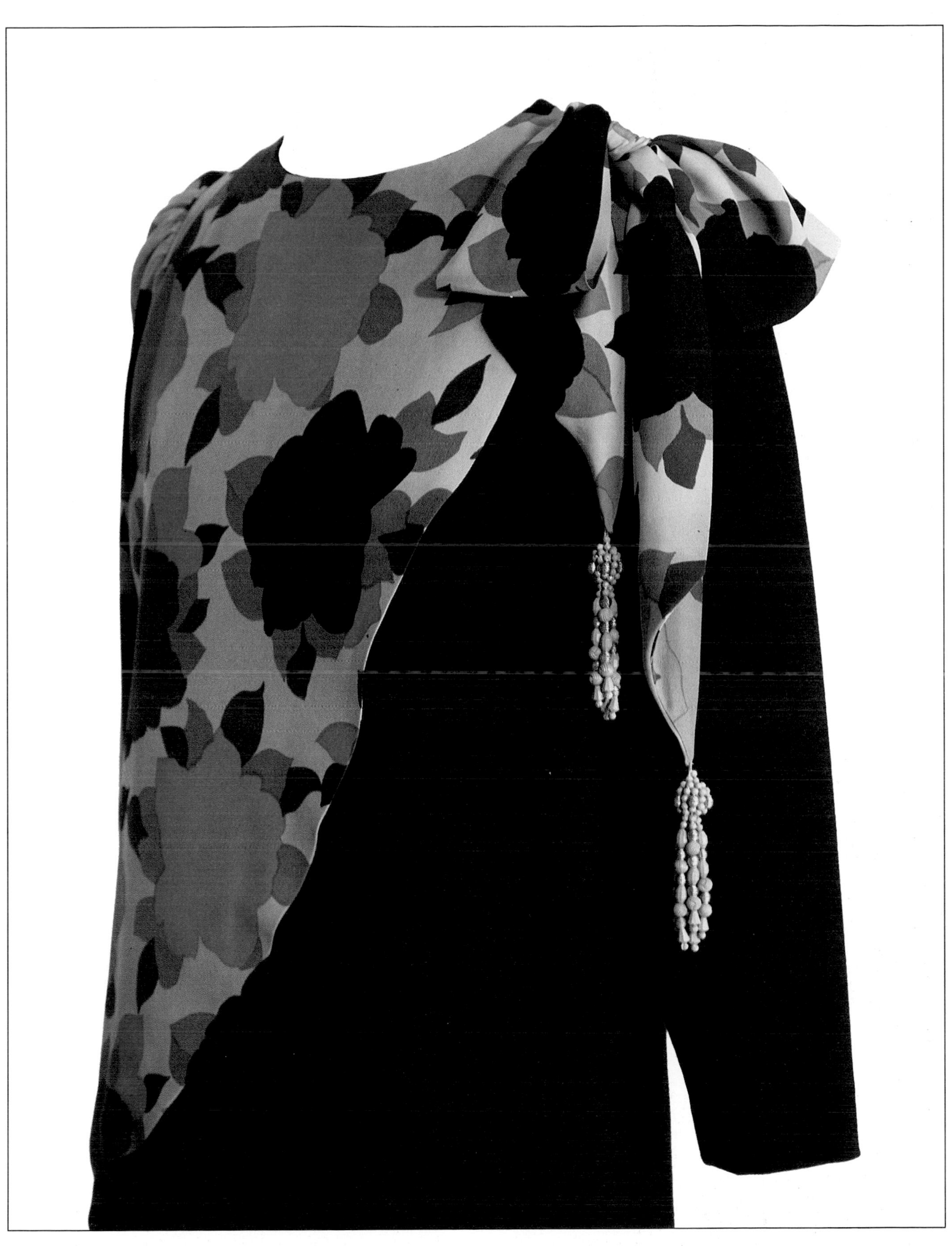

Beaded tassels complete the tails of the bias bow at the shoulder of this wool crepe dress. The silk crepe de Chine print drapes beautifully.

Scalloped edges of neck, front and tulip sleeve are easy, as linen takes a hard press. Linen is underlined in silk organza to resist wrinkles.

Rows and rows of pre-pleated gros-grain ribbon create this stunning sleeve. A soft braid rings neck to tie in back above zipper.

This heart-shaped sleeve in black linen was inspired by Pierre Cardin. Simple epaulet holds scarf in place.

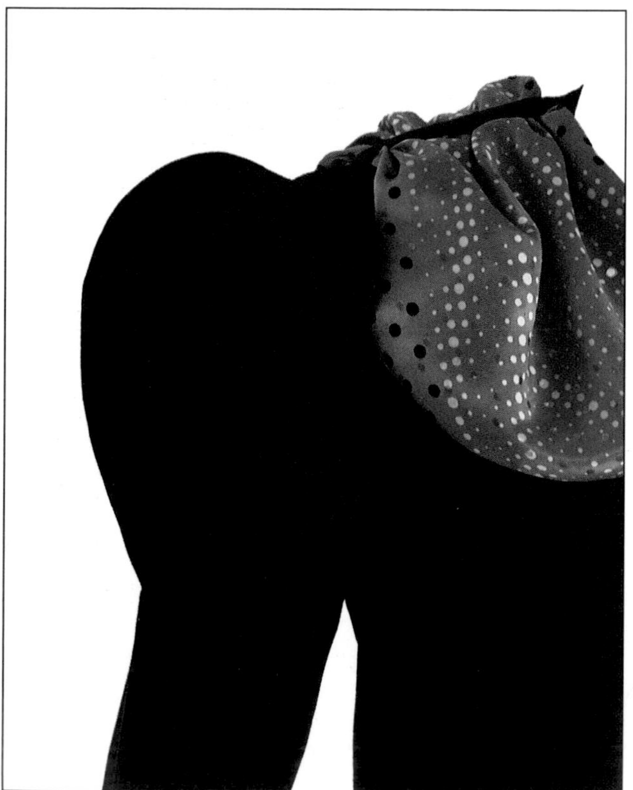

Wool plaid highlights this unique sleeve. A strap cut on the straight grain and an insert cut on the bias create a play of patterns.

The upper left cuff is fake—a rectangle folded and topstitched in place before bias binding is sewn at wrist. Covered buttons are acorn style. At upper right the cuff is detailed with channel stitching and Chinese ball buttons. One button was unraveled to yield braid for matching button loops. Below that, cranberry piping defines the cuff and holds gathers in an upright position. Loop buttonholes are piping with seam cut away. In the lower left multi-striped fabric has been chevroned (see page 77). In the cuff area fabric is pieced to remove all but the red.

The details make the difference. A circular pocket in contrasting fabric makes a garment special.

Triangle buttonhole variations are endless. At left are a few of the possibilities!

The buttons below are but a few from my collection.

Here's a sampling of couture fabrics:
upper left: silk chiffon with a satin stripe woven through
upper right: a navy and silver brocade is matched perfectly at the zipper
lower left: a combination of sheer cottons and cotton faille suggest the couture details
lower right: two brocades in wool with metallic threads

CHAPTER 14

Gathers

Throughout The Couture, the art of gathering appears in ruffles, sleeves, skirts, and in seams within the body of a garment. There is an art to gathering. The time spent in calculating the ratio of gathers, in the preparation of the gathered seam, and in its application to the garment all result in easier stitching and beautiful, perfectly even gathers.

Ratio of Gathers

In what used to be called "kitchen curtain" ruffles, a $2^1/_2$-to-1 ratio is used. That means the length of the ruffle is $2^1/_2$ times the length of the curtain edge. For example, 20″ (51cm) of curtain needed 50″ (127cm) of ruffle fabric, gathered back to 20″ (50cm). A $2^1/_2$-to-1 ratio is considered the norm, a basis for calculating other ratios for more or less fullness.

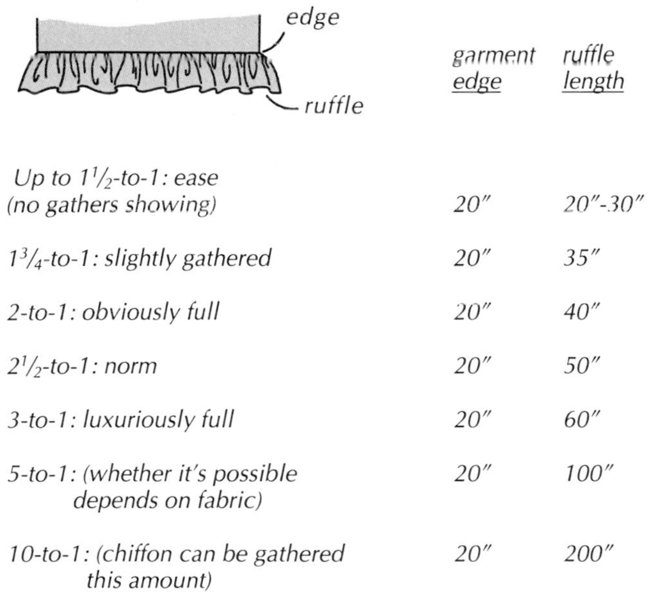

	garment edge	*ruffle length*
Up to $1^1/_2$-to-1: ease (no gathers showing)	*20″*	*20″-30″*
$1^3/_4$-to-1: slightly gathered	*20″*	*35″*
2-to-1: obviously full	*20″*	*40″*
$2^1/_2$-to-1: norm	*20″*	*50″*
3-to-1: luxuriously full	*20″*	*60″*
5-to-1: (whether it's possible depends on fabric)	*20″*	*100″*
10-to-1: (chiffon can be gathered this amount)	*20″*	*200″*

(Note: for metric equivalents, see chart on page 36.)

Gathering Rules:

1. When calculating fullness, consider the fabric's density (thickness). Obviously, a thin fabric such as chiffon can be gathered more closely together than a heavier fabric such as taffeta.

2. Consider design. Silk crepe de Chine can be gathered in a 3-to-1 ratio, but for a particular look you may only **want** a 2-to-1 ratio.

3. The wider the ruffle, the less full it will appear. For example a 1″-wide (2.5cm) ruffle gathered 2-to-1 may look as if it has the same fullness as a 5″ (12.5cm) ruffle gathered 3-to-1.

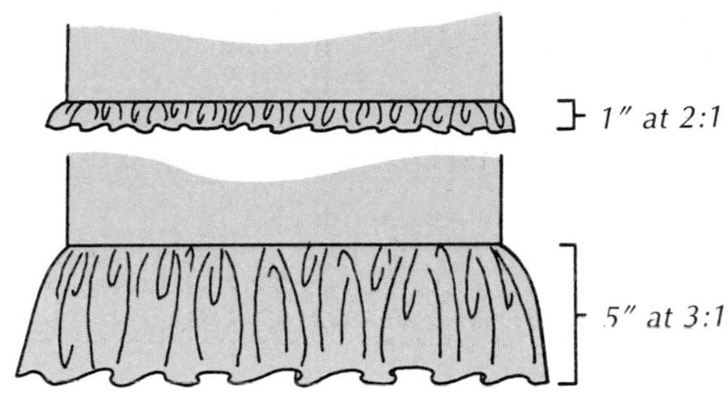

4. If a ruffle is cut on the bias, you can increase the ratio and cut a ruffle with more fullness.

5. Gathering stitches are **never** removed and should **never** show in the finished garment.

6. Make all rows of gathering stitches within the seam allowance. Never stitch beyond the seamline.

7. Use a matching thread in the needle but a high-contrast thread in the bobbin so you can easily see the stitches when pulling them up and when sewing the gathered edge to the garment. This is especially helpful on black or dark fabrics where stitches otherwise might barely show.

8. Three rows of gathering stitches provide good control. Four rows help to keep a seam flat, as on a sleeve cap. Four rows also increase your ability to ease difficult fabrics, such as silk lining in a sleeve cap.

9. The shorter the distance in each section of gathers, the greater the chance for perfection. Long rows of gathering stitches can lead to more thread breakage, a fate worse than death!

How to Gather

1. Divide the garment edge into equal units—quarters, eighths or sixteenths, and mark carefully.

2. Divide the edge to be gathered into the same number of units. Mark carefully.

3. Stitch six stitches per inch (2.5cm) with the bobbin thread on the side from which you will be working. Generally, this is the wrong side of the fabric.

4. Sew the first row of gathering **in the seam allowance**, as close as possible to the stitching line, starting and stopping at unit marks and leaving thread tails.

5. Space each additional row of gathering stitches 1/8″ (.3cm) apart into the seam allowance. To ensure even spacing of gathers in the finished garment, start and stop gathering stitches at the same place in each row.

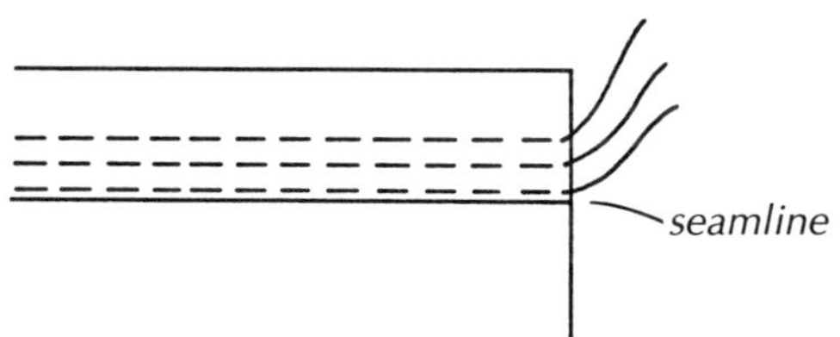

6. Subsequent sections of gathering stitches should begin one stitch back and just below the previous row. Staggering gives good control. Return stitches to the correct line as soon as possible.

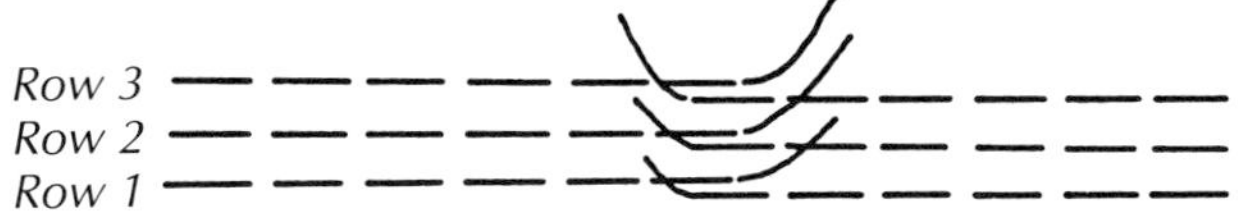

7. Draw up gathers to fit the garment edge.

8. Once the correct measurement is reached, the thread ends of each section can be tied together so there is no interruption in the even flow of gathering. Tie off each end of each row by pulling the top threads to the bobbin side and tying square knots.

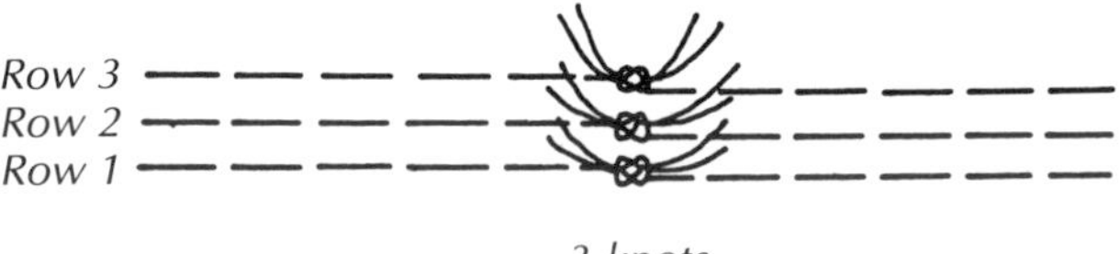

3 knots

9. Now adjust the gathers. Patiently even them out with your fingernail, the best and handiest built-in sewing tool.

10. Then, holding the seam edge flat under your thumb, pull the gathers at right angles to the stitching line so the fabric is straight.

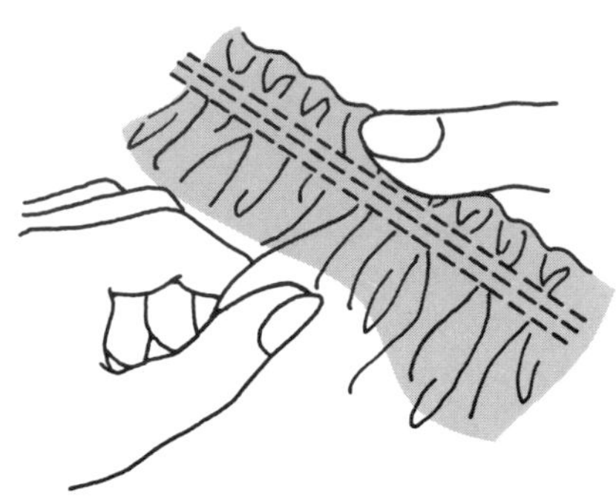

11. A gathered edge is inherently bulky with all that fabric packed together. To lessen the bulk, press the seam allowance hard with the edge of an iron to within 1/4″ (.6cm) of the stitching line. Steam, and use a clapper to flatten.

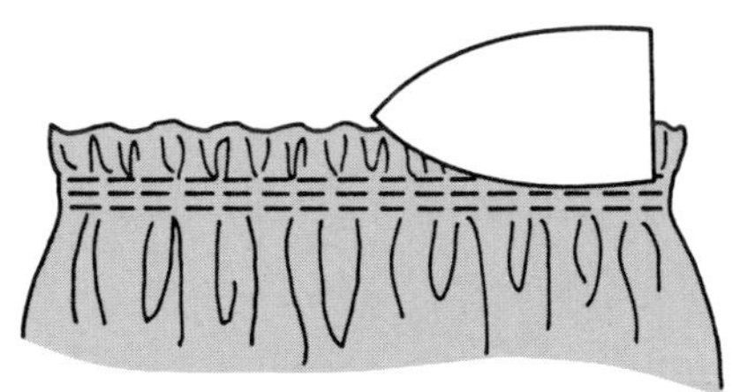

This pressing can be done before attaching the gathered edge to the garment straight edge, and again after stitching.

Attaching a Gathered Edge to a Garment Edge

1. Match all marks and pin **between** the gathers to avoid disturbing the even ripples and to prevent tucks from appearing after stitching. Slippery fabrics may need to be hand basted, but generally pinning will be sufficient.

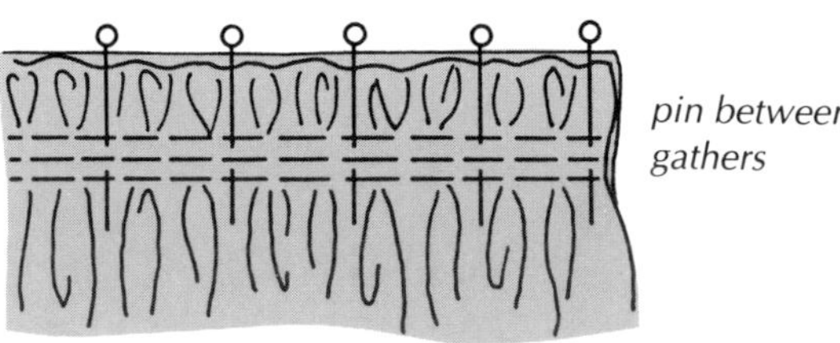

pin between gathers

2. Stitch with the gathers on top, holding the work taut as it goes through the machine. At the same time, be sure the gathers are always at right angles to the machine stitching line. Remove pins just before the needle reaches them.

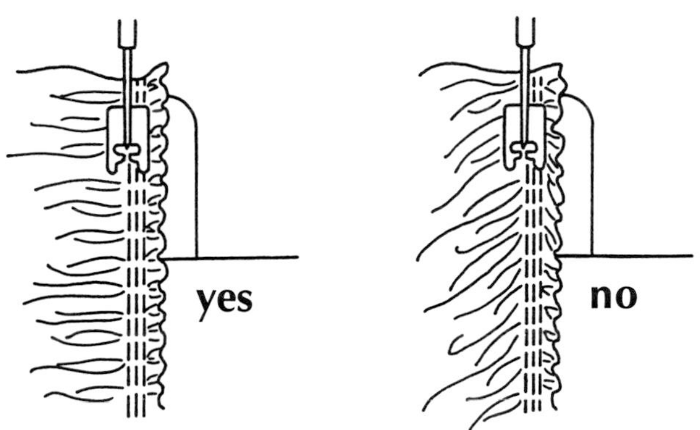

3. Grade seams to remove bulk, but beware of trimming a gathered seam too close to the stitching line. If it needs grading, always cut close to a row of gathering stitches, but never closer to the seamline than $^1/_4$" (.6cm). A gathered seam that is too narrowly trimmed will surely produce a ridge.

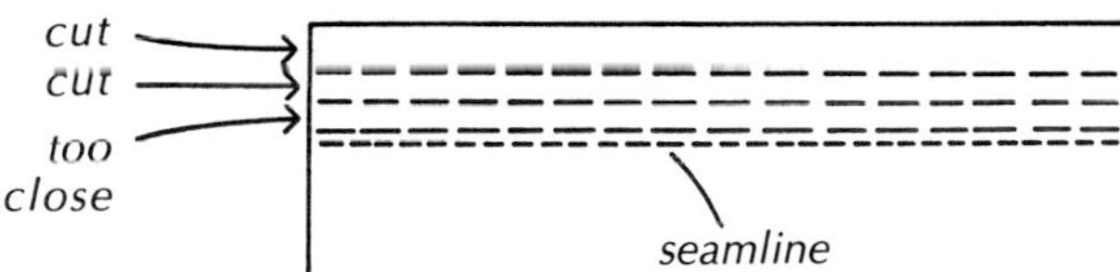

Inserting Gathers Between Two Straight Edges

When inserting gathers between two pieces of fabric, as around a neckline with a facing, keeping the gathers straight is a real feat.

1. Using a contrasting color thread, hand baste the ruffle to the main garment first, basting very close to the first row of gathers.

2. Pin, then baste the facing in place, using a different color thread from step 1.

3. Machine stitch, using the hand basting stitches (done in step 1) as a guide.

Double-layer Ruffles

Fold fabric in half and gather to create double-layer ruffles. Use these for sleeve heads or any place where a "pouf" is the goal. Gently pull the ruffle apart to "pouf." **Caution:** Do **not** pull apart the two fabric pieces until **after** they have been permanently stitched to the garment. Resist! Do not be tempted!

To pouf, hold the upper half of the ruffle in one hand, the under half in the other hand, close to the gathers, and gently pull the layers apart. Each fabric will support the other and a beautiful, soft pouf will result.

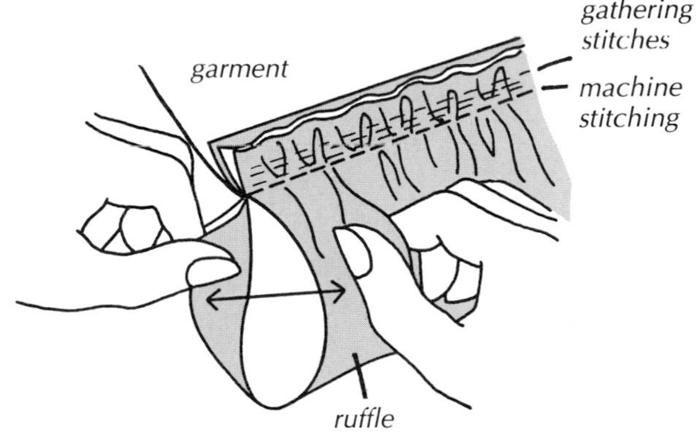

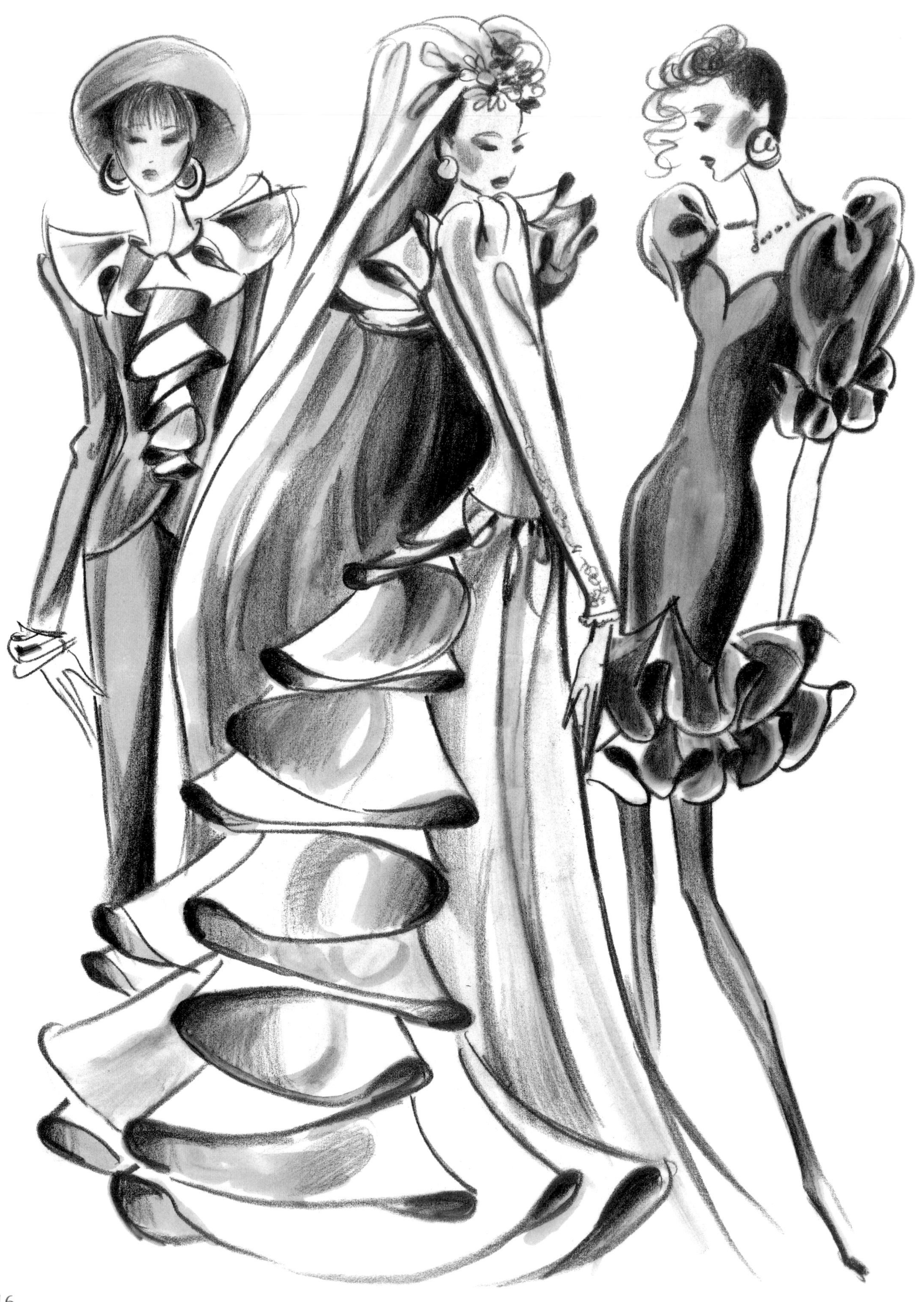

CHAPTER 15

Circular Ruffles

It's fun to look at fashion magazines—those beautiful clothes, billowing skirts, ruffles that flutter about, oversize bows, and surely, a silk flower tucked here or there. Perfectly lovely. And then a little voice whispers, "But you have no place to wear it." or "It's not you." Ah, but they are a source of inspiration, to copy, to adapt, to make yours in a way that will be beautiful for you!

Circular ruffles are an example. They always look exciting, as if perfectly arranged, and they stay that way. Why? Because a circle has all grains, can ripple, can be wide or narrow, gently fluid or stiffly gathered. There's that creativity again. Circular ruffles can be used anywhere, can be any size, and can worn by anyone!

Elements of a Circle

The concept of circular ruffles is a lesson in mathematics right out of the 7th grade. Once you understand circles, the variations are effortless.

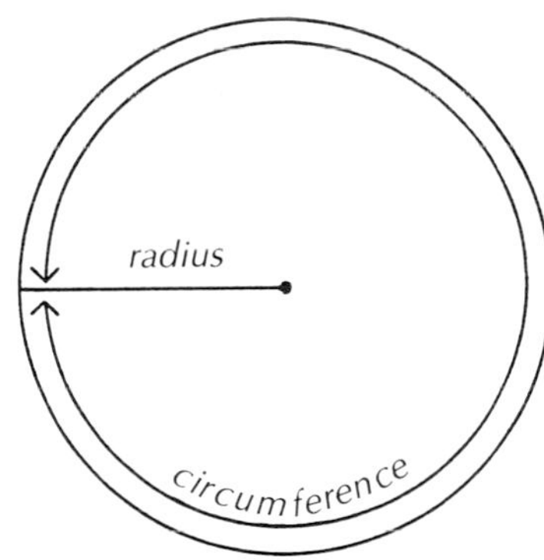

Circumference (C)
the perimeter (outside edge) of a circle

Radius (R)
a line from the center of a circle to the perimeter

pi π
a number representing the ratio of the circumference to the diameter of a circle. The transcendental number is 3.14149265. (Take heart! We use 3.14)

Note: Pi comes from Medieval Greek "periphireia," a word from which we derive perimeter.

The formula for determining the circumference of a circle is:

$$C = 2\,\pi\,R$$

$$C = 2 \times 3.14 \times R$$

$$C = (6.3)\ R$$

Note: Due to the amount of numbers in this chapter, we will not include metric equivalents. Refer to chart on page 205 if you'd like to fill in metric numbers when calculating your own circular ruffles.

Understanding the Concept

What may look complex at first glance is easy if you'll follow the exercises below in sequence.

There are inner circles and outer circles. In a skirt the inner circle is the waist, the outer circle the hem.

For example, let's make an inner circle with a 26" circumference:

Let C = inner circle

C = 26"
C = 2 π R
C = 6.3 R
26" = 6.3 R
26" ÷ 6.3 = R
4 1/8" = R

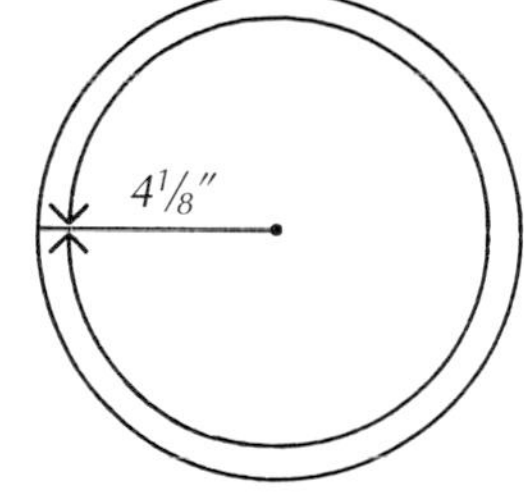

circumference = 26"

The radius of the inner circle is $4\frac{1}{8}$". By using a compass or a pencil with a string $4\frac{1}{8}$" long, you can make a circle that is exactly 26" around.

pin or pushpin
4 1/8"
pencil
string

Now we need to find the circumference of the outer circle that is 28″ away from the inner circle. The radius of the outer circle would be $4\frac{1}{8}$″ (radius of inner circle) PLUS 28″, for a total of $32\frac{1}{8}$″.

$R = 32\frac{1}{8}$″
$C = 2\pi R$
$C = 6.3\ R$
$C = 6.3 \times 32\frac{1}{8}$″

Answer: C = 202″

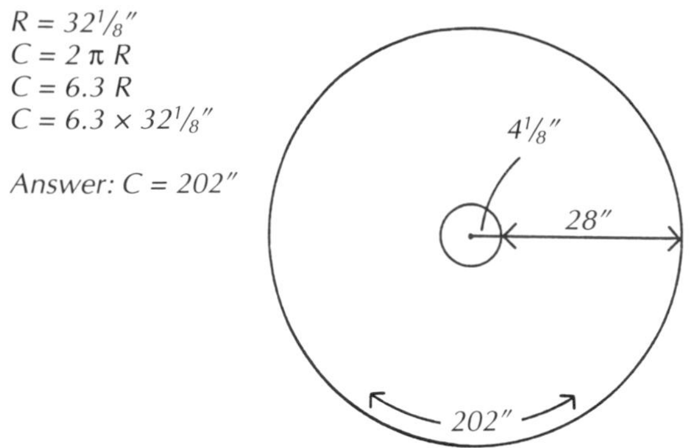

The above calculation is an important one to understand, for if you wanted to bind the hem of a circular skirt, for instance, you'd want to know how much bias binding to make—202″ ($5\frac{3}{4}$ yards).

How to Add Seam Allowances

If you were to make a circular skirt, you need a way to get into it! Therefore, to calculate the waist circumference of the skirt to fit a 26″ waist, you must add seam allowances.

26″ waist + $1\frac{1}{4}$ (two $\frac{5}{8}$″ seam allowances) = $27\frac{1}{4}$″

$C = 27\frac{1}{4}$″
$C = 2\pi R$
$C = 6.3\ R$
$27\frac{1}{4}$″ = 6.3 R
$27\frac{1}{4}$″ ÷ 6.3 = R

Answer: $4\frac{3}{8}$″ = R

Calculate the outer edge (hem) in the same way. The radius would be $32\frac{3}{8}$″ (28″ skirt length plus $4\frac{3}{8}$″ waist radius).

Now add a seam allowance at the waist and a hem allowance at the outside edge.

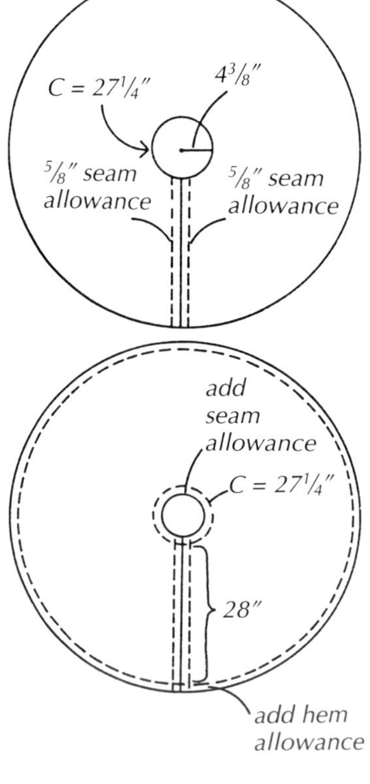

Making a Gathered Circular Skirt

Calculating Waist Measurement for a Gathered Skirt

What if you wanted to gather the circular skirt? How much fullness would you want to add to the waist circumference?

Ratio:

$1\frac{1}{2}$-to-1	=	slightly gathered
2-to-1	=	obviously full
$2\frac{1}{2}$-to-1	=	normal
3-to-1	=	luxuriously full

Let's choose $2\frac{1}{2}$-to-1 for fullness.

26″ waist x $2\frac{1}{2}$ = 65″.
65″ + $1\frac{1}{4}$″ (two ″ seam allowances) = $66\frac{1}{4}$″

$C = 66\frac{1}{4}$″
$C = 2\pi R$
$C = 6.3\ R$
$66\frac{1}{4}$″ = 6.3 R
$66\frac{1}{4}$″ ÷ 6.3 = R

Answer: $10\frac{1}{2}$″ = R

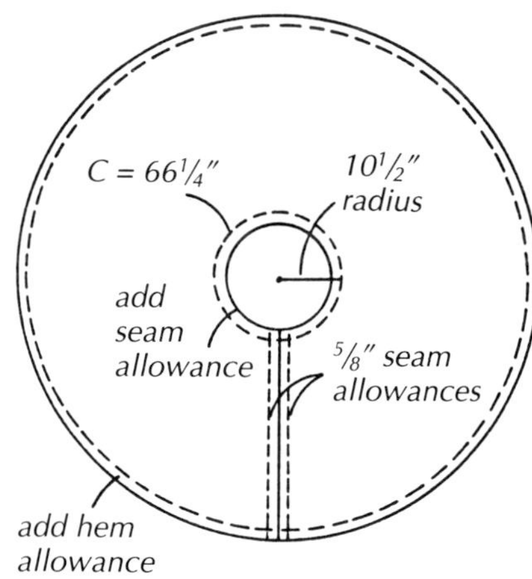

Make a circle using a $10\frac{1}{2}$″ radius. Calculate outer circle (hem edge). Add seam allowance at waist and hem allowance at outer edge. Gather to fit 26″ waist.

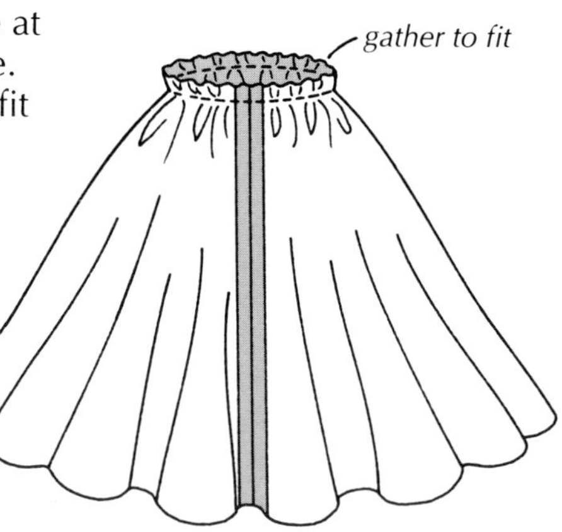

Now for the Fun Circular Ruffles!

Circular ruffles can outline a neckline or hem, ring a wrist and continue up a sleeve. Sleeves can be covered with circular ruffles. Since the ruffle is not **gathered** onto the neckline, if just one circle were used, it would look flat like a facing. To achieve a rippling effect, use more than one circle. How many circles? COUTURE IS JUDGMENT. Experiment. The thickness of the fabric, the fullness desired and the hem finish all contribute to ripple quality.

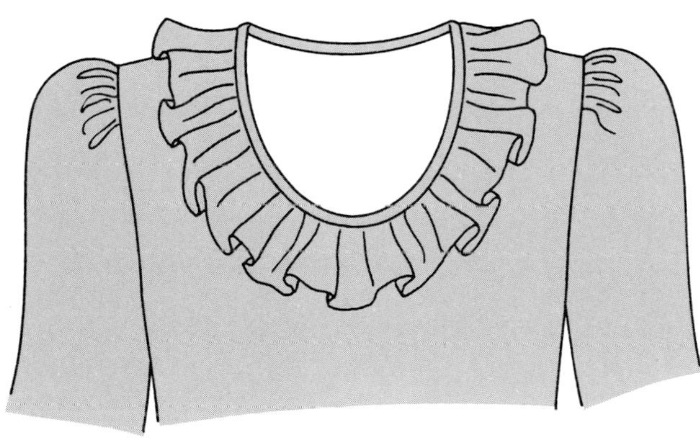

As an example, let's take a 27″ neckline and six circles. To join the circles, add two $1/4$″ seam allowances, totalling $1/2$″, to each one. Six circles would be 6 × $1/2$″ = 3″ you would need to add for seam allowances.

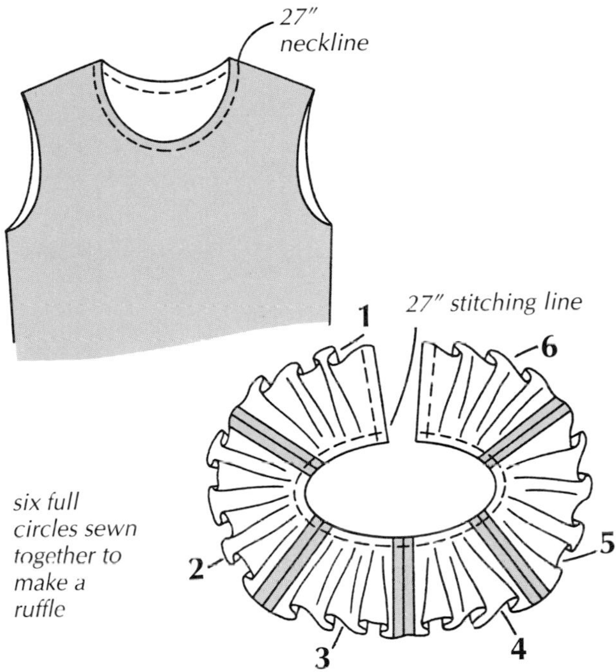

Neckline = 27″ + 3″ for seam allowances = 30″.

We need 30″—not in one circle, but in six circles.

30″ divided by 6 = 5″.

The circumference at the **stitching line** (inner circumference) of **each** circle is 5″.

Seam Allowances for Circular Ruffles

The circles will be sewn together so **each** needs seam allowances. You also need seam allowances on the edge to be sewn to the garment and on the ruffle's hem edge. The size of these seam allowances varies with the size of the circles.

Small circles need $1/4$″ seam allowances on the edge to be sewn to the garment. Larger or deeper circular ruffles can handle $1/2$″-$5/8$″ seam allowances. The hem allowance will be determined by the hem finish you choose.

Now Calculate Radius to Stitching Line of Each Circle

C = 5″

C = 2π R
C = 6.3 R
5″ = 6.3 R
5″ ÷ 6.3 = R
Answer: $3/4$″ = R

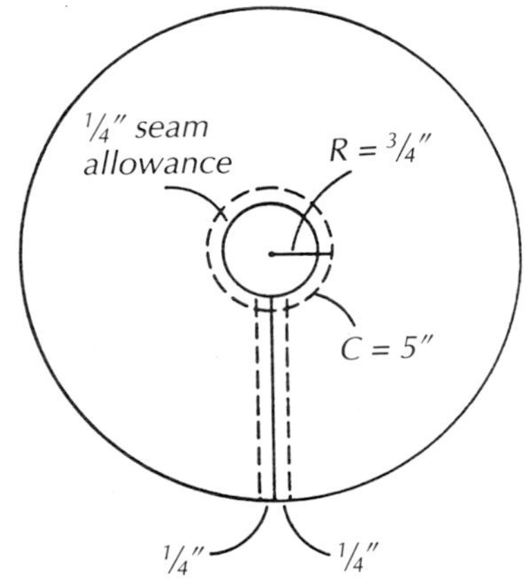

$3/4$″ is the distance from the center to the stitching line. Now add a $1/4$″ seam allowance to create a cutting line.

Now Determine the Width of Each Ruffle

To make a 2″ wide ruffle, draw another circle $2^3/_4$″ from the center ($^3/_4$″ from center to first stitching line plus 2″ ruffle width). Add desired hem allowance.

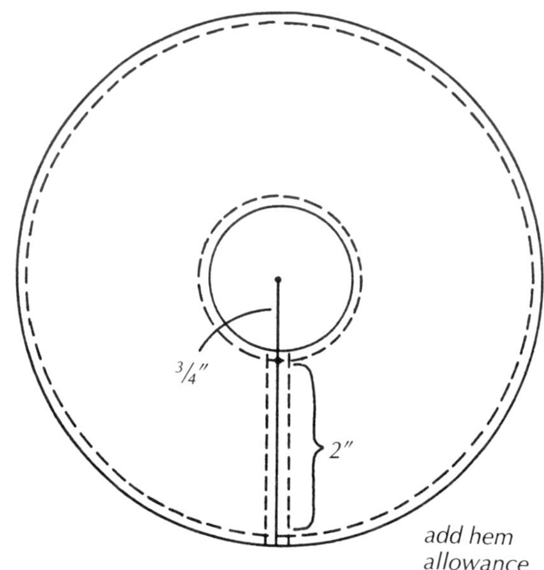

Sew the Ruffle from Six Circles

Cut six of these circles, then cut each circle apart **on the straight grain**. (This rule should be followed no matter how many circles are used or how wide.)

Sew circles together using $^1/_4$″ seam allowances. Use French seams in sheer or thin fabrics. (See French Seams, page 61.)

The stitching line of the ruffle should now measure 27″, the same as the neckline of the garment. Sew together.

When attaching circular ruffles, sew in a 1-to-1 ratio using a $^1/_4$″ seam allowance. No stretching, no easing and no clipping allowed. Can you hear me shouting **no clipping!** I know you will have a great urge to clip here. Please resist! It's simple, if the circular neckline measures 27″ and seamline of the ruffle measures 27″, no clipping should be needed!

Press at right angle to stitching line to meld stitches, making sure iron does not rest on the ruffle.

Now You Can Clip!

Clipping a circular ruffle will cause it to ripple everywhere there is a clip. As the designer you can determine how many ripples you want and how deep. The closer the clips, the more ripples; the farther apart the clips, the fewer the ripples, but the ripples will be deeper.

Clip ruffle seam allowance only, clipping straight to the stitching line at even intervals. Every time you clip a ripple will occur.

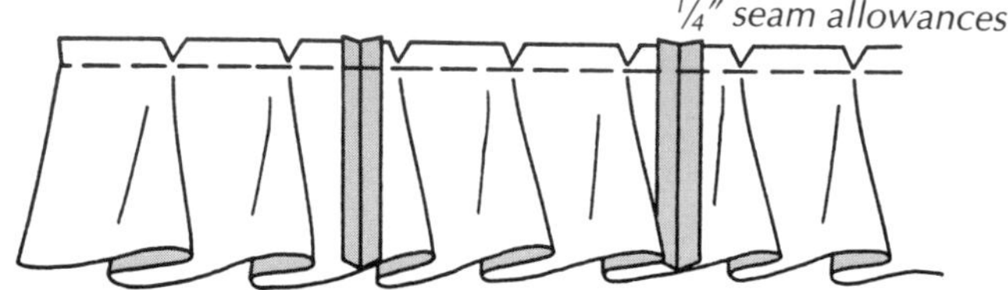

Circular ruffles can be attached to a neckline using a traditional facing. Ruffles will then tend to turn toward neck.

ruffles attached with traditional facing

Circular ruffles bound to a neck edge with bias binding will fall toward the garment.

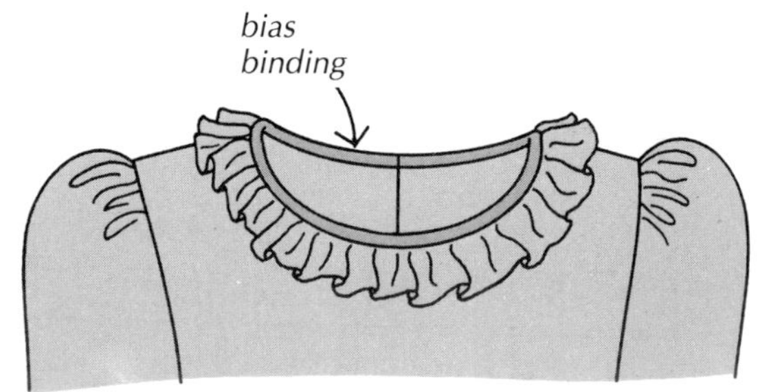

Ruffle Hem Finishes

The hem finish on a circular ruffle adds to the intensity of the ripple as well as the overall effect. There are many choices including the following:

1. Narrow hem. (See page 63.)
2. Bias bound edge (See Bias Binding, page 85.)
3. Lined. Cut exactly the same number and size ruffles out of lining as you did for the fashion fabric. Make both ruffles, then sew outside edges right sides together. Press. Trim seam allowance to $^1/_8$", turn right side out and press. Sew ruffle to garment.
4. Line with fashion fabric following same directions as in #3.
5. Pipe the edge first (page 93), then line or face.
6. Machine roll edge.

Double Circular Ruffles

A double circular ruffle is hand stitched to the garment after it is completed rather than being inserted into a seam during construction. A double circular ruffle can have both sides the same width or one side narrow and the other wider.

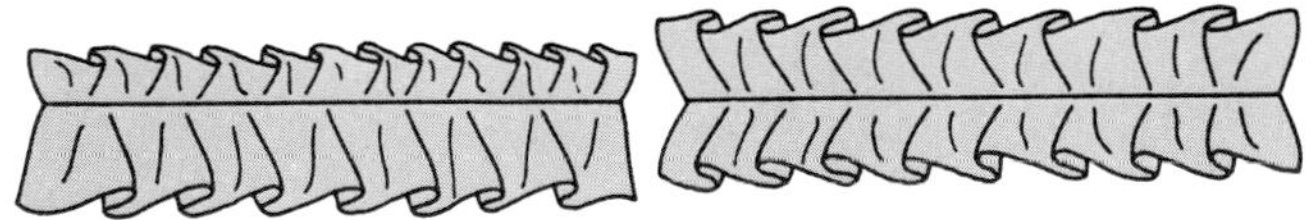

1. Cut twice as many circles as needed to "travel the distance" (a way to think of the length of the edge to which they will be sewn). Be sure to add seam allowances for sewing circles together if using more than one circle. Make them the desired width plus hem allowance at lower edge and seam allowance at edge of inner circle.
2. Stitch circles together in two continuous ruffle strips.

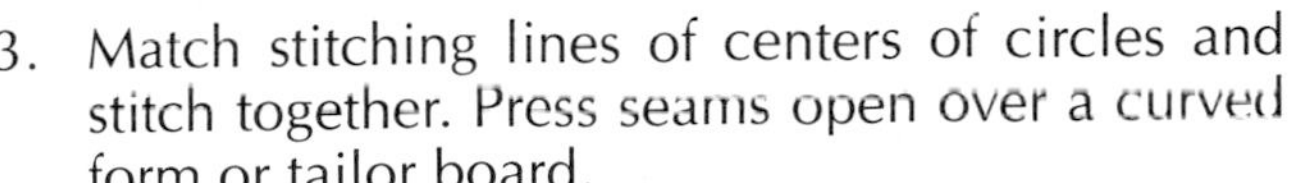

3. Match stitching lines of centers of circles and stitch together. Press seams open over a curved form or tailor board.

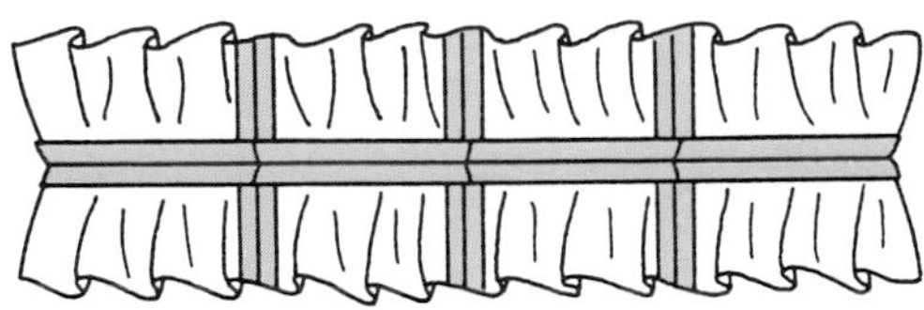

4. Hem both outside raw edges of circles.

Lined Double Circular Ruffle

A double circular ruffle is particularly beautiful when it is lined or faced. Start by renting the video of "Gone With the Wind."

1. Cut **four** times the number of circles needed.
2. Stitch circles together in four continuous ruffle strips.
3. Stitch strips 1 and 2 together on center of circles.
4. Stitch strips 3 and 4 together on center of circles. Now you have two long strips of double circular ruffles.

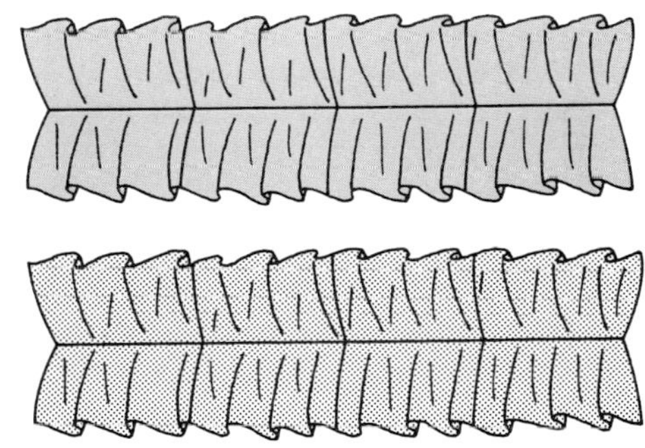

5. Press seams open over curved form or tailorboard.
6. Place strips **right sides together** and stitch outside edges together. You now have a tube.

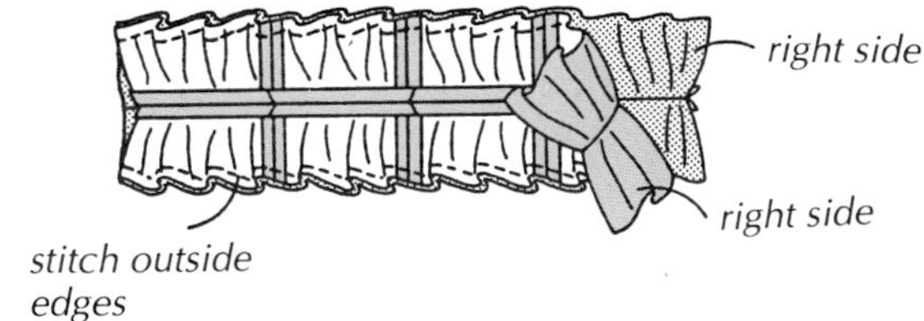

7. Trim seam allowances to $^1/_8$". Turn tube to right side.

8. Press hem edges. Finish ends by hand, turning in $^1/_4$" seam allowances and slip stitching closed.

9. Stab stitch center seam to hold together. (See page 39.)

When Rhett Butler says "Frankly, my dear, I don't give a damn"—you won't either!

Uneven Double Circular Ruffles

The centers will all be the same radius; the width of the ruffle will be different. The procedure for sewing together is the same as if they were of equal size.

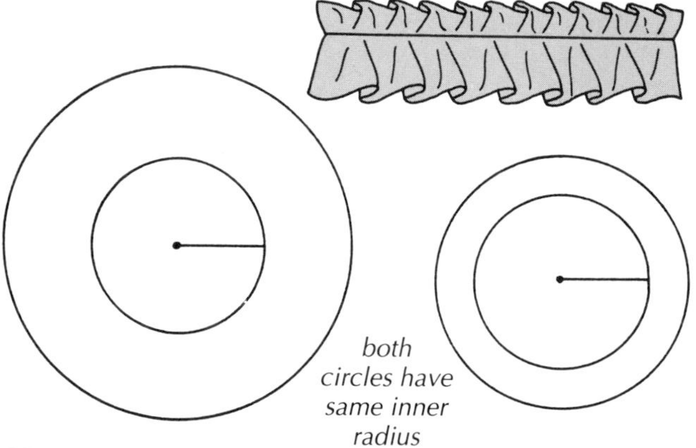

Haute Couture

The ultimate is a double circular ruffle boa (see photo, page 32). The following instructions are for a finished boa 60" long with 5"-wide ruffles. It is made with 10 circles in each half. Try this in silk organza for evening wear; make in white pique for a summer garden dress or in taffeta for a stiff ruffle.

Finished length at center of double ruffle = 60"
Added length for seam allowances:
10 circles × $^1/_2$" (two $^1/_4$" seam allowances) = 5"

Total needed = 65"

65" ÷ 10 circles = $6^1/_2$" inner circumference of each circle.

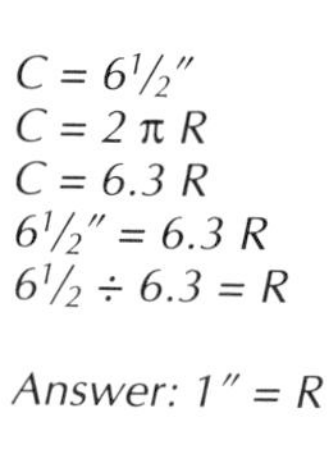

$C = 6^1/_2$"
$C = 2\pi R$
$C = 6.3 R$
$6^1/_2$" $= 6.3 R$
$6^1/_2 \div 6.3 = R$

Answer: 1" = R

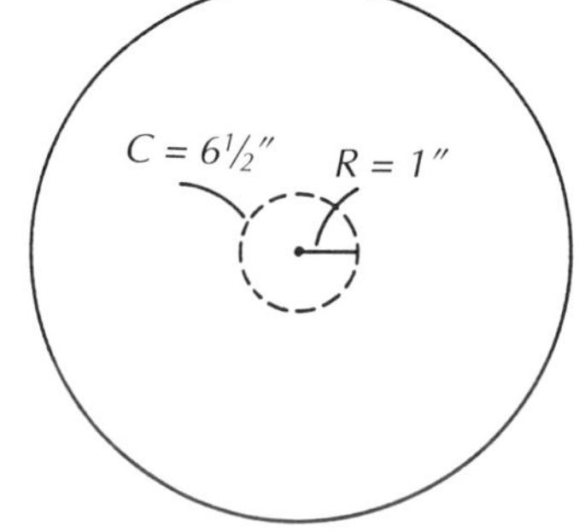

Each circle will have an inner radius of 1", a ruffle width of 5", and $^1/_4$" seam allowances on inner and outer edges.

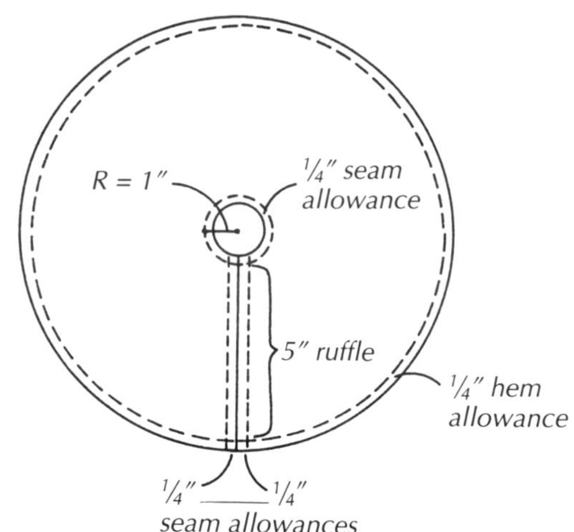

For this double circular ruffle boa 20 circles are needed—10 on each side. However, because it should be self-faced, you will need a total of 40 circles. Follow instructions for constructing a lined double circular ruffle, page 121.

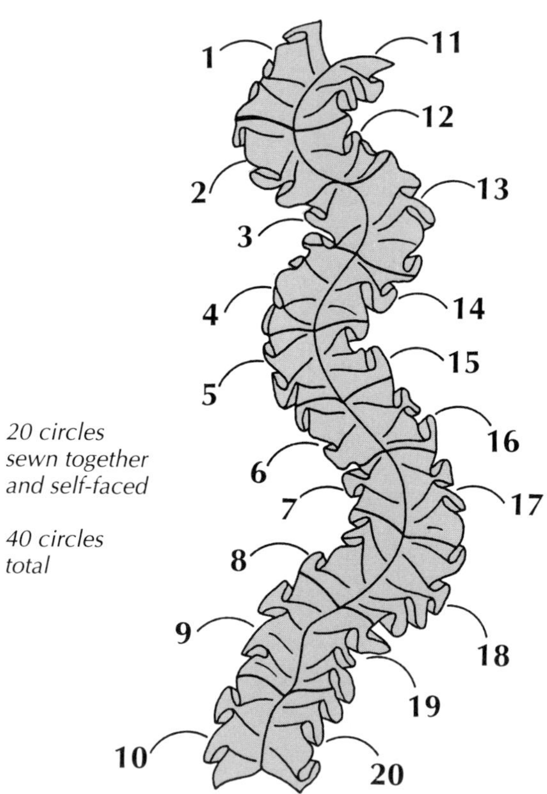

Question: How much fabric is needed?

Each circle will need a 12½″ square of fabric. Forty circles are needed.

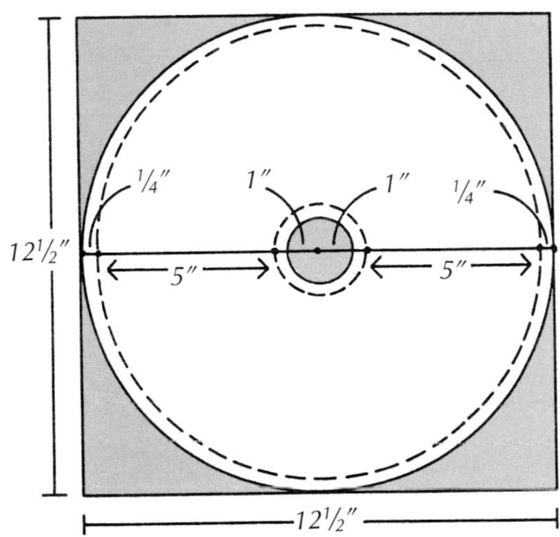

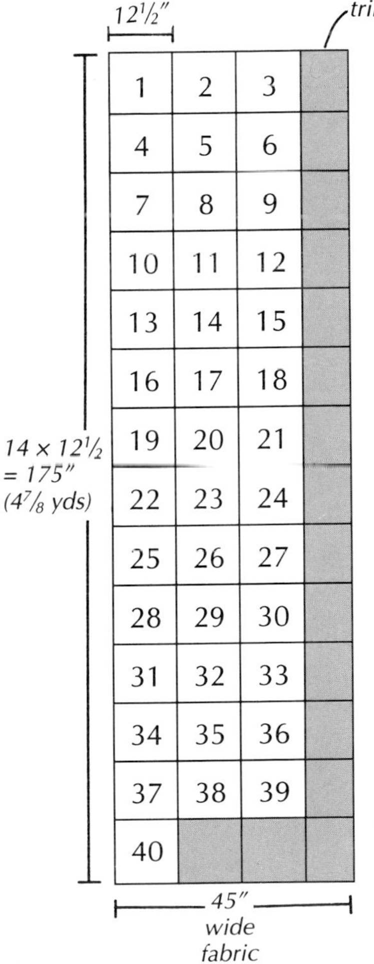

cut 40 12½″ squares

Answer:
4⅞ yards of 45″ fabric or
3½ yards of 55″ fabric.

COUTURE Tip For a really dramatic boa make ruffles 10″ wide and hand sew beads to hem edge.

Haute Haute Couture— Test Your Skills

Try a gathered, lined, double circular ruffle boa.

- How long do you want the boa?
- What ratio of gathers?
- How many circles?
- How deep a ruffle do you want?

1. Add additional length for seam allowances to finished boa length.
2. Calculate the radius of inner circle (see page 119).
3. Calculate radius to hem edge based on depth of the ruffle (page 120).
4. Add inner seam allowances and outer hem allowances.

Calculate yardage needed.

Cut, stitch circles together, gather, stitch strips together, turn. Press.

Wear it with flourish! You win the prize!

CHAPTER 16

The Princess Line

The princess line is used throughout couture for fit or design. As a design line, it is one of the most universally beautiful lines on the female body. It enhances the small-busted figure, and adds necessary fullness for good fit over a large bustline without the need for a dart. The princess seam is unique, with special rules and methods for stitching and pressing.

The princess line originates either in the shoulder or the armhole, crossing the bust point and continuing through the waist to the hem. A princess line can also cross the bust up to $\frac{1}{2}$″ (1.3 cm) past the apex toward the side seam.

Understanding the origin of the princess line is foundation knowledge in couture sewing. The line is created simply by relocating the original underarm dart of the basic sloper to either the armhole or the shoulder.

A princess line going into an armhole should be curved.

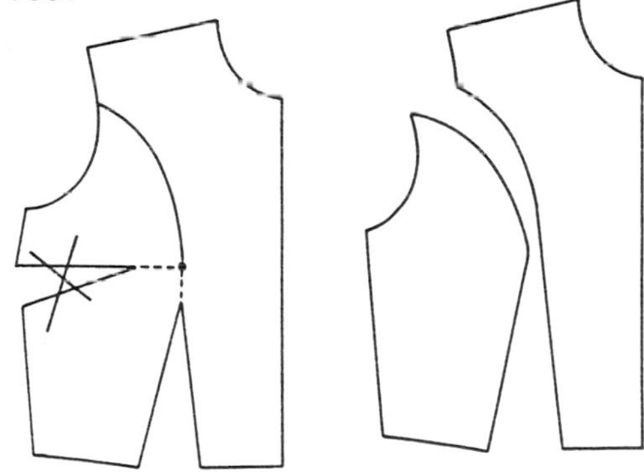

A princess line that runs into the shoulder will usually be a relatively straight line, but may have a slight curve.

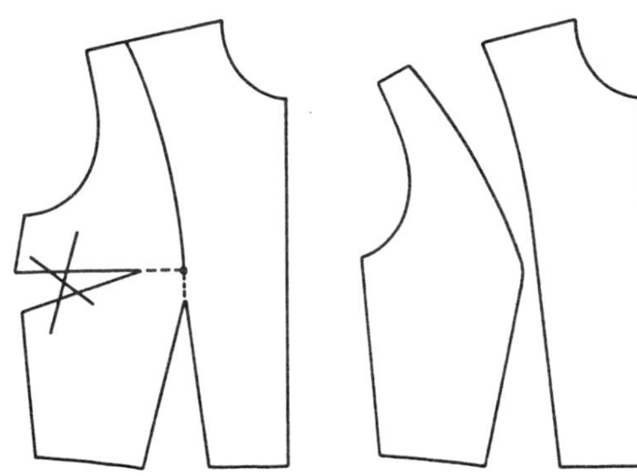

The amount of ease in the princess seam depends on bust size. The larger the bust, the larger the darts; thus, the princess seam will be more curved. The reverse applies for a princess line for a smaller figure.

You must understand this concept when fitting a garment with a princess line. When there is too much fabric in the chest and armhole area, the natural tendency is to make the seam deeper. But that only makes the "dart" larger, producing more fullness. Instead, let out the seams to make the garment lie flat in the chest/armhole area.

If the garment is too tight (compressing the bust), increasing the seam allowance will provide more fullness for the bust.

The increase or decrease for fitting should be taken on the side front piece, leaving the center front as is.

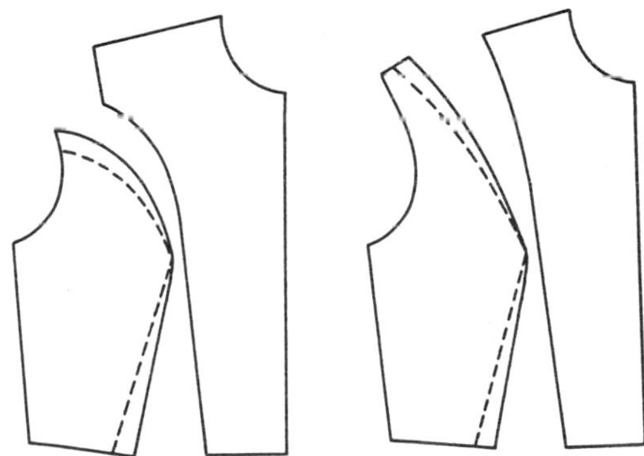

increase curve for a large bust

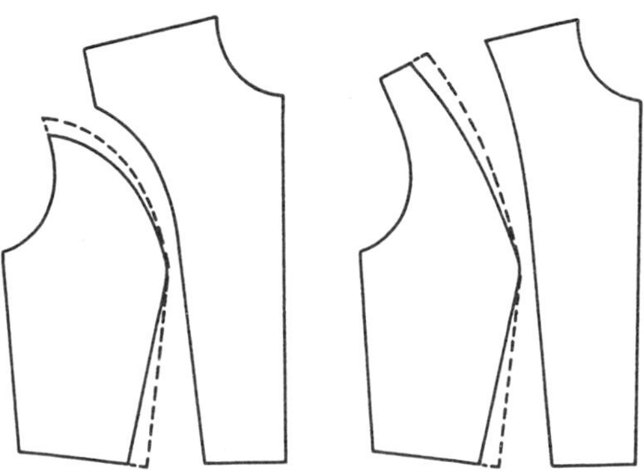

decrease curve for a small bust

If an alteration is done in paper or fabric, the shoulder line or armhole curve must be re-marked and the waistline circumference adjusted.

Changing the Grain

We often read that a particular couturier was a good "cutter." No one ever says someone really understood grain. But changing the grain of a particular garment segment can enhance a design's fit and look. For example, cutting the side piece of a princess design on the bias causes the garment to follow the body contours for a clean, fitted look.

Now **you** become the designer.

Changing the grain of the princess side piece also can be used to create a different configuration of stripes and plaids.

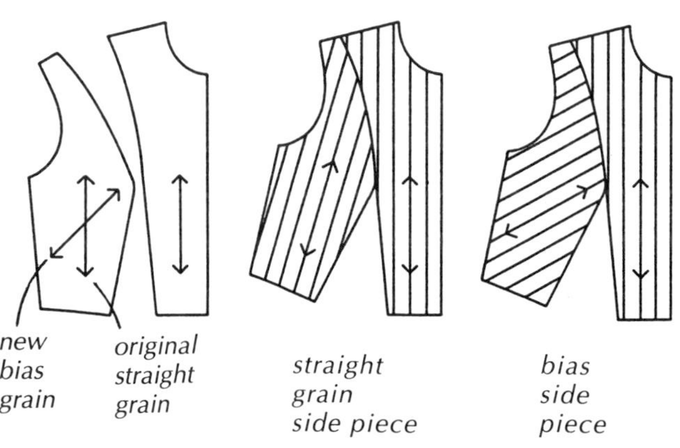

Using the pattern's original grainline, draw a bias grainline (45-degree angle) and place that line on the fabric's straight of grain.

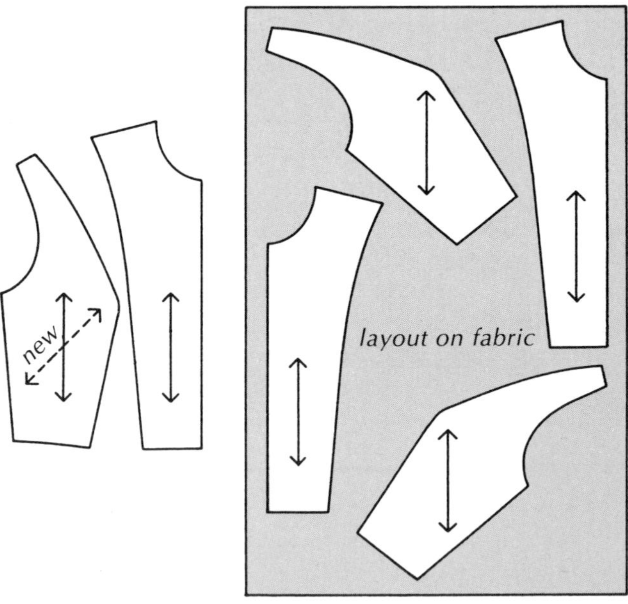

When underlining and/or lining the garment, cut it on the same grain as the fashion fabric.

If you're cutting the side piece on the bias for decorative purposes only, the underlining can be cut on the straight grain and the entire piece will act as if both pieces were cut on the straight grain.

Sewing a Princess Seam

A princess seam should always be slipstitch basted from the right side.

1. Working over a ham, fold under the seam allowance along the marked stitching line on the side piece, and position it at the marked stitching line of the center front or center back piece. Remember, the rule is **fold the seam with the greater curve onto the straighter seam.**
2. Pin from shoulder or armhole to $1^1/_2$" (3.8cm) from bust point.
3. Pin from hem up to $1^1/_2$" (3.8cm) from bust point.
4. Shift ham for a strong curve under the bust area and place pins close together over the bust point. Ease if necessary by gently stretching the stitching line of the center front piece.

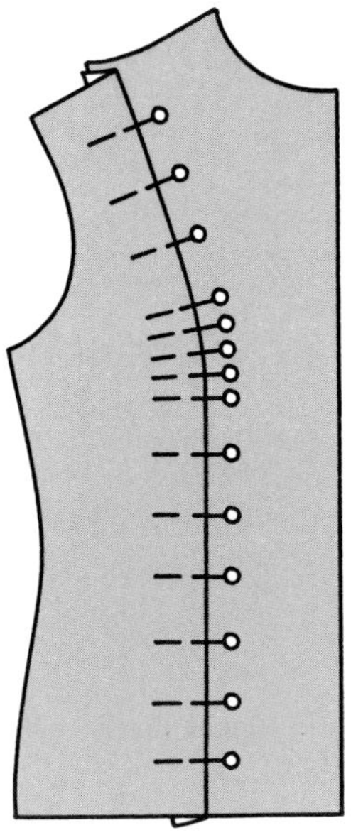

5. Slipstitch baste along seamline, with fabric shaped over a ham. Space stitches more closely together over the bust point.

6. Fold fabric right sides together and machine stitch, remembering the mixed grain rule:

   Sew with the weakest grain or greatest curve on top. In a princess seam, the side piece is always on top. Sew from the bottom up on the right side of the garment and from the top down on the left side of the garment. Stitch as close as possible to the basting stitches. Hold work **taut** and sew at moderate speed.

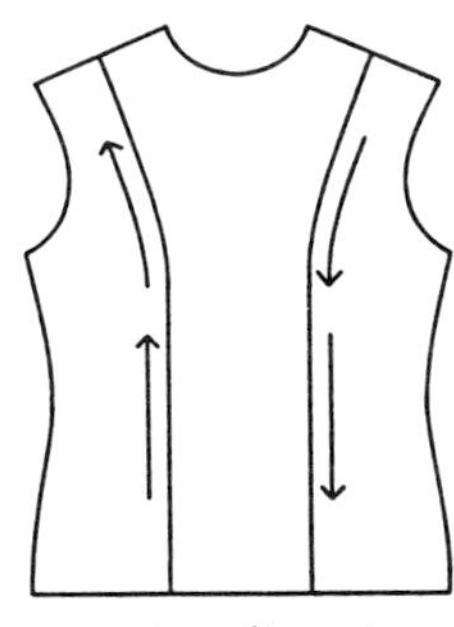

sewing direction

7. Remove all basting.

8. Meld stitches (both sides of seam) with the edge of the iron.

9. Press seam open over a ham.

COUTURE Tip Although you generally press in the same direction as you sew; with a princess seam, press over a ham from the hem to bust point and from the shoulder or armhole to bust point. Move the ham often to get the exact curve you need under the work.

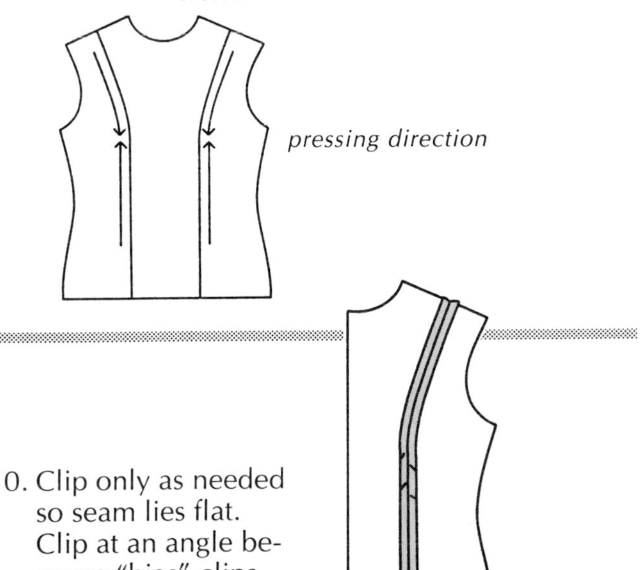

pressing direction

10. Clip only as needed so seam lies flat. Clip at an angle because "bias" clips will not ravel.

Princess Design Ideas

The princess seam can be sewn as a slot seam or welt seam. (See Topstitching, pages 163-165.) Use this when show-through (light-colored fabrics or sheers) is likely. Because all excess seam allowances can be cut away, little is left to show through.

The princess seam can be pressed toward the center front and topstitched parallel to the seamline. When the original princess line is 1/2" (1.3cm) away from the bust point, the topstitching then will cross the bust point exactly, giving the garment a more slender look. Grade the seam allowance which lies next to the body to 3/8" (1cm) and the remaining seam allowance to 1/2" (1.3cm).

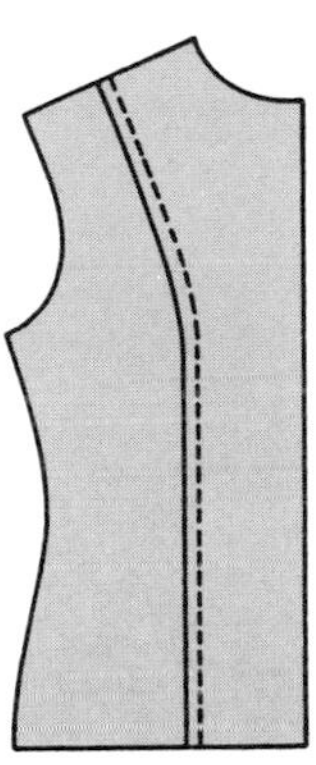

Princess Linings

Construct lining the same as the garment (steps 1-10). From the wrong side, hand baste the lining seam allowances to the body of the lining. For smooth and stable seams, topstitch from the right side 1/4"-1/2" (.6-1.3cm) away from the seamline on each side. Trim away excess seam allowance next to topstitching. This creates a very smooth and stable seam when silk or other thin lining fabric is used in a garment with princess styling.

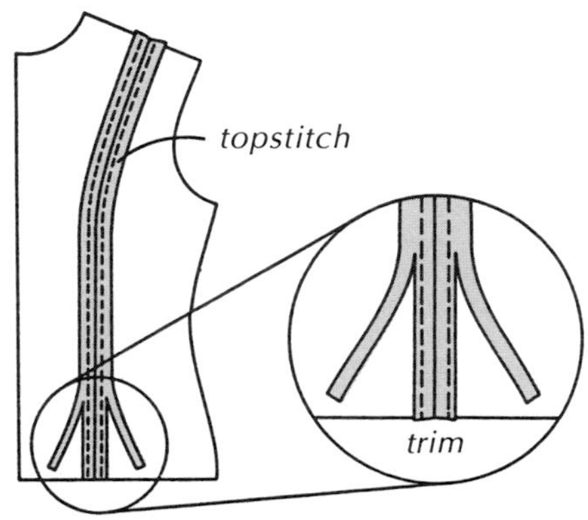

CHAPTER 17

Sleeves—Glorious Sleeves!

Sleeves are fashion. Sleeves are Couture. Sleeves make a statement. They can be decorative or plain. They can be one-piece or two, cut on the lengthwise or crosswise grain or on the bias. They may have cuffs. Sleeve caps may be gathered, darted, or eased to fit the armhole. Some sleeves are very fitted while others are full. Length can vary from cap sleeves to elbow-length to long.

You could make a lifetime study of sleeves. Nothing changes the look of a dress faster than a sleeve. The mark of a skilled tailor or seamstress is the sleeve.

Anatomy of a Sleeve

To design and sew beautiful sleeves, you must understand the anatomy of a sleeve.

1. Cap point matches shoulder seam.
2. Lengthwise grainline runs from cap point to wrist.
3. Crosswise grainline, 2″ (5cm) below cap point, is the ease area in the traditional set-in sleeve.

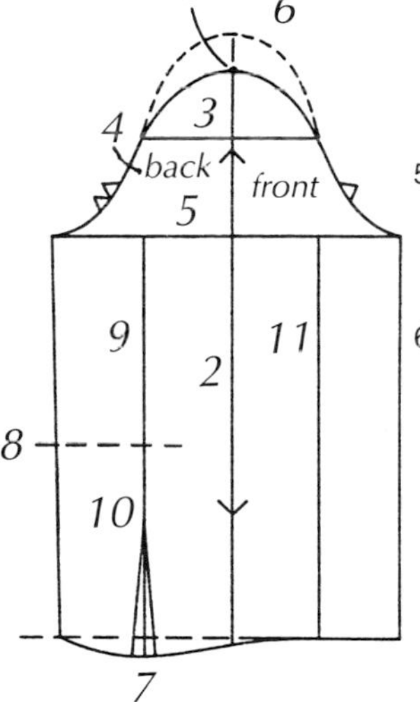

4. The midpoint of the back is halfway between the underarm and the cap.
5. The underarm line is on the crosswise grain.
6. Loft is the amount the sleeve rises and extends past the natural shoulder line. Loft requires support, added during construction.
7. Drape at the bottom of the sleeve allows for ease over the elbow in a cuffed sleeve. (This ease results when the elbow dart of a sloper is transferred to the wrist and becomes ease.)
8. Elbow line is at your elbow.
9. Half-of-back line is located halfway between back underarm seam and center grainline.
10. Opening is located on the half-of-back line.
11. Half-of-front line is located halfway between front underarm seamline and center grainline

Preparing the Sleeve Pattern

1. Use 1″-wide (2.5cm) seam allowances. Wider seam allowances make it easier to shrink the sleeve cap and to shape a two-piece sleeve. Also, if you decide to set the sleeve further into the shoulder, you'll have the extra fabric needed on the sleeve cap.

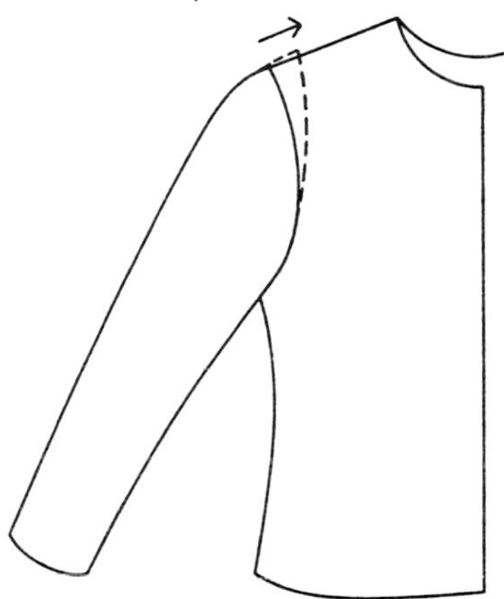

2. Draw a crossgrain line across the cap 2″ (5cm) down from the cap point if the cap is to be eased.
3. Mark every place where two seam cross, to indicate match marks for putting the pieces together in a one- or two-piece sleeve.

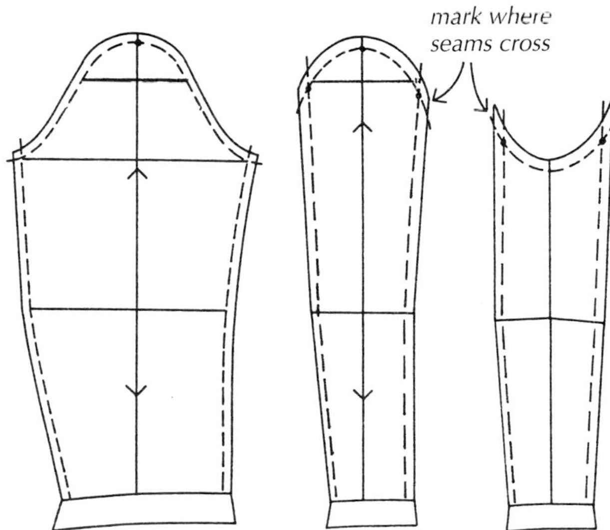

4. After cutting, transfer all marks to fabric using silk thread.

Wrist Drape

In couture, a cuffed sleeve drapes softly at the wrist. On a hanger it looks as if an arm is in the sleeve. How much drape is a judgment call, a feel, a look, based on the overall garment design and its relationship to the sleeve, the fabric, the person who will wear it, and how it will be worn.

Adding Wrist Drape

Begin with a paper pattern for a sleeve that fits you. You will simply be making a change on a commercial pattern.

1. Trim away all seam allowances. (You will put them back after you make the design change.)
2. Draw the underarm line.
3. Draw lengthwise grainline.
4. Divide back in half and draw half-of-back line.
5. Divide front in half and draw half-of-front line.
6. If the sleeve has drape and you want to change the amount, you will need to remove existing drape first. Where half-of-front line crosses the wrist seamline, mark the point with an X. Draw a cross grainline through this point and cut off excess pattern below the line.

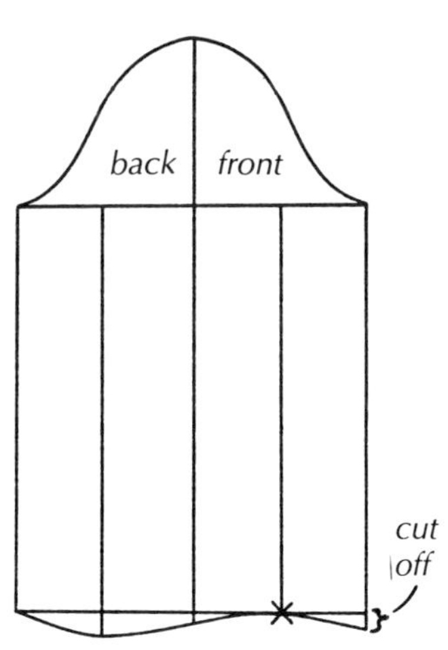

7. Attach extra pattern paper and draw a $1\frac{1}{2}''$ (3.8cm) rectangular box at the bottom of the sleeve. Divide the box in half horizontally. Extend vertical lines into the box.

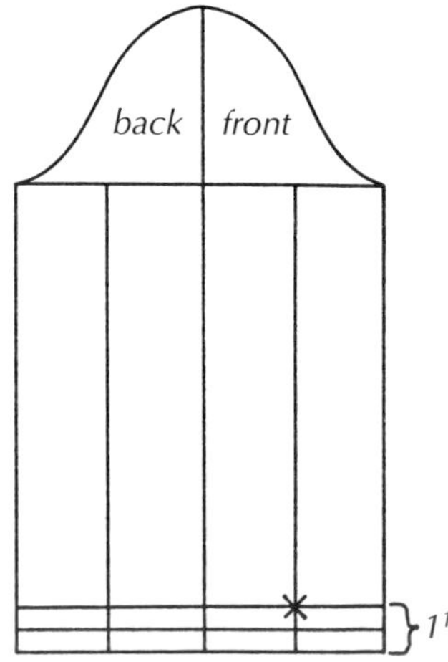

COUTURE Tip The amount of drape depends on the curve at the bottom of the sleeve. Where you place your X's in step 8 determine the fullness.

8. Mark X's on the lines as shown:

For more drape: This method should be used on blouses and dresses that will be worn without a jacket.

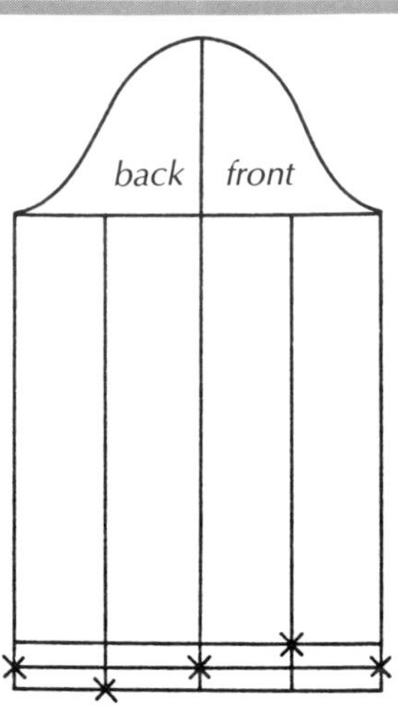

For less drape: This method flattens the line across the front of the sleeve, reducing fullness. It is suitable for blouses worn under jackets.

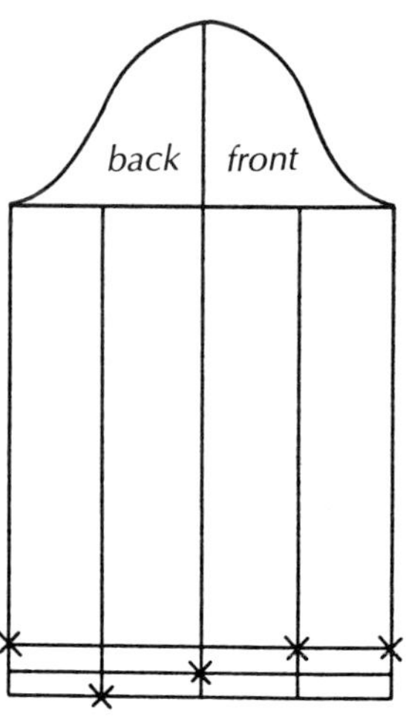

9. Connect the marks to form an elongated "S" curve. Use two French curves for a smooth, continuous line. They should touch at the center line.

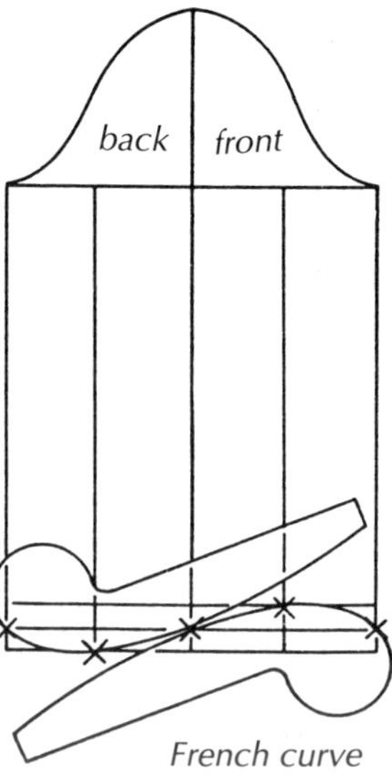

10. Mark opening on half-back line.

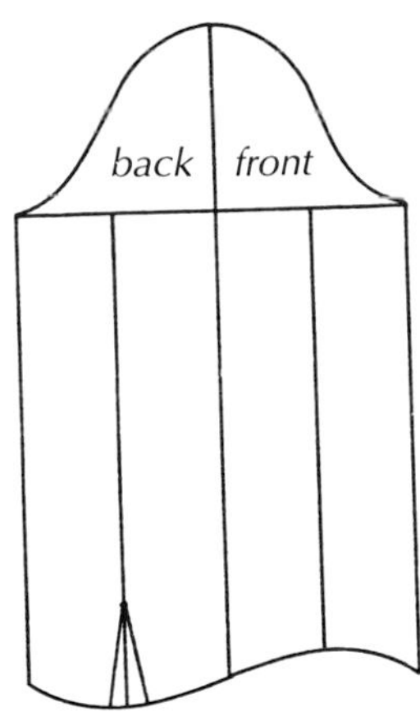

COUTURE Tip In step 7, the original size of the box can be increased up to 5" (12.5cm) for a dramatic drape. This is especially beautiful in a full chiffon sleeve.

Set-In Sleeve Loft

A perfect, traditional set-in sleeve hangs straight, with no evidence of gathering in the cap (only ease), and the cap is rounded (supported by a sleeve head). The amount of "roundness" depends on the amount of loft.

Loft is added to a traditional eased-in sleeve cap to achieve a more rounded, soft cap line, a characteristic of the couture. Loft may also be added to a gathered sleeve cap for increased pouf—a more dramatic look.

When loft is added, there is more fabric to ease into the armhole. Thus, fabric that shrinks easily is more suitable for a sleeve with high loft. Wool flannel, for example, eases better than a rigid, tightly woven fabric such as gabardine.

To Add Loft

1. Trim away seam allowances from pattern.
2. Find the midpoint of the back of the sleeve cap by drawing a straight guideline from underarm point to cap point. Measure the line and divide by 2. At that point draw a perpendicular line. The point at which this line crosses the stitching line of the sleeve is the midpoint of the back.

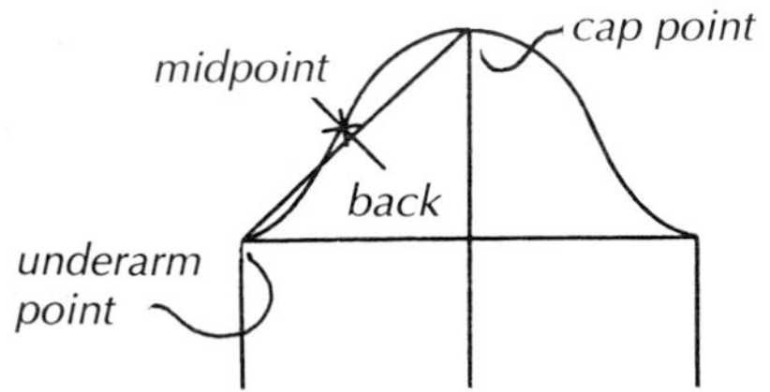

3. Draw a crossgrain line from back midpoint to sleeve front, parallel to the underarm line. Mark the point where the crossgrain line crosses the sleeve stitching line.
4. Mark a point about ½"-¾" (1.3-2cm) above cap point.

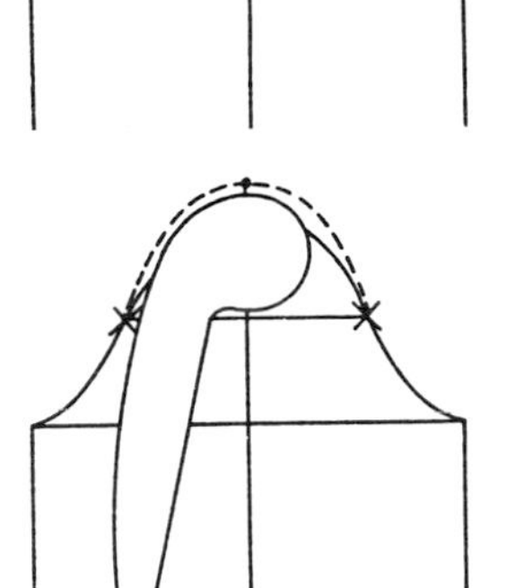

5. Using a French curve, re-draw cap from back midpoint to new cap point and from front point to new cap point. Be sure cap point is rounded.
6. Use this new line as the stitching line. Add seam allowances.

Easing Sleeve Cap in a Set-in-Sleeve

When making a traditional one-piece or two-piece, set-in sleeve, keep the easing stitches in the "ease" area. To outline this area, draw a crossgrain line 2" (5cm) below the cap point. The shape of this area is different in a full sleeve than in a fitted sleeve.

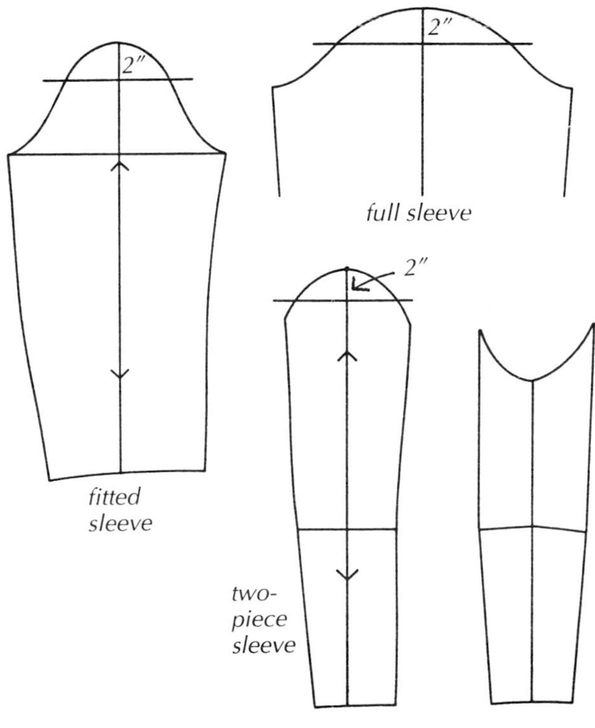

1. Starting just below the 2" (5cm) line, with the **right side of the sleeve up**, stitch three rows of easestitching. (Bobbin thread will be on **wrong** side of sleeve.)

2. Begin stitching with 20 stitches per inch (2.5cm) and change to 6 stitches per inch at the 2" (5cm) line. Stop stitching 3/8" (1.3cm) from cap point and clip threads, leaving only thread tails. Repeat on remaining half of the cap.

Stitch the first row of easestitching on the seamline and the remaining rows in the seam allowance, spaced 1/8" (.6cm) apart.

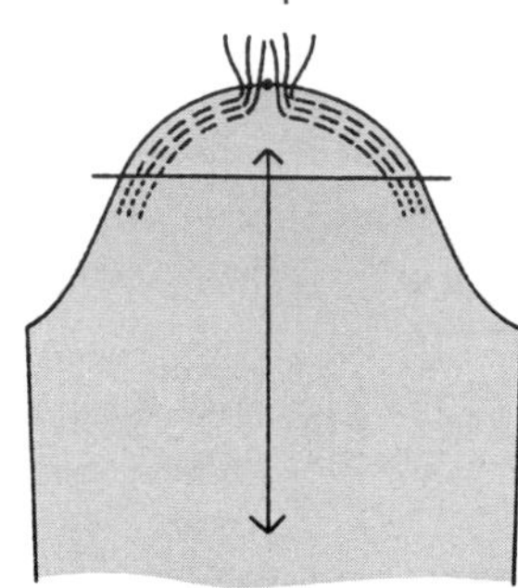

3. Stitch or hand baste seams together. Draw up cap ease and test for exact placement, hang and fit of sleeve.

4. Once the sleeve cap fits into the armhole, tie off easestitching. You'll have six knots!

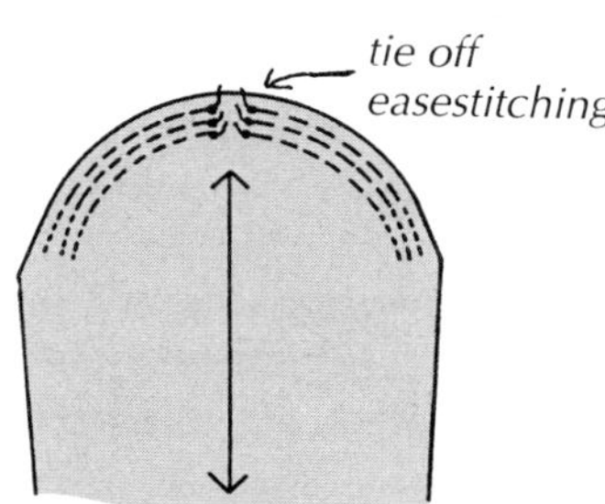

Shrinking a Sleeve Cap

One technique that ensures a perfectly smooth sleeve cap is shrinking out excess fullness in the seam allowance. Do this only after finalizing sleeve fit.

1. With the tailor's ham upright (in ham holder), pin the sleeve cap stitching line to the seam on the ham with the sleeve seam allowance on the ham's wool side. Make a fence of pins, inserting them straight up.

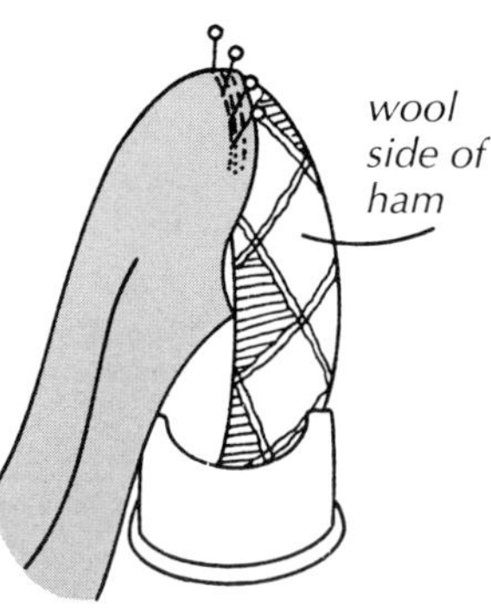

2. With a damp press cloth and dry iron, apply heat with the tip of the iron to seam allowance only; ease stitches with your thumb. Repeat about three times across the cap to shrink the seam allowance only, getting it as flat as possible. Allow to dry, at least half an hour.

Setting In a Sleeve

In The Couture, setting a sleeve begins with "hanging the sleeve" from the outside of the garment. This can be difficult to do alone. But it **can** be done on a dress form or a hanger with large shoulder pads attached to duplicate the body.

1. Complete steps 1-4, "Easing Sleeve Cap in a Set-in Sleeve."

2. Fold under sleeve cap seam allowance and place on garment against basted or chalked armhole seamline. Pin sleeve cap in place from right side.

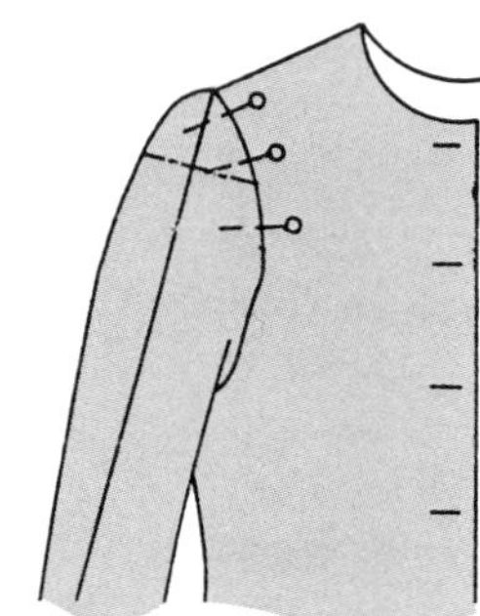

3. If the sleeve is not at **your** correct shoulder point, move it in or out using more or less sleeve cap seam allowance.

COUTURE Tip If you change the seamline on the sleeve cap, you must re-stitch ease stitching. (See "Easing Sleeve Cap in a Set-In Sleeve.")

4. Lengthwise grain should be **perpendicular to the floor** and crosswise grain should be **parallel to the floor**. If they are not, **do not rotate sleeve**. Instead, pull up or release gathering stitches until crossgrain lines are perfectly aligned.

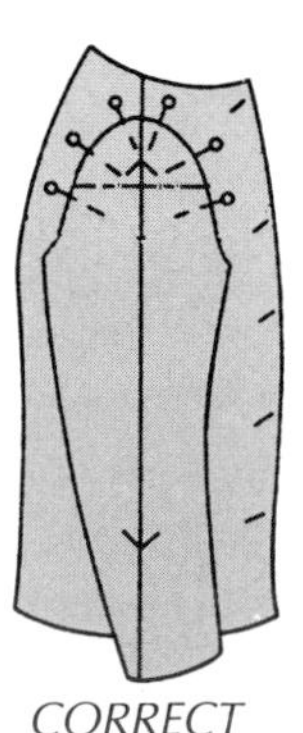

CORRECT

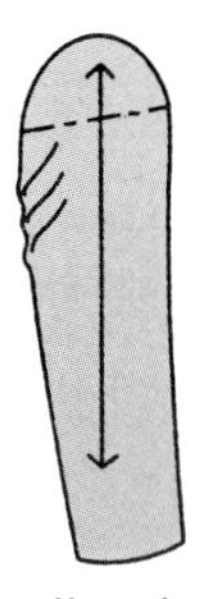

pull up back

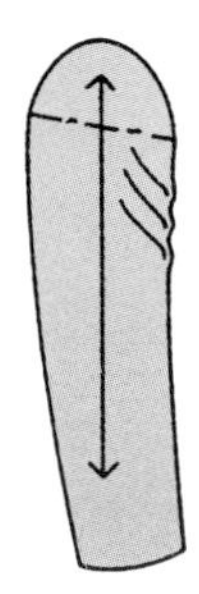

pull up front

5. Cross mark on sleeve and garment with thread basting before unpinning, so you will be able to set it back in the right place.

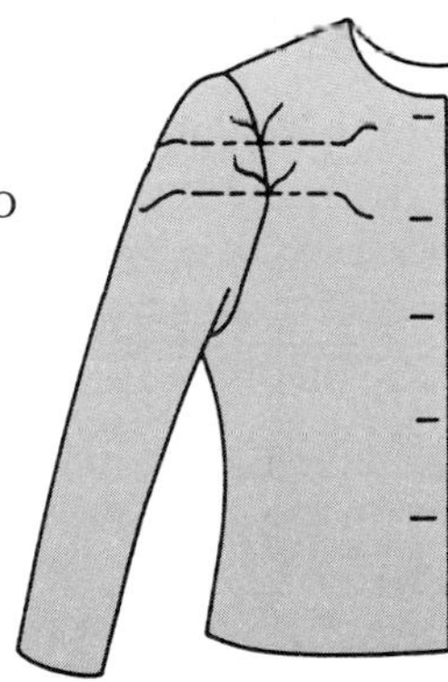

6. Remove the sleeve, tie off ease stitching, and shrink the sleeve cap. (See Shrinking a Sleeve cap, page 132.)

7. Set sleeve into armhole (step #2) matching cap and cross marks.

8. Slipstitch from the right side of the garment in the cap area only.

9. On the inside, match underarm stitching line of sleeve and garment. Baste.

10. Machine stitch around entire armhole.

11. In underarm area, machine stitch again $\frac{1}{4}$″ (.6cm) away from original stitching. Trim to stitching.

12. **Hand** overcast underarm seam.

13. Trim sleeve cap seam to $\frac{5}{8}$″ (1.5cm). It can be hand overcast if fabric is very ravelly, pinked or left unfinished. Do not serge or the edge will be too rigid.

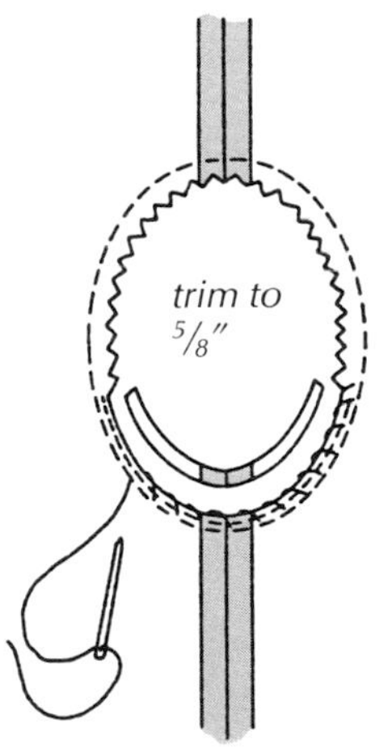

14. Lightly press sleeve cap **seam allowance only** to meld threads.

In a traditional eased sleeve cap, the seam is turned toward the sleeve. In a pleated or gathered cap, the seam goes toward the garment.

Shaping a Two-piece Sleeve

Although a two-piece sleeve has inherent shape, further shaping with steam helps perfect the fit and gives the sleeve permanent shape that reflects the curve of the arm hanging naturally at your side.

1. Stitch both front and back seams, meld stitches and press seams open over a seam roll.

2. To **stretch and shape the back seam**, turn sleeve wrong side out. With seam allowances together, even though you just pressed them open, apply steam and press back sleeve seam, using your hand to **stretch** and curve as you go. Stretch from wrist to elbow and underarm to elbow.

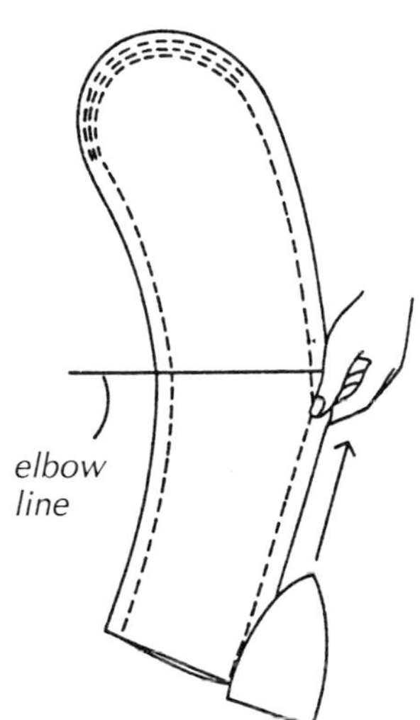

COUTURE Tip When working from underarm to elbow, flip the sleeve over to keep the iron in the seam allowance only, and stretch with your other hand.

3. To **shrink the underarm seam**, curve it and steam from wrist to elbow and underarm to elbow.

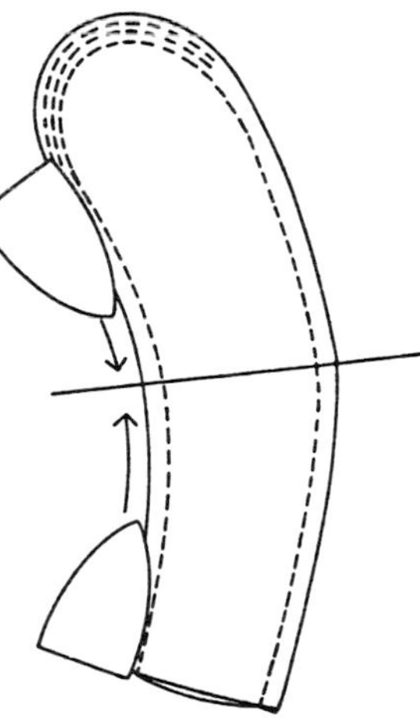

4. Return sleeve to seam roll and press seam open again, working in the seam allowance **only**.

5. Trim seam allowance to $\frac{5}{8}$″ (1.5cm).

Shape the sleeve lining for a two-piece sleeve the same way. This is a bit more difficult in silk or rayon lining fabrics than in the garment fabric. Polyester cannot be shaped at all.

Gathered Cap

Gathers often conjure up the image of a little girl with "puff" sleeves, but gathers can add softness, grace or drama. The secret of "**adult gathers**" is to turn the cap seam toward the garment rather than into the sleeve. That one difference changes "puff" to elegant, little girl to sophisticated woman.

1. Stitch three rows of gathering stitches at six stitches per inch, placing the first on the marked stitching line and the others into the seam allowance $^1/_8$" (.3cm) apart. Stitch with the bobbin thread on the wrong side of the fabric.

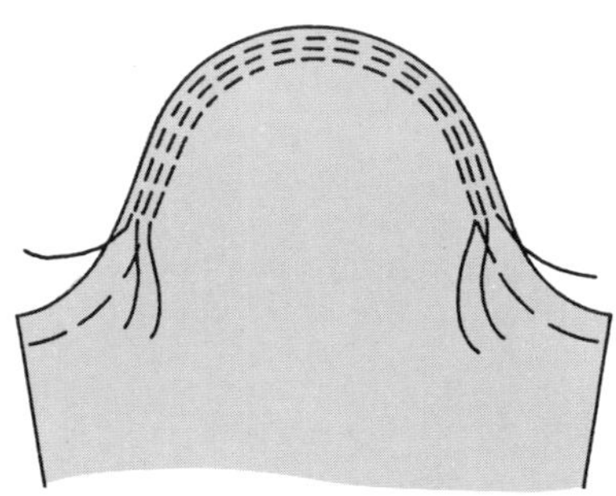

2. Pull up bobbin thread to gather the cap the correct amount and tie off the ends of each row (6 knots). This creates an evenly gathered seam allowance without a "blurp" where the gathers end.

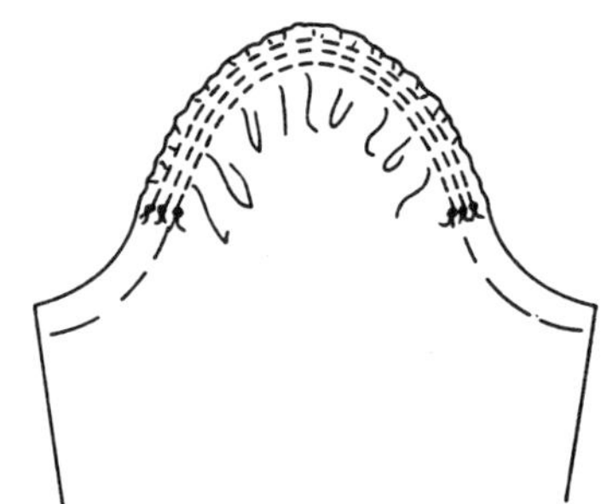

3. Use your fingernail to spread gathers evenly.

4. Sew sleeve underarm seam.

5. Pin sleeve into garment so that pins fall between folds. This prevents little tucks from occurring between gathers. **Hand** baste on stitching line.

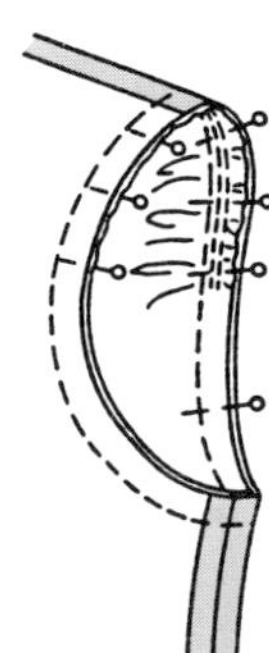

6. Permanently machine stitch a hair away from the basting. Stitch again close to the first stitching in the underarm from notch to notch.

7. Press cap seam allowance flat, using the edge of the iron along the stitches but do not press into sleeve, past the seamline. Steam, apply pressure, then flatten with the edge of a clapper.

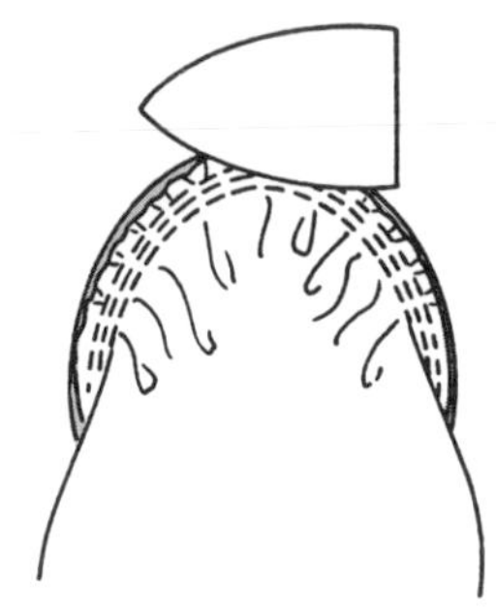

8. Trim the seam to $^1/_2$" (1.3cm) to remove excess bulk. Do not trim away any gathering stitches.

9. Clip almost to seamline just below where gathers start and end, so the cap seam can be turned toward the garment.

10. Trim underarm to $^1/_4$" (.6cm) and hand overcast.

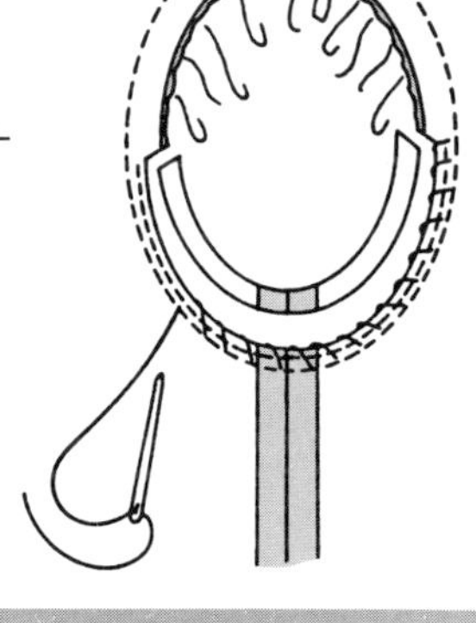

COUTURE Tip If it is difficult to keep the seam toward the garment, pin the seam in place from the **right side** of the garment, hand baste if control is needed, then topstitch from the garment right side $^1/_8$"-$^1/_4$" (.3-.6cm) into garment through all layers. As a more decorative alternative, topstitch two rows $^1/_4$" (.6cm) apart.

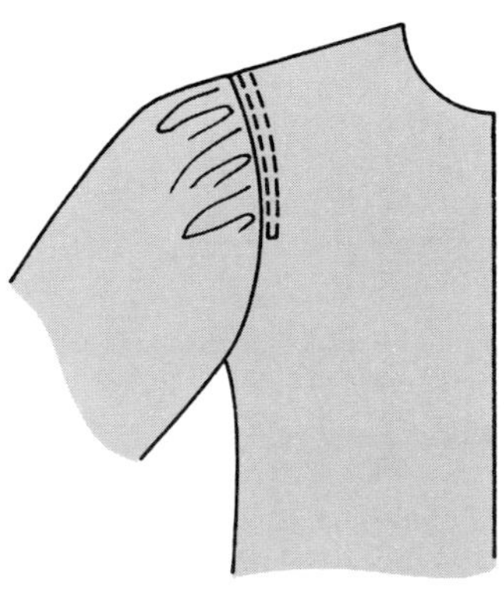

Lined Short Sleeves

In couture, short sleeves often make a strong fashion statement. Valentino cuts short sleeves on the crossgrain to achieve a cylindrical effect. Then the hem edge is cut on perfect lengthwise grain. The lining should be cut on the same grain as the sleeve.

How to Line Short Sleeves

1. Cut sew-in interfacing on the bias the width of the hem + $1\frac{1}{4}$″ (3.2cm).

2. Interface the hem edge so $\frac{5}{8}$″ (1.5cm) of the interfacing extends past the fold into the hem allowance. Slipstitch fold of interfacing to fold of hem and catchstitch interfacing to garment on ends nearest underarm seam.

3. Cut a rectangle of lining fabric slightly larger than the sleeve, on the same grain as the sleeve.

4. Machine stitch lining piece to sleeve hem.

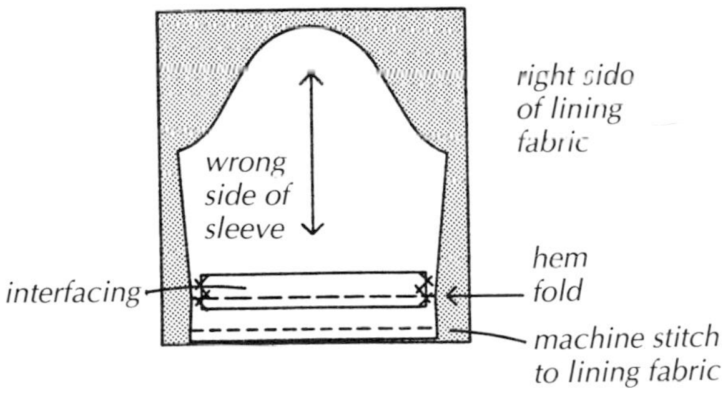

Press to meld stitches; press seam open.

5. Fold hem and lining up to wrong side of sleeve and lightly press hem edge.

6. Pin sleeve to lining rectangle and cut out lining exactly like sleeve.

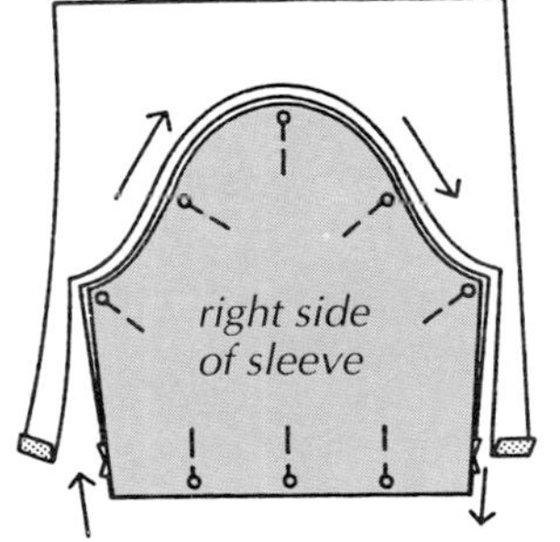

7. Remove pins and open out sleeve and lining. Pin underarm seam in sleeve and lining. Stitch.

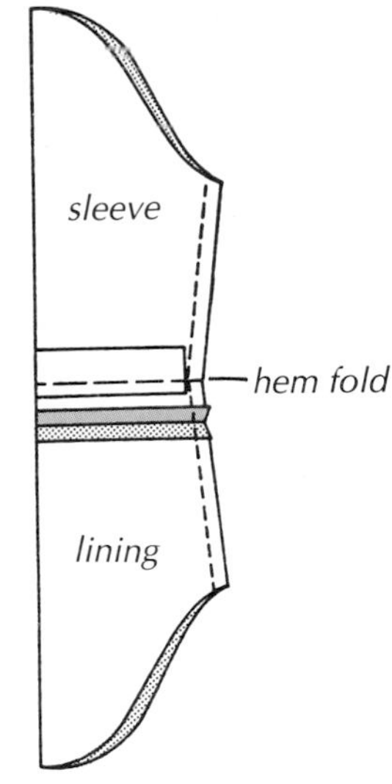

8. Press to meld stitches. Press seam open, clipping on either side of hem fold.

9. Turn lining back into sleeve and insert sleeve into garment, choosing one of these methods:

   a. **If garment is not lined**, baste sleeve and lining together and set into garment as one unit.

   b. **If garment IS lined**, set fashion fabric sleeve into garment and hand stitch lining sleeve cap in place, turning under cap seam allowance.

Cuffs

Cuffs on blouses or dresses attached to a pleated or gathered sleeve at the wrist are play-time to me. Yes, there's a couture method of construction that ensures a smooth cylindrical unit, but there's nothing easier or smaller in all of sewing where you can be the designer.

Cuffs can be cut on any grain, pieced, tucked, stitched, scalloped, piped, or trimmed. Button and buttonhole possibilities abound.

You can experiment on a cuff—try something new—and you only have to do it in a small amount. As many times as I say make a sample, there are techniques in which making the sample in fashion fabric can result in a beautiful cuff.

Here are some wonderful examples of couture cuffs.

1. Slot seam in center of cuff using a contrast color underneath (page 164).

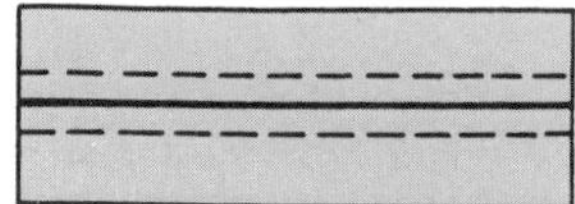

2. Double-needle tucking with cord underneath (page 67).

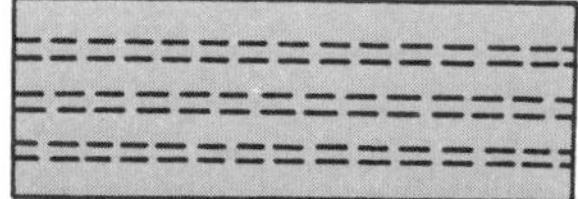

3. Pleated cuff in a striped fabric, designed so one color is pleated out and the cuff is a different configuration of stripes from the original.

4. Channel stitched using very small stitches (20 stitches per inch) with shiny rayon thread or buttonhole twist.

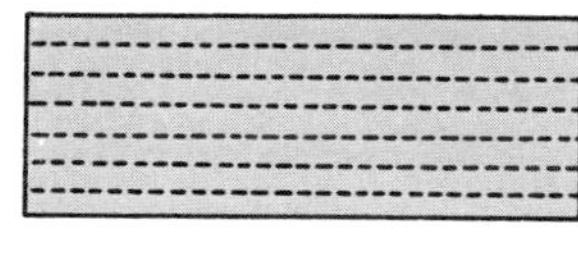

5. Piping around all edges (page 93).

6. Loop buttonholes (page 60).

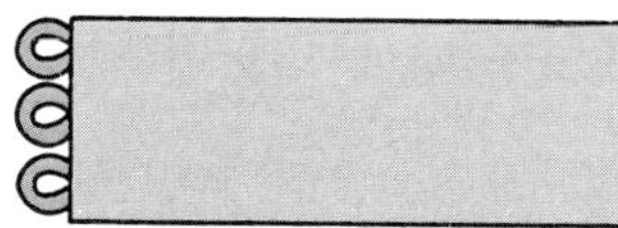

7. Triangular buttonhole (page 189).

8. Seminole patchwork—a good example of a technique to try in small quantities.

See additional cuff ideas in the color section, especially page 111.

Anatomy of a Cuff

Cuff facing*—cut on the bias.*

Outside cuff*—cut on any grain and interface.*

Buttonhole *(measurement from end of buttonhole to edge of cuff equals diameter of button, minus 1/8")*

Underlap *(twice the diameter of the button)*

Note: Most often commercial pattern companies give a cuff pattern in one piece with a fold at the wrist. This is fine for a plain cuff. But for cuffs with decoration, and those that fit beautifully, a separate facing piece cut on the bias is ideal. Cut pattern in half and add seam allowances.

Preparing a Decorative Cuff

1. Decorate outside cuff.
2. Clearly mark stitching lines, buttonhole and button placement.
3. Interface cuff with sew-in interfacing, cut on the bias. Catch stitch on all edges.

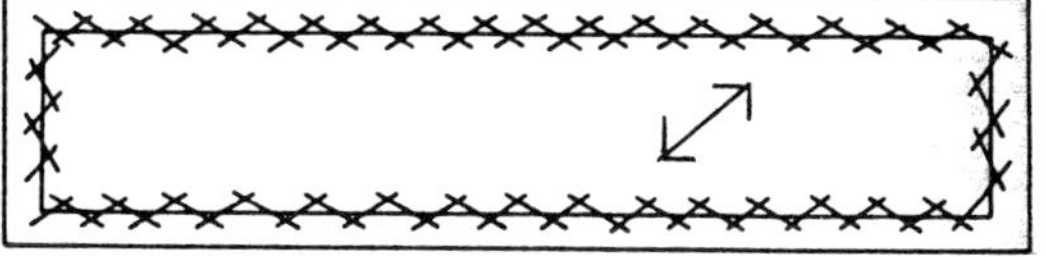

COUTURE Tip To add extra body to cotton batiste or silk organza, apply a fusible interfacing to it first. Then attach by hand to cuff.

4. Make buttonhole.
5. Sew cuff facing to cuff along one long side. Press seam open, then closed. Grade so longest seam allowance is to the outside.

COUTURE Rule Remember to **always** press with full seam allowance first, then trim and grade.

6. Baste cuff to garment, matching notches and other construction marks. Seam allowances on front of cuff will extend beyond opening edge. Underlap will extend beyond opening edge.

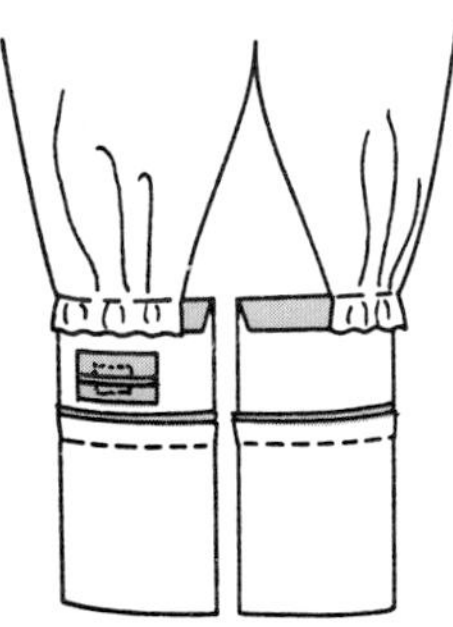

7. Sew cuff to garment; meld stitches. If there are gathers, press them flat in seam allowance. Trim seam allowance to 1/2″ on cuff and 3/8 ″ on cuff facing.

8. Press seam allowances at each end of cuff to wrong side, making absolutely sure the ends are straight and at right angles to hem edge.

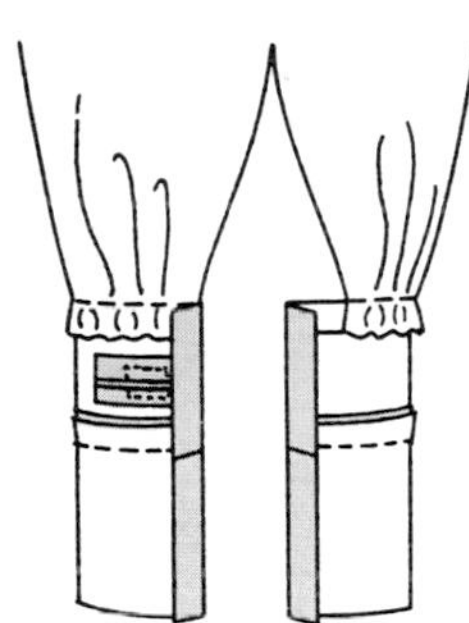

9. Miter corners of extension in both facing and cuff.

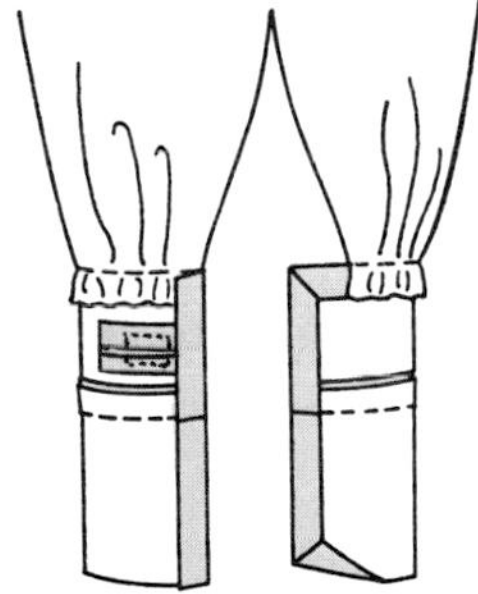

10. Working from the right side of cuff, smooth facing into place on the inside of the cuff and pin from right side.

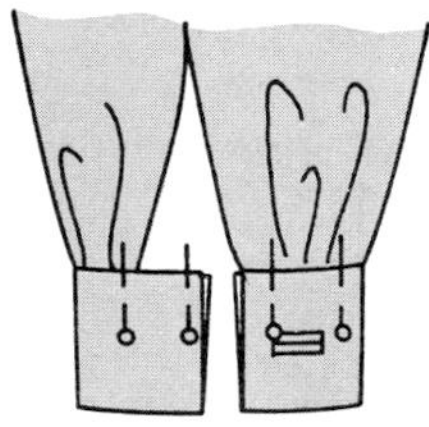

Note: This ensures a smooth inner cuff.

At this point I remind you this is couture. What follows sounds like more work and it is, but I promise you, it takes less than 10 minutes and you'll smile for years every time you wear it.

11. Having pinned the facing from the right side:

   a. On wrong side, match mitered corners of underlap on both facing and cuff. Turn under raw edge of facing to just touch original stitching line. Turn under buttonhole end of facing, checking to be sure it cannot be seen from the right side.
   b. Pin in place.
   c. Baste turned seam allowances of facing, removing pins as you go. Remove pins on outside cuff.
   d. Open out cuff facing and press facing seam allowances hard.
   e. Trim seam allowance to 3/8″.
   f. Finish back of buttonhole (see page 192).
   g. Re-pin cuff facing in place.
   h. Hand slip stitch all edges of facing to cuff.

10 minutes are up!

12. Wrap cuff around a seam roll. Pin ends by slipping pin in seam where cuff is sewn to sleeve. Shoot steam at cuff; pat with your hand to establish shape; let dry; repeat.

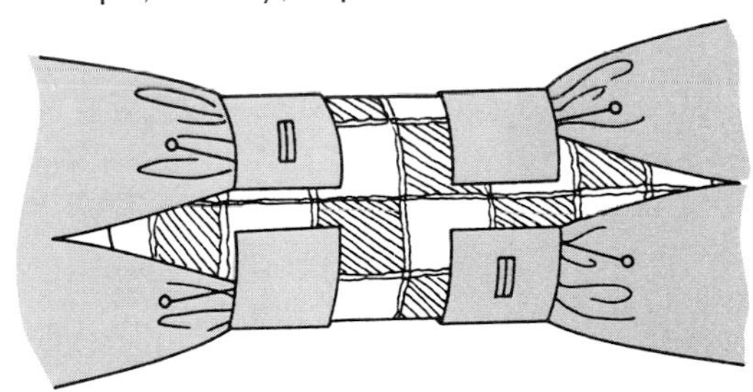

This is one of those tasks that is left to dry while you do other things. Go back several times to give it another shot of steam (wool—about three times, linen and silk—up to 5 times, my pink dress with channel stitching on the cuffs—20 times!). The cuff is "done" when it holds a circle after being removed from the seam roll.

CHAPTER 18

Sleeve Heads

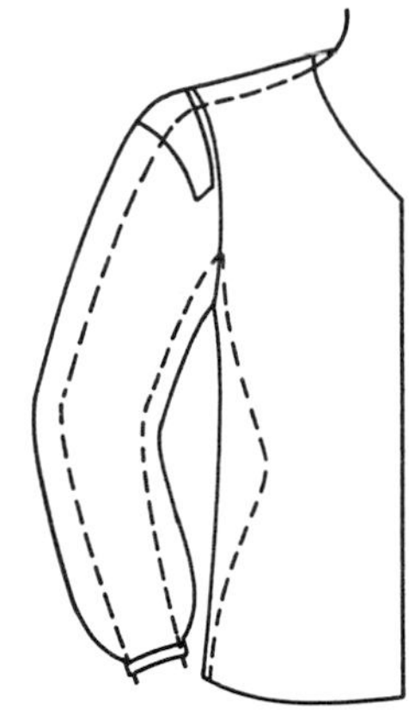

The cap of a sleeve, by virtue of its placement on the body, leaves the shoulder and does not touch the arm. Therefore, a hollow area exists. The potential for the sleeve to collapse in the cap is great. This can be prevented by adding a sleeve head for support. Couture is support!

Sleeve heads take many forms and shapes, depending on sleeve design. It is important to note that sleeve heads are independent of shoulder pads; each serves a totally different function.

Sleeve heads can be made of Armo Wool, hair canvas, fashion fabric or silk organza, **depending on the desired results**.

Inserting a Sleeve Head

Insert sleeve heads **after** the sleeve is machine stitched to the garment. It is sandwiched between garment and sleeve seam. Use a "float" stitch to attach it.

1. Center the sleeve head in the cap so the edge of the sleeve head just touches the sleeve stitching line.
2. With a fine needle, take a stitch in the edge of the sleeve head, then insert the needle under a machine stitch on the sleeve, not catching the garment or the seam allowance.

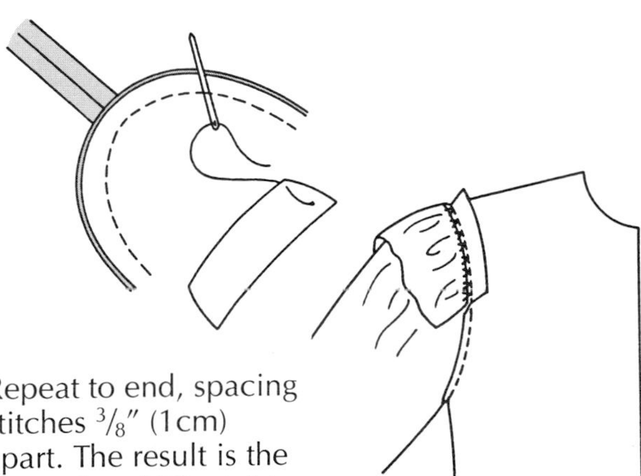

3. Repeat to end, spacing stitches $^3/_8$" (1cm) apart. The result is the sleeve head "floats" in the cap, not pulling on the garment or sleeve.

Sleeve Head for Gathered Sleeves

There are two types of sleeve heads for gathered sleeve caps and they can be used separately or together.

Gather Sleeve Head and Sleeve Cap as One

This method helps support a lightweight fabric.

1. To make a **pattern**, draw a crossgrain line, connecting gathering points. Fold down the cap on that line. Trace the cap curve onto the sleeve pattern to create an "oval" shape.

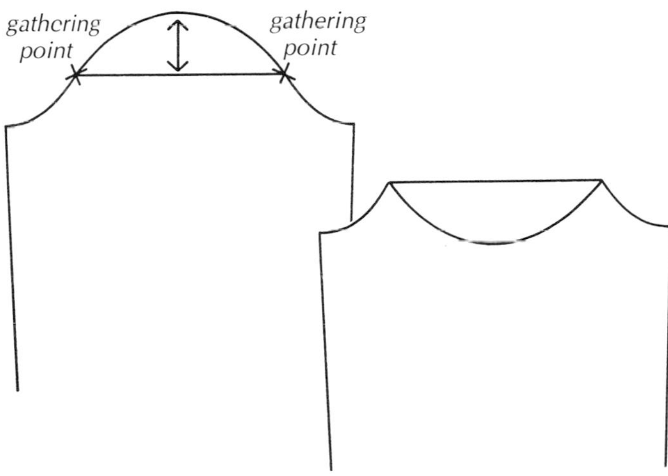

2. Cut this oval sleeve head shape from silk organza on the straight of grain (crisp) or bias (soft).

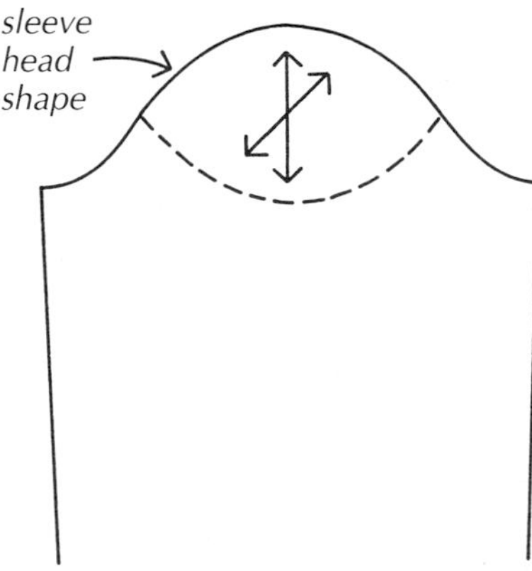

3. Position this sleeve head on the wrong side of sleeve, and gather the two layers together as one.

Note: To enhance gathers at the wrist, this technique can be used. Cut a bias piece of silk organza about 5″ (12.5cm) wide, shaped to follow the shape of the bottom edge of the sleeve. Position on wrong side of sleeve and run a long basting stitch through both layers so you can gather them as one.

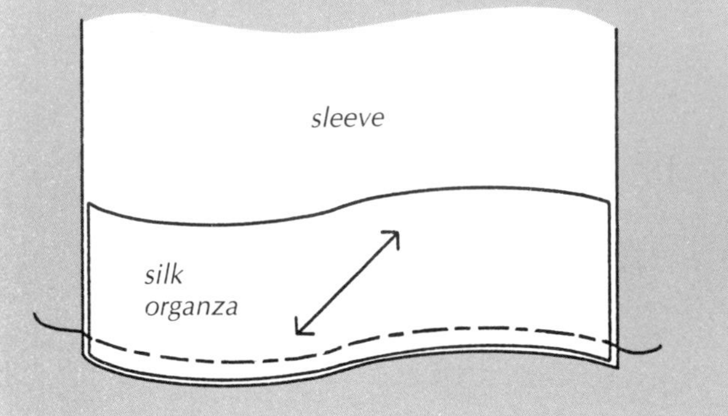

Gather Sleeve Head and Sleeve Cap Separately

Use this method for a sleeve with a great amount of loft.

1. Measure the garment between gathering match points on front and back of armhole on bodice and multiply by 2.

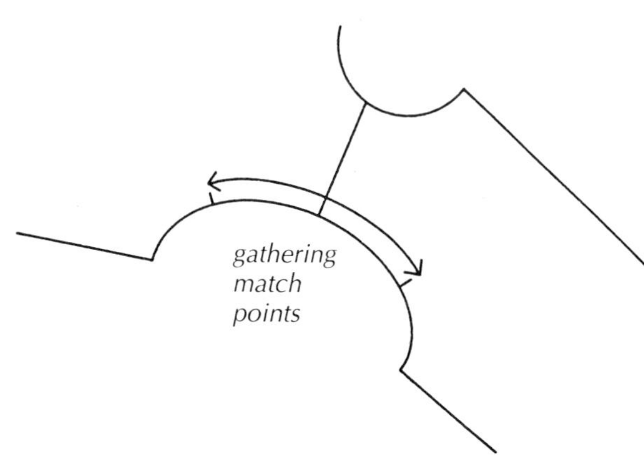

2. Cut a 5″-wide (12.5cm) strip of bias organza the length determined in step 1.

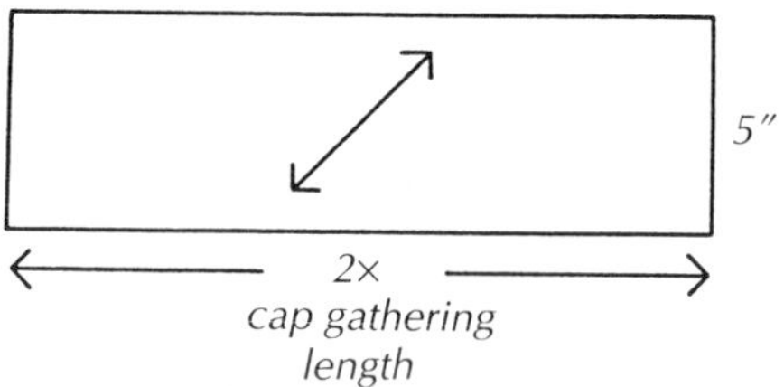

3. Fold down 2″ (5cm) on the long edge of the bias strip and stitch two rows of gathering stitches (6 stitches per inch) as close to the fold as possible.

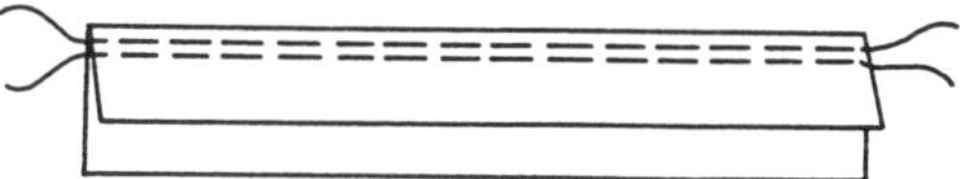

4. Draw up gathering stitches so sleeve head is original cap length.
5. Stitch one row of regular stitches across the gathers to hold them in place, or serge folded edge. Press edge hard.

6. Gather sleeve cap and set in sleeve.
7. With the wider side of the sleeve head next to the sleeve, float stitch (page 139) the fold of the sleeve head to the sleeve stitching.

Sleeve Head for Tailored, Set-in Sleeve

When a traditional sleeve is stitched into a garment, the cap often appears to have dimples even if the stitching line is very smooth. That's because the seam allowance is not sufficient to fill out the roundness of the cap. It needs a sleeve head.

Use Armo® Wool, a loosely woven wool or hair canvas with a high wool content if the sleeve is fuller or made from a heavy fabric such as wool coating.

1. Cut a 5″-wide (12.5cm) bias strip of the wool about 12″ (30.5cm) long. Fold down 2″ (5cm) along one long edge of the bias strip.

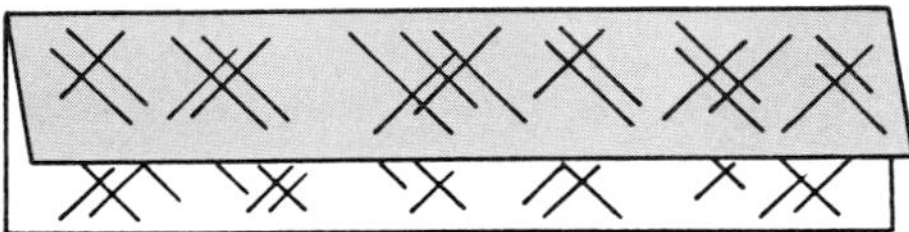

2. With the wider side next to the sleeve, place the strip into the sleeve cap under the seam allowance, with the fold touching the sleeve stitching.

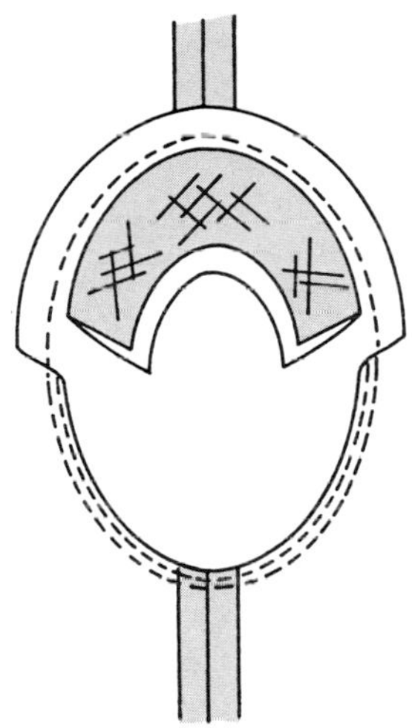

3. Float stitch (page 139) to sleeve stitches.

Because the sleeve head is cut on the bias, it will fill in the cap as needed.

Sleeve Roll

If loft has been added to the sleeve cap, a simple sleeve head may not be enough. Then add a soft sleeve roll to the original sleeve head as follows:

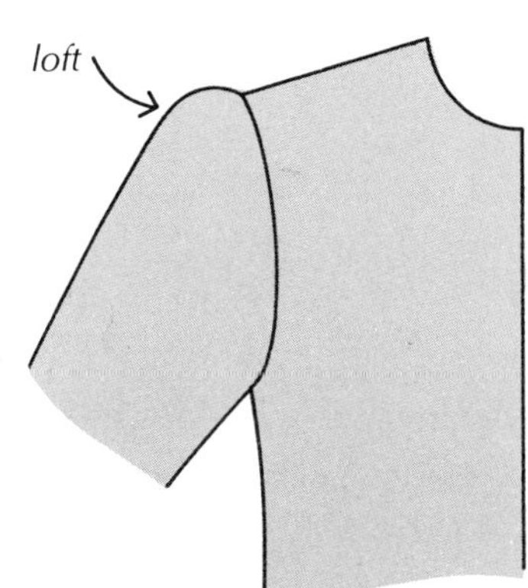

1. Cut a 3″ × 12″ (7.5 × 30.5cm) bias strip of Armo Wool.

2. Fold long edges to the center, then fold in half lengthwise to make the piece 3/4″ (2cm) wide. Catchstitch folded edges together.

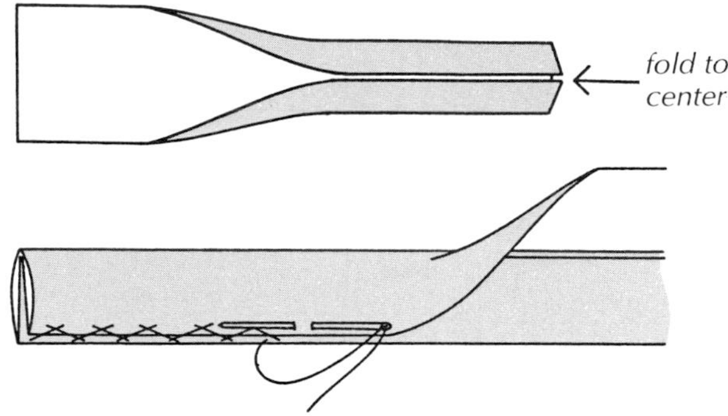

3. Sandwich the roll between the two layers of the traditional sleeve head. Float stitch the roll to the sleeve head, without catching the stitches in the garment.

The more loft in the sleeve cap, the greater the need for support. Armo Wool can be rolled more tightly if a harder sleeve head is needed. The goal is to fill out and round the cap permanently.

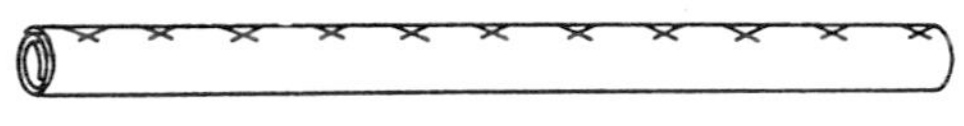

As the designer, don't hesitate to experiment until the look is right, adding width, layers or thickness. If you add too much, you can always remove it.

Sleeve Head Pouf for Darted or Pleated Cap

A darted or pleated sleeve in a blouse or dress needs support from a sleeve head "pouf" you make from polyester fleece such as Thermolam or Pellon Fleece.

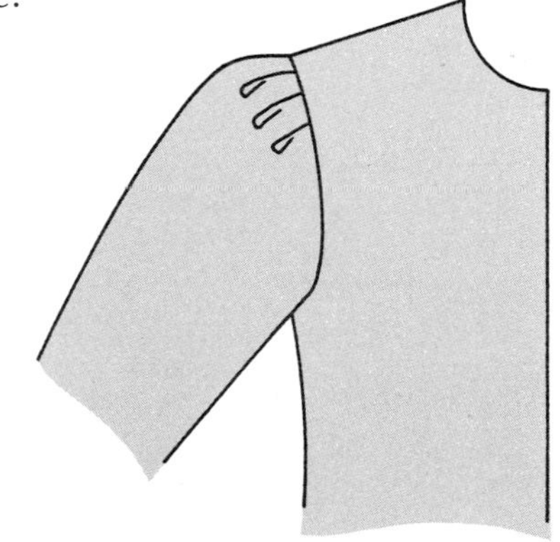

1. Cut football shapes on the straight grain as indicated for **each** pouf:
   Cut two 3″ × 8″ (7.5 × 20.5cm)
   Cut one 2″ × 7″ (5 × 18cm)
   Cut one 1″ × 6″ (2.5 × 15cm)

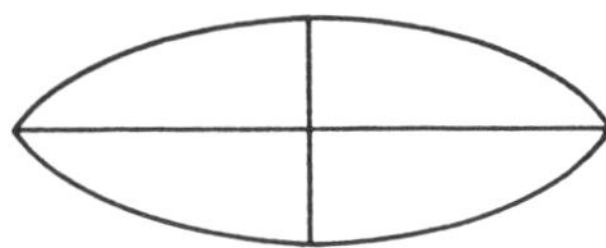

2. Stack one on top of the other with largest layers on the **bottom and top**. Machine stitch down the center through all layers.

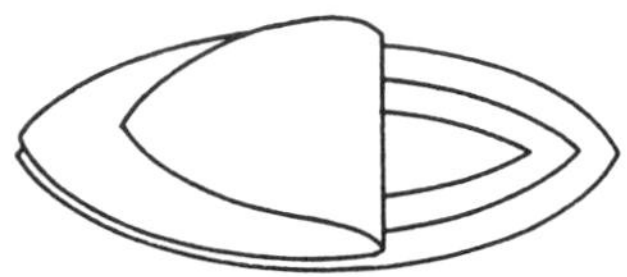

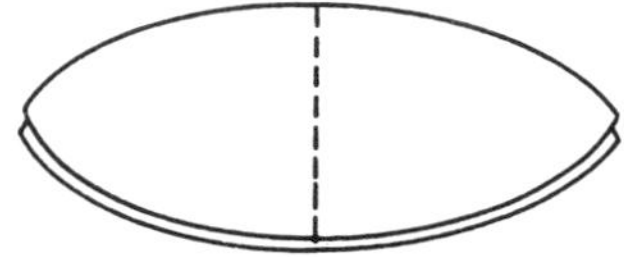

stack layers

3. Cut two football shapes, each 3″ × 8″ (7.5 × 20.5 cm), from a soft, lightweight silk fabric. Place both pieces on top of the stack and pin in place. Stitch 5/8″ (1.5cm) from the raw edge on one half through all layers.

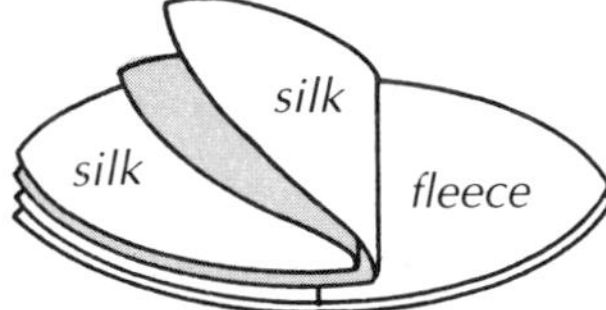

COUTURE Tip You can make a dramatic difference in the edge of this sleeve head. For a very soft edge, include the polyester fleece in the seam allowances. For a flatter edge, trim away the seam allowances after stitching silk to fleece. To compare, make a sample, trim away fleece on half, and feel the difference.

4. Pull one silk layer around and over the seam to encase the layers between the two silk pieces.

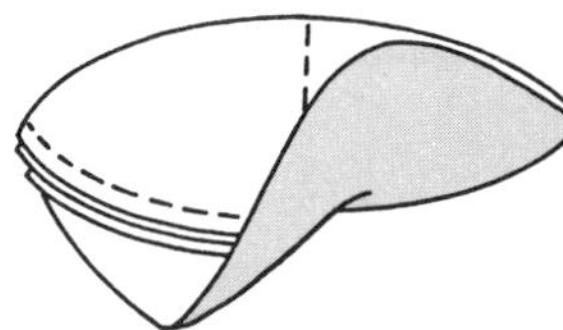

5. Serge raw edges together or hand stitch closed, folding under the raw edges.

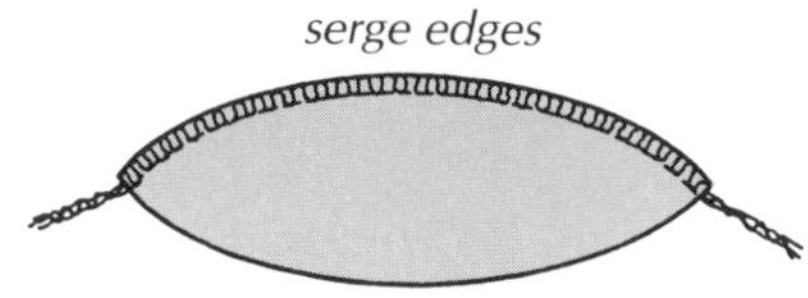

6. Place serged or hand stitched edge of pouf in sleeve cap and float stitch to sleeve stitching line.

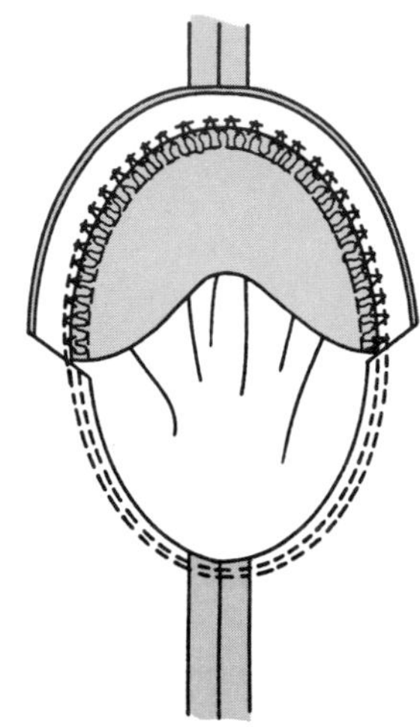

Rigid Sleeve Head for Darted or Pleated Cap

A variation on the "pouf" is a rigid sleeve head for a darted sleeve cap or pleated sleeve cap. Use it in a garment made from stiff or heavy fabric such as gabardine. This method would be more appropriate in a tailored jacket, whereas the "pouf" is appropriate for dresses and blouses.

1. Cut two 3″ × 6″ (7.5 × 15cm) football shapes from the straight grain of self fabric.

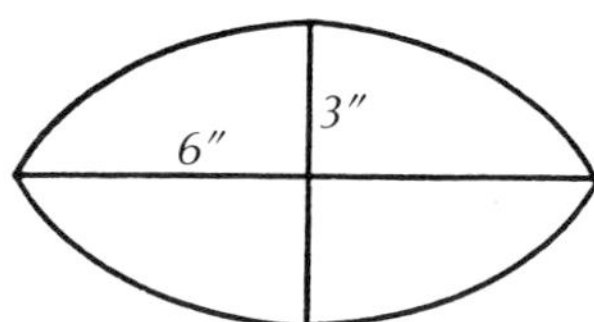

2. Apply a 2″ × 5″ (5 × 12cm) piece of fusible interfacing to one piece.

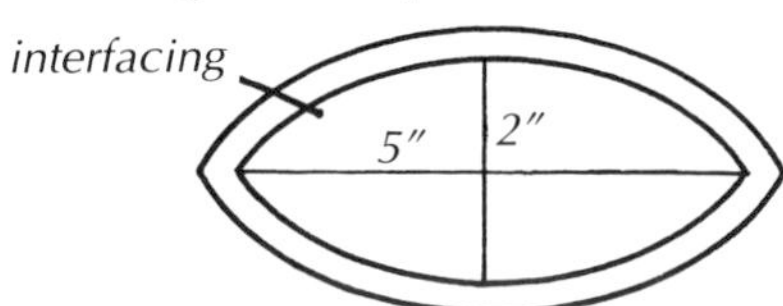

3. Machine stitch the two shapes right sides together using a 1/2" (1.3cm) seam allowance, leaving an opening. Trim seam to 1/4" (.6cm).

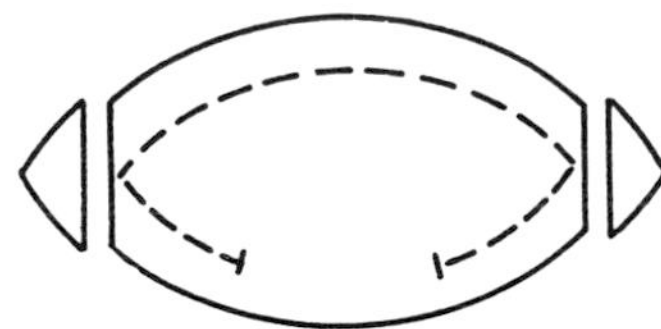

Turn right side out. Press edges hard.

4. Stitch row after row of machine stitches, 1/8" (.3cm) apart, until the desired amount of stiffness is achieved. It's OK to cover the shape completely with stitches.

5. Place in sleeve cap with edge along stitching line; float stitch (page 139) to stitching.

Underlined Large Pouf Sleeve

Large, full sleeves need extra support from underlining in the entire sleeve. **Nylon organza** makes a perfect underlining because it retains its stiffness through repeated washings or dry-cleaning, and it is comfortable, not scratchy to the touch. Simply cut a piece of nylon organza the same size as the sleeve and baste it to the wrong side of the sleeve. Handle the two layers as one as you follow the pattern guidesheet. If the sleeve has a gathered cap, the organza also will act as a sleeve head. To reduce bulk and stiffness in the underarm seam, trim organza from the underarm seam allowance after the first stitching.

To underline soft fabrics, fuse a soft, nonwoven, all-bias fusible interfacing, such as Pellon's Sof-Shape, to cotton batiste. Use this fused fabric in place of nylon organza.

Underlining large sleeves is particularly appropriate when the sleeve has no set-in cap, as when an elastic casing holds the "sleeve" in place over the shoulder.

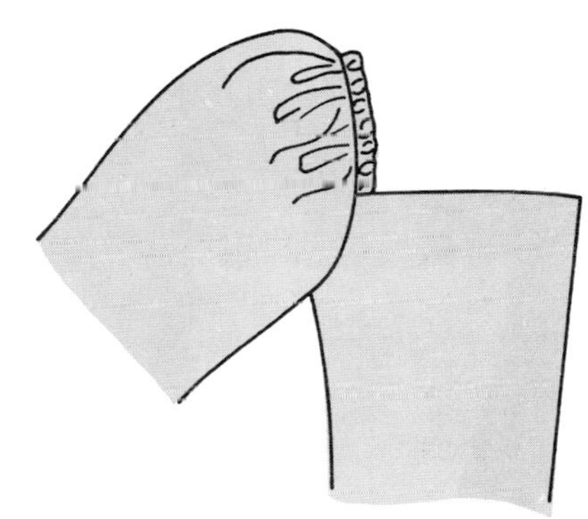

CHAPTER 19

Shoulder Pads

Shoulder pads are an integral part of a design. I'm sure the minute you hear the name Joan Crawford, a vision appears of a broad, straight-shouldered suit. The shoulder line is a design line supported by a shoulder pad. Square versus rounded shoulders run at the whim of fashion. Extended versus natural shoulder lines change as fashion changes.

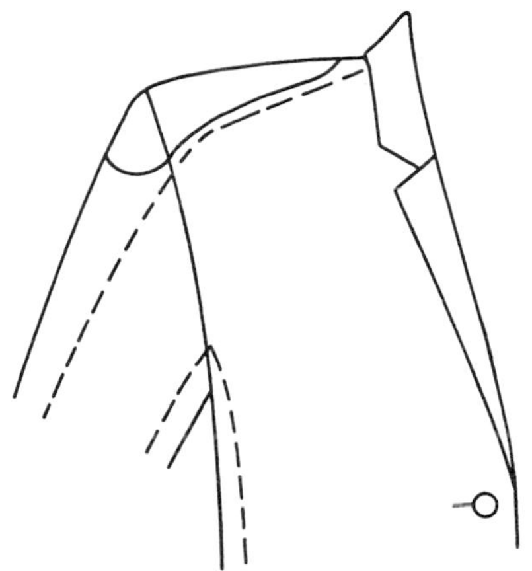

If a garment is designed for a shoulder pad, one is needed to execute the design. In tailoring, shoulder pads are essential to create a smooth line from the shoulder over the bust.

The size and shape of a shoulder pad is relative to the design of the garment. The height (thickness) is the difference between you and the garment's designed shoulder line.

For example a wide (size), raglan (shape) would be appropriate for everyone, but a person with a sloping shoulder might need this pad 1″ (2.5cm) thick to achieve the look while a person with square shoulders might **need** this pad only ½″ (1.3cm) thick to achieve the same look. Both people need a shoulder pad if the garment was designed to have one.

I am always distressed when a student says, "I don't need shoulder pads because I have square shoulders." That's like saying you're not going to eat at the banquet because you'll be hungry later anyway.

The other comment I hear often is, "I don't want to look like a football player." Then I become very sad, because it simply means that this person has not had perfect shoulder pads that enhance her figure.

The shoulder pads in ready-to-wear should not be used as the criteria for what shoulder pads should look like or what they should do.

Couture is custom! And shoulder pads are custom, specific to one garment and one person, and they should be perfect! Couture!

Common Shoulder Pad Shapes

Angel wing—the tiny shoulder pad used in a blouse to be worn under a suit jacket. It allows the sleeve to hang free without conforming to the upper arm.

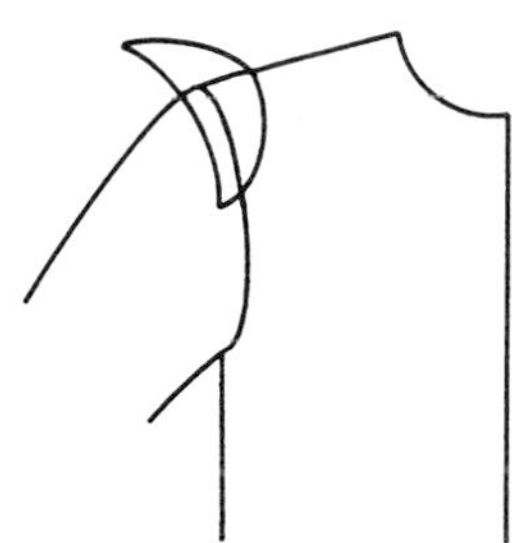

Traditional suit/coat—usually shaped and covered with hair canvas interfacing.

Raglan—triangular shape with a broad edge to support the wide area of a raglan sleeve. Raglan shoulder pads vary in size, according to garment design.

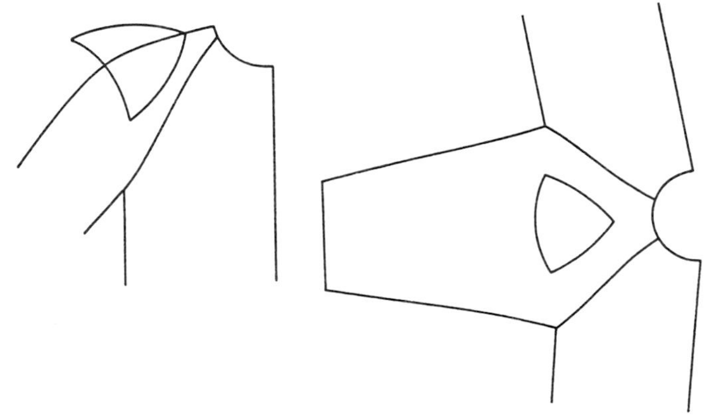

Extra large raglan—soft with smooth surface. Excellent for extended shoulders and coats.

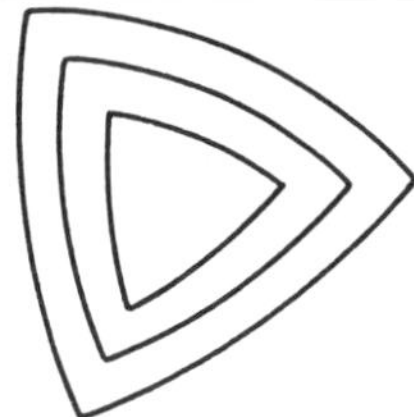

Darted cap—the edge of the shoulder pad has three darts to round the edge so it follows shoulder contour, serving as a **partial** sleeve head. A sleeve head may be used in addition to this pad.

Yoke—edges are straight to follow the lines of the yoke. See page 149 for custom instructions.

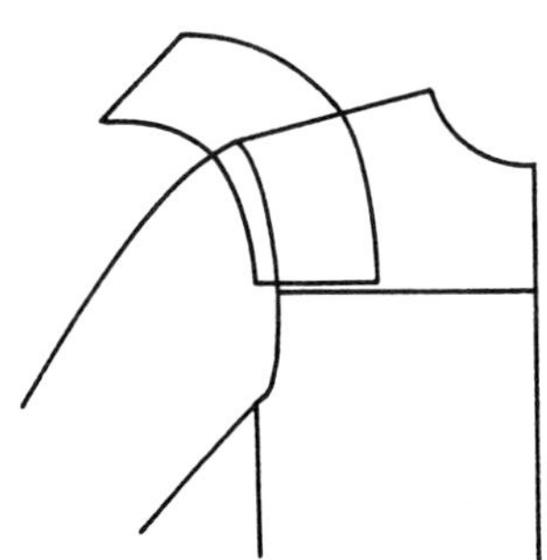

With soft sleeve head—traditional tailored shape with padded material actually sewn-on, incorporating sleeve head and shoulder pad in one unit.

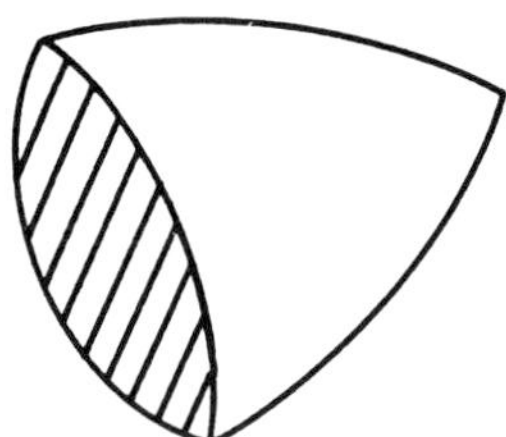

Molded—A permanently shaped pad, usually designed for a specific fashion look. Molded pads come close to being a "fad" because that they change as fashion changes.

I could write four more chapters and still not cover every shoulder pad shape. And, then there are "one-of-a-kinds" - uniquely shaped shoulder pads cut for a certain garment or to compensate for the shape of one's body.

Experiment, test, try. If the shape works, use it. Don't try to make a shoulder pad "look like" a shoulder pad if it doesn't work. Be as inventive as you need to be to make the garment look right.

Remember a shoulder pad must relate to the garment **and** body; a sleeve head relates **only** to the sleeve design.

Molded vs. Soft-Shaped Shoulder Pads

Soft-shaped shoulder pads are fitted to and placed into the garment **before** putting the garment on the body.

Molded shoulder pads have a permanent hard shape which cannot be flattened. Place them on the body first, put on the garment, and pin pads in place.

Shoulder Pad for Tailored Garments

A perfect shoulder pad extends into the armhole seam, 1/2" (1.3cm) past the stitching line. **The extension should be exact for the entire edge of the shoulder pad.**

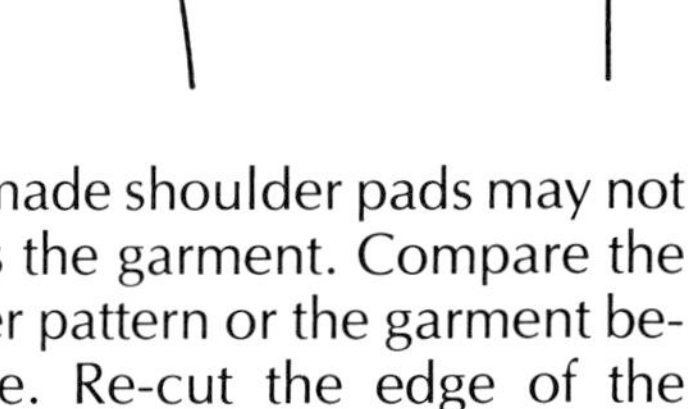

The curve on ready-made shoulder pads may not be precisely the same as the garment. Compare the shoulder pad to the paper pattern or the garment before inserting the sleeve. Re-cut the edge of the shoulder pad if necessary.

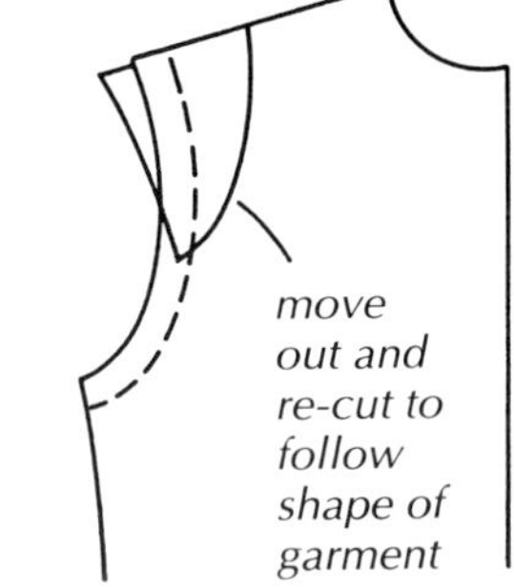

A Tailored Shoulder Pad

No matter what the design, a tailored garment requires a clean, smooth shoulder line. Though the shape of a shoulder pad is related to the garment design and the thickness related to the body, the surface of a tailored shoulder pad should be smooth and relatively rigid. Covering the pad with hair canvas achieves this goal.

1. Use a correctly fitting shoulder pad and trace a pattern, marking the shoulder line on the bias.

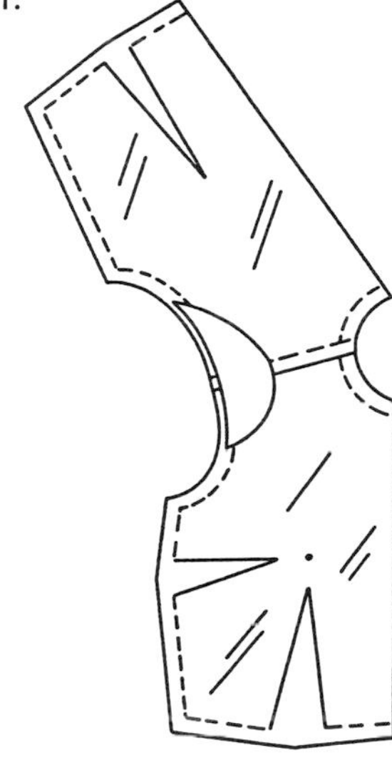

2. Add $^1/_2$" (1.3cm) on curved edge. Keep armhole edge the same as the shoulder pad.

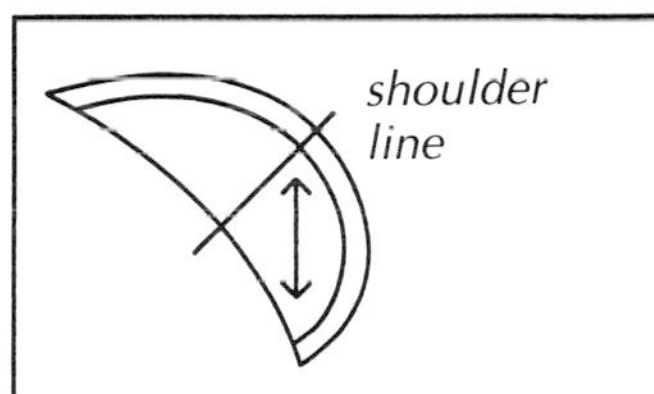

3. With the shoulder line on the bias, cut this shape from hair canvas. Place on top of the shoulder pad while holding the pad over your hand to create a roll. Pin in place and diagonally tack loosely to hold in place.

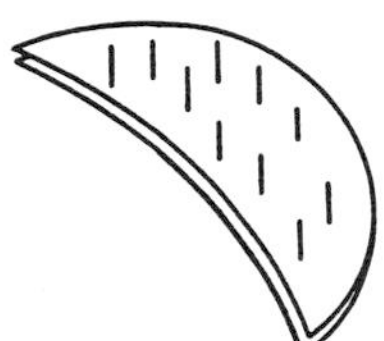

4. Pin pad over edge of ham and shoot with steam. Allow to dry. Shoot with steam again and allow to dry thoroughly. This shapes the pad permanently.

5. Insert in shoulder with hair canvas next to garment.

COUTURE Tip

If you don't know which end of a shaped shoulder pad is the front, remember FAT FRONT, SKINNY BACK.

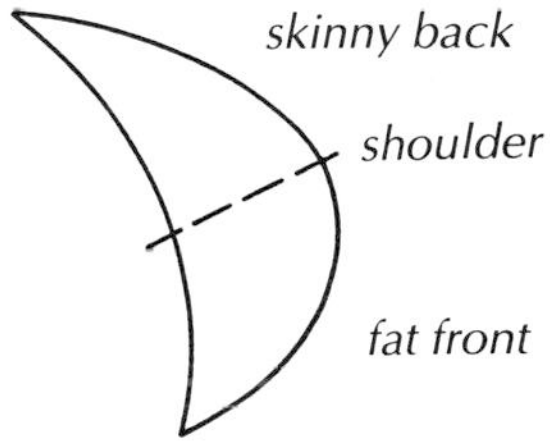

skinny back

shoulder

fat front

How to Insert Shoulder Pads

1. Once shoulder pads have been fitted, clip pad to indicate shoulder line. 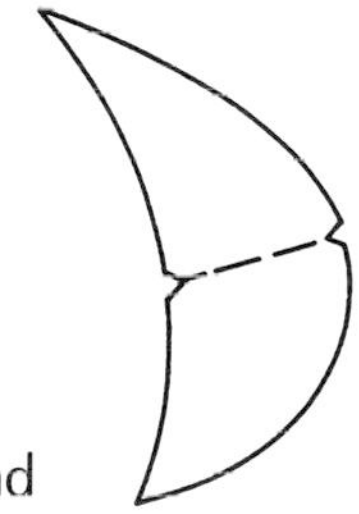
2. Fold pad on this line and place fold along shoulder seam line in garment. Float stitch in place, taking one stitch in the shoulder pad, then one stitch in garment **stitching** line. **Do not** attach pointed ends of pads to the seam allowances. They hang free.

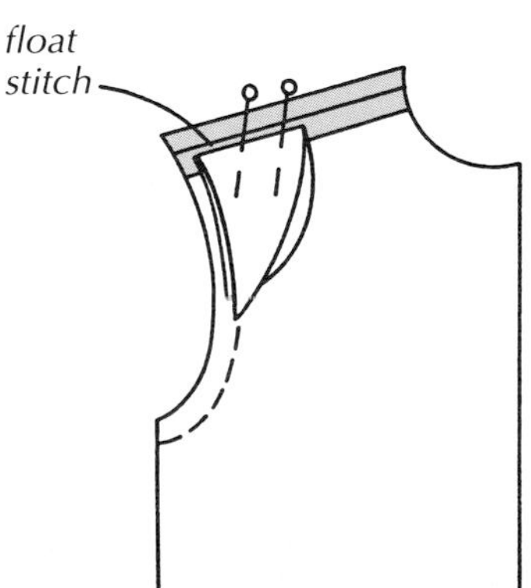

How to Insert a Raglan Shoulder Pad

Some raglan sleeves have no shoulder seam, so the raglan shoulder pad can show through and form a ridge. To avoid this and make insertion easier, apply the pad to a piece of underlining cut from organza or lining fabric. If the garment is unlined, you can cut the underlining from fashion fabric instead for a neater appearance inside.

1. Cut a piece of underlining from the raglan sleeve pattern, from the neck edge to about 10″ (25.5cm) into the sleeve, curving the bottom edge.

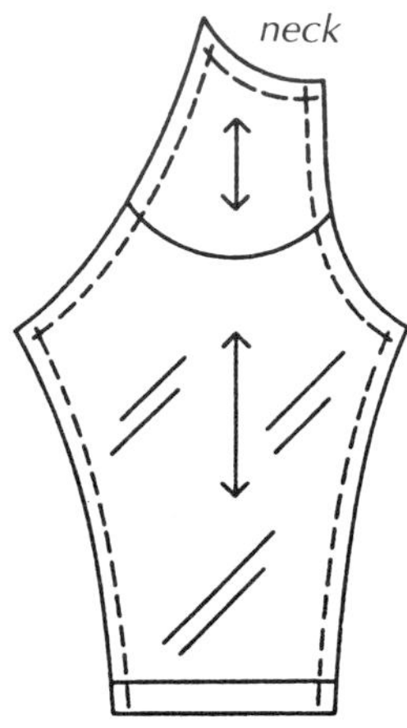

2. Pin underlining to wrong side of sleeve to try on garment, and pin shoulder pad in the correct location.

3. Mark outline of pad on underlining piece; remove from garment.

4. Catchstitch pad to underlining piece. Or machine zigzag it in place if stitches won't form a ridge on right side of finished garment.

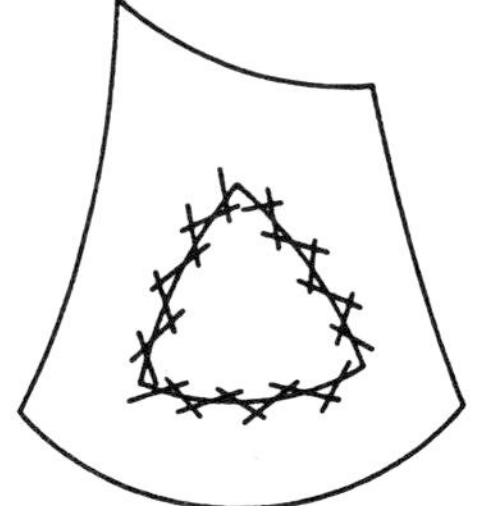

5. Place underlining on wrong side of sleeve and baste to seam allowance. When sleeve seams are sewn to the garment, the underlining will be caught in the seam automatically.

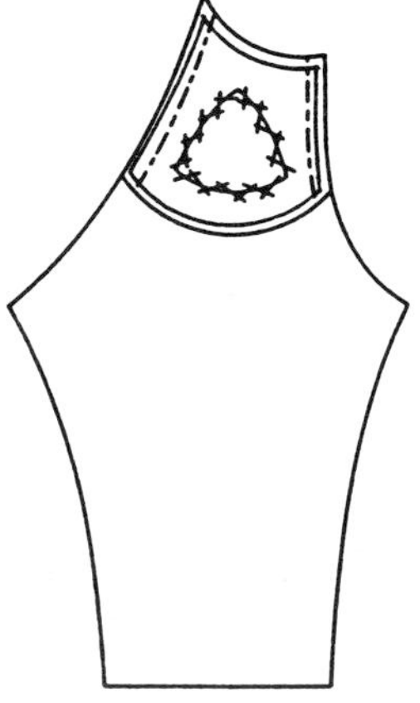

6. For an unlined garment, another layer of fashion fabric can be placed over the shoulder pad and underlining before stitching the sleeve seams, so the shoulder pad will not show from the inside.

How to Cover a Shoulder Pad

Unlined garments require covered shoulder pads, as do some lined garments if the fabric's texture might cause the pad to stick or catch on the fabric. The method for covering a shoulder pad is the same no matter what the shape.

1. Cut a circle of lining fabric and mark the bias.

2. Place armhole edge of the shoulder pad on the bias line.

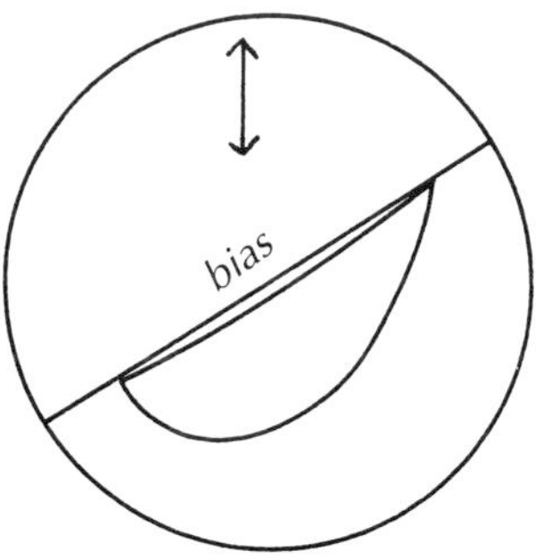

3. Fold the circle in half sandwiching the pad inside. Hold the pad over your hand to create a curved shape. Smooth lining over the top of pad first, working excess fabric out to the edges.

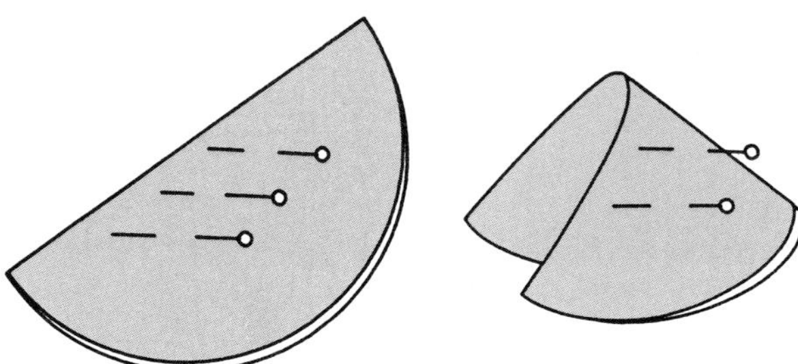

4. Retaining the curved shape, turn the pad to the underside, and take up one or two tucks to remove excess fabric. Pin in place.

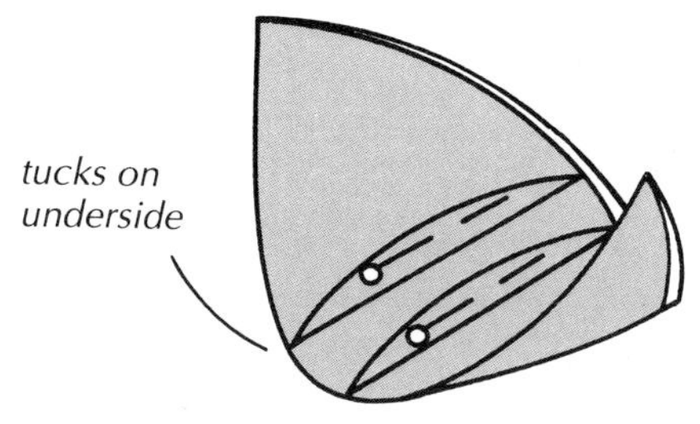

5. Trim the excess lining, leaving about $^1/_2''$ (1.3cm) extending beyond the pad to allow for a natural grade and prevent shadow-through. Finish the raw edges by serging, pinking, or straight stitching and hand overcasting; or turn under raw edges and slipstitch them together.

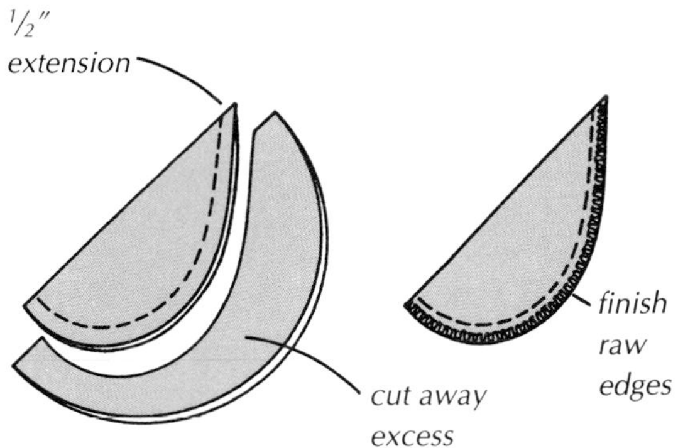

Shoulder Pads for a Yoke

Padding the shoulder line in a yoked garment poses an interesting challenge: having the correct thickness and retaining a smooth line without a ridge showing to the right side.

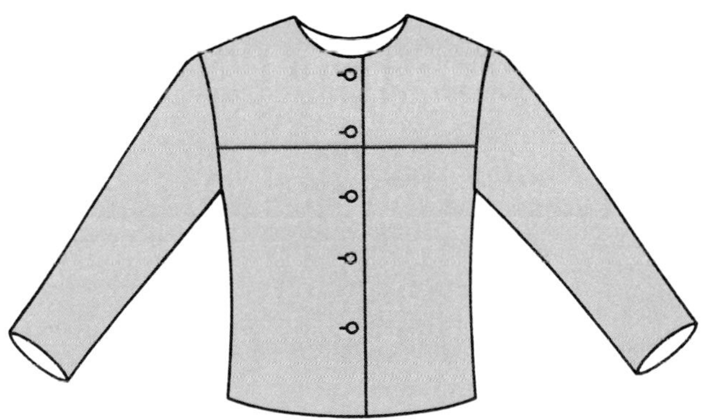

It's easy to achieve this by making the shoulder pad part of the yoke facing.

1. Trace the shape of the yoke—armhole, front, and back.

2. Draw a curved line from front to back, $1^1/_2''$ (3.8cm) away from the neck.

3. Cut four or five pieces of polyester fleece, making each piece the same at the armhole edge, but $^1/_2''$ (1.3cm) smaller on the other edges, so layers are progressively smaller.

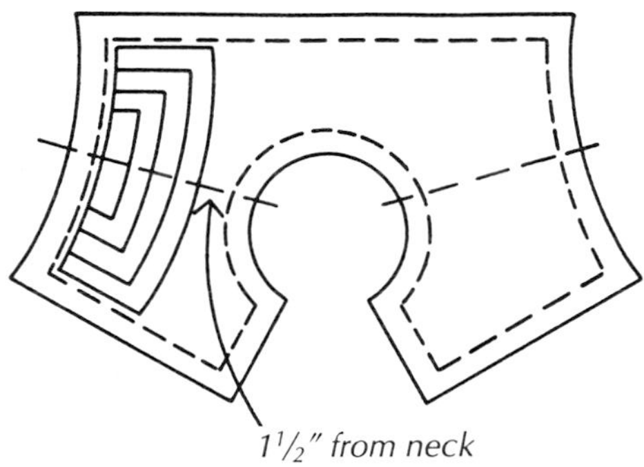

4. Layer the pieces with shoulder edges matching and baste through the center to hold.

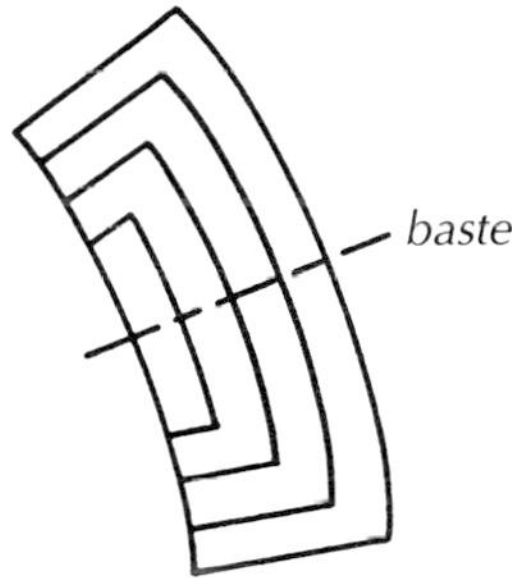

5. Place pad, with the smallest piece of fleece down, on the wrong side of the yoke facing.

6. Stitch parallel rows $^1/_2''$ to $^5/_8''$ (1.3cm to 1.5cm) apart, working from the neckline toward the armhole. Leave $1^1/_2''$ (3.8cm) at armhole edge free of stitches. Do not allow stitching to extend into garment seam allowance.

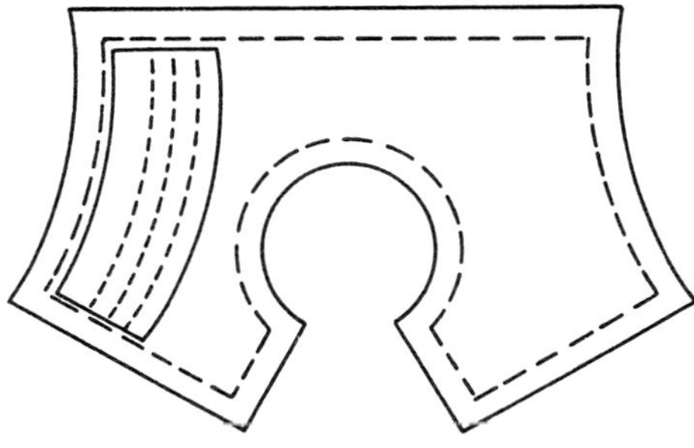

The shoulder pad is now a permanent part of the yoke facing. Complete the construction of the garment as directed on pattern guidesheet.

CHAPTER 20

Designing Sleeves

The Couture is innovation, a change of grain, a seam moved to create an illusion. That's the role of the couturier to be executed by the patternmaker. You can be a designer, too. Sleeves are fun! You don't need to be a master patternmaker, or an artist, just disciplined enough to follow a step-by-step progression of lines and cuts and moving pattern pieces to form a new configuration.

The designs that follow are often seen in The Couture and rarely offered by the pattern companies.

These are sleeves that set one apart from the ordinary. Each is unique and spans the changing waves of fashion.

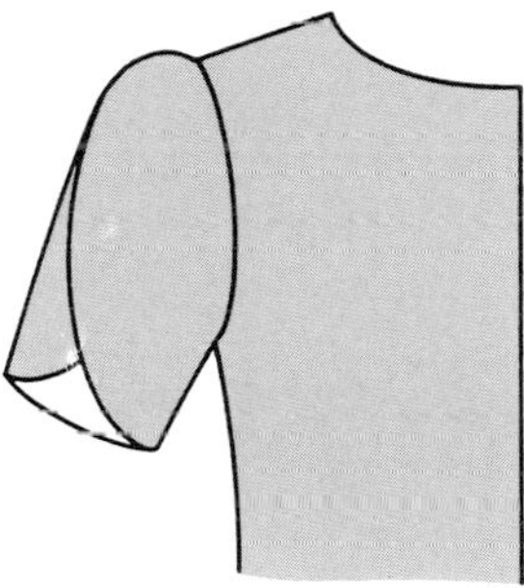

Tulip Sleeve

Pattern Drafting Step By Step

1. Start with a simple, short **set-in** sleeve pattern. Be sure the length is correct. **Remove all seam allowances from tissue.**

2. Trace pattern so you have two identical copies. Clearly mark front and back on each sleeve pattern.

3. About 3″ (7.5cm) down from the cap point draw a crossgrain line. This will dictate where the tulip will wrap. Also draw a center line down middle of sleeve.

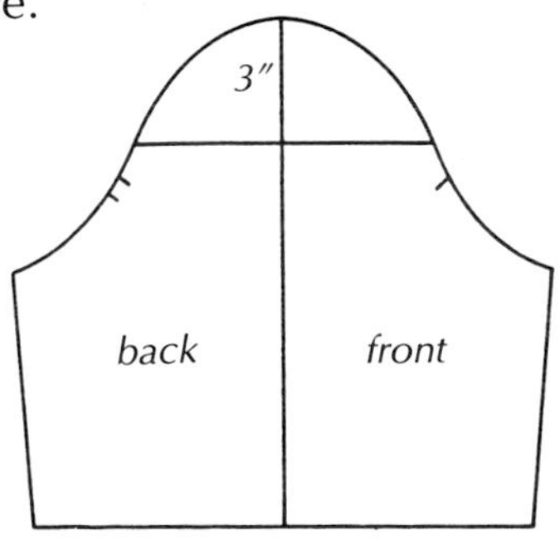

4. From the back underarm seam at the hem, draw a curved line to the wrap point on the front using a French curve. From the front underarm seam at the hem draw a curved line to the wrap point on the back. Be sure that both lines cross **exactly** on the center line.

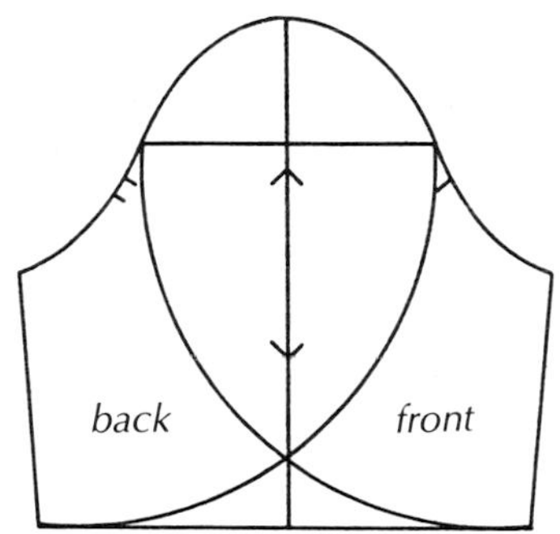

5. Trace the curved lines onto the second sleeve pattern, as well as all construction symbols.

6. Cut one pattern apart on the curved back line, one on the front curved line.

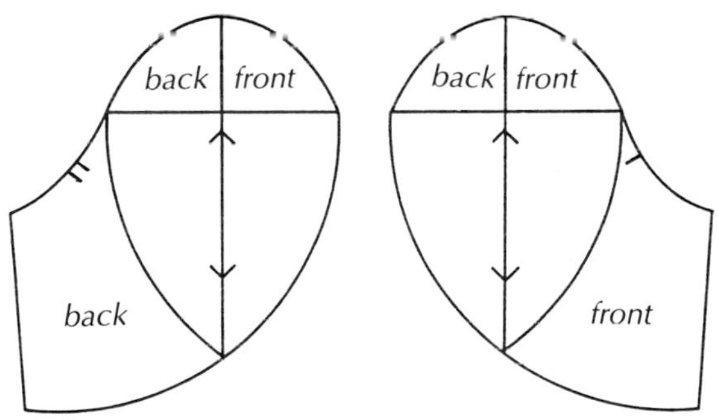

7. On a clean piece of paper, draw straight grain and crossgrain lines, perpendicular to each other. Place each half of the sleeve pattern so that the underarm points touch and both front and back straight grainlines are parallel. If the underarm seams are not on the straight grain, simply fill in at the hem. Add seam allowances and the new sleeve pattern is complete.

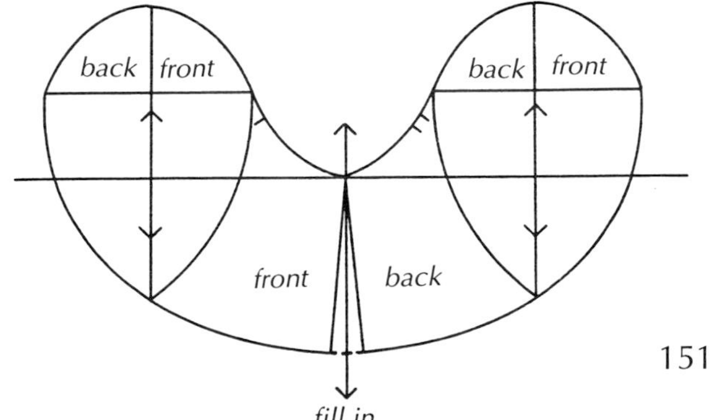

Sewing Instructions

1. Finish hem first. There are several ways to do this:

   a) Narrow hem. (See page 63.)

   b) Face. Cut facing exactly like edge of sleeve on same grain, about 1″ to $1^1/_2$″ (2.5cm to 3.8cm) wide.

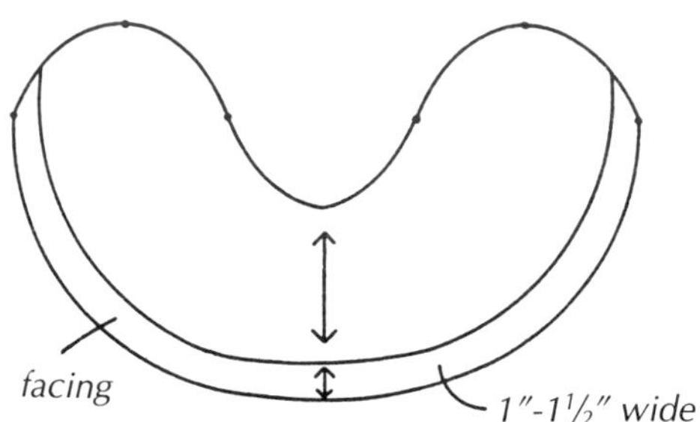

   c) Bind edge. Use bias in same or contrasting fabric. (See Chapter 12, Bias Binding, page 85.)

   d) Line. Cut sleeve from lining fabric. With right sides together, sew together at hem, and turn lining to inside. Press. Grade seam. Baste lining to fabric around the sleeve cap.

   e) Pipe. Use a facing (b above) or lining (d above) to finish.

   f) Scallop the edge. Face or line and sew scallop shapes.

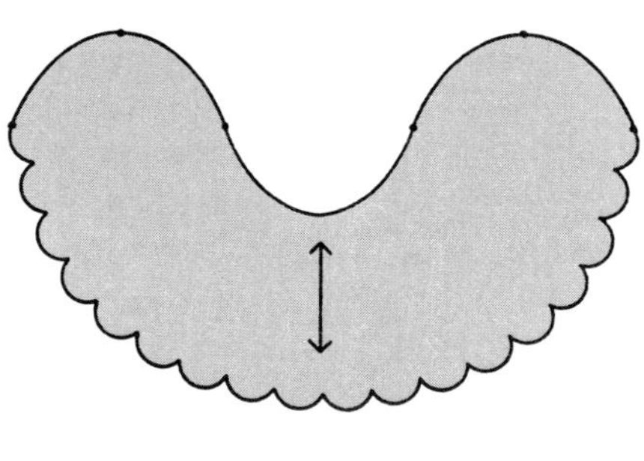

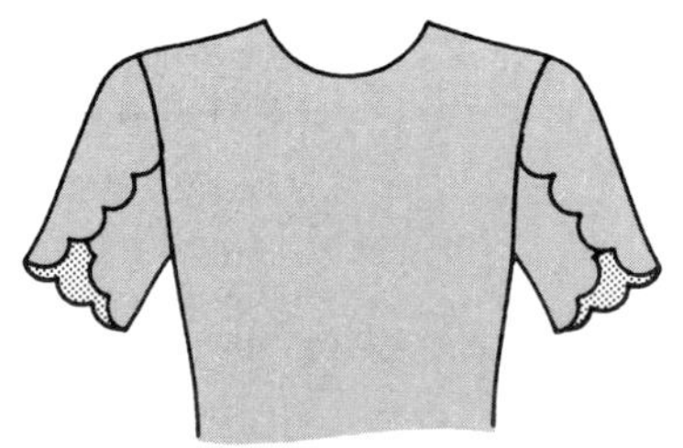

2. Lap front over back or back over front, as you please, carefully matching marks; pin together; baste across cap.

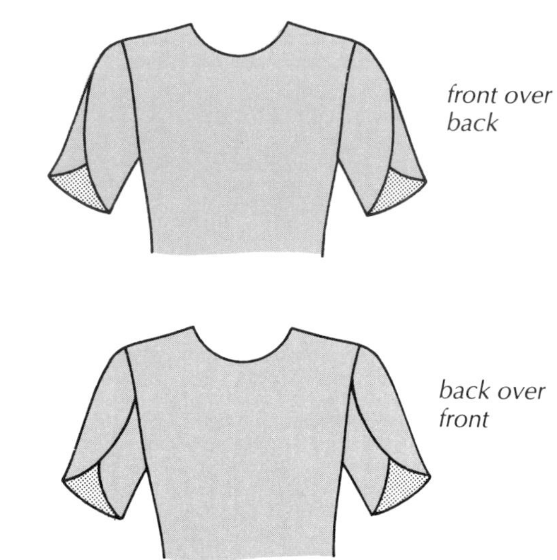

COUTURE Tip Back over front will draw the eye up to the face. Lapping front over back will visually widen shoulders and make the waist appear smaller.

3. Run two rows of ease stitching across sleeve cap.
4. Set sleeve into garment.

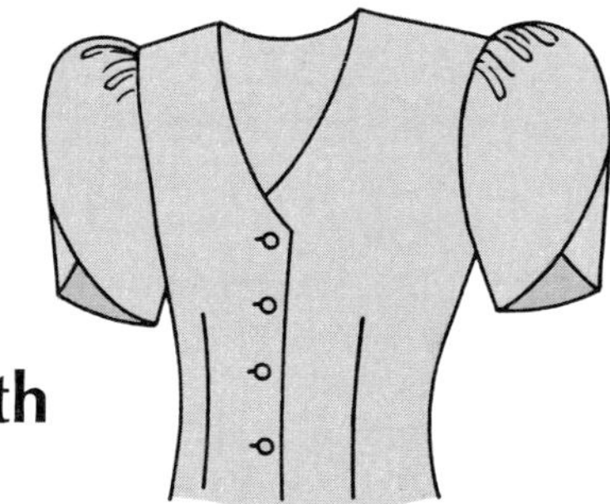

Tulip Sleeve With Gathered Cap

Once you have mastered the traditional set-in tulip sleeve, it is easy to create a gathered tulip. The advantage is that the hem becomes a straight line which can be cut along a stripe or border print for an intriguing look. A gathered tulip sleeve can be cut on any grain.

Drafting the Pattern

1. Follow steps 1-5, page 151, to establish base pattern.

2. Draw lines parallel to the center line about $^1/_2$" (1.3cm) apart on both sleeves as shown. The more lines you draw, the easier this is to do and the gathers are prettier.

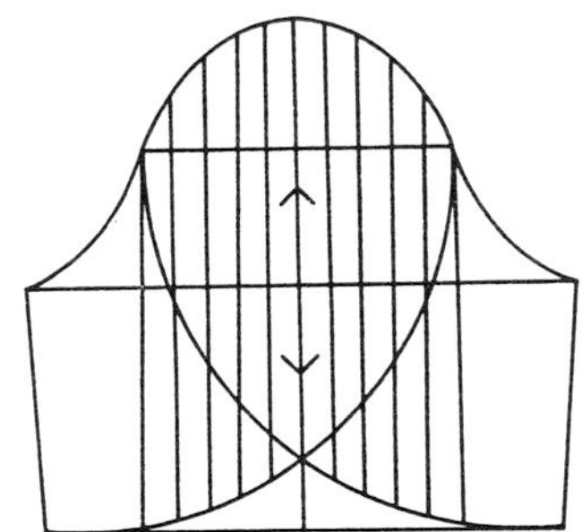

3. Cut one pattern on back design line, one on front design line. Match at underarm. (See step 7, page 151.)

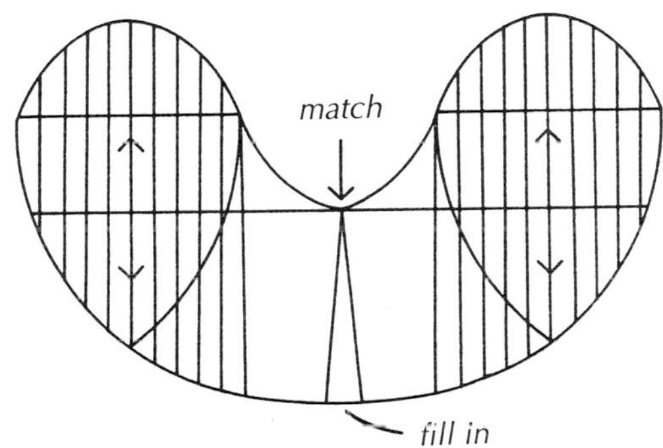

4. Cut on parallel lines to, but not through, the lower edge. Spread until hem is as close to a straight line as possible.

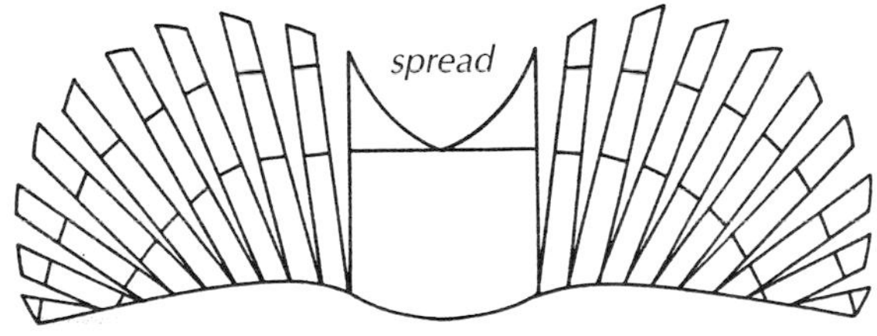

5. Draw a straight line on a piece of paper. Place lower edges of new sleeve on straight line.

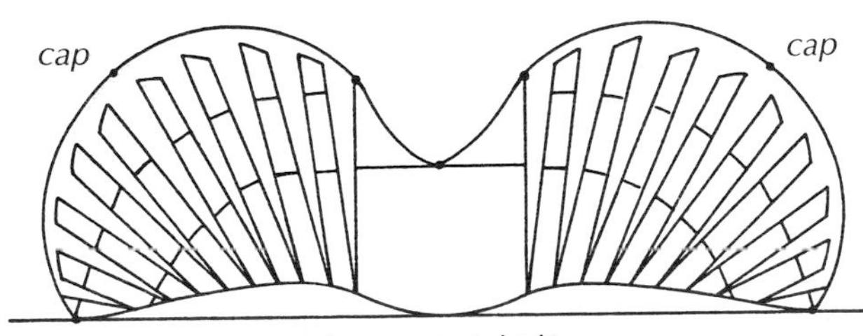

6. Re-draw cap using a French curve. Do not cut off any of the original pattern. In fact, it may be necessary to add a little height (loft) at the top of the cap to make a smooth curve.

7. Cut out and fold paper front over back. Check to see that cap **curve** matches exactly on both front and back placement marks.

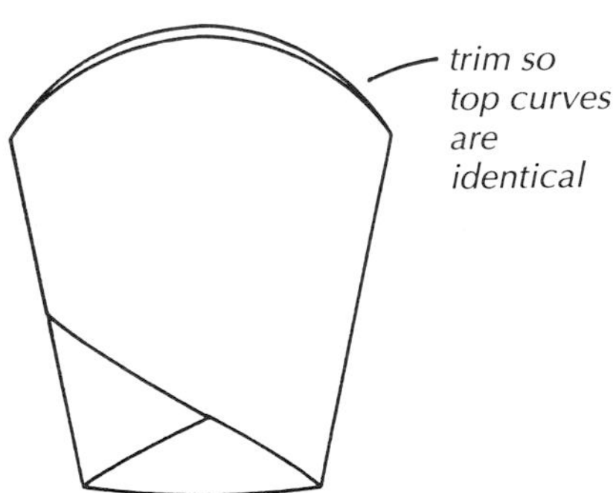

8. Hem finishes and sewing instructions are the same as a traditional tulip sleeve with one exception. The cap will be gathered rather than simply eased into the garment.

Tulip Sleeve With Gathered Cap Design Variations

- Cut on cross grain for a stripe or use a border print.

- Cut double with hem on the bias to self-line the sleeve. The hem edge will be very soft. This is a beautiful sleeve in silk chiffon, underlined with organza.

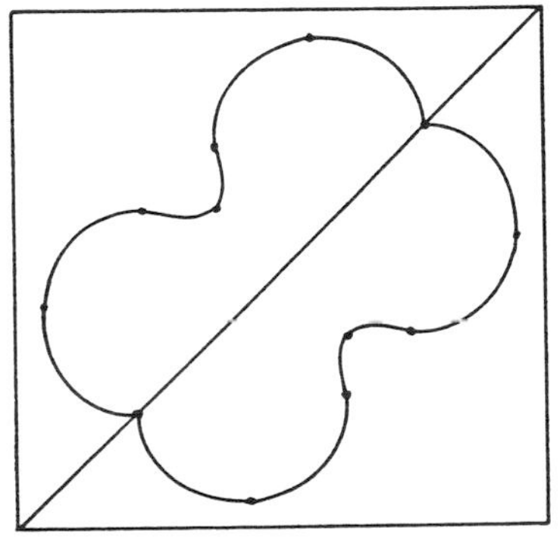

- Be creative with grain and hem finishes to achieve an elegant look.

Strapped-cap Sleeve

A strapped-cap gives the appearance that the sleeve has a "strap" or band over the cap.

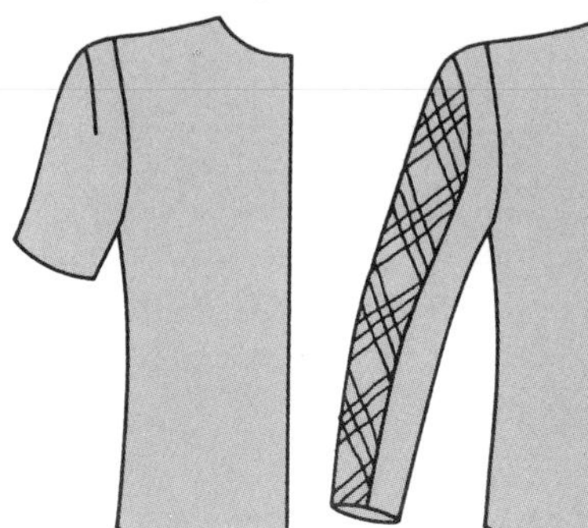

A strapped-cap sleeve is evidence of effort. It is Couture in a most intriguing way. It can be made in a short sleeve or long. While the short sleeve is cut in one piece, the long sleeve is cut in two pieces with no underarm seam. The center piece can be cut on the bias, which is particularly effective in a plaid.

Every time I make this sleeve, I remember learning about spatial relationships in school and thinking, "When will I ever need this information?" Well, now I know. Don't let all the letters and lines overwhelm you. Take it slow at first. Try it once in muslin so you can mark front, back, and notches right on the fabric. This will be your guide whenever you make this sleeve.

Start with a semi-fitted, one-piece set-in sleeve. All ease in the cap will be **removed** so the sleeve is set directly into the armhole. Consider using this sleeve in fabrics that are difficult to ease.

Pattern Drafting for a Strapped-cap Short Sleeve

1. Use a pattern for a short fitted sleeve that's the correct length; remove all seam and hem allowances.

2. Draw a line from the sleeve cap point to the hem, parallel to the grainline.

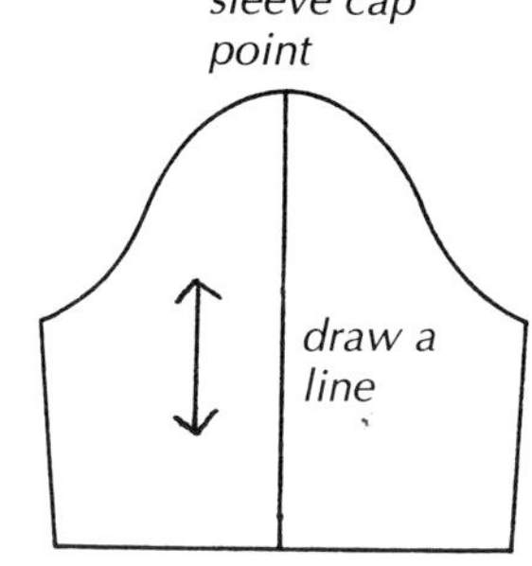

3. Measure the armhole of the garment on the stitching line and the sleeve along the edge. You removed seam allowances, so edge is stitching line. Determine how much larger the sleeve cap is than the armhole.

4. Mark ½ this amount on each side of the cap point (D and E) for "ease" marks.

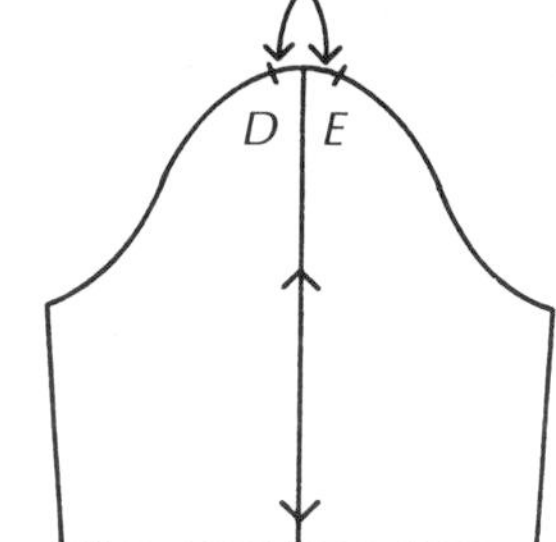

5. Mark points A and B just a hair above the midpoint (half way between cap point and underarm).

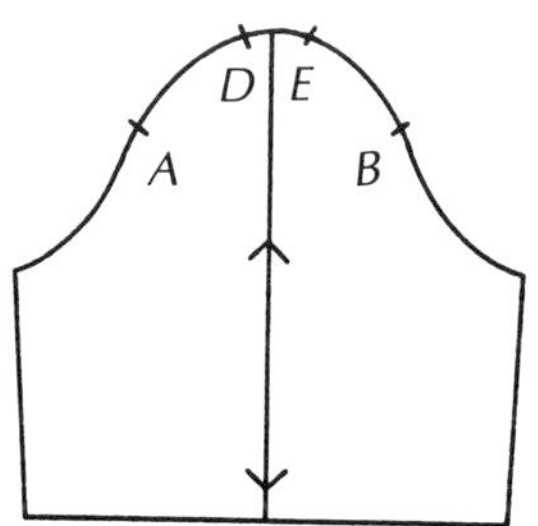

6. Draw a new cap line 1⅛" (2.8cm) into sleeve cap A¹ to B¹. This will become the strap. Mark point C at the center of new cap line.

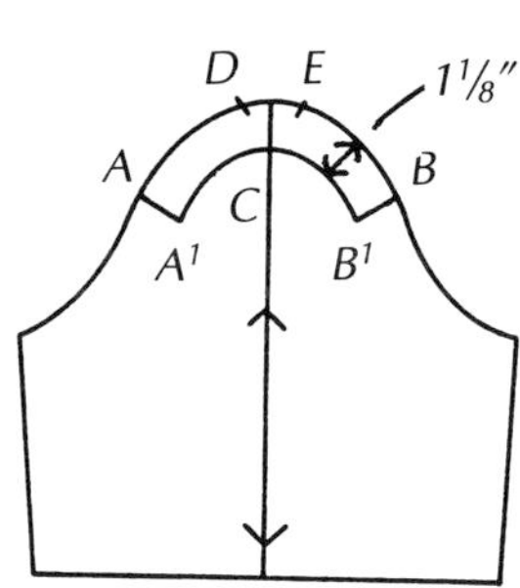

7. Divide the new cap from A¹ to C and C to B¹ into four equal sections.

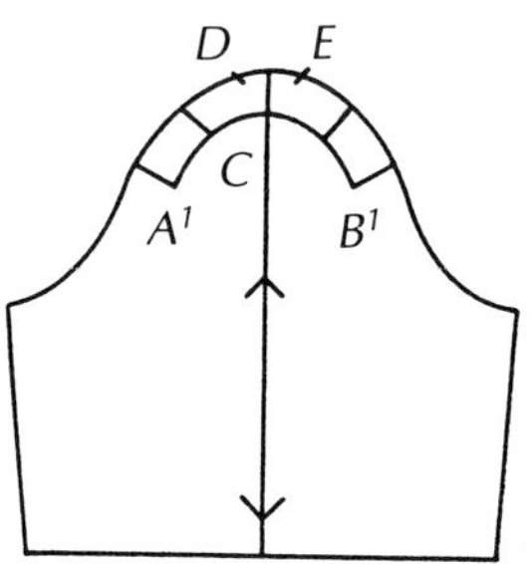

8. Connect ease marks (D and E) to center of strap line (C) and cut out to remove ease.

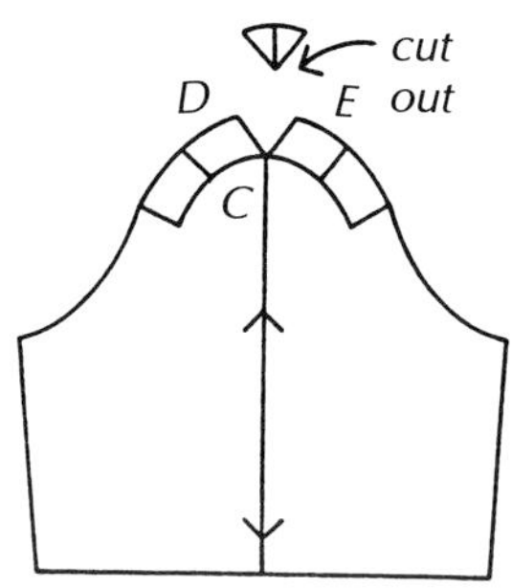

9. Slash on the center line to bottom edge of sleeve. Spread 1″ (2.5cm) at cap to nothing at lower edge.

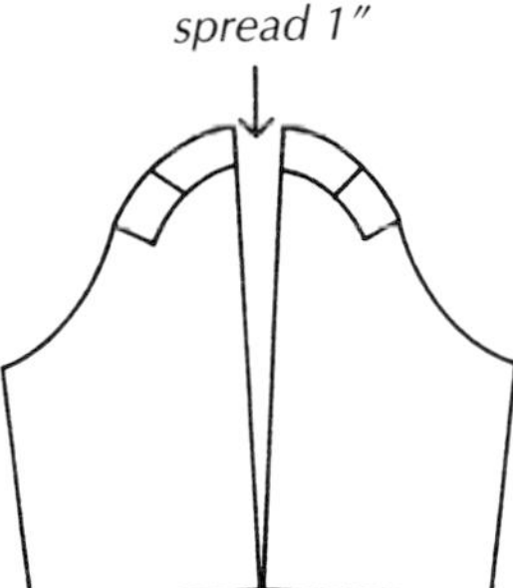

10. Cut on strap lines. Cut on section lines to but not through the sleeve cap edge.

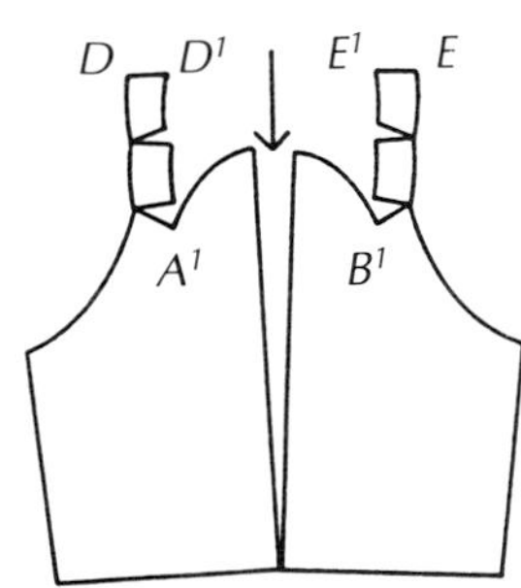

11. Raise cap 1½″ (3.8cm) and redraw using a French curve. Mark cap point (C[1]).

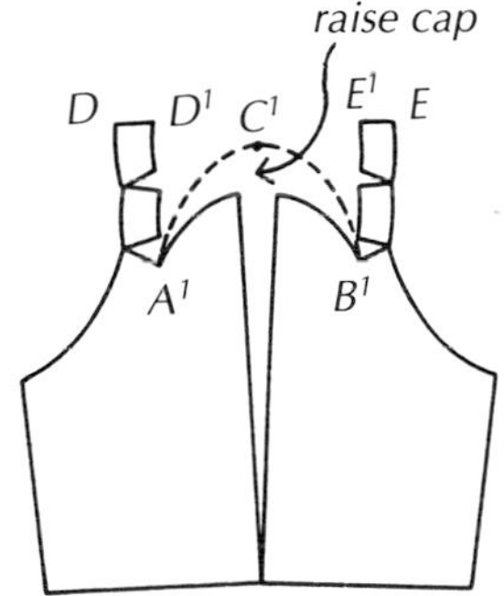

12. Spread strap sections until the slashed edges (A[1]-D[1] and B[1]-E[1]) equal the measurements of A[1]-C[1] and C[1]-B[1]. Be sure the amount you spread is equal in each slash.

13. Trace new pattern on a clean sheet of paper and add seam allowances. Carefully transfer all marks to fabric.

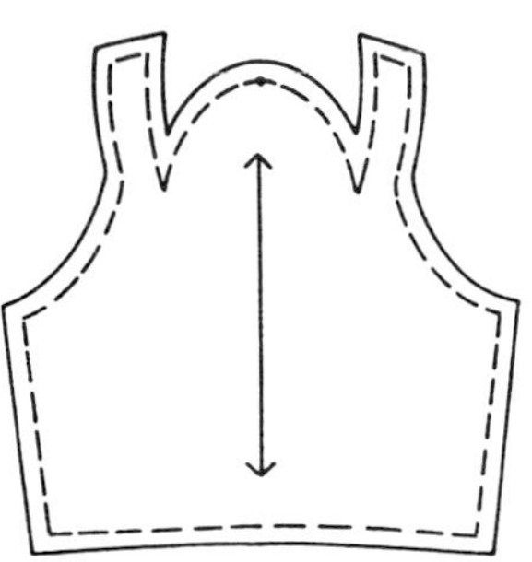

14. Hem edge will need to be faced as it has become slightly curved. Cut a 1½″-wide (3.8cm) facing on the bias.

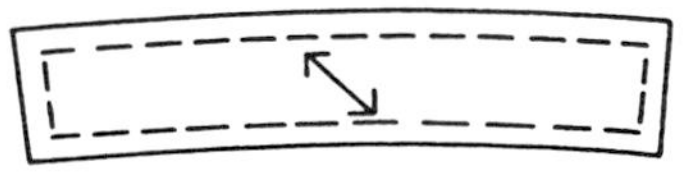

Sewing Instructions for Short Strapped-cap Sleeve

1. Sew the short ends of the strap together (D-D[1] to E-E[1]).

2. Sew the strap to the sleeve cap, matching the seam in the strap to the cap point (C[1]).

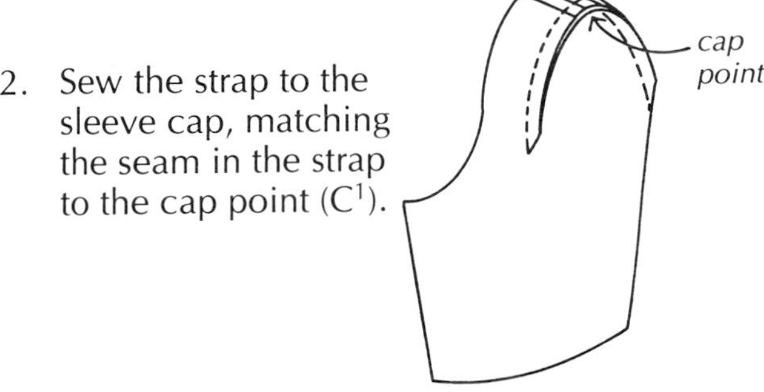

3. Interface and face hem, as it is a curve and cannot be turned up straight.

Long Sleeve Strapped Cap

1. Create strapped cap as shown for short sleeve, steps 1-12.

Note: In step #9 you will be slashing the center line to the **wrist**.

2. At the wrist measure and mark half the distance from the center line to each underarm edge (G and H).

3. Extend strap lines to wrist back (A[1] to H) and front (B[1] to G). Curve lines **slightly**, curving out on the back and in on the front.

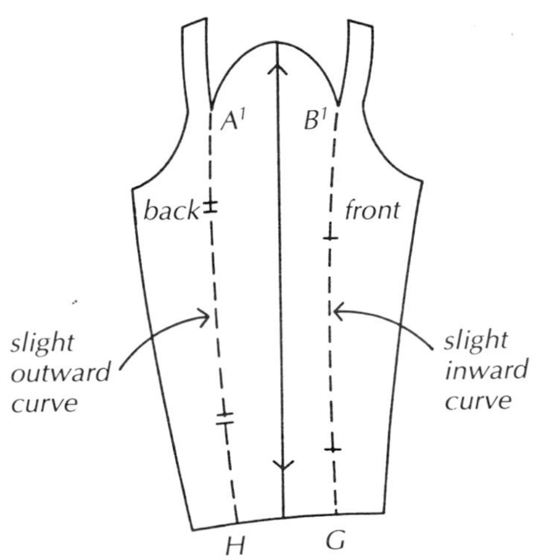

4. Mark matching points.

5. Cut pattern apart on strap lines A^1 to H and B^1 to G.

6. To create the front and back one-piece underarm section for the sleeve, Match B and A strap sections at underarm and wrist. **Do not worry if they do not meet in the middle**. Draw a straight line from underarm to wrist to establish the grainline. Cut as one piece.

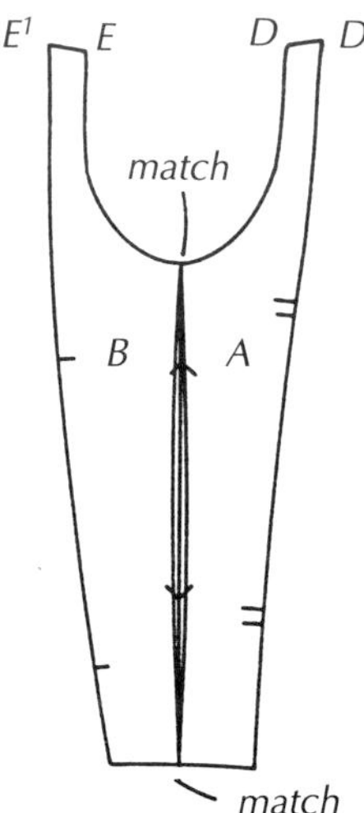

7. On the front edge of the sleeve center section, mark 3/8" (1cm) in from the edge at the midpoint. Draw new curve (B^1 to G), using shallow side of a French curve. Extend matching marks.

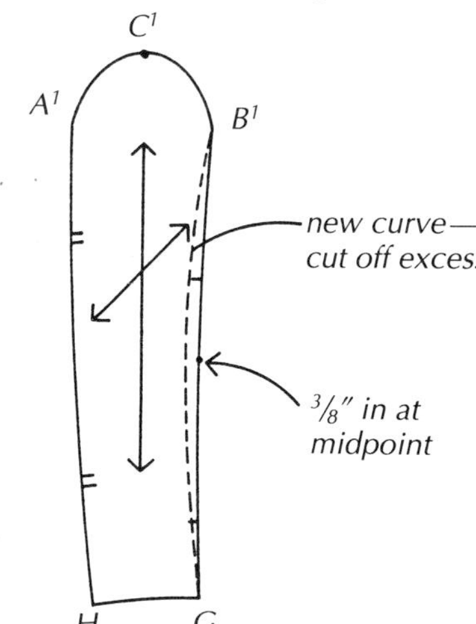

8. Establish grainline. It can be straight or bias. (If cutting this piece on the bias see page 80 for layout.)

9. Add seam allowances. to both underarm and center sections.

10. Add hem or use facings.

Sewing Instructions for Long Strapped-cap Sleeve

1. Stitch strap seam first (D-D^1 to E-E^1).

2. Pin center section to strap, baste and stitch with center section on top, stitching from G to B^1 to C^1 (strap seam) to A^1 to H.

Note: Match all fronts, backs, circles and matching points precisely.

Piping can be inserted between center section and strap for a visual definition. Apply piping to the center section before sewing to the strap edge. (See Piping, page 93.)

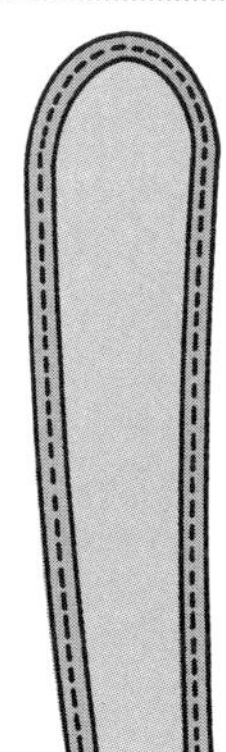

Short Cowl Sleeve

Here's a fun, simple short sleeve that looks wonderful in silk or lightweight cotton for summer. The cowl (bias drape), hangs free on the arm letting a sliver of skin show through.

How to Draft a Cowl Sleeve Pattern

Start with a pattern for a short set-in fitted sleeve the length you desire.

1. Trim seam and hem allowances from pattern. Draw a line down center of sleeve and cut on that line to separate back and front.

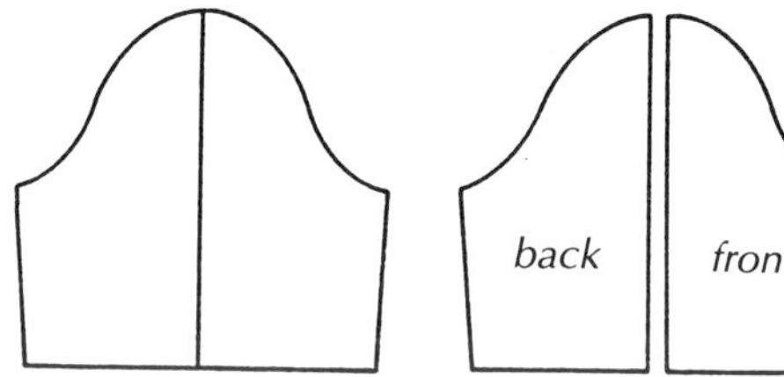

2. On a piece of paper draw two lines at right angles perpendicular to each other.

3. Place sleeve back and front on these lines as shown.

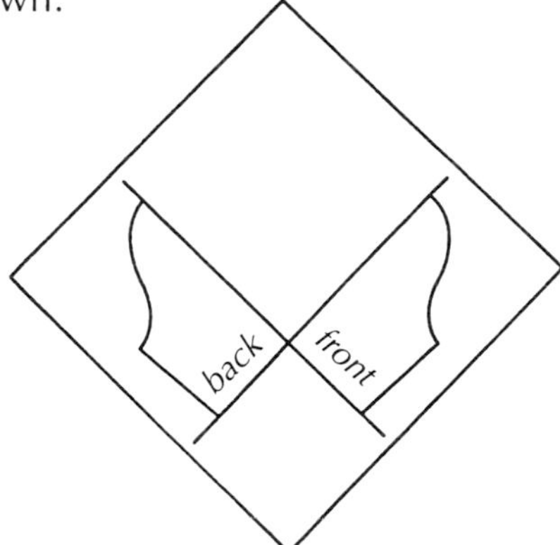

4. Draw a straight line connecting cap points.

5. Draw another line $1\frac{1}{2}''$ (3.8cm) above and parallel to the first line as shown. This will become a self-facing.

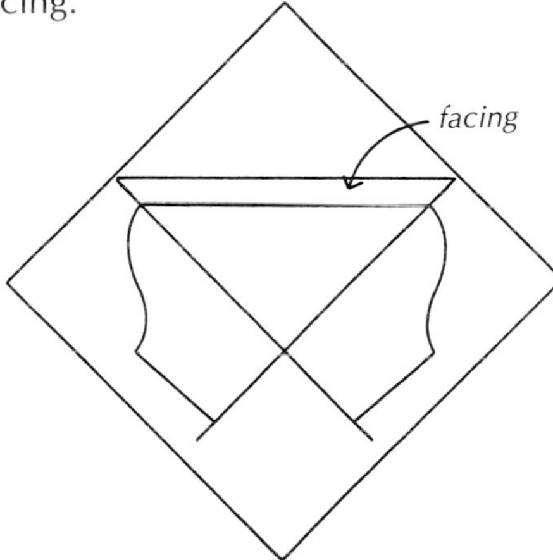

6. Connect hem A to B with a curved line. The distance around the hem is now shorter than the original pattern. Measure A curved to B to be sure it is 2″ (5cm) greater than your arm. If you need to add width, add equally front and back at the hemline.

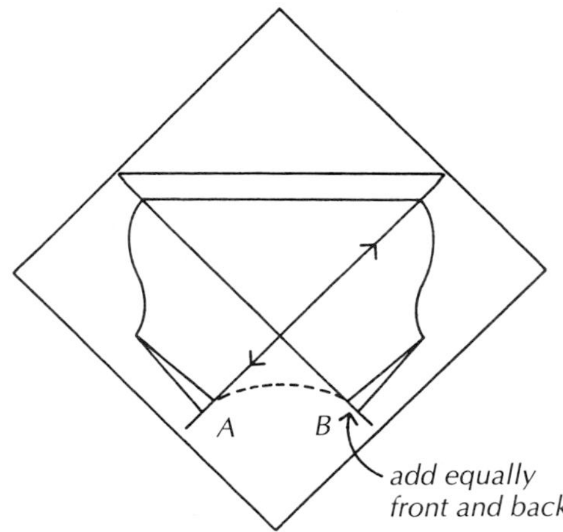

7. Establish grain as shown so sleeve will be cut on the bias. Add seam allowances.

How to Construct the Cowl Sleeve

1. Finish self-facing edge by pinking.

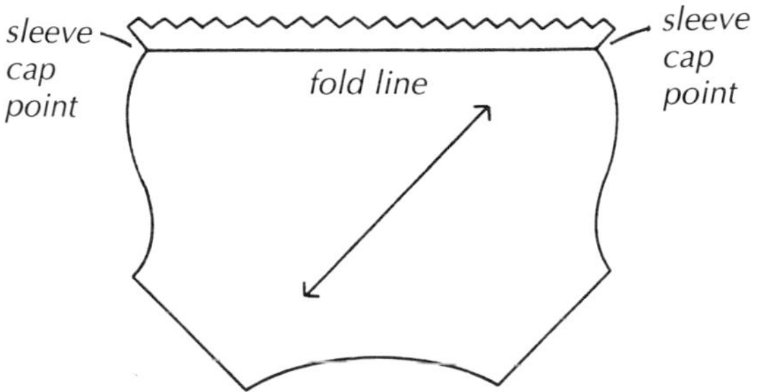

2. Fold facing to inside and press.

3. Bring cap points together. They will just meet, not overlap. Baste or tack them together in the seam allowance.

4. Make two rows of ease stitching in cap seam allowance.

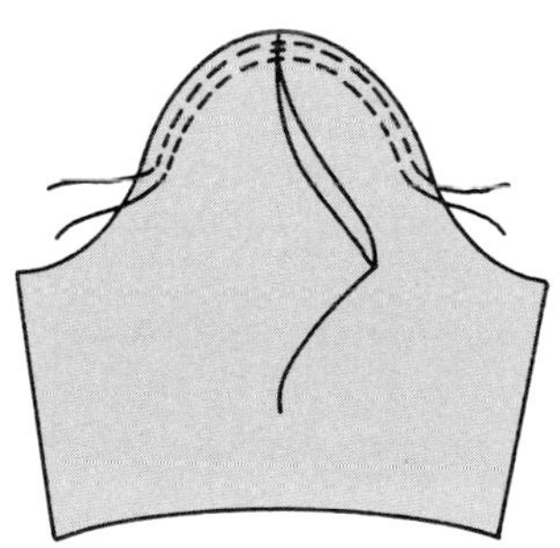

5. Stitch underarm seam, press open.

6. Finish the bottom edge. Try a bias facing, adding piping, or binding with matching or contrasting bias strip.

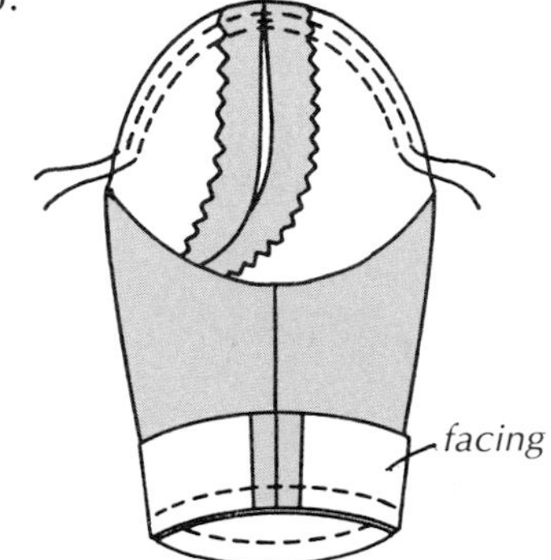

7. Set sleeve into garment.

Heart-shaped Sleeves

Pierre Cardin is most famous for his geometric shapes, especially when they appear in sleeves. This type of sleeve is fanciful, fun, and a real attention-getter, to be sure. (See color photo, page 110.)

It can be designed with a subtle approach or full-blown drama. The concept is the same. The final shape is three-dimensional.

A close-fitting one-piece sleeve is the basis for this design. This sleeve works best in fairly firm fabrics such as cotton gabardine or poplin or linen. The cap shape can be interfaced to firm it up.

How to Draft a Pattern for a Heart-Shaped Sleeve

Select a fitted set-in sleeve pattern for use in drafting the heart-shaped sleeve.

1. Trim seam and hem allowances from pattern.
2. Draw a line down the center of the sleeve. Cut sleeve on the center line. Mark on pattern which is front and back half.
3. Mark a dot 5/8″ (1.5cm) down from the cap.

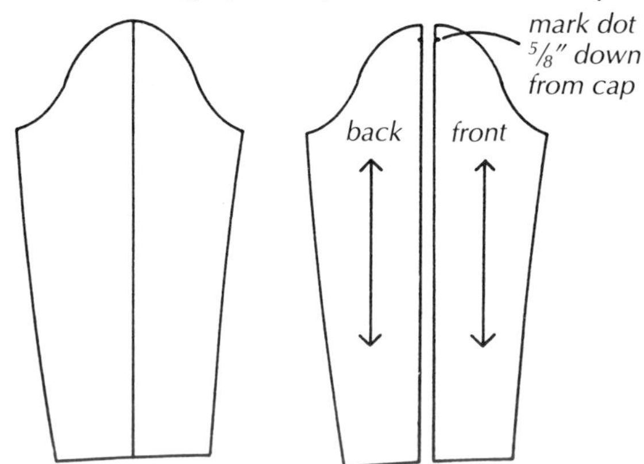

4. Draw a shape of your choice such as hearts, circles or diamonds. Make a second copy of the shape and cut one shape in half.
5. Place half of shape on front and half on back sleeve pattern with top at the 5/8″ (1.5cm) dot.

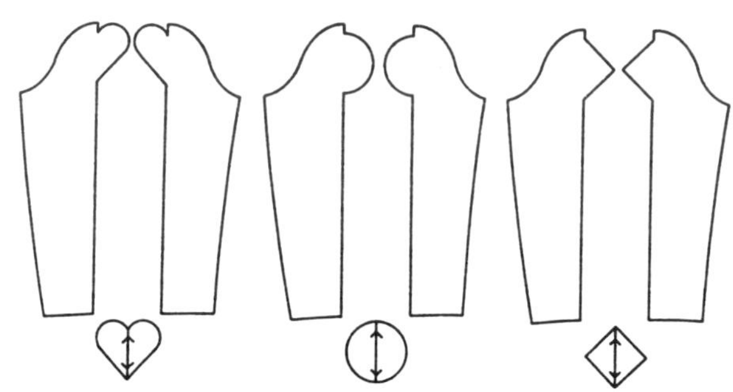

6. Add seam and hem allowances to new sleeve pattern pieces and heart shape.

To Sew Heart-Shaped Sleeve

1. Machine stitch front to back for 5/8″ (1.5cm) from cap. Hand baste on center line through shape. Then machine stitch to bottom edge of sleeve. (Remember, use 20 stitches per inch for 1/2″ (1.3cm) on either side of the opening.)

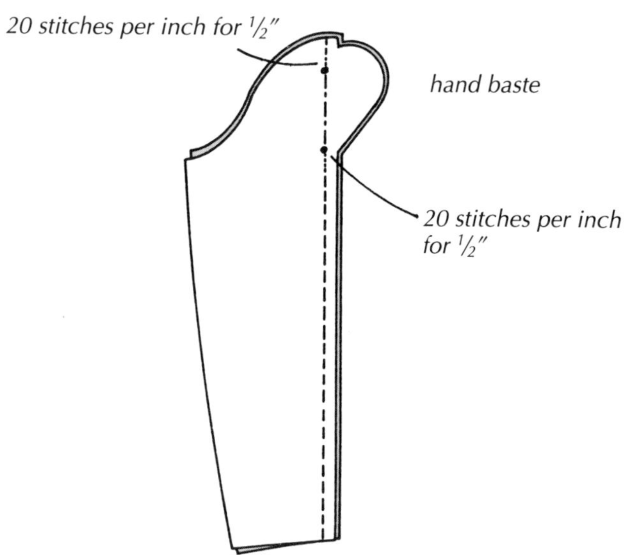

2. Press seam open. **Do not** press basting.
3. Cut a separate shape piece.
4. Place it right sides together on top of open shape on sleeve.

5. Stitch around shape ending with 20 stitches per inch as you reach center seam. It is easier to sew one side, then rearrange at machine and sew second side.

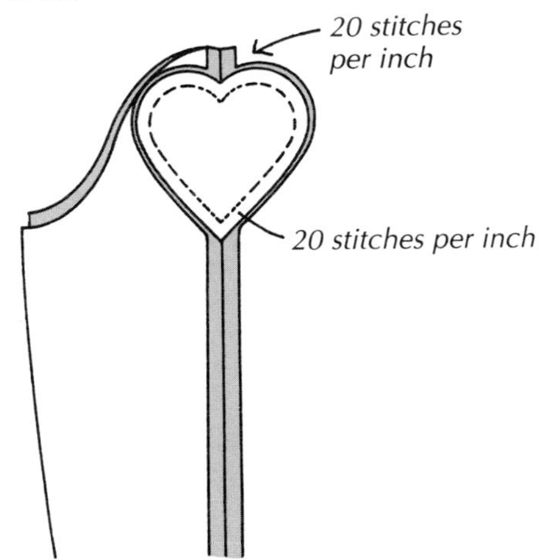

6. Remove basting.

7. Press shape seam open carefully over tailor-board.

8. Clip at right angles into main sleeve seam at top and bottom of shape.

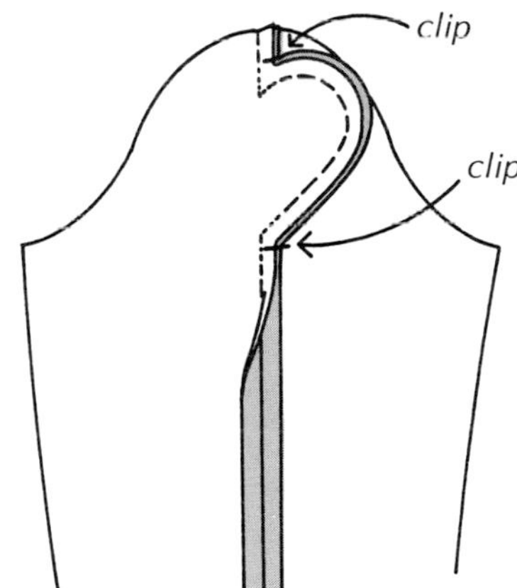

Lay shape to one side. Clip. Repeat for opposite side.

9. Grade seams of shape to $^3/_8''$ (1cm) and $^1/_4''$ (.6cm) or narrower, depending on fabric.

10. Turn shape to right side, pushing it through the opening.

11. Press edges of shape flat slowly and carefully, using a press cloth.

12. Edges of shape can be topstitched to add rigidity and/or decoration.

Variations

Geometric shapes can be made of contrasting fabric. Circles can be easily piped. Pipe the second circle shape before applying to sleeve. Shape can be tucked first with double needle before attaching to sleeve. Tuck fabric first, then cut shape. (See Double Needle Stitching, page 66.)

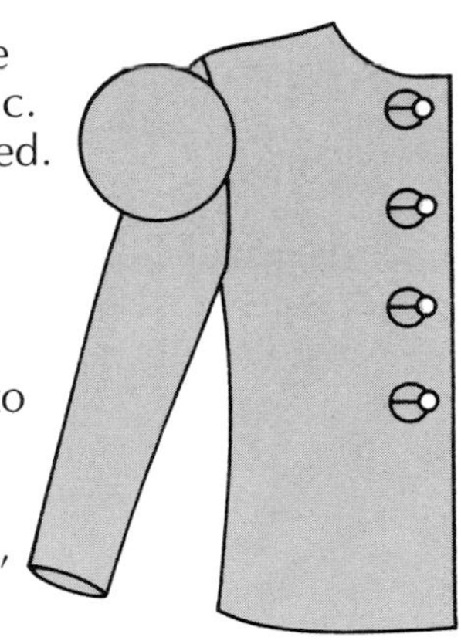

Haute Couture

Sometimes in couture what constitutes **haute** couture is a concept or technique that is expanded to its largest form or reduced in size and used in multiples. Such is the case here.

Following the same cutting and stitching instructions, design the sleeve with several shapes running the length of the sleeve.

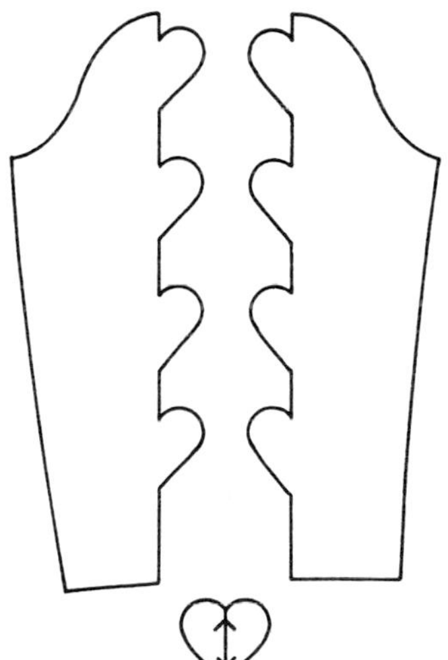

Cut each shape in a different color for a festive mood. This sleeve is absolutely wonderful for casual couture using brightly colored cottons of fairly substantial weight.

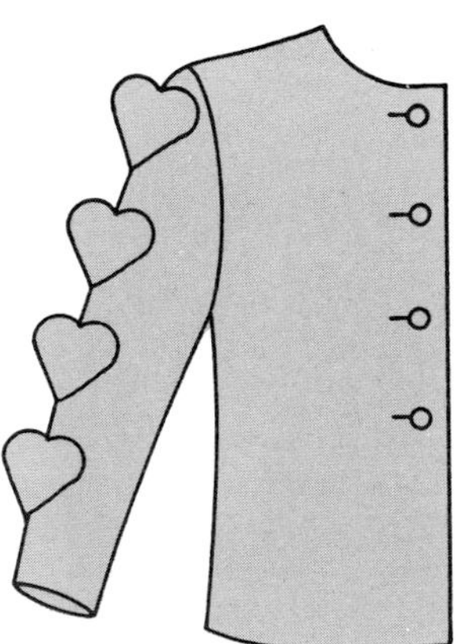

CHAPTER 21

Topstitching

Topstitching is seen most often in couture clothes as a decorative detail, but it often serves a functional purpose, too. Variations in topstitching are created by changing the stitch length, the number of rows of stitching, the space between rows, and the thread color and type.

Channel Stitching—Multiple rows of topstitching, usually done by machine.

Saddle Stitching—Longer-than-average stitches, usually done by hand.

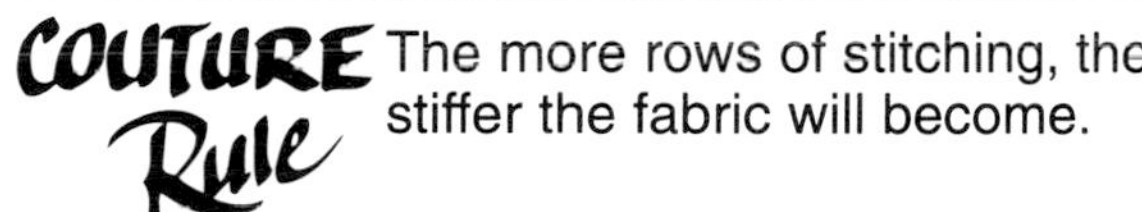

The more rows of stitching, the stiffer the fabric will become.

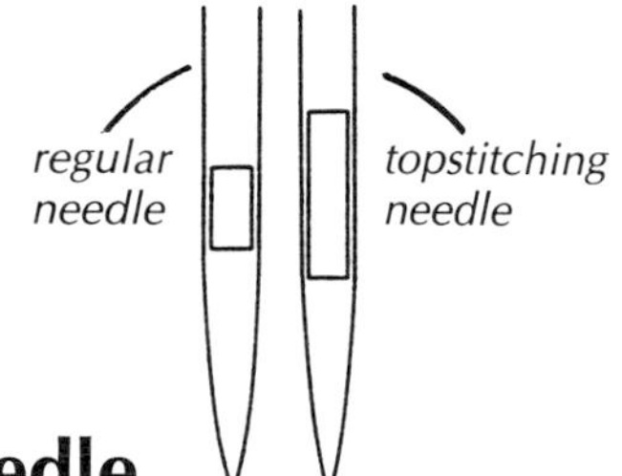

Topstitching Needle

Perfect topstitching is achieved when the thread passes easily through the machine needle eye so the thread can flow evenly with each stitch.

Topstitching needles, available in sizes 70, 80, and 90, have a long eye which allows a thicker thread to pass through without fraying the thread as stitches form.

Topstitching Thread

Cotton Thread—Usually matching the fashion fabric in color, it imbeds itself in the fabric to form a line of demarcation. It can be very effective when channel stitching. Use in the bobbin also.

Buttonhole Twist—preferably silk. This thick thread "rides" on the fabric surface and has a high sheen. For machine stitching, use it with cotton thread in the bobbin.

Rayon Thread—Available in a large number of colors, this thread has a high sheen. It can be used in a color that matches, blends or contrasts with the fashion fabric. It also can be used in the bobbin.

Metallic Thread—This glittery thread can appear "skimpy" in single rows. Sew in multiple rows or with decorative machine stitches rather than a straight stitch. Use with cotton thread in bobbin.

When topstitching, consider using a contrasting bobbin thread to make the topstitching stand out. For example, if you are using red thread to topstitch on navy, use navy thread in the bobbin. This will define and separate each stitch on top, preventing it from looking simply like a straight line.

Channel Stitching

Channel stitching consists of evenly spaced rows of machine stitches of the same length. Because it stiffens fabric, channel stitching often eliminates the need for interfacing or allows the use of a thinner, softer interfacing.

How to Channel Stitch a Garment Edge

1. Channel stitching is done on a finished edge, so apply the facing or hem the edge, as required.

2. With silk thread, **cross baste** (page 46) every 2″ (5cm) at right angles to the finished edges to retain grain, prevent puckering, and eliminate the need for pins.

3. On scrap fabric, **test** stitch length and spacing between rows.

4. From fabric **right side**, stitch first row the desired distance away from the edge. Then, to ensure the stitching doesn't gradually throw the edge off grain, straighten and press lightly from the right side. Use a press cloth and press at right angles to the stitching line.

COUTURE Tip Remember, if you basted with silk thread, pressing over your basting won't leave permanent thread imprints.

5. Continue to add the desired number of rows, remembering to press all previous rows **each time** you add a row of stitching. Leave 4″-6″ (10-15cm) thread tails when ending a row.

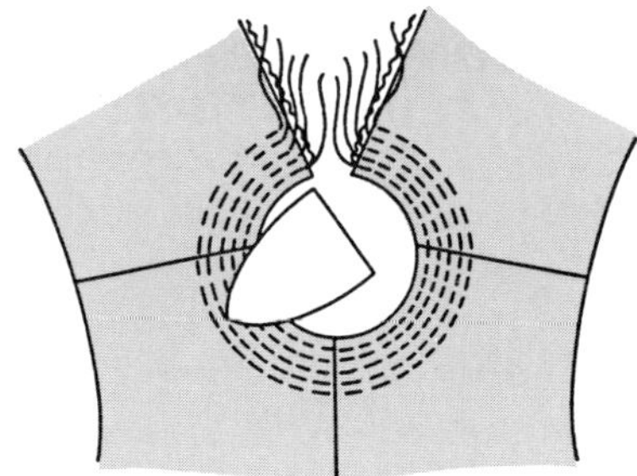

6. To tie off threads, choose one of the following methods:

    a. Bring top thread to wrong side and tie a tiny square knot. Clip thread ends close to knot.

    b. Bring top thread to wrong side, thread into a hand sewing needle and weave thread into facing fabric along stitching line with tiny stitches. Weave bobbin thread and top thread individually, not together.

7. Remove basting stitches.

8. Final press, using press cloth and light steam.

How to Channel Stitch a Garment Segment

Chanel stitch on the garment section first, then attach to the garment. Although the concept of channel stitching here is similar to channel stitching a garment edge, a few additional "rules" apply.

1. Choose a backing. Use elephant flannel (cotton tailor's flannel) or very lightweight polyester fleece (Thermore) for a quilted effect. If you leave a wider space between rows, you will get the appearance of a welt. If you apply a woven interfacing, the garment section will have a flatter appearance.

2. Cut out the fashion fabric piece (collar, yoke, pocket, sleeve cap, collar or cuff), allowing 1″ (2.5cm) seam allowances all around. Carefully mark stitching lines, notches, and all construction marks.

3. Cut backing the same size as the fashion fabric. (Backing will be trimmed from seam allowances later.)

4. Cross-baste backing to fabric **with silk thread**.

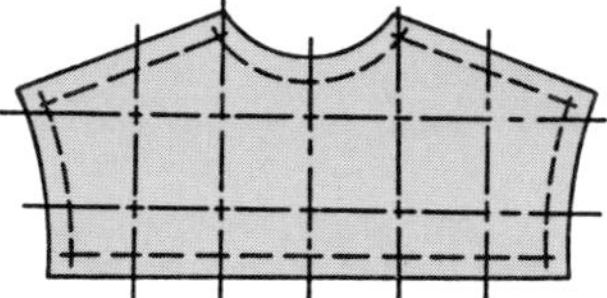

5. Begin stitching, using one major seamline as a guide. For example:

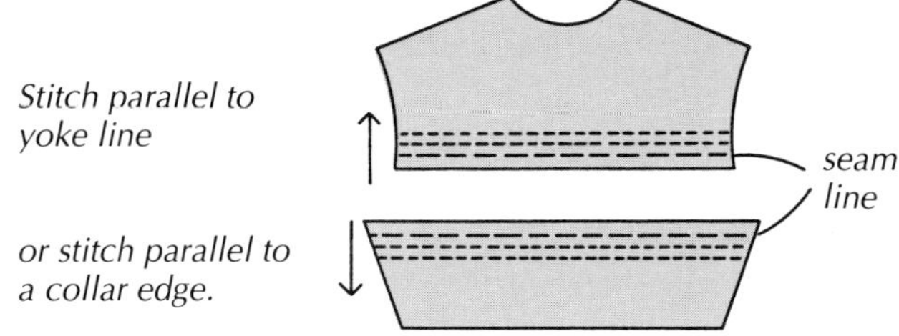

6. Begin stitching about $\frac{1}{8}$″ (.3cm) inside seam allowance at 20 stitches per inch (8 stitches per centimeter), then switch to desired stitch length at seam line. Return to 20 stitches per inch $\frac{1}{8}$″ (.3cm) into opposite seam allowance.

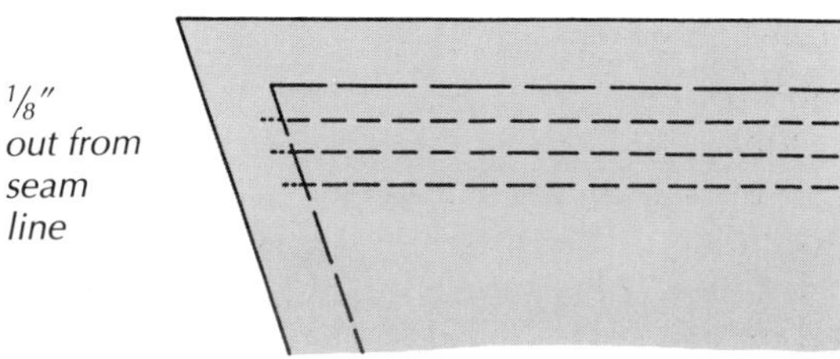

7. Pressing may become difficult when using a "fluffy" backing. You can eliminate pressing as long as you hold the work perfectly flat. Or use a bristled press cloth and press from the right side.

8. Once all channel stitching is completed, place paper pattern on topstitched piece and re-mark, because it is likely the stitching has drawn up the piece and made it smaller.

9. Resume normal sewing sequence for the garment. Sew, meld stitches, and press seam. Then trim backing from seam allowances.

Topstitching Variations

If ever there were a place to emulate The Couture, it is in topstitching. Topstitching in ready-to-wear is labor-intensive, thus seldom seen in its most beautiful execution.

It is common to see topstitching as two single rows about 3/8" (1 cm) apart. For a couture treatment, stitch two sets of two rows, very close together.

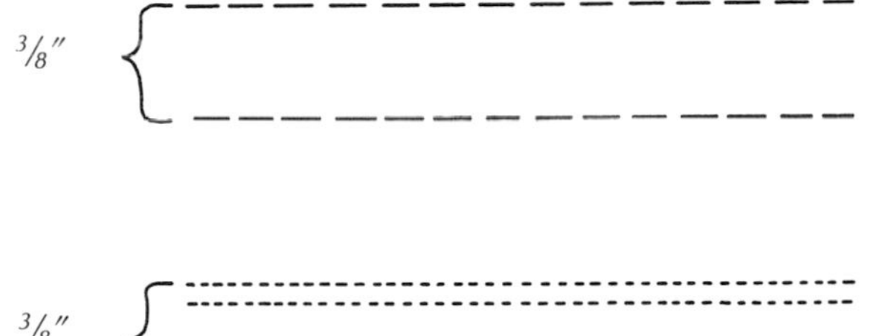

I remember seeing a white, sheer wool crepe coat by Patou with princess lines and contrived lines repeating the princess curve, all topstitched at 20 stitches per inch. It looked like beads on a chrysalis.

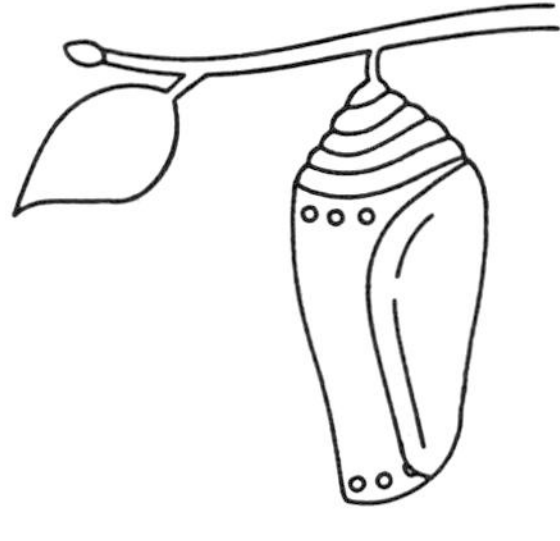

When stitching parallel rows of topstitching, **every** stitch in **every** row should be a mirror image of the next. That's easy on straight rows, but what about a curve? If an outside curve in a hem is stitched first, as the progressive inner curves are stitched, the stitch length must be **shortened**. The eye will then see all the stitches as even.

The reverse is true on a neckline where the smallest curve is sewn first. The stitches become longer in each successive row.

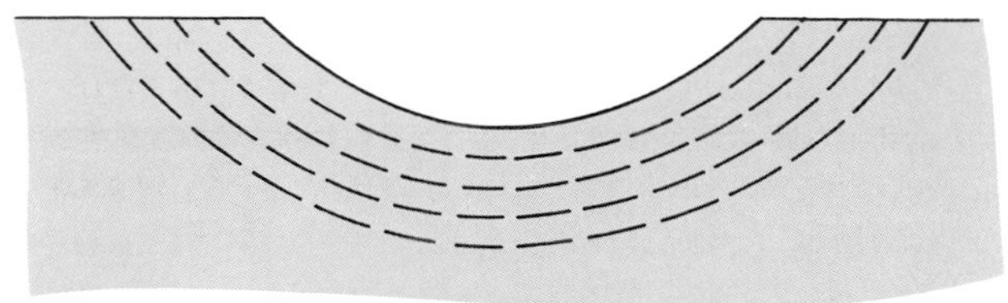

Functional Topstitching

Decorative topstitching always seems like more fun, but topstitching also serves practical purposes. The following techniques solve common problems. My students often say, "Oh! If I had only known that." Well, here it is, for you to know and use.

The Welt Seam

A welt seam is a traditional seam pressed open and topstitched from the right side through the seam allowance.

Choose a welt seam to stiffen the seam allowances and make it more stable, or if you want to trim away excess seam allowances on white or sheer fabrics.

Welt seams can be stitched on either straight or curved seams and can be placed in any area of a garment. Remember that all machine stitching, hand basting and pressing should be done in the **same direction** when creating a welt seam.

1. Machine stitch seam.

2. Press seam open from wrong side; clip only as needed, as little as possible!

3. Pin seam allowances from the right side, perpendicular to the seamline. Hand baste seam allowances in place.

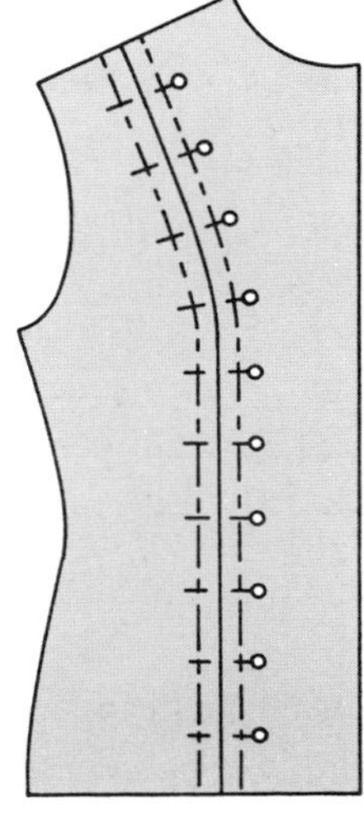

If fabric does not slip and can be controlled, pinning may be adequate. Do **not** stitch over pins.

4. Topstitch one or two rows on each side of the seamline. Thread can be a contrasting or matching color, shiny or matte. Changing stitch length will change the appearance, too.

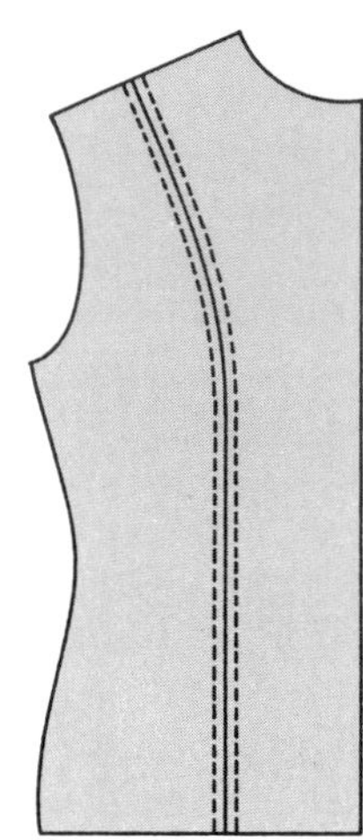

The Slot Seam

In couture, we often see a surprise—the unexpected—a dash of color—a sliver of shocking pink on a black suit, for example. A topstitched slot seam, a variation of the welt seam, is one way to create this detail.

1. Hand baste seam.
2. Machine baste seam together using six stitches per inch.

The seam may have been hand basted for fitting, but you must machine baste, too, so you can press the seam open and get a hard edge. If the seam were only hand basted, it would look uneven.

3. Remove **hand** basting stitches only.
4. Press seam open from wrong side over an appropriately curved shape. Clip only as needed, as little as possible.
5. Cut a $1\frac{1}{2}''$-wide (4cm) **bias** strip of fashion fabric the length of the seam. Be creative! Use a contrasting color in the fabric of your choice. This will become the sliver of color that shows through the "slot."
6. Place the strip, right side out, behind the seam. Pin from the **right side** to ensure the seam holds its shape and the bias strip doesn't "grow." Periodically check inside to ensure that the strip lies evenly over the seam.

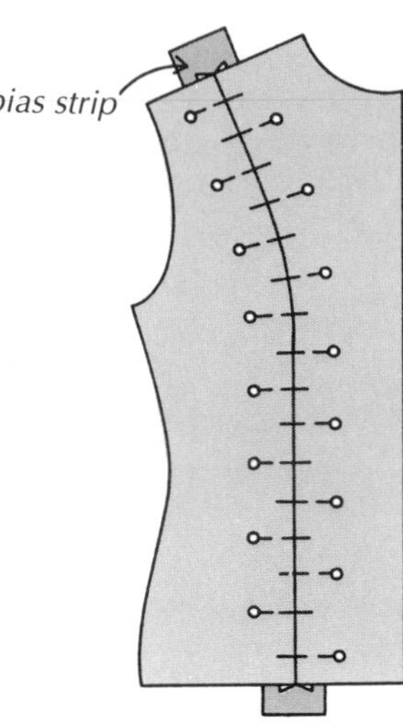

7. Hand baste from the right side about $\frac{1}{2}''$ (1.3cm) away from seamline; remove pins.
8. Machine stitch $\frac{1}{2}''$ (1.3cm) away from seamline, close to but not on top of hand basting.

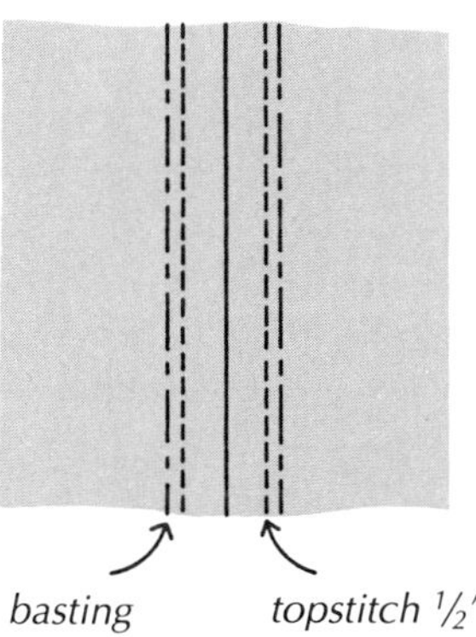

9. Remove hand basting.
10. **Carefully** remove machine basting from seamline.
11. Steam the seam from the right side, using a press cloth to protect the fabric.

VOILÀ! A hint of contrast shows through the slot.

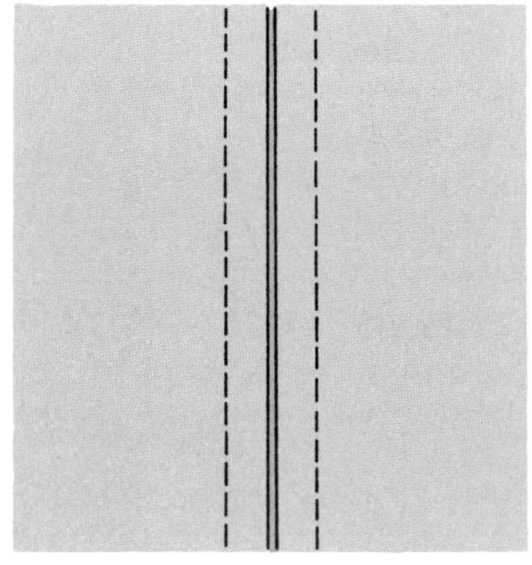

Welt Seam in Two-Part Sleeve

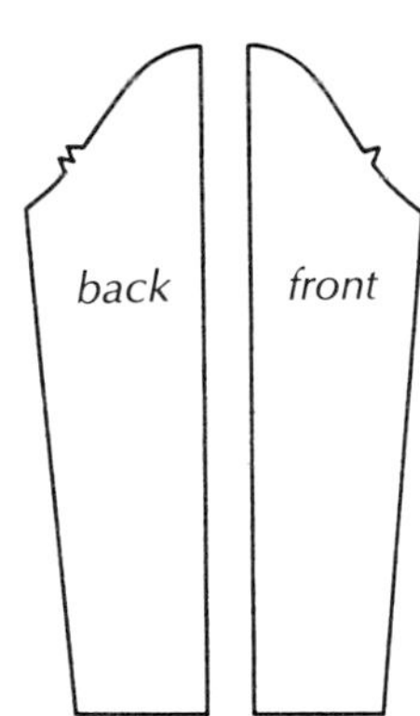

A **two-part** sleeve (as opposed to a **two-piece** sleeve seen on many tailored jackets) is seamed down the center of the sleeve and at the underarm.

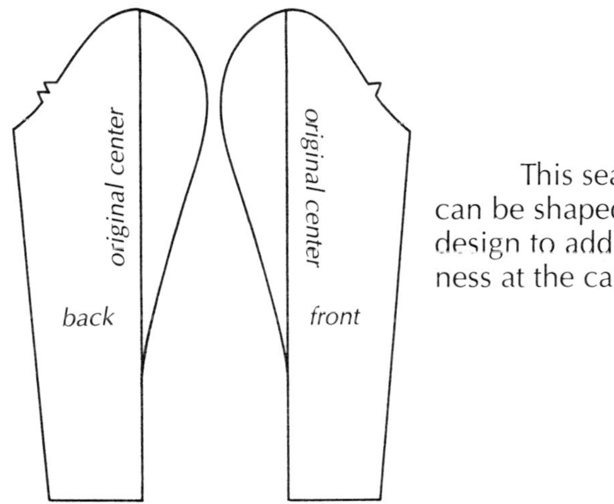

This seam can be shaped by design to add fullness at the cap.

Whatever the shape, this seam needs to be stabilized to hold the shape. Follow the steps for a slot seam with the following changes:

Step #1: Machine stitch permanently.

Step #5: Cut a $1\frac{1}{2}$"-wide bias strip, not from fashion fabric, but from elephant flannel or Armo® Wool, or silk organza if the sleeve fashion fabric is very thin. The thicker the fabric, the more "welt" effect you will get.

bias elephant flannel or Armo wool

seam pressed open

The sleeve may be sewn into the armhole in the traditional way or you may stitch the sleeves to the garment first. Then sew welt or slot seam from the neck edge, across the shoulder and down the sleeve to the wrist.

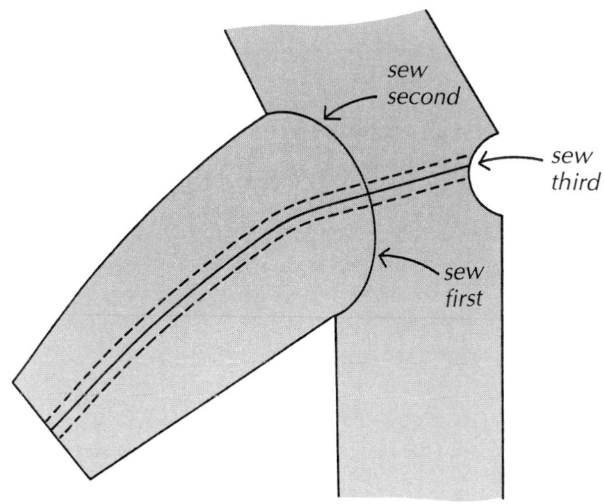

How to Finish Topstitching

To finish topstitching, draw the top thread to the underside, thread into a hand sewing needle and bury the thread between the garment and facing for about $1\frac{1}{2}$" (3.8cm). When the needle exits the fabric, clip thread close to the garment surface. Bury the top and bobbin threads separately.

Remove basting stitches and lightly press from right side with press cloth and steam.

CHAPTER 22

Pockets

Coco Chanel said pockets are to be used. Any little boy knows that as he carries a frog in his pocket, or rocks, a piece of string, a little Ninja turtle, or maybe a miniature dinosaur.

For women of fashion, a pocket may carry a silk handkerchief, theatre tickets, money or keys. A couturier decides the purpose in the design stage and designs the pocket accordingly—type of fabric, short/shallow pocket vs. long/deep pocket, and placement perfectly proportioned to the garment and the person who will wear it.

Pockets can also be a grand decorative detail. A welt pocket, for instance, can have contrast welts or a zipper—true couture touches.

Knowing many different techniques to construct pockets as well as having a repertoire of pocket shapes and designs becomes an asset for the couture sewer.

Single-Faced Pocket

A single-faced pocket is formed by the pocket being placed on the **wrong side** of the garment and topstitched to hold it in place. It is ideal for a side seam where you want no gaping.

Compatible thread color can be used or a contrasting thread for a more decorative look. The shape of the pocket can vary for different effects. A single-faced pocket is a substitute for the traditional pouch pocket put in a side seam.

A patch pocket is bulkier than a single-faced pocket, because seam allowances are turned under on the edges. Also, a patch pocket has a top opening which may not be appropriate for the design. Knowing about the single-faced pocket technique gives you an option.

Single-faced Pocket Shape Ideas

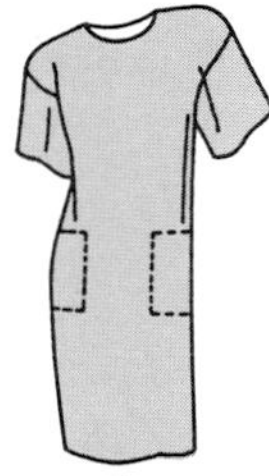
A

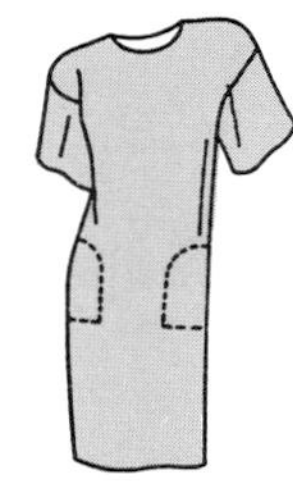
B

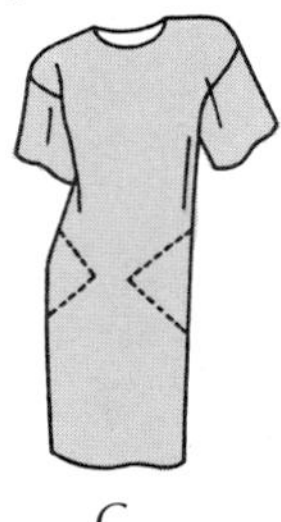
C

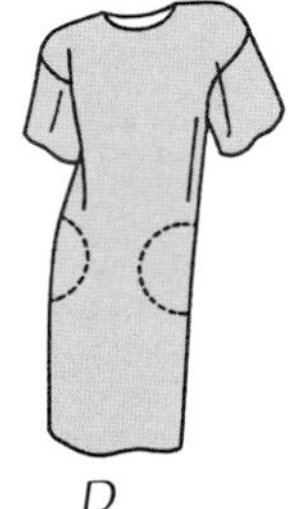
D

Sewing a Single-faced Pocket

It is very important to follow the directions in **sequence**.

1. Determine pocket pouch shape—rounded, square, circular, or triangular.
2. Cut one piece of fabric for each pocket, 10″ long and 9″ wide in the desired shape. Finish all edges by pinking, serging or with mock Hong Kong finish (see page 62.) The seam finish will not show through if you select one appropriate to the fabric.

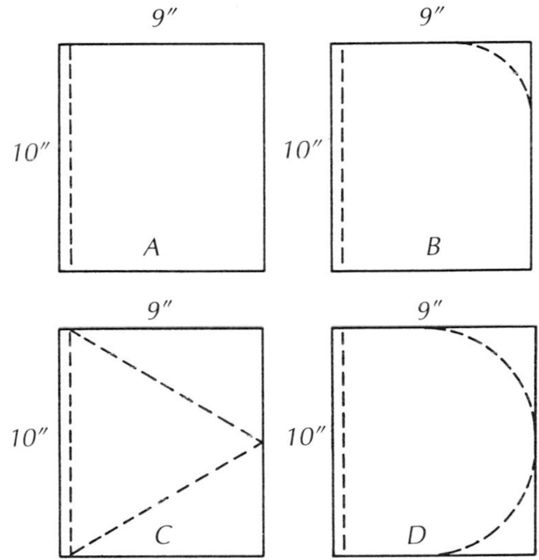

3. Cut a $1\frac{1}{2}''$ × 10″ (3.8 × 25.5cm) piece of fusible or sew-in interfacing on the straight of grain.

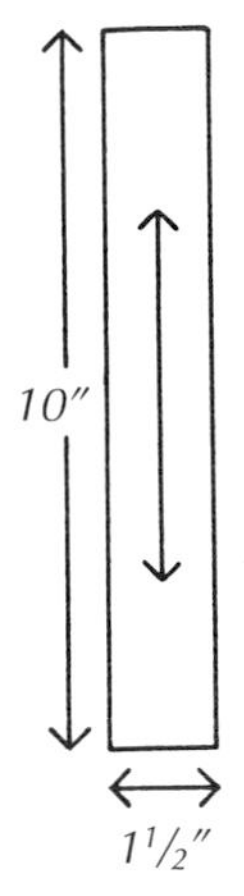

4. Determine pocket opening by trying on pinned-together garment and putting your hand where you would like your hand to enter the side seam. Mark with pins. Then mark on wrong side of garment front and back with chalk. The pocket opening should measure 6½″ (16.3cm). Mark pocket placement lines 1″ (2.5cm) above and 2½″ (6.3cm) below pocket opening. Now thread trace so marks show on right and wrong side.

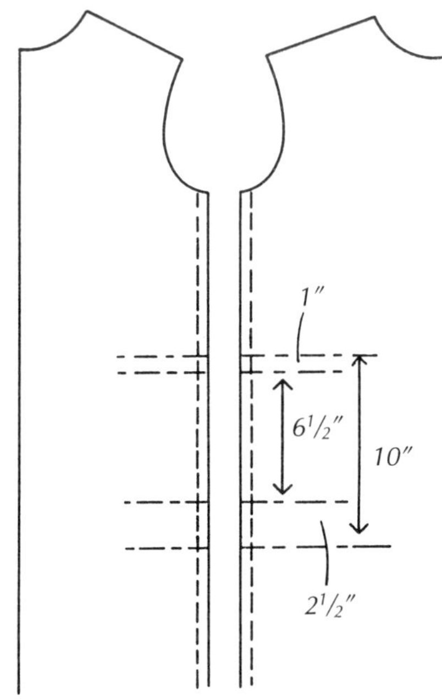

5. Sew side seam, hem to armhole, machine basting at 6 stitches per inch along the 6½″ (16.3cm) which will become pocket opening. For about ½″ (1.3cm) on either side of the opening stitch 20 stitches per inch to reinforce without needing to tie off at a later time. Do not backstitch, the short stitches **will** hold.

6. Press seam open.

7. Apply interfacing to wrong side of front only, ½″ (1.3cm) into seam allowance with 1″ (2.5cm) in garment. Fuse or baste in place on stitching line.

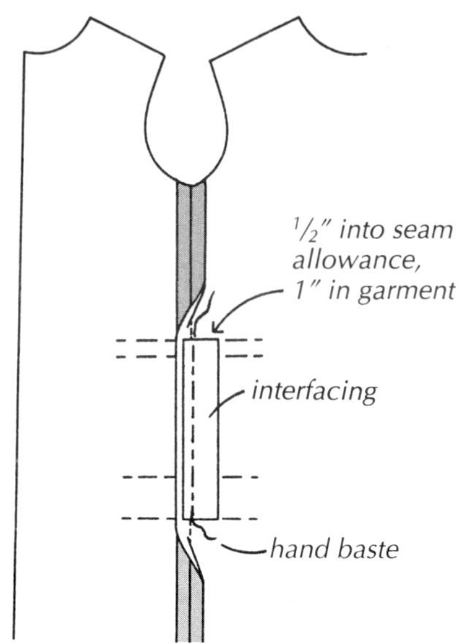

8. Re-press seam open. Quickly hand baste front seam so it will stay flat.

9. Topstitch front seam allowance from right side, making two rows ⅜″ (1cm) apart. Start and stop ⅜″ (1cm) inside pocket placement marks. Leave thread tails. This will allow for remaining topstitching to cross in the correct place.

This step is essential to success and must be done now as there will be no way to get back here after pocket pouch is applied.

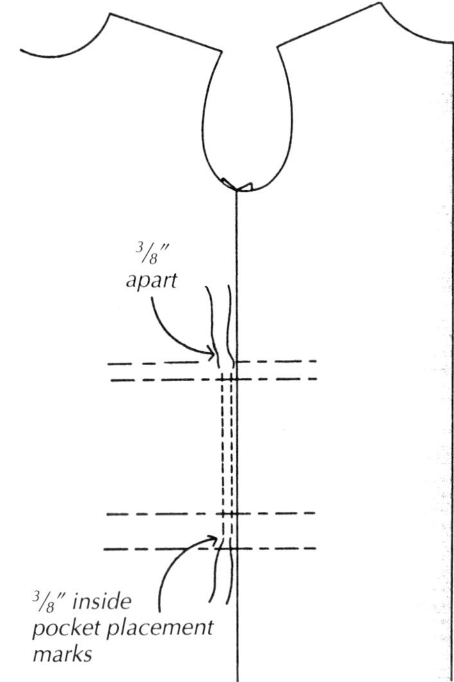

10. Working from the **wrong side**, stitch pocket to back seam allowance of garment with zipper foot as close to original stitching as possible. Be careful to stitch pocket to the back seam allowance **only**, not the garment.

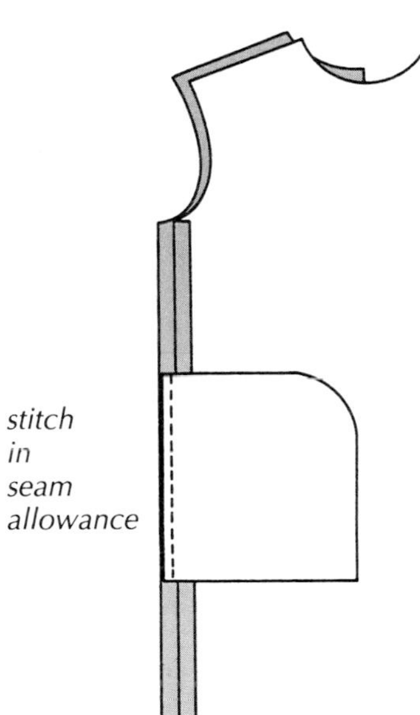

11. Pin remainder of pocket pouch on the wrong side of front of garment. Hand baste close to pocket edge making sure long stitches show on right side. These will be your guide for topstitching.

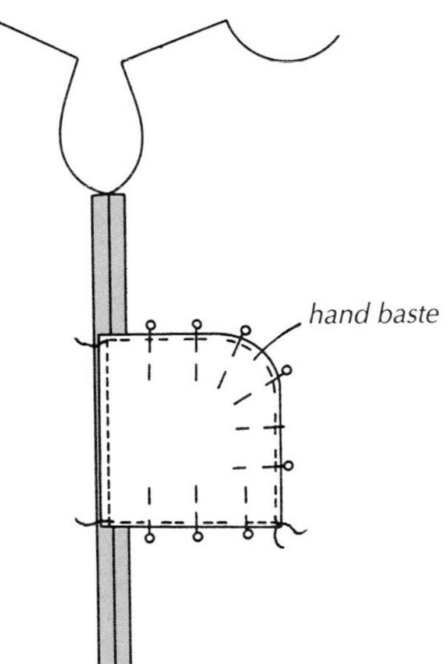

12. Turn garment to right side and topstitch 2 rows 3/8" (1cm) apart along back next to seam and around pocket. Stitch parallel to front seam, turn, cross above and below row of hand basting and proceed around pocket.

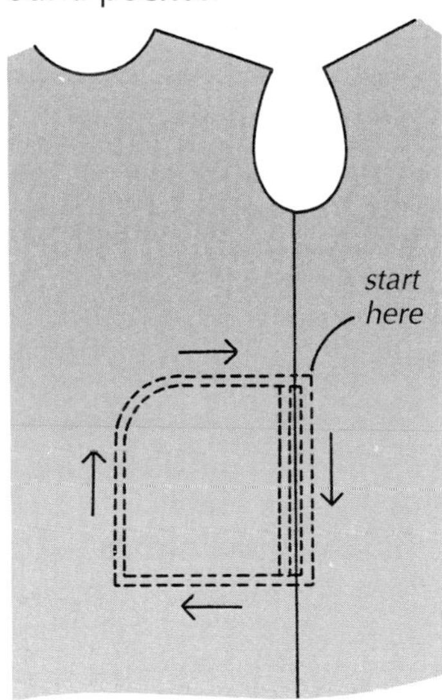

13. Now check your thread tails. This is the KEY to perfection. Look at the topstitching. If a row was started one stitch short, thread the tail into a needle and sew a stitch until rows are even. If you stitched too far, pull out a stitch. When perfect, pull all threads to the wrong side and tie off, one knot for each thread.

14. Remove hand basting. Press flat from wrong side and carefully remove machine basting stitches at pocket opening.

The Perfect Patch Pocket

Considerations for a perfect patch pocket:

In planning your sewing strategy for the perfect patch pocket, consider the fashion fabric. Is it thick or thin? Does it need some sort of stabilizing such as an underlining? What type of interfacing will best firm up the opening edge which gets the most wear. Will topstitching add the needed stiffness on the edge or will it be purely decorative? Can the lining be used as support?

COUTURE Tip Many times it is best to interface the **lining** with a lightweight fusible interfacing such as Silk Weight or Touch of Gold instead of underlining the fashion fabric.

What pocket shape is best suited to the garment? To you? Rounded or square corners? Consistency will give a complete look to the garment. If you have a notched lapel with all edges square, a square pocket might be more appropriate. If the lower front of the jacket is rounded, rounded pockets may look better.

Anatomy of a patch pocket:

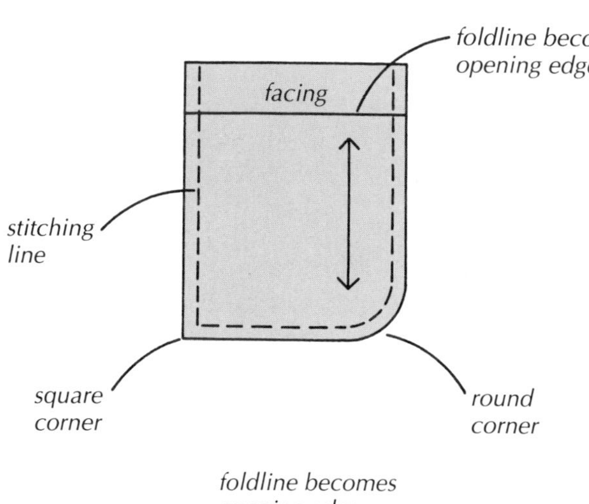

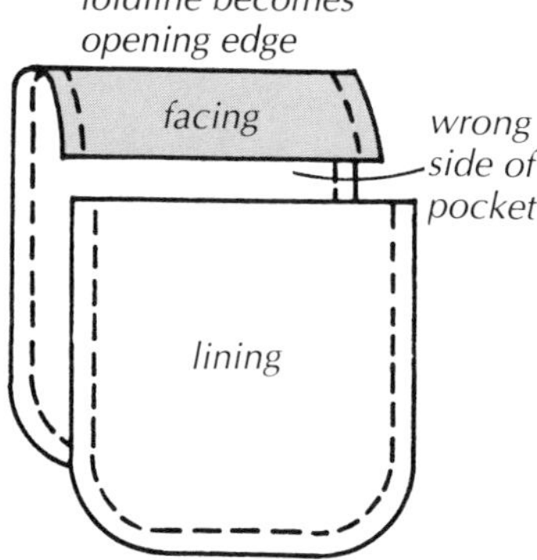

The perfect patch pocket has even corners, whether round or square; the opening edge is firm and topstitched, if you choose. Pocket edges are flat, not bulky. The lining is smooth and enhances rather than detracts from the finished pocket.

Both the fashion fabric and the lining should be cut on the straight of grain unless the fashion fabric is being cut on the bias to create a design. Regardless, cut the interfacing on the straight grain.

COUTURE Tip On a fitted jacket or any garment where the side seam curves out in hip area, the outside edge of the pocket nearest the side seam should be slightly off grain in the same direction . This will give the illusion of a smaller waist and follow the contours of the body. Simply mark out 1/2″ at the bottom edge of the pocket nearest the side seam and draw a slightly curved line to the original corner of the opening edge. Use this as the new cutting line (or stitching line if you've trimmed away seam allowances).

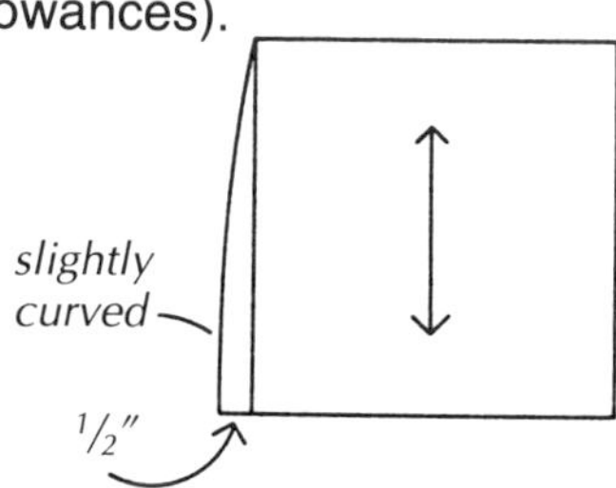

This can be done on round or square corners.

How to Construct Perfect Patch Pockets

1. Select pocket shape.

2. Whether you are using a commercial pattern or you create a pocket shape of your own, it is best to make a template without seam allowances or facings out of heavy paper. A file folder is great! This ensures accuracy and helps you to mark stitching and fold lines easily and accurately.

3. Cut a piece of fashion fabric slightly larger than the size needed for the pocket and grain-up fabric. Yes, AGAIN! Even Pati Palmer, speed sewing champion, regrains pocket fabric!!

4. Place pocket shape on fashion fabric and mark all stitching lines with chalk on wrong side of fabric and thread trace foldline for pocket facing. Add seam allowances and facing. Cut out pocket.

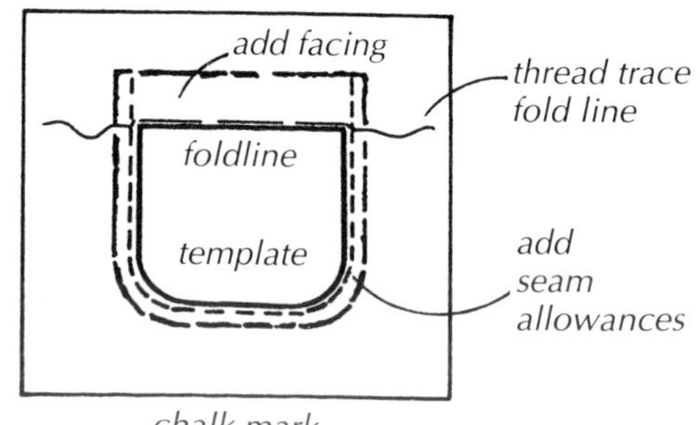

5. Interface the facing:

For fusible interfacing cut interfacing the width of the pocket facing plus 5/8" (1.5cm). Do not include interfacing in any seam allowances. Fuse interfacing to facing with 5/8" (1.5cm) of interfacing extending beyond foldline following manufacturer's instructions.

For sew-in interfacing cut interfacing without seam allowances, making it the width of the pocket facing plus 5/8" (1.5cm). Pin to wrong side of facing with 5/8" (1.5cm) of interfacing extending beyond foldline. Turn back 5/8" (1.5cm) of interfacing along fold line and slipstitch to pocket. Catch stitch interfacing to stitching lines.

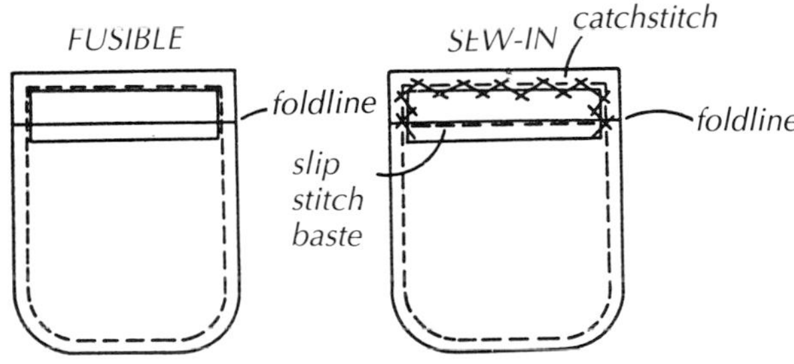

COUTURE Tip Pocket may be entirely interfaced if needed for stability; however, do not include interfacing in seams.

6. Stitch a piece of straight-grain lining fabric slightly larger than pocket to pocket facing edge. Leave a 2" (5cm) opening in the center of the seam to use later for turning.

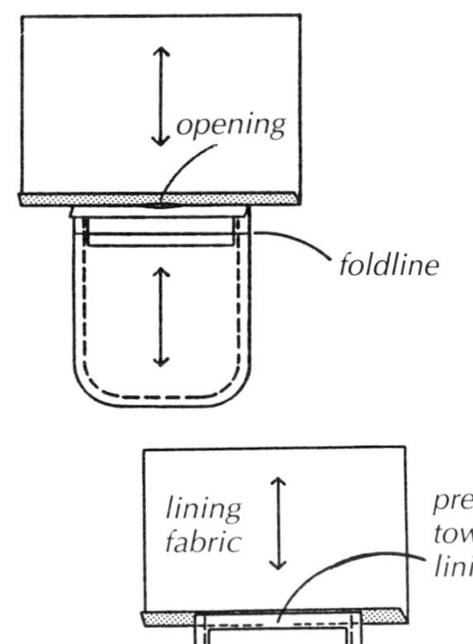

7. Press to meld stitches. Press seam toward lining.

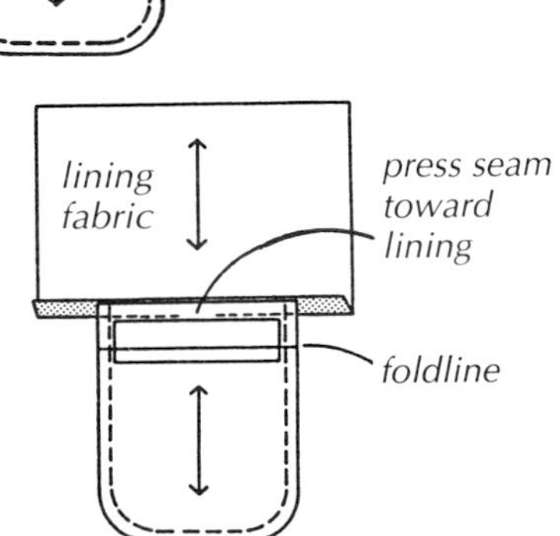

8. Fold on facing foldline and press from right side over ham to create a slightly curved edge.

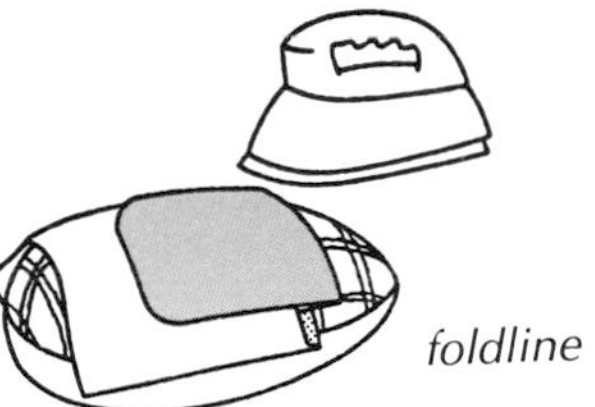

9. Pin lining to fashion fabric and cut lining exactly the same as fashion fabric pocket.

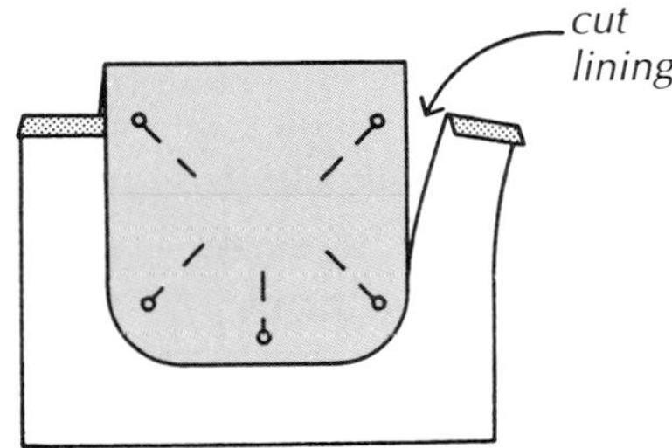

To prevent the lining from showing, you'll need to make the lining a bit smaller. How much depends on the thickness of the fashion fabric. Lay out pocket flat. With thin fashion fabric, trim away 1/16" (.15cm) from edge of lining. With thicker fashion fabric, trim away 1/8" (.3cm) from edge of lining. Taper to nothing at foldline of facing.

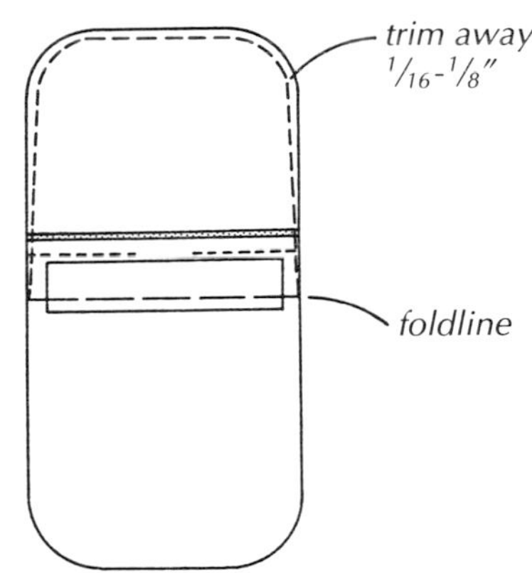

10. Fold pocket with **right sides together** matching cut edges of fabric and lining exactly. Pin at right angles to stitching line. Hand baste lining to fashion fabric **if necessary**. In some cases pinning at this stage will be sufficient.

Machine baste at 6 stitches per inch on marked stitching line.

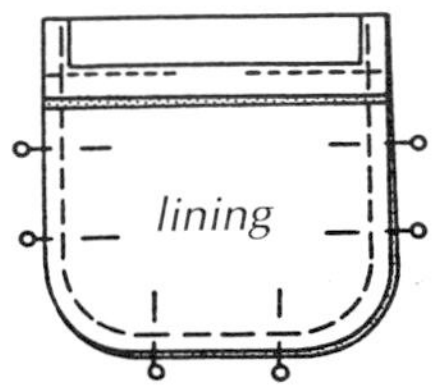

On square corners, remember to stitch 2 basting stitches across corner. This will prevent a dimple at the point.

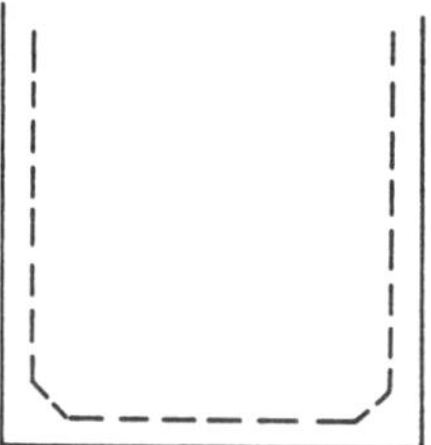

Miter both lining and fashion fabric pocket corners now before turning. (See page 66.)

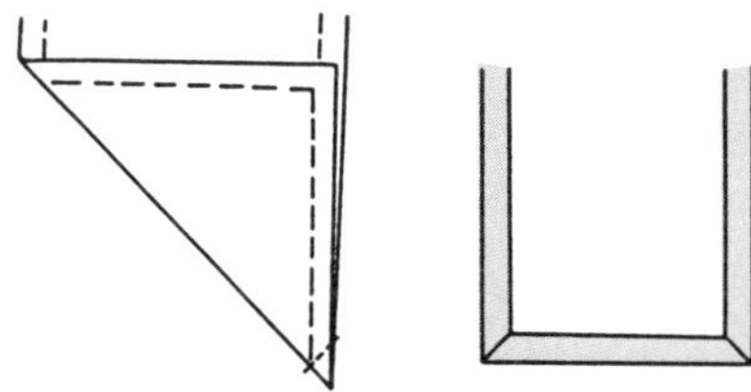

11. Press to meld machine basting stitches. Do not trim away remaining seam allowances at this time.

12. Turn pocket to the right side through opening left between facing and lining. Working first from the lining side and then from the fashion fabric side, gently press seam at right angles to the stitching line.

    Be patient! Use a damp press cloth and the tip of the iron. As you flatten the seam, use a clapper. Remember the full seam allowance is still in there.

13. Remove machine basting stitches and open pocket so that it lies flat. Remember, the machine basting was done in order to get a hard press. A slight ridge will appear on fold line at top of pocket. This is good—do not flatten.

Additional pressing of seam allowance can now be done from the right or wrong side to achieve a sharp edge on both the fashion fabric and lining. Further shrinking of the seam allowance of rounded corners can be done now. On the fashion fabric pocket, insert template under seam allowance to prevent seam from causing a ridge to show through to the right side. This also protects against shrinking the pocket itself.

Topstitching and Optional Buttonhole

Now's the time for the topstitching and to add a buttonhole if desired. See Chapter 21, page 161, for topstitching possibilities and Chapter 23, page 186, for buttonhole ideas.

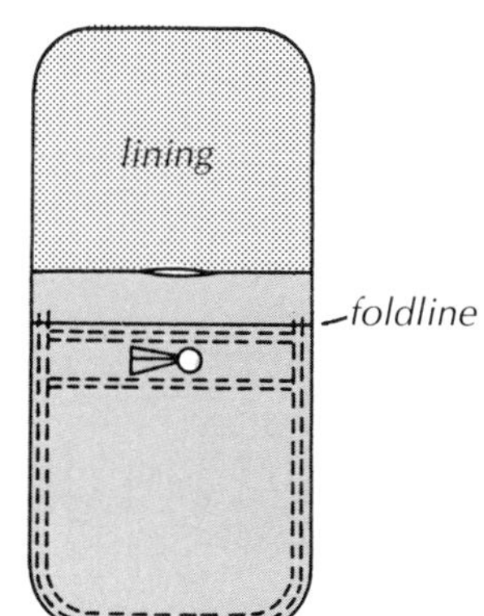

1. Topstitch fashion fabric in any way you choose (for example, single row/double row) extending stitching past fold line. Pull last stitch through to the wrong side and tie off with a square knot.

2. Make buttonhole on pocket. If buttonhole is for decorative purposes only, you do not need to make a finished opening in the facing. Sew button to outside of finished buttonhole.

3. Trim fashion fabric seam allowances close to topstitching. Do not trim lining seam allowance. Quickly slipstitch opening between facing and lining. Final press pocket.

Apply Pocket to Garment

1. Place pocket on garment, lining side down. Be sure the opening edge is not lying absolutely flat; leave a little slack so your hand can go in without stretching the pocket.

2. Pin pocket lining **only** in place on each side of opening, slipping pins under fashion fabric pocket. Flip pocket up and pin remainder of pocket lining in place. Now stitch lining to gar-

ment. Using 20 stitches per inch (8 stitches per centimeter), stitch 1/2" (1.3cm) **along foldline**, turn corner and stitch 1/2" (1.3cm) to secure corners. Then continue around pocket lining, using 12-15 stitches per inch. Finish second corner as the first, using 20 stitches per inch.

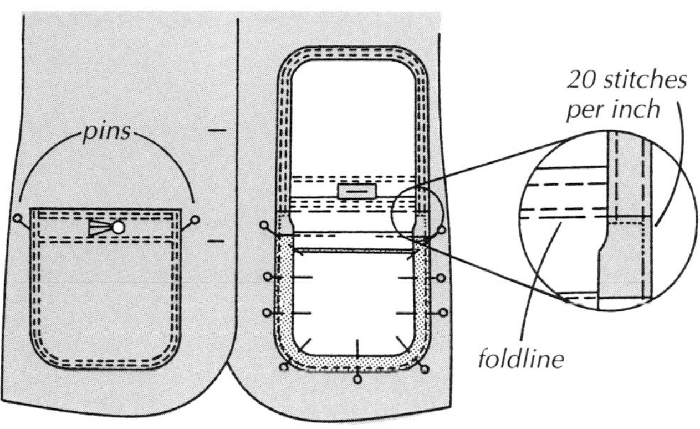

3. Press. Trim seam allowances close to stitching.

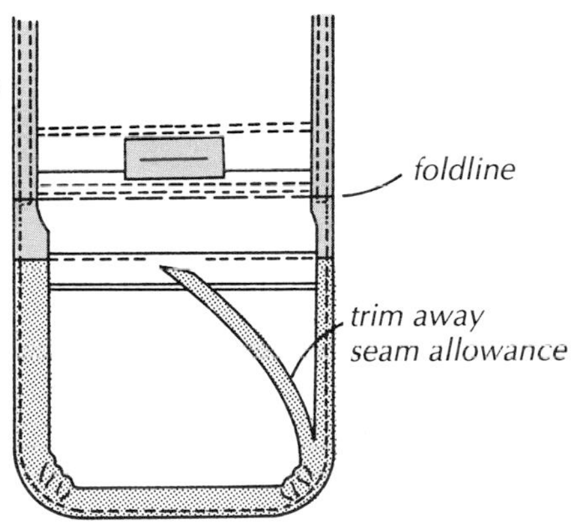

4. Fold pocket down over lining, making sure that pocket covers the lining exactly. Pin in place.

5. Hand slipstitch pocket to garment with a single thread. Be sure to slide needle to underside of pocket edge so there is no evidence of stitches.

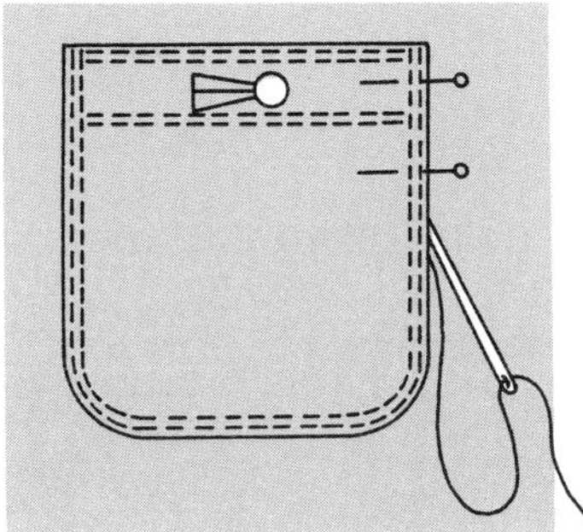

Hard-edge Welt Pocket

The hard-edge welt pocket is particularly attractive in couture sportswear. The opening created is very stable and durable. The narrow welt is created during construction and is not a separate piece. The welt can be made from the garment fabric or from a contrasting fabric. When made in a facing for an inside pocket, lining fabric can be used.

The pocket pouch can be deep or shallow. Two welt pockets add drama. Because of the construction method used, the pocket opening can be placed at any angle on a garment.

Couture Tip The measurements given here are for a 6"-wide (15cm) opening which can be **lengthened or shortened**. Shorten for a breast pocket. The depth of the pocket pouch can also vary, depending on its intended use. A breast pocket can be shallower.

1. Stabilize the wrong side of the garment where the pocket opening will be placed with a **lightweight** interfacing (fusible or stitchable) cut on the **same grain** as the garment. Cut the interfacing 2" (5cm) wide and 2" (5cm) longer than the desired finished length of the pocket opening. For a standard 6"-long (15cm) welt pocket, cut interfacing strip 2" × 8" (5cm × 20.5cm).

2. Cut two pieces of lining fabric for the pocket pouch each 6″ × 8″.

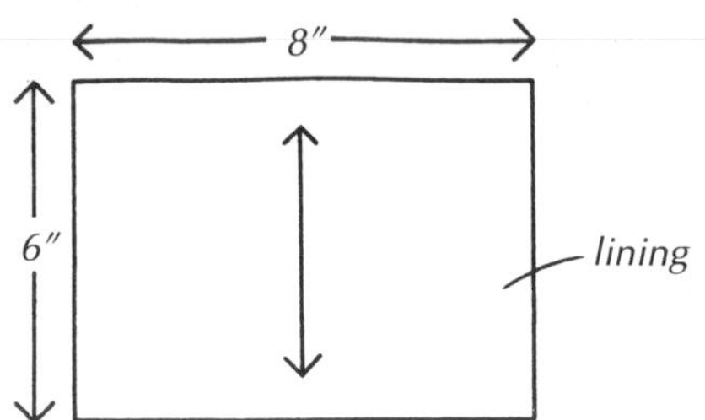

3. Cut a 3″ × 8″ (7.5cm × 20.5cm) bias piece of fabric for the welt.

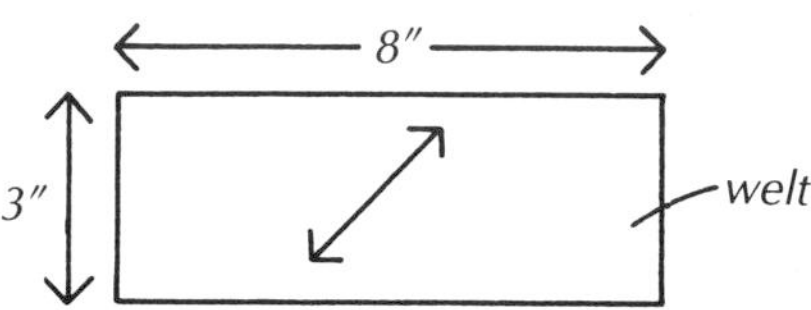

4. Cut a 2″ × 7″ (5cm × 18cm) bias piece of fairly stiff **woven** fusible interfacing.

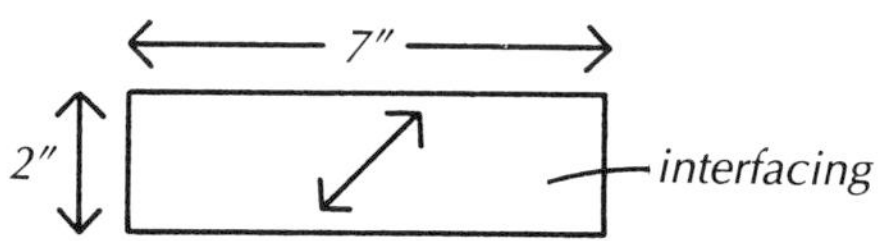

5. Draw a 6″ (15cm) long opening in center of interfacing.

6. Fuse interfacing to wrong side of welt, positioning the interfacing "off center" with a 3/8″ (1cm) seam allowance on one side, 5/8″ (1.5cm) on the other.

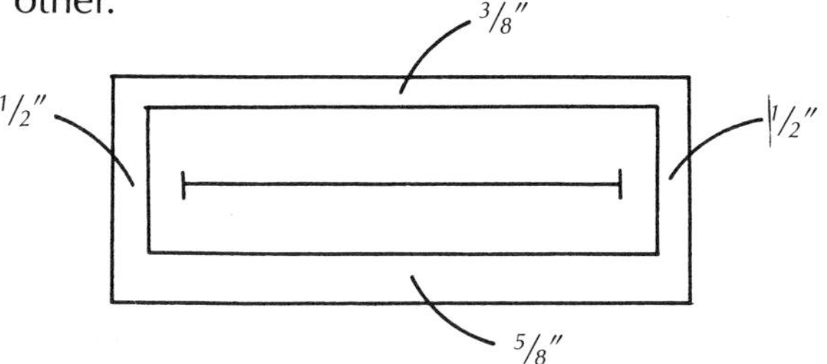

7. Fold 5/8″ (1.5cm) seam allowance toward interfacing and press **hard**. Stitch folded edge 20 stitches per inch.

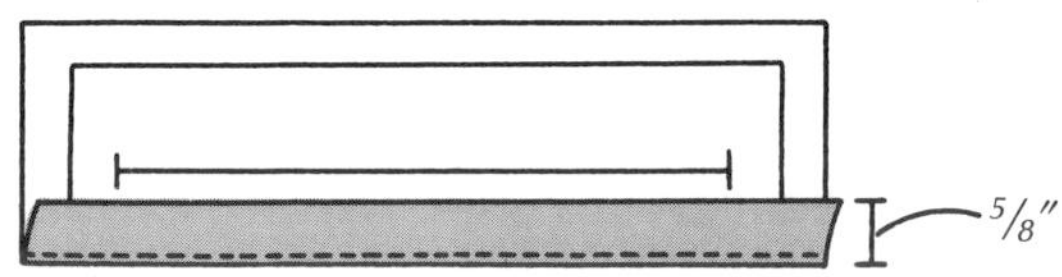

8. Place wrong side of one lining piece (pocket pouch) on **wrong side** of garment so that top of lining is 1 3/8″ (2.8cm) above pocket opening. Place welt on **right side** of garment with opening line directly over marked opening line on garment.

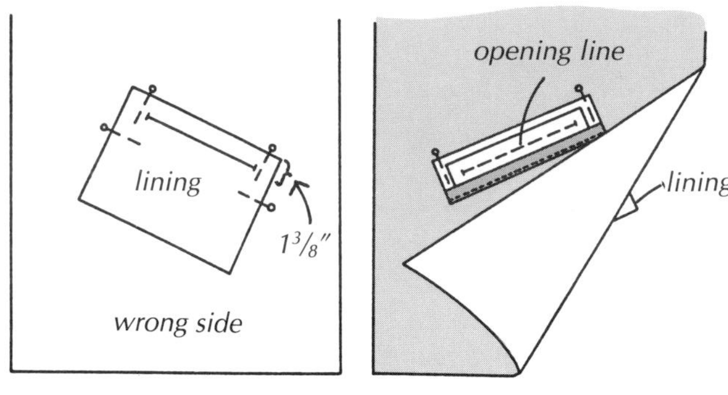

9. Hand baste together through all thicknesses on marked opening line. Thread-baste across ends.

10. Using 20 stitches per inch, stitch 1/8″ (.3cm) from marked opening line to create a 1/4″ (.6cm) "box."

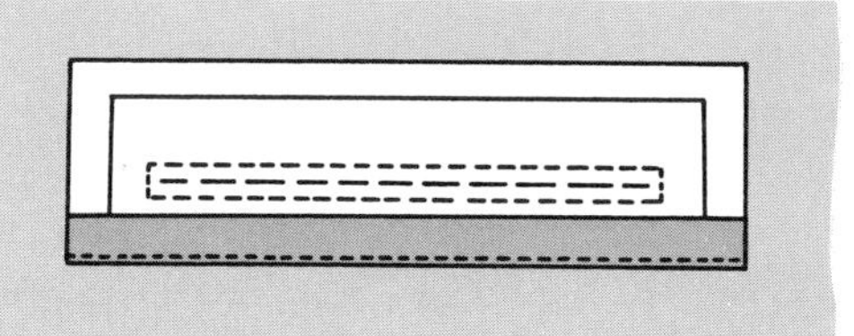

11. Cut **exactly** on center line of box through all thicknesses and into each corner.

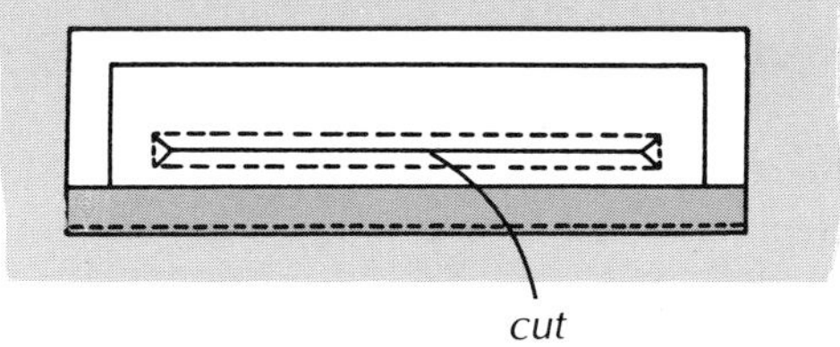

12. Pull welt through hole to wrong side. Press, allowing each 1/8″ (.3cm) seam allowance to act as a "lip."

13. Diagonally whipstitch lips together.

14. From right side, stitch 20 stitches per inch 1/8″ (.3cm) away from welt on both ends and lower edge. Leave tails.

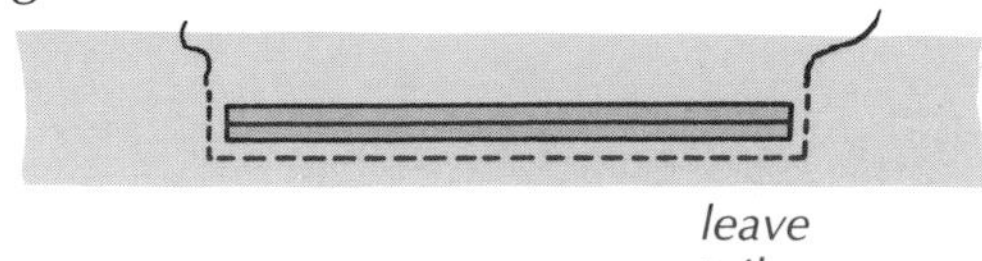

15. On inside of garment, place remaining pocket pouch on top of first **right sides together**. Pin all raw edges together.

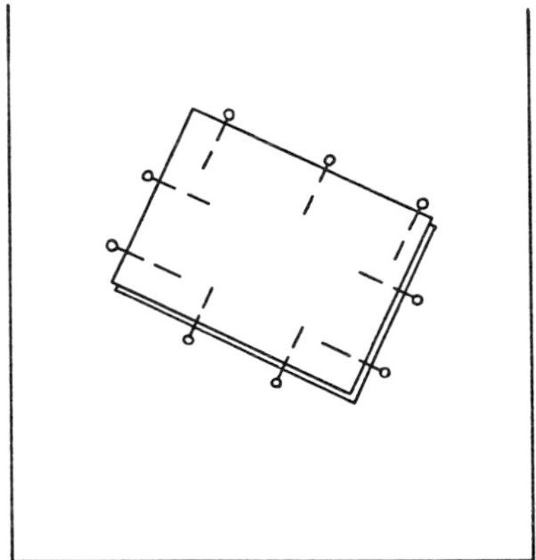

16. From right side, stitch through all thicknesses 1/8" (.3cm) from top of welt, finishing the box. Leave tails.

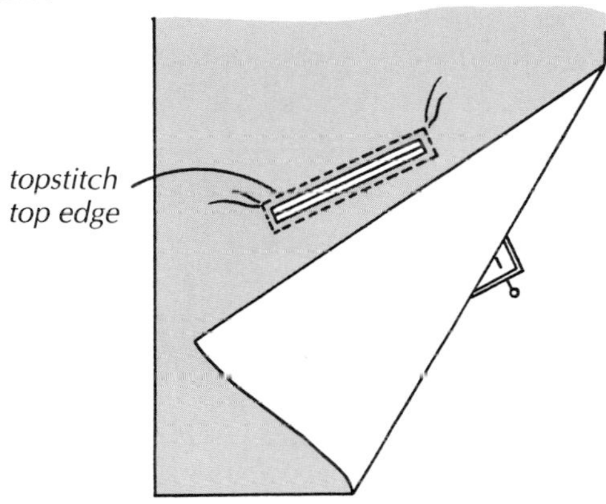

17. Now check your thread tails. This is the KEY to perfection. Look at the topstitching. If a row was started one stitch short, thread the tail into a needle and sew a stitch until rows meet at corners. If you stitched too far, pull out a stitch. When perfect, pull all threads to the wrong side and tie off, one knot for each thread.

18. On **wrong side** of garment, stitch pocket pouches together using 1/2" (1.3cm) wide seam allowances, rounding bottom corners.

Circular Pocket

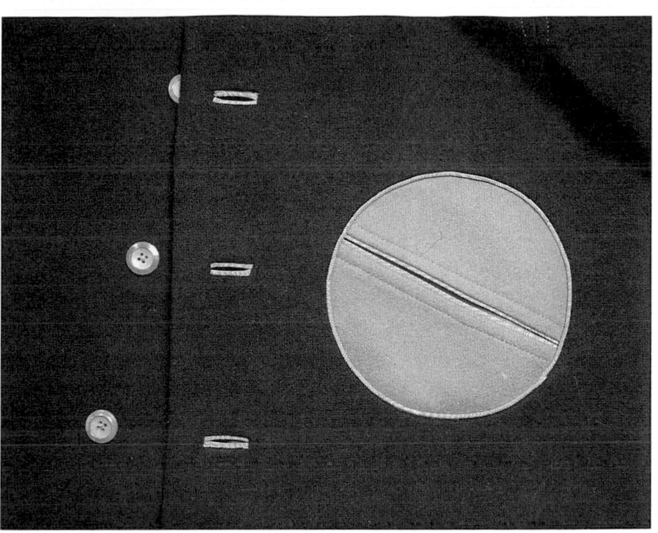

Couture details always look remarkable in the finished garment. Many times they look difficult, but in reality most are easy to construct if you know how. That sounds funny as I write it, but it's true. Such is the case with circular pockets. Understanding the basic concept and construction gives you the freedom to create.

First, read this section in its entirety to grasp an overall understanding of the concept. As a couture student, I am sure your mind will be racing with ideas. The possibilities for using circular pockets are limitless.

You may want to try the pocket in paper first. It's a quick and visual way to understand each of the components. Glue together different colors for garment, insert, and pocket pouch. Cut and glue-stick together rather than stitch.

Anatomy of a Circular Pocket

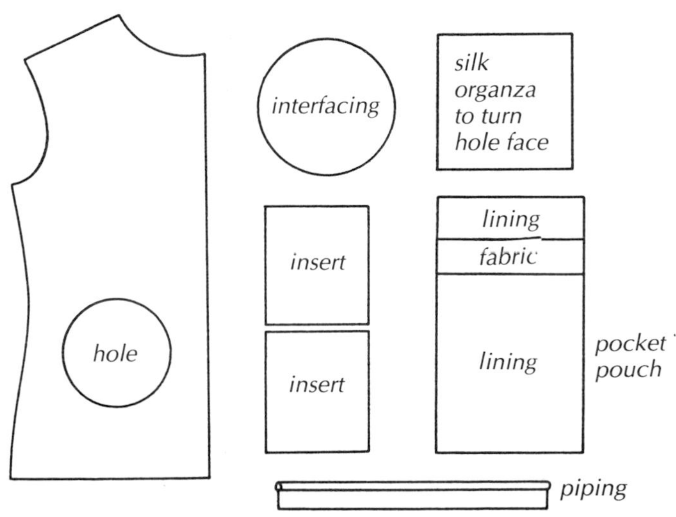

Circular Pocket Construction

1. Prepare the opening. Interface the garment on the wrong side where the circle will to be made. This can be done with fusible interfacing (if it doesn't show through) or with a piece of sew-in interfacing cross- basted to the garment. Interfacing will automatically be secured when stitching the pocket. Cut the interfacing with a diameter 4″ greater than the desired diameter of the finished circlular pocket opening and on the same grain as the garment. The interfacing also prevents pocket show-through to the outside of the garment.

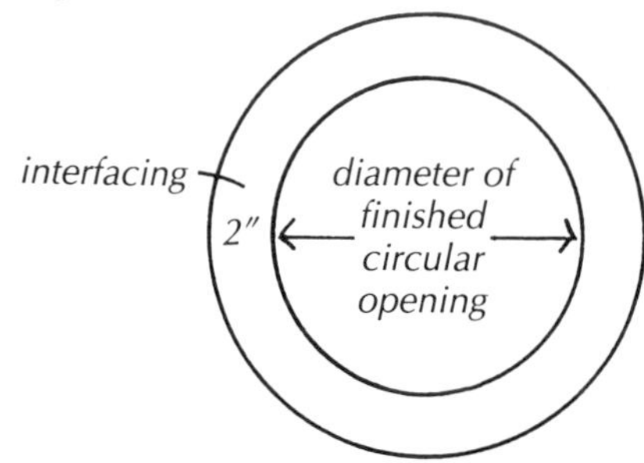

2. Draw a circle on the right side of the fashion fabric exactly where the pocket is to be located, making it the exact size desired.

COUTURE Tip If you want the outside edge piped, attach piping now. (See Applying Piping, page 94.) Place piping with cording outside of the circle and the raw edges to the inside. Overlap to join in lower left hand edge of circle. Using zipper foot, machine stitch piping in place.

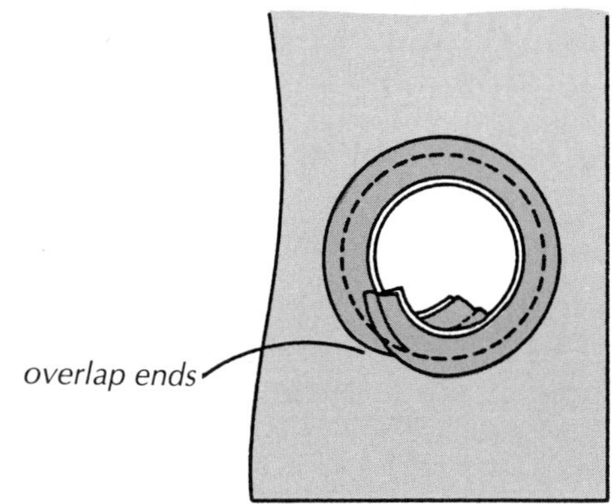

3. Cut a square of silk organza **at least** 3″ (7.5cm) larger on all sides than the circle and place over the marked circle on the **right side** of fabric. Thread trace the circle stitching line.

4. Machine stitch on circle, using 15-18 stitches per inch. If the pocket has been piped, use zipper foot for this step.

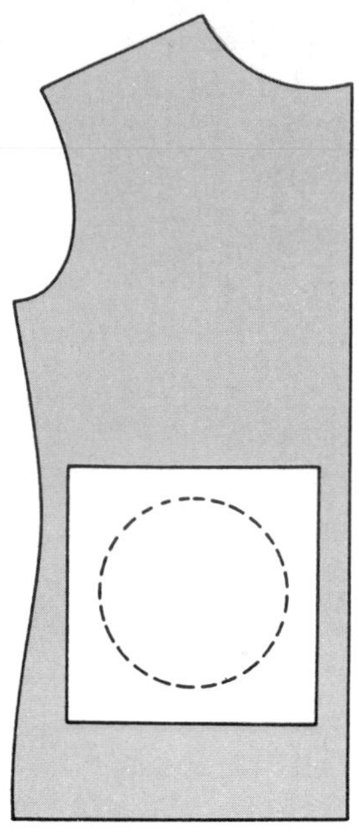

5. Cut through organza and fashion fabric in wedges like a pie, cutting to, but not through stitching. If a large circle, the center can be removed first.

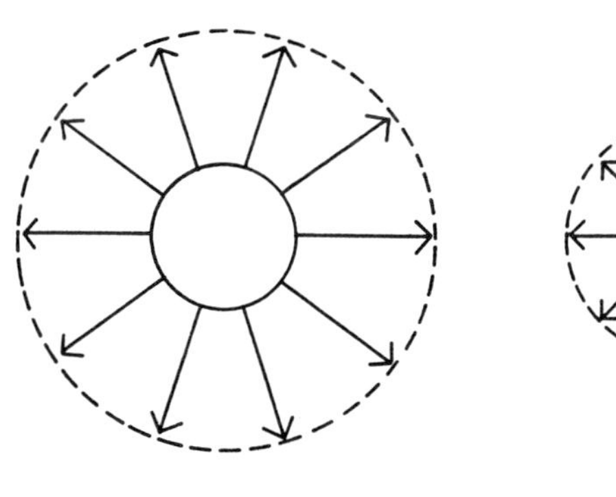

6. Turn organza through opening to wrong side and press, gently at first, then hard to create a sharply pressed edge. You have created a **faced hole** in the garment.

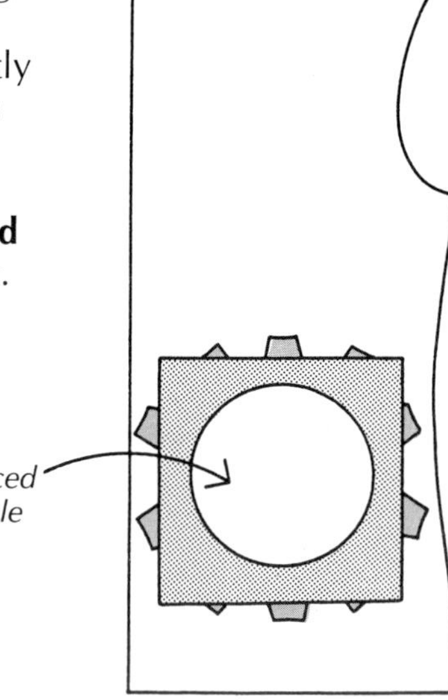

Make Circular Pocket Insert

The insert is made in two sections which will be centered in the circle to create a pocket opening. Make the pocket insert of your choice. (See instructions for variations on page 178.)

COUTURE Tip The opening can be parallel to the hem or at an angle.

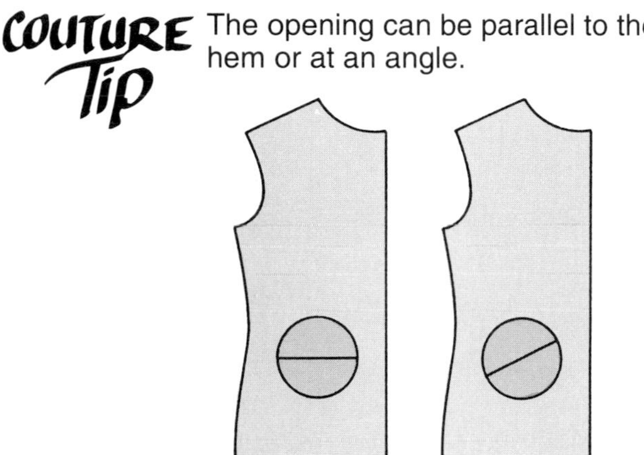

1. Cut two **squares** of fabric, each 2″ (5cm) wider than the diameter of the hole you've created in the garment.

2. Interface the **wrong side** of what will become the outside of the insert, extending interfacing past the fold $^{5}/_{8}$″ (1.5cm).

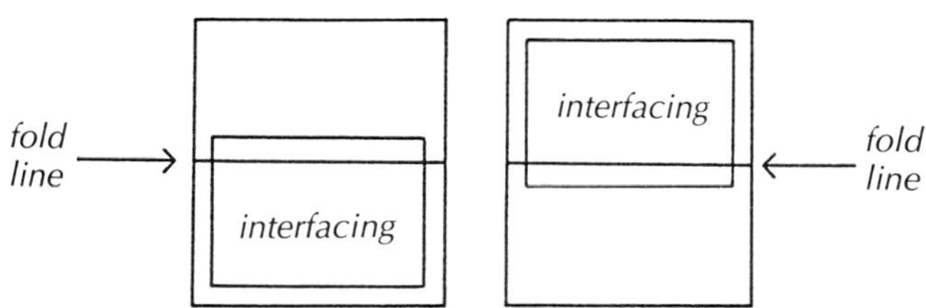

3. Fold each square in half and press. From the right side, topstitch 3-4 rows starting at the fold. Two rows of traditional topstitching can also be used to create a welt look.

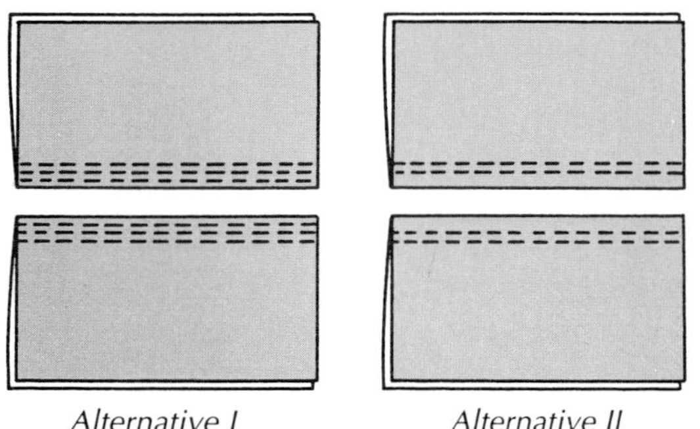

4. Butt folded edges together; diagonally whipstitch to hold. Then hand baste around all outside edges.

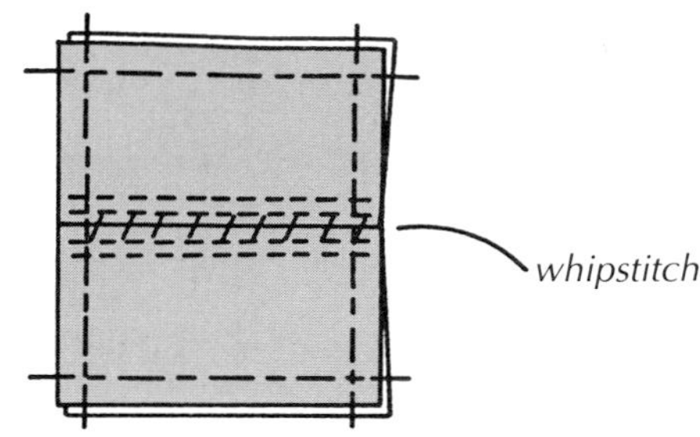

5. Place insert under the hole in the garment and slipstitch in place from the right side, making sure pocket opening (insert) is centered in circle. Remove pins before machine stitching.

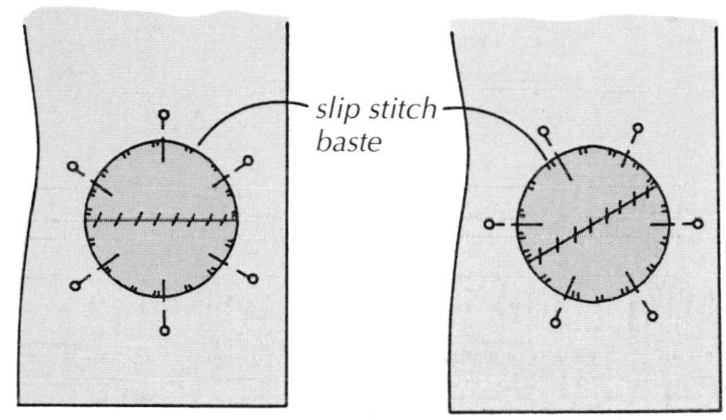

6. From the inside machine stitch around edge of circle using a **zipper foot**. Lift the garment away from the pocket and stitch around circle through little pie shape wedges and the insert. This is relatively easy to do. Just be patient and sew slowly.

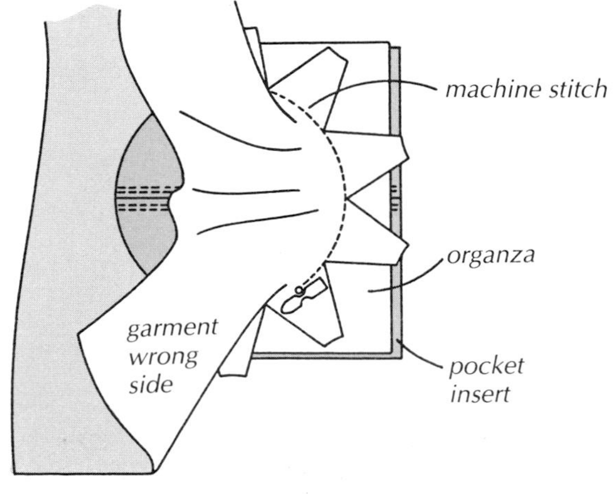

7. Remove basting stitches.

Make a Pocket Pouch

Create the pocket pouch and the back of the pocket in one piece as shown. The pocket pouch is one long strip cut from lining. The fabric directly behind the pocket opening will be seen from the outside; therefore, a strip of fashion fabric will be attached in that area.

1. For pocket pouch, cut a piece of silk lining fabric 2″ (5cm) wider than pocket hole and long enough to fold back on itself making a pouch.

2. Sew one end of silk strip to bottom of insert.

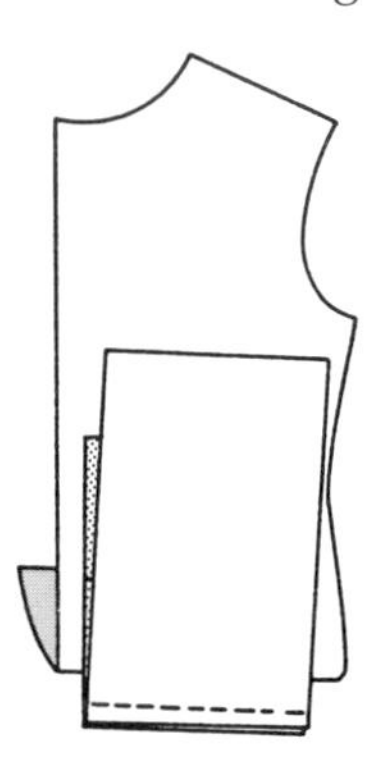

3. Fold so that raw edge of pouch (silk) matches top edge of insert. Press the fold.

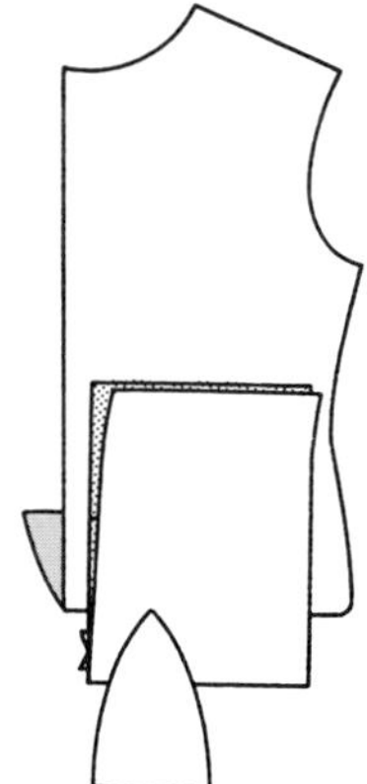

4. Mark location of pocket opening on silk; cover this line with a 2″ (5cm) strip of fashion fabric. Topstitch or zigzag in place.

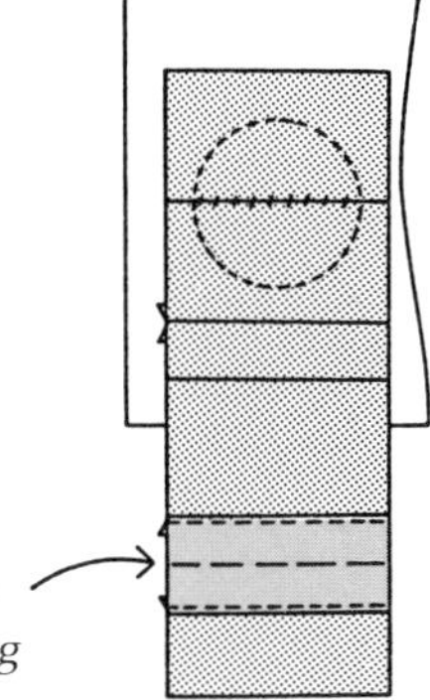

5. Re-place raw edge of pouch on top edge of insert and pin all edges together.

6. Machine stitch $^5/_8$″ (1.5cm) from raw edge rounding corners.

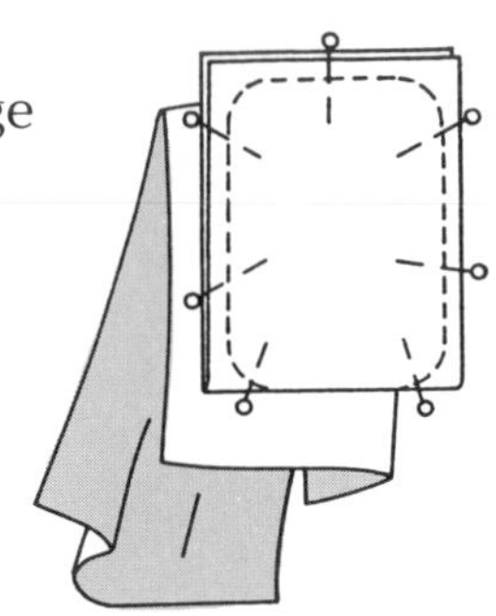

7. Grade seams: seam to outside to $^1/_2$″ (1.3cm); seam nearer body to $^3/_8$″ (1cm).

Variations of Pocket Inserts

The insert can be made with or without a seam in the opening edges, and with or without piping or topstitching. The fabric can be cut on a grain different from the garment to highlight a print or stripe. The insert for a large circle should be interfaced.

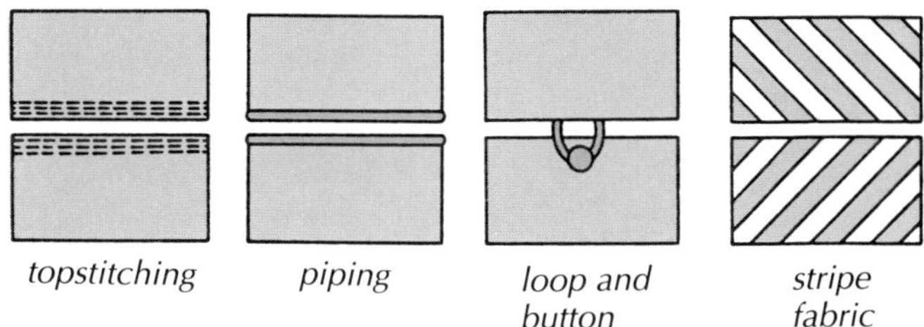

Piped Insert

1. Cut four pieces of fabric, each 2″ (5cm) wider than circle diameter and half of circle diameter + 1$^5/_8$″ (4cm) in length. This provides for a $^5/_8$″ (1.5cm) seam allowance on edge that will become the opening.

2. Sew piping to the right side of one edge of two of the pocket pieces.

3. Interface the remaining two pocket pieces.

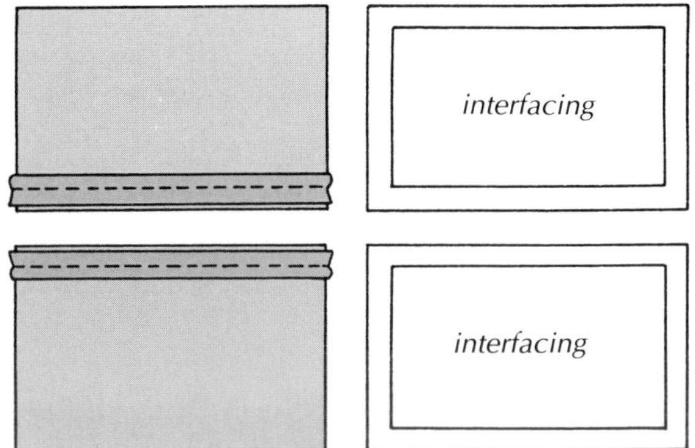

4. Stitch interfaced piece to piped piece, right sides together.

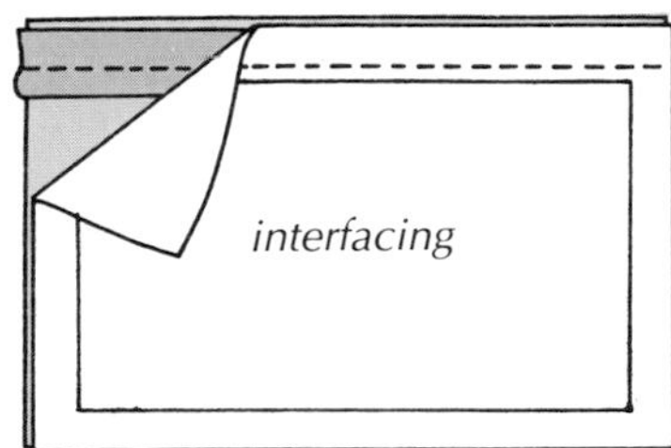

5. Press to meld stitches. Press seams open, then closed. Grade seams, but **do not** grade piping. Press with heavy duty press cloth.

6. Hand baste raw edges together.

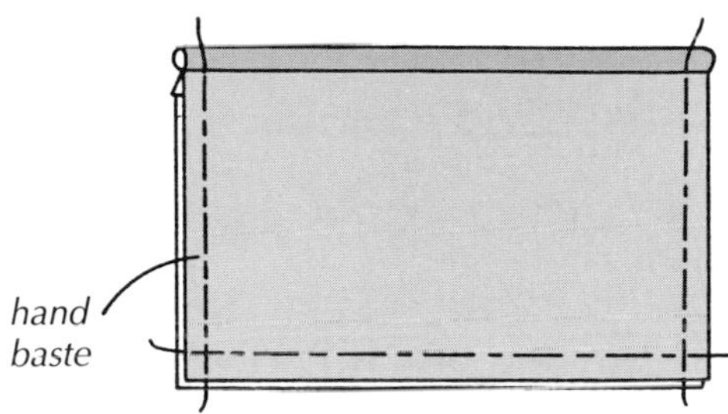

7. Butt piped edges together and diagonally whipstitch together.

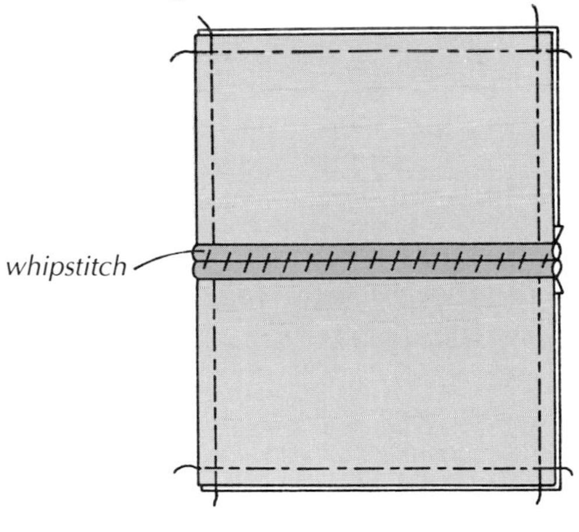

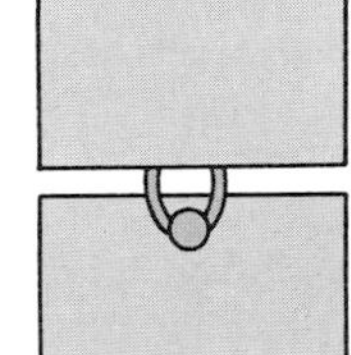

Button and Loop Insert

This variation is a good choice when the circular pocket is large, as in a coat. The loop and button prevent any possible gaping.

The insert edges can be piped or not depending on the design and the desired finished effect.

1. Following the instructions for the piped insert, cut and interface your pocket pieces.

2. Center a piece of cording to form a loop to fit the button on **right side** of one pocket edge and permanently stitch to seam allowance using 20 stitches per inch. (See Tiny Loops, page 60.)

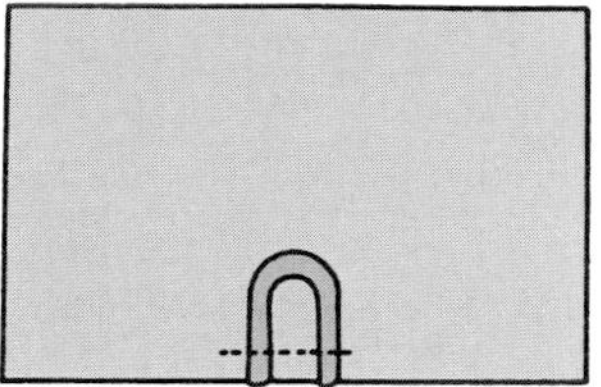

3. Complete both halves of pocket as in piped insert.

4. Butt center edges together, diagonally whipstitch and baste outer edges.

5. Sew button in place on lower half of pocket insert.

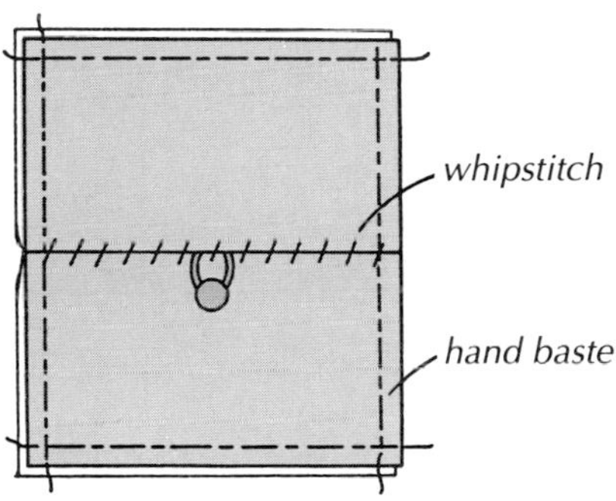

Designer Inserts

Now that you understand the concept, design your own inserts. For example, cut pocket on the bias from a plaid or stripe to create interest. Or, use a contrasting color or type of fabric or a print for the insert. Make parallel rows of tiny tucks throughout the pocket insert fabric before cutting the insert.

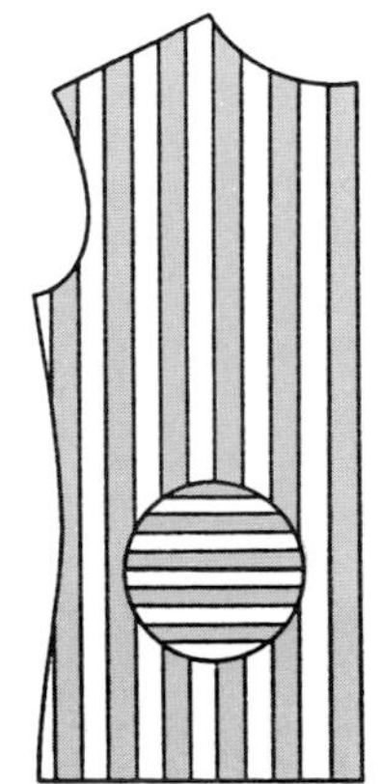

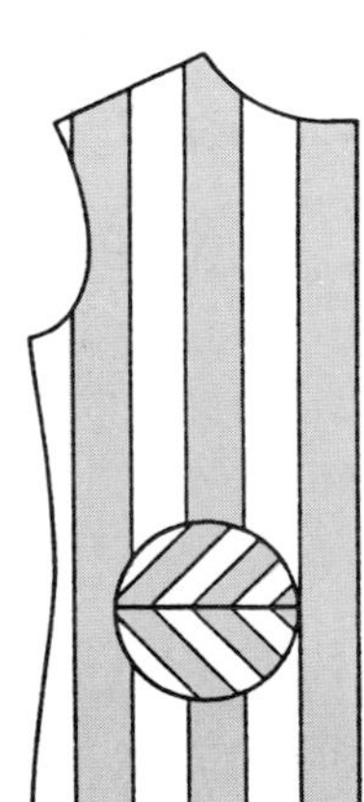

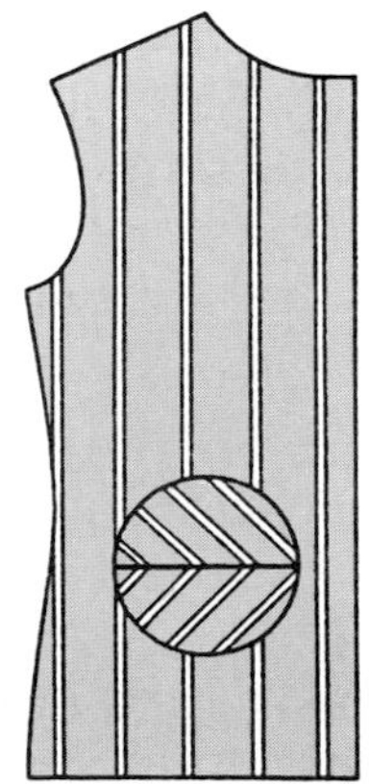

COUTURE Tip The technique of creating a circular pocket can be used to make a circular buttonhole. Any geometric shape is fair game when using this technique, whether for a pocket or buttonhole. However, it is not the best method for making a "triangular" buttonhole (page 188) as it leaves the points too fragile. Be creative! Experiment! And, always make a **test sample**.

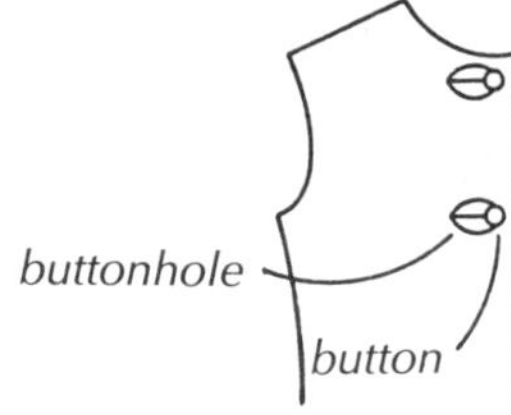

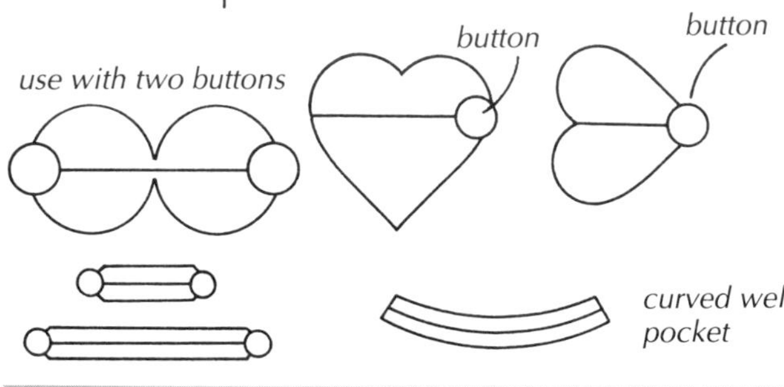

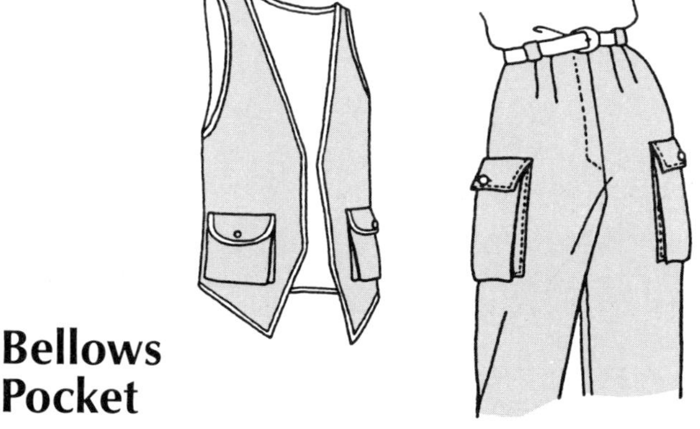

Bellows Pocket

A pleated bellows pocket lends itself to casual couture. It is often seen in couture clothes when a safari look is in fashion. It lies flat against the garment, but can expand because of pleats on the **sides and bottom**. Ideal for travel clothes, a bellows pocket is equally wonderful in sophisticated sportswear.

A pocket flap keeps the pocket closed and can be made with or without a button and buttonhole. Flap shapes can be varied, piped, or cut on any grain to achieve a particular effect.

A bellows pocket without a flap can be secured with a button on the garment and a buttonhole in the pocket. A triangular buttonhole in the flap would be the ultimate. (See Triangular Buttonholes page 188.)

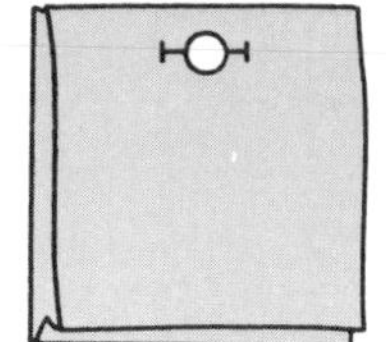
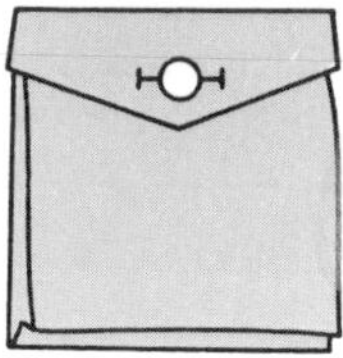
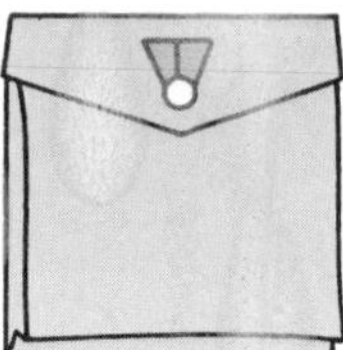

A bellows pocket can be small or large, but a primary consideration is the thickness of the fabric. Because a pleat is the design detail and there are three thicknesses of fabric plus a seam allowance on the sides and bottom of this pocket, it is best to choose a lightweight fabric or one that can be given a hard press.

Use interfacing to stabilize the opening edge and/or the flap as the fabric requires. The pocket opening edge should be firm but not bulky.

The first step in developing a bellows pocket is to make a pattern. Decide on the size of the pocket and the width of bellow (pleat). An attractive pocket is slightly longer than it is wide, for example, 6" (15cm) wide and 7" (18cm) long. To allow room to expand without becoming bulky or unmanageable, plan on a 1½"-wide (3.8cm) bellow (pleat).

Draft the pocket pattern on graph paper using a see-through lined ruler to keep all lines very straight and **exact**. This is what the final pattern will look like.

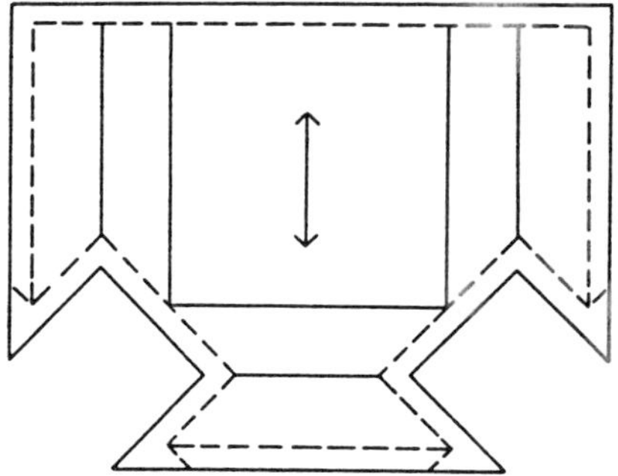

Draft the Pocket Pattern

1. Draw pocket in desired size extending opening edge line (A-A[1]).

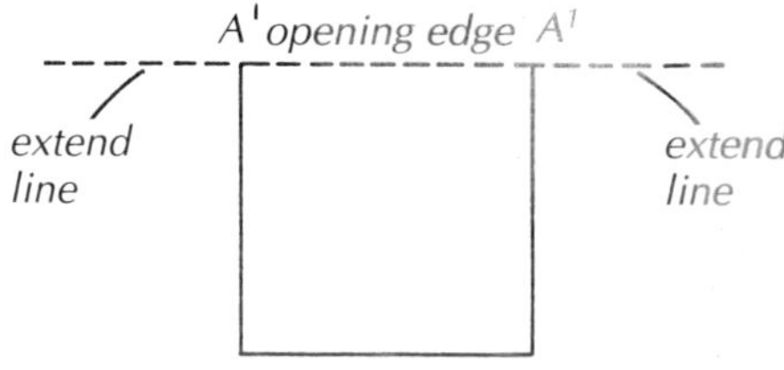

2. Draw a true bias line across lower corners (B,B^1).

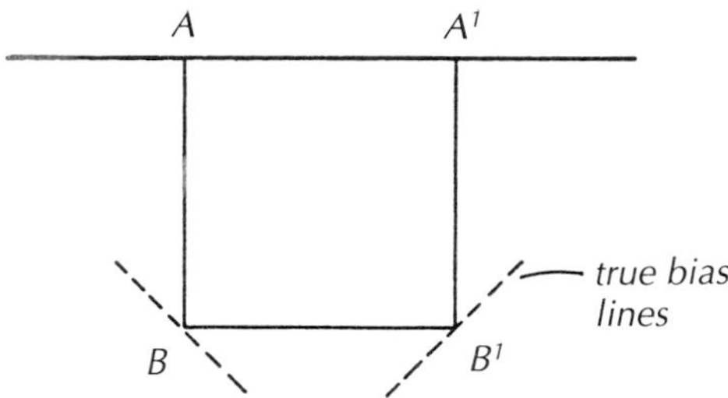

3. Draw 2 lines 1½" (3.8cm) away from and parallel to the pocket sides (C,C^1) and bottom of pocket D.

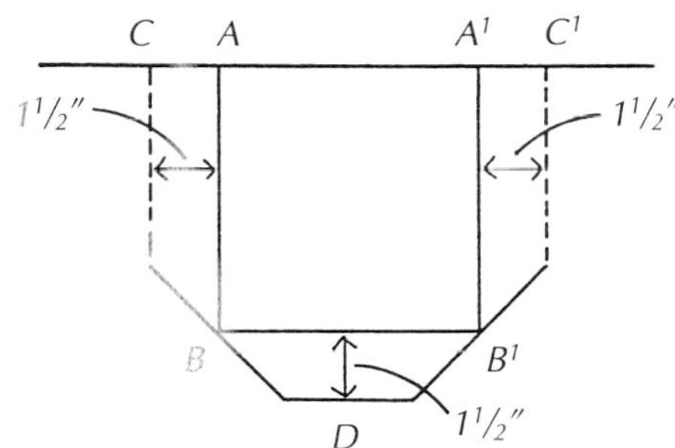

4. Draw additional lines 1½" (3.8cm) from lines C and C^1 and D and parallel to pocket sides (E,E^1) and bottom of pocket (F).

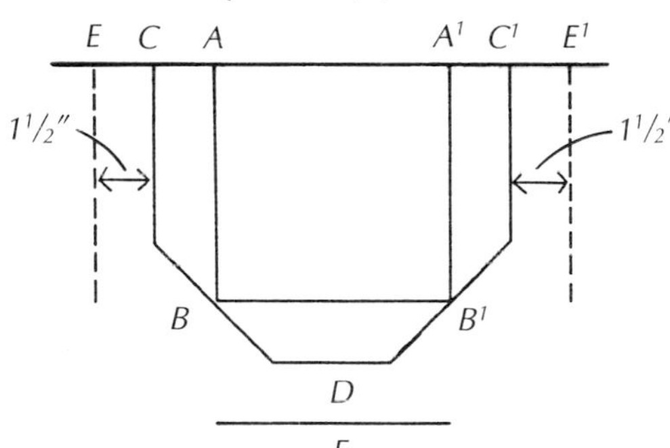

5. Draw two lines (legs) at right angles to lines B and B^1 connecting with E and E^1, and bottom F.

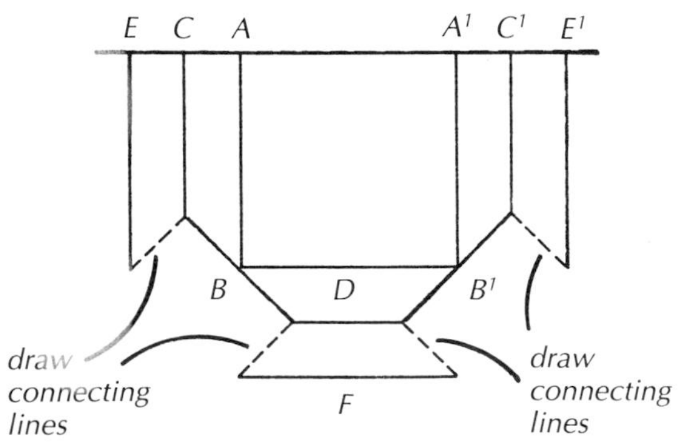

6. Add ½" (1.3cm) seam allowances to all edges. Indicate miter line in seam allowance as shown.

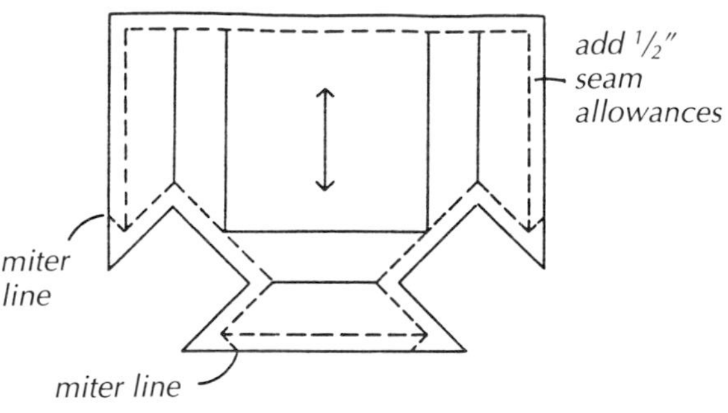

7. Indicate inner and outer fold lines on pattern.

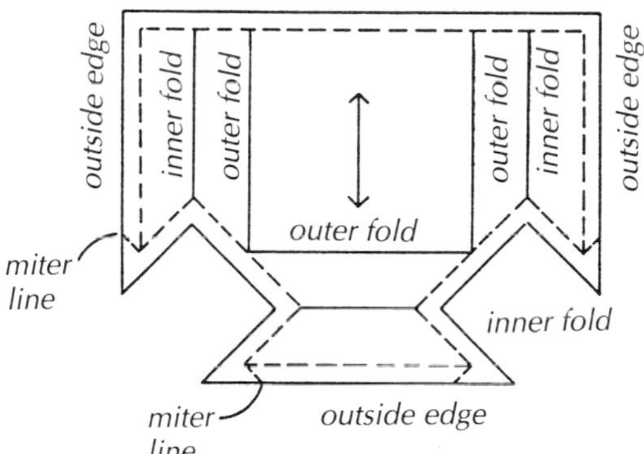

Draft the Flap Pattern

Although the flap can be designed in many shapes, traditional proportions are given here.

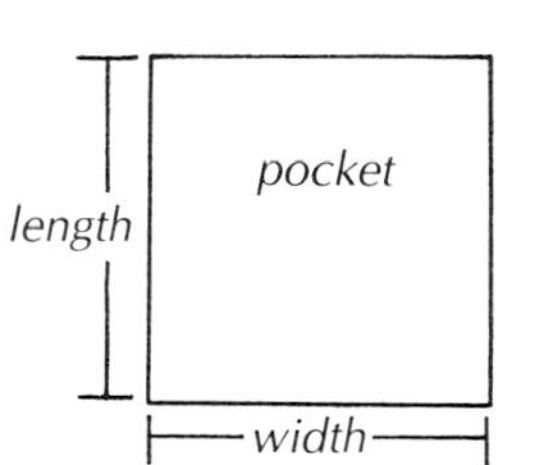

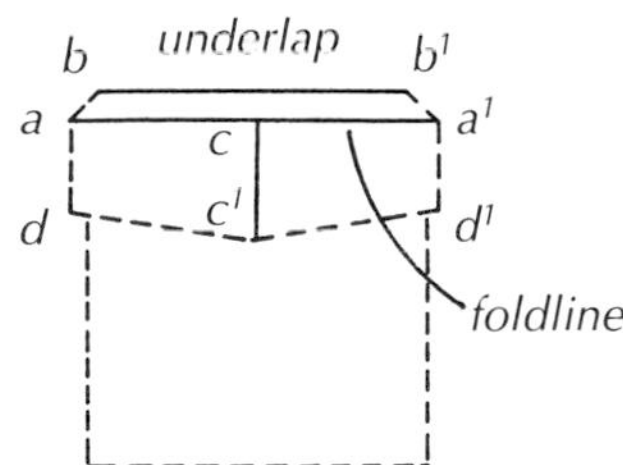

1. Draw fold line the width of pocket **plus** 1/4" (a-a').
2. Draw underlap the width of pocket **minus** ¼" (.6cm) and ½" (1.3cm) above opening edge (b-b^1).
3. Make the distance to point of flap one third the length of the pocket (c-c^1).
4. Make the sides one quarter the length of the pocket (a-d, a^1-d^1).
5. Add seam allowances to all sides except underlap edge.

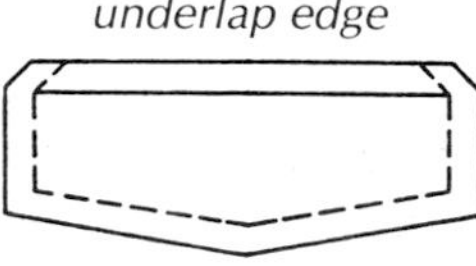

To Cut and Stitch Flap

1. To cut flap, place underlap edge on fold of fabric. This eliminates a seam here and keeps pocket from getting too bulky at the opening.

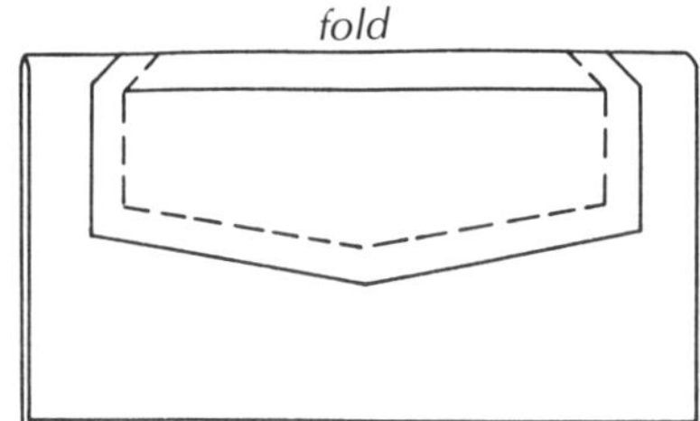

2. With right sides together machine stitch flap edges together and leave an opening for turning. Stitch 2 stitches across corners.

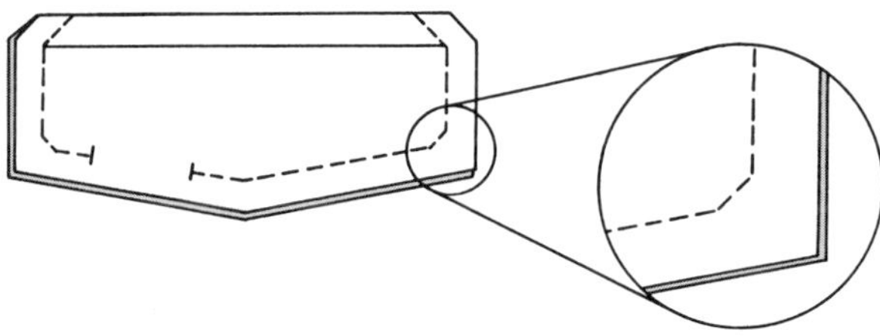

3. Trim seam allowance at all points.

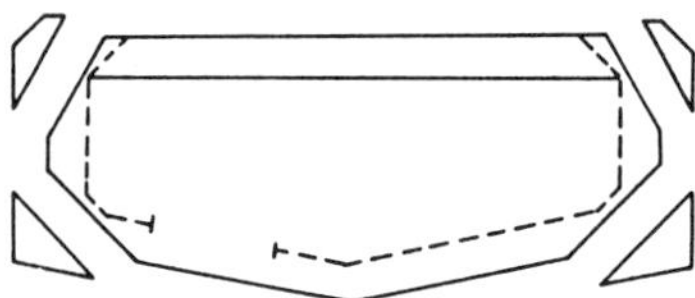

4. Meld, turn and press flap. Quickly slipstitch opening for turning. Press again from right side over a ham to create a slight curve in the finished flap.

Note: The flap can be interfaced, if desired, on the front side. It can be topstitched for emphasis. A bound buttonhole must be made prior to stitching the flap together. A machine buttonhole can be made after flap is constructed.

To Cut and Construct Bellows Pocket

1. With fabric perfectly on grain, cut pocket and transfer all fold lines and stitching lines. Chalk and thread trace with silk thread for maximum accuracy.

2. Interface the pocket section only, not the bellows.

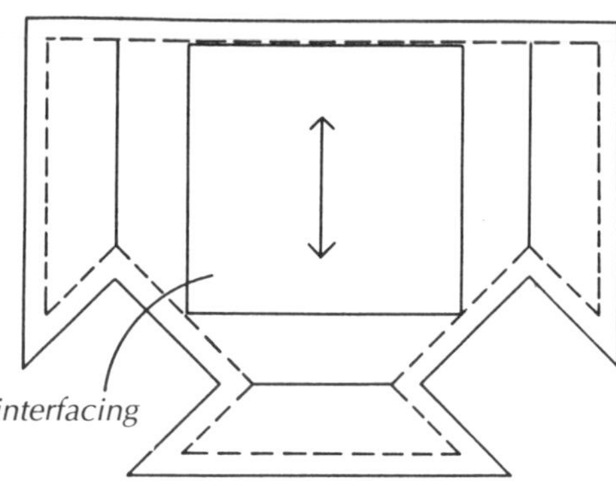

3. Face the opening edge with lining or self-fabric (if not too bulky). Turn to inside and press. Trim. As an alternative finish, turn under the top edge of the pocket and topstitch. This is especially appropriate for tightly woven cottons.

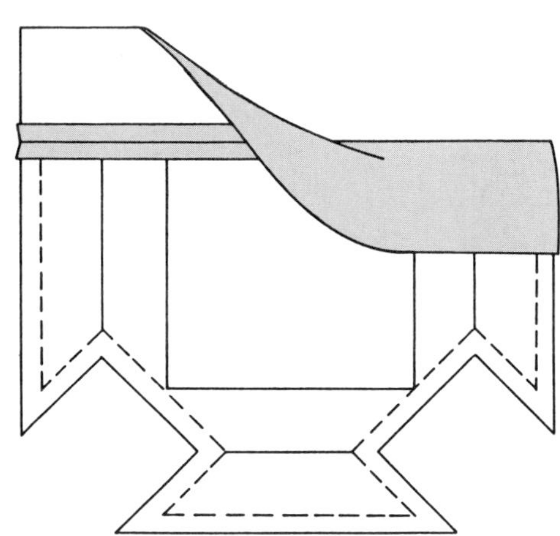

4. If no flap is being used, make a buttonhole in the pocket now.

5. Fold side edge to bottom, right sides together, (line E aligns with line F). Machine stitch corners using 20 stitches per inch. Clip to inner corner. Trim seam allowances at points. Press seams open over point presser. Trim seams to $^1/_4$″ (.6cm). Repeat on other half of pocket.

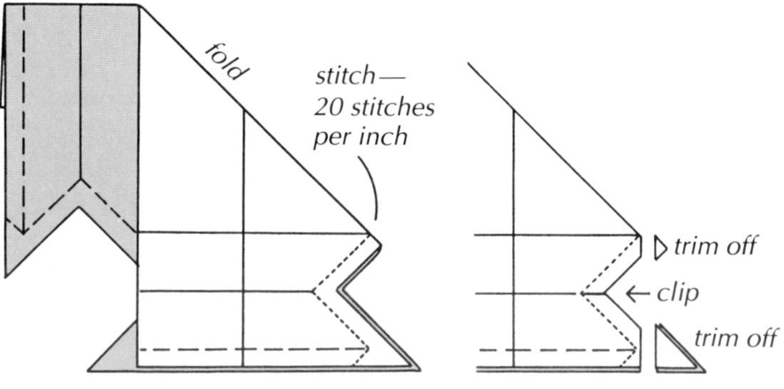

6. Turn carefully and press seam allowances at outside edges to the inside at sides and bottom.

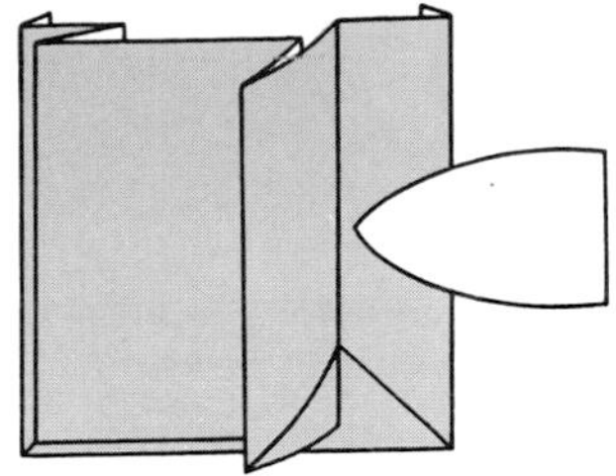

7. Fold on outer fold lines of original pocket and press hard. Match outer folds of pocket to outside edges and press again. This creates the inner fold.

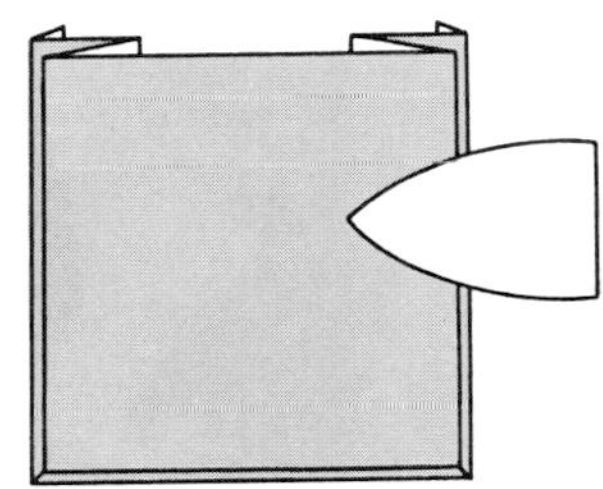

8. Attach flap first, stitching along edge and along fold line.

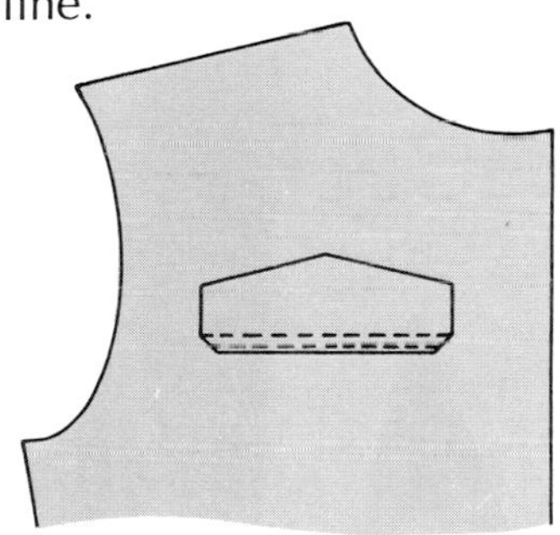

9. Place pocket on garment with opening edge just touching the flap edge. Lift bellows pleat out of the way and edgestitch pocket in place, using 15-20 stitches per inch.

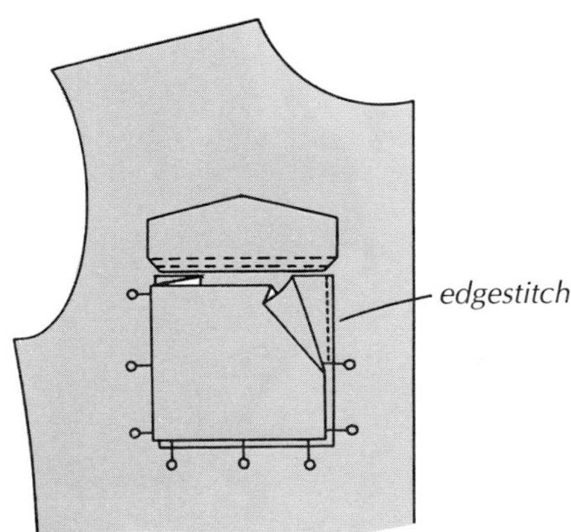

10. Turn flap down onto pocket and press with press cloth.

The original pocket can be made with additional detail and the pleats sewn on as separate pieces.

Caution: When cutting pocket apart, be sure to add $1/2''$ seam allowances. Stitch and press toward center of pocket. Pocket should be flat and look exactly like the original pattern before starting the step-by-step construction.

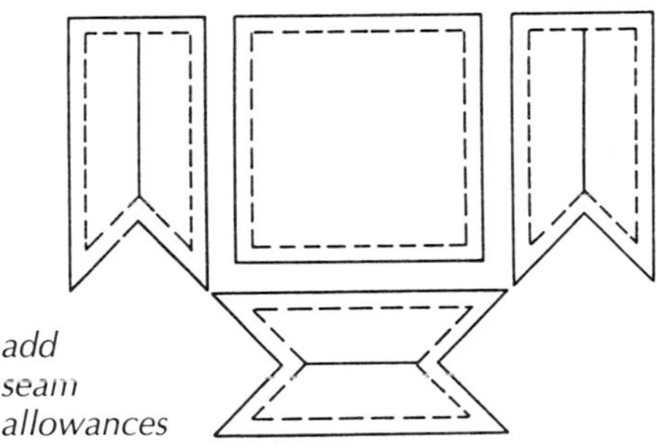

Let your creativity flow!

Here are some ideas for starters:

A slot seam (see page 164) could be used in the center of the original pocket.

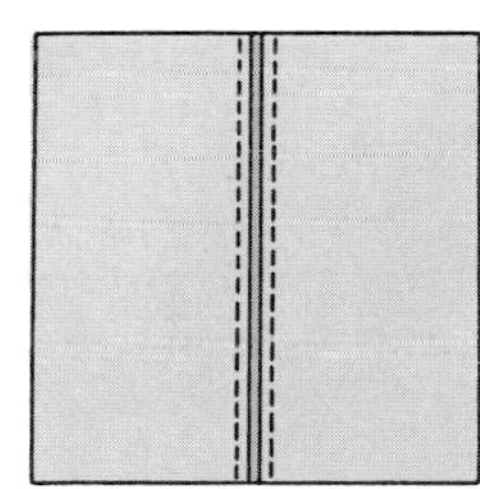

An additional box pleat can be added to the original pocket first.

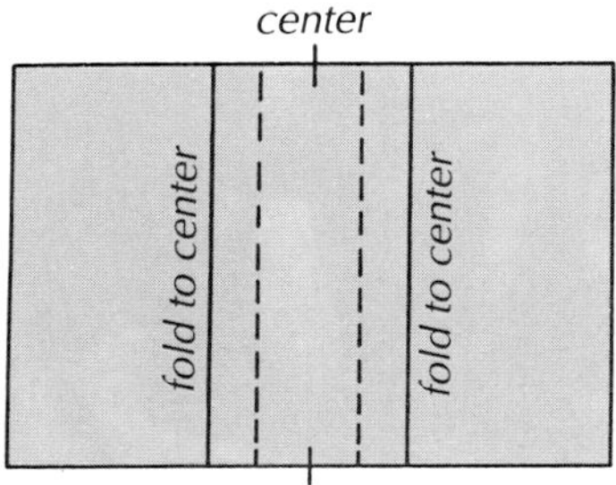

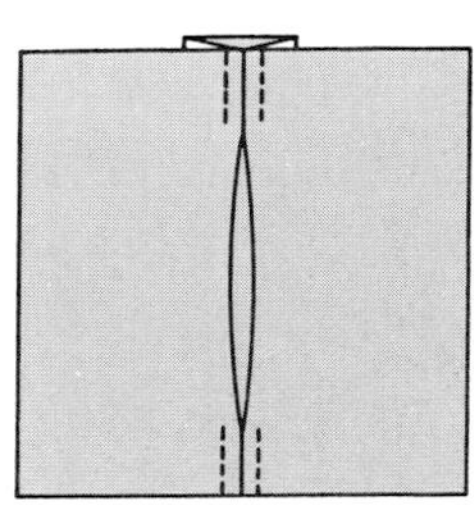

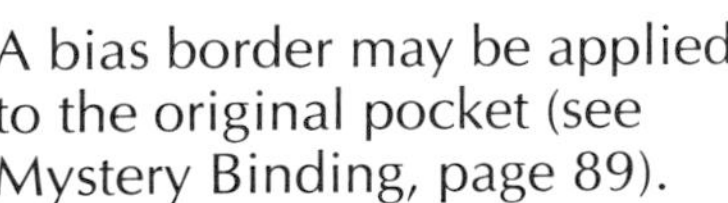

A bias border may be applied to the original pocket (see Mystery Binding, page 89).

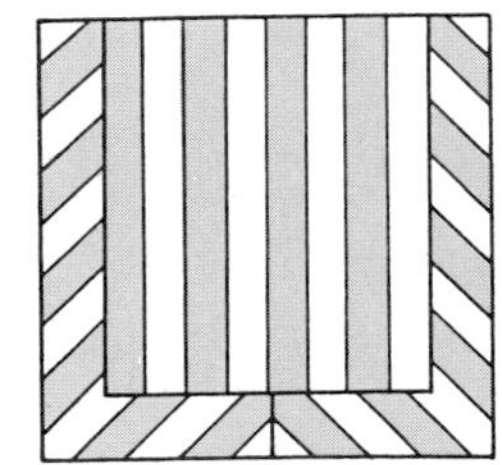

CHAPTER 23

Buttonholes

Let's talk about buttonholes. In The Couture, details often distinguish a garment as couture rather than pret-a-porter (ready-to-wear). It is clearly the difference between custom and manufactured.

Without a doubt, the cost of meticulous buttonholes, as labor intensive as they are, prevents manufacturers from including these fine details in most ready-to-wear.

Here's where the home sewer and dressmaker can add beautiful details and, in fact, become a designer by incorporating special buttonholes in a garment.

A bound buttonhole is made of fabric, can take a variety of shapes and with some methods can be made long enough to be used as a welt pocket. No matter what the shape of the opening, it is formed by two pieces of fabric called lips which allow a button or, in the case of a pocket, a hand to pass through easily.

Bound buttonholes offer limitless possibilities for design as the fabric used for the buttonhole itself need not be the same as the garment. Drama can be achieved by using a contrasting color or a completely different fabric for the buttonhole lips.

Interfacing for Buttonholes

Always interface behind a buttonhole for stability and durability no matter what method or design placement you use.

If sew-in interfacing has been used it will already be in place in the garment. This is particularly true in tailored garments.

If the fabric can tolerate fusible interfacing without show-through, fuse to the wrong side of the garment.

If fusible interfacing has been used on only the facing piece, you must add interfacing to the garment behind each buttonhole location for support. After testing to make sure you don't get show-through, fuse a circle or oval piece of interfacing behind each buttonhole location. If your garment **cannot** tolerate fusible on the garment, use sew-in interfacing and baste it in place.

Always cut interfacing on the same grain as the garment.

Buttonhole Lips

The buttonhole method used will determine whether or not you can interface the lips. Fabric for the buttonhole lips must be pre-shrunk and grained-up.

Caution: It is imperative that fabric for bound buttonhole lips be perfectly on grain before buttonhole lips are cut out, even if it was grained-up prior to cutting out the garment.

Buttonhole Placement

Buttons are measured in lines. A line 40 button is 1″ (2.5cm) in diameter; a line 20 button ½″ (1.3cm), a line 60 button 1½″ (3.8cm). When determining buttonhole size, it is always wise to actually measure the button; the thickness will add to the buttonhole length.

The length of a buttonhole is the **diameter** of the button plus ⅛″ (.3cm); for a ball or dome button, it is the measurement **around** plus ⅛″ (.3cm). **Always make a test buttonhole to be sure of size.**

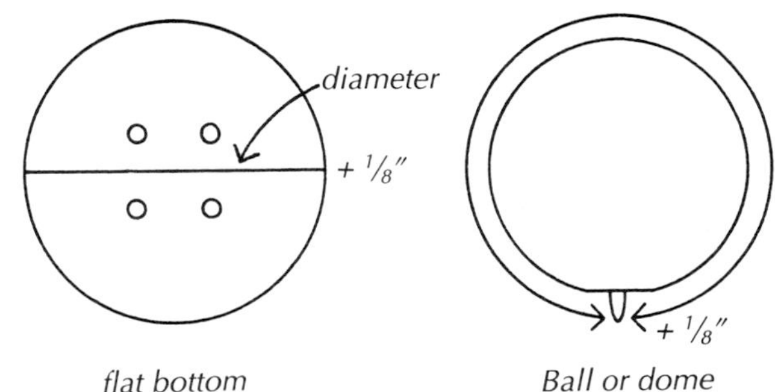

flat bottom *Ball or dome*

The placement of buttonholes is the designer's perogative, close together, far apart, double or any combination.

Some Traditional Placement "Rules"

- The width of the fabric extending past the center front is equal to the diameter of the button. The goal is to give the appearance that there is the same distance from the center front to the edge of the button as from the edge of the button to the edge of the garment.

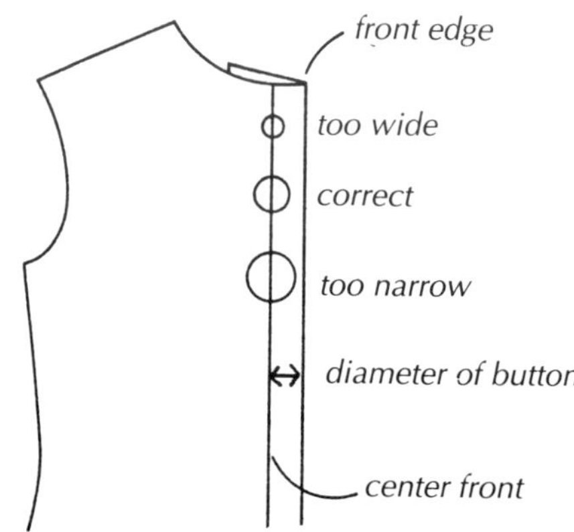

Note: If you change the size of the button from what the pattern recommends, be sure to check the width of the extension and adjust accordingly. Facings must be adjusted also.

- Buttonholes should start 1/8" (.3cm) past the center front into the extension.

- The first buttonhole at the neck should be set below the neckline a distance equal to the diameter of the button plus 1/4" (.6cm).

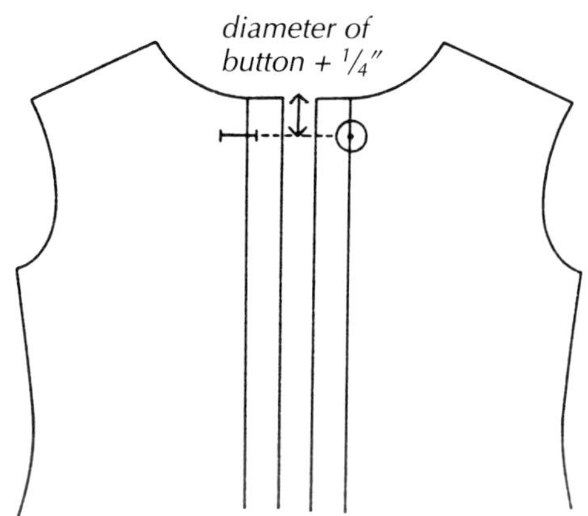

- To space buttonholes:

  - **In general**, set the neck buttonhole first; then one at the waist or 3/8" (1cm) above it. Divide the space between those two buttonholes by the remaining number of buttonholes plus 1. For example, for 3 remaining buttonholes, divide the distance between neck and waist by 4.

  - **Place one buttonhole at the bustline** or slightly above or below (3/8") (1cm). With proper fit, a buttonhole exactly at the bustline isn't necessary.

  - **Place the lowest buttonhole above the hem** in an amount equal to 1 1/2 times the buttonhole spacing or MORE—never less. The distance from the hem to the bottom buttonhole can be even more in a shirtdress.

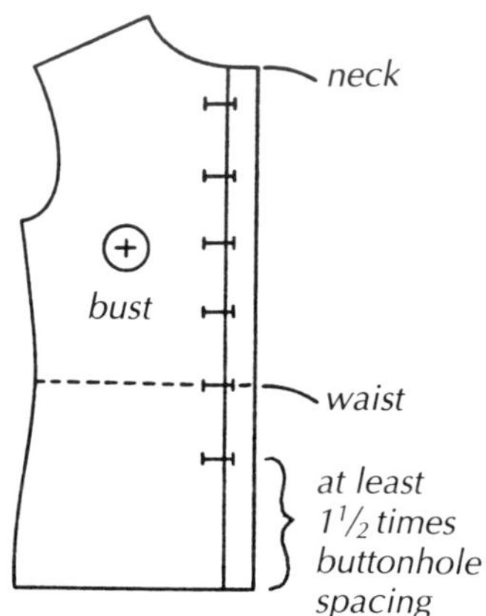

  - **For garments with belts**, do not place a buttonhole at the waistline. A button there would be uncomfortable. Space buttonholes so the distance between them is the same as buttonhole to edge of buckle.

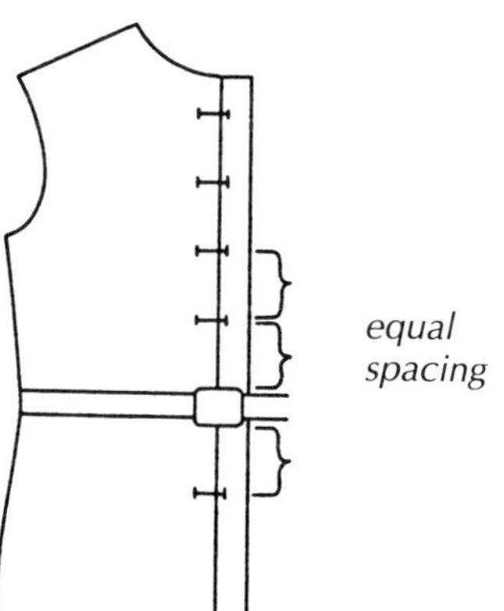

  - **For garments without belts**, place one buttonhole at the waistline. If there is a waistline seam, create an opening in it for the buttonhole. Add a seam to the facing at the waistline behind opening to allow button to pass through.

  - **For garments with a lapel** or open collar, the first buttonhole is placed at the base of the roll line, making sure that the button is not covered by the lapel. Test this, especially for large or dome buttons.

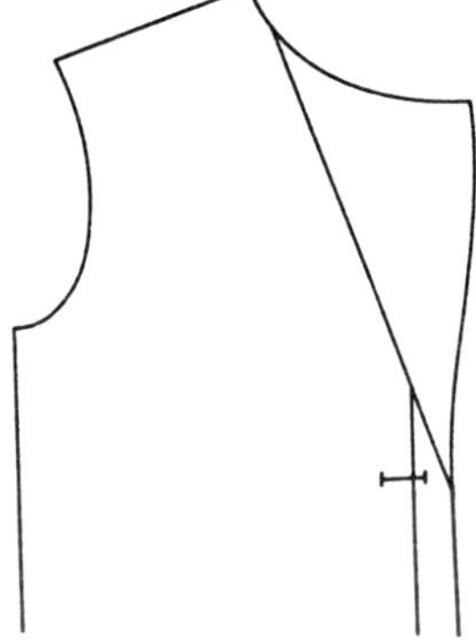

• Place the buttonhole in the center of the **waistband on skirts**. The first buttonhole should be set below the waistband a distance the diameter of the button plus 1/4" (.6cm). The distance from the hem to the bottom buttonhole needs to be at least 1 1/2 times the buttonhole spacing used, but can be more.

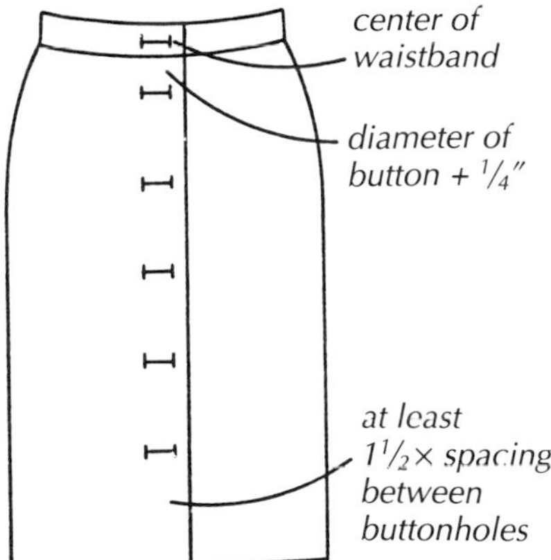

• **Diagonal buttonhole placement** is a design detail but can be very practical as well. For example, on a very ravelly fabric, the buttonhole will be on the bias and bias doesn't ravel. Or, on bias-cut garments, a diagonal buttonhole will be on straight of grain. Interfacing will add stability to any design placement.

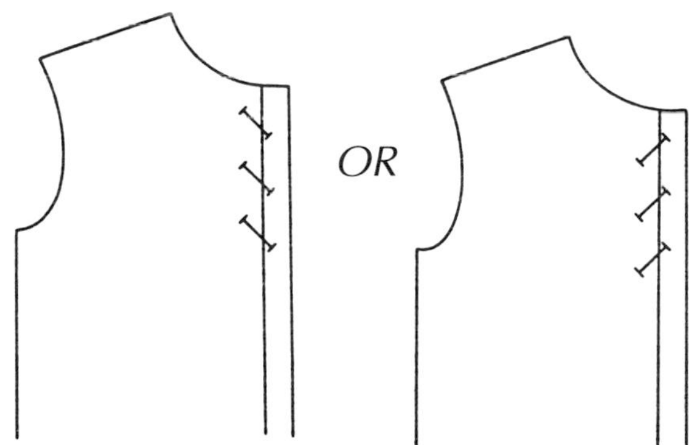

Spanish Snap Buttonhole

Frequently used by the designers, this buttonhole has very thin lips that can hardly be seen. I like to call them "invisible" bound buttonholes. The advantage of a Spanish snap buttonhole is that it can be made very small—as one might use on a silk blouse. On the other hand, Spanish snap buttonholes are equally effective used on a tweed or nubby fabric with the lips made from wool flannel or worsted.

Spanish snap buttonholes make great decorations on sleeve vents and waistbands where an opening is not needed on the backside.

The concept and success of a Spanish snap buttonhole is dependent on the use of the bias grain of the fabric down the center of the buttonhole, which becomes the lips. Therefore, it is imperative that the fabric be exactly on grain prior to cutting the buttonhole lip patches.

Always Make a Test Sample

1. Chalk mark buttonhole placement lines on wrong side of garment. Mark the center front, buttonhole width and placement lines on wrong side of garment. Thread trace to right side of garment with silk thread.

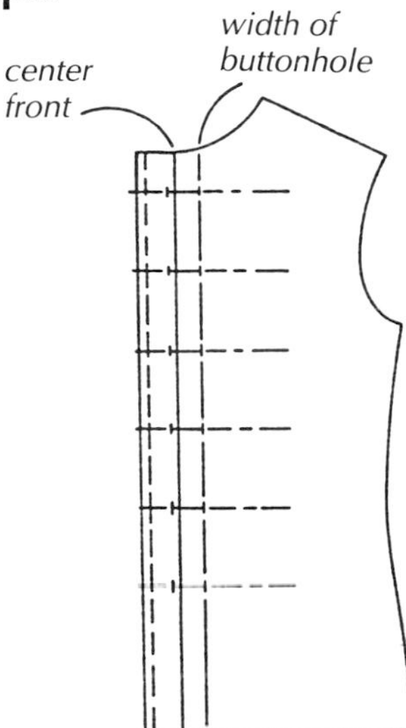

2. Make an egg-shaped template 2" × 3" (5 × 7.5cm). Draw a line through the center.

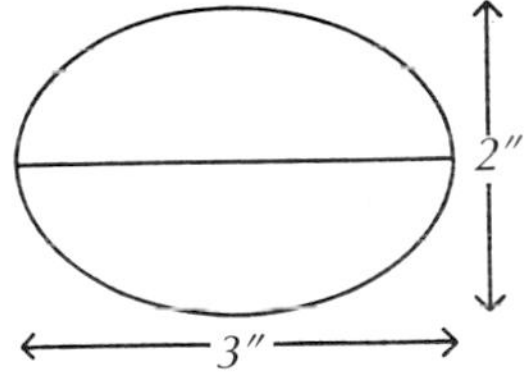

3. Grain-up a piece of fabric large enough to cut as many egg shapes as needed for buttonhole lips.

4. Chalk precise **bias** lines on your buttonhole lip fabric.

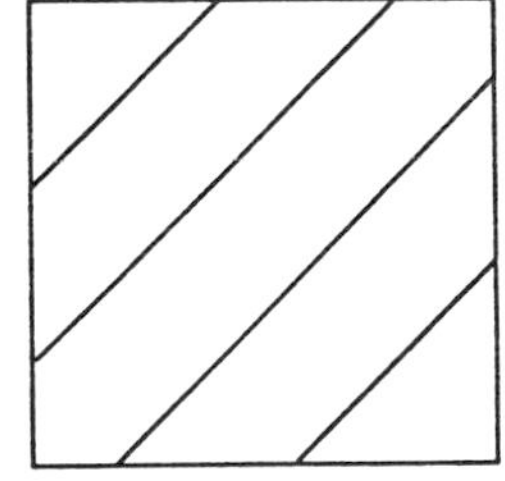

5. Using eggshape template, trace and cut as many patches as needed. The chalked line will appear in the center of each patch.

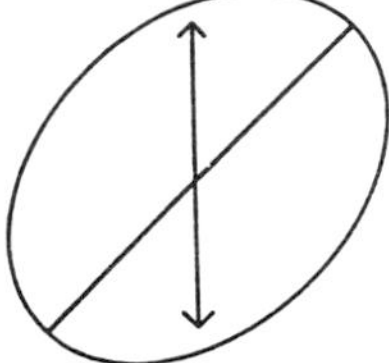
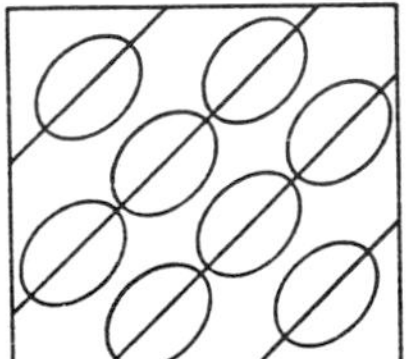

Note: The patch for a Spanish snap buttonhole **cannot** be interfaced or you will not be able to "snap" it and get the full effect of the bias.

6. Pin patch to garment, right sides together, so that the bias line of the patch goes across placement line. Chalk mark the center front and buttonhole width line across all patches. Use a see-through ruler for accuracy.

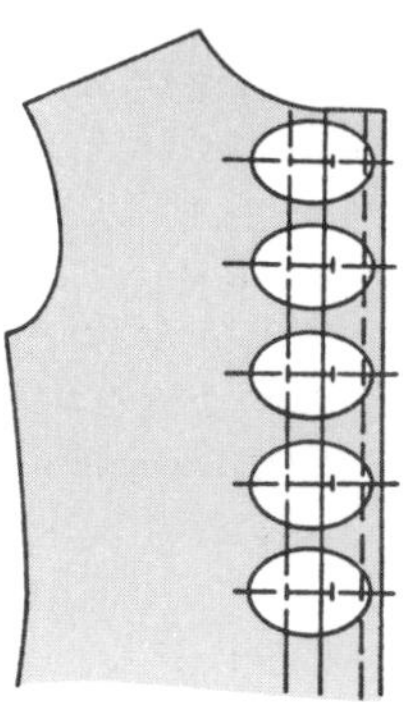

7. Machine stitch a skinny football shape, starting on one long side and pivoting at each point using 20 stitches per inch (8 stitches per centimeter).

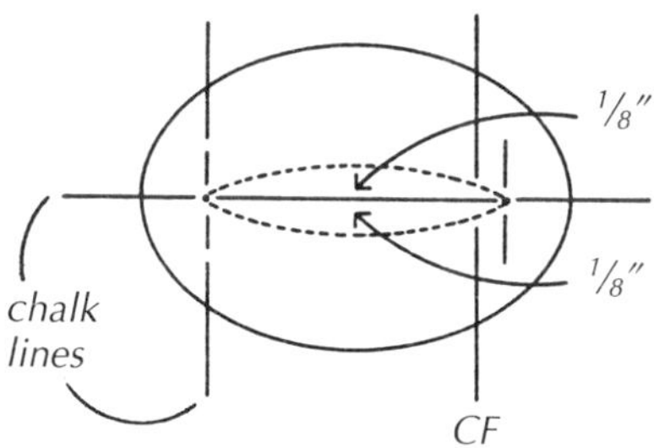

The space at the center of the football shape (lips) should not exceed $\frac{1}{4}$" (.6cm), so lips will each be $\frac{1}{8}$" (.3cm) wide. Stitching at each end should be far enough apart so you can easily cut to the points.

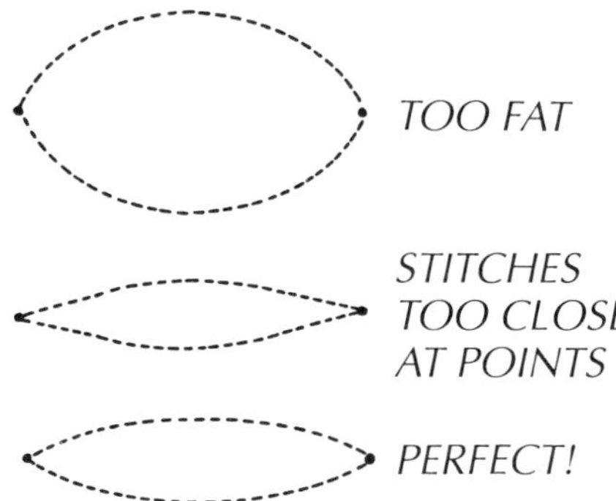

8. Press to meld stitches. (See page 52.)

9. Slash through center of patch **and** garment, using small sharp scissors (pelican scissors are best) and cutting all the way to the point without breaking through the stitch at the point. Put a pin across point to protect it from your scissors to be safe.

10. Turn patch to wrong side through opening.

11. Holding each end of the egg shape patch with the thumb and forefinger, pull in a snapping motion. One good "snap" and the bias will wrap around the $\frac{1}{8}$" (.3cm) seam allowances and automatically create tiny narrow lips.

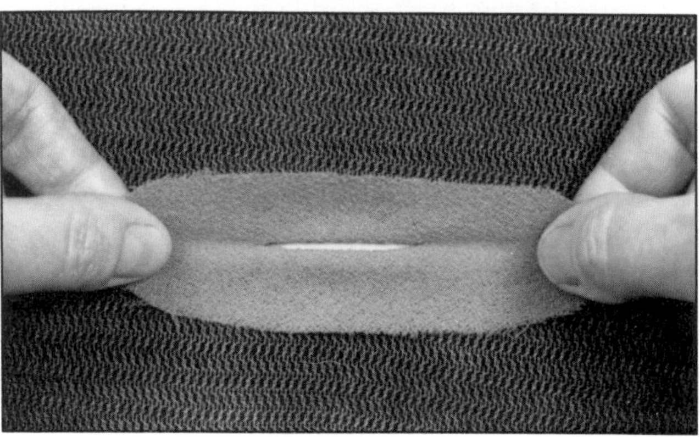

12. Press from wrong side.

13. Apply a **dot** of fusible web under the patch at each end and fuse down to hold ends in place. **No additional stitching is needed.**

14. The buttonhole is finished! After attaching the facing to the garment front, finish the backs of the buttonholes, following the directions on page 192.

When making Spanish snap buttonholes down the front of a garment, trim off the patch at the front edge so it does not extend into the seam allowance at the front edge.

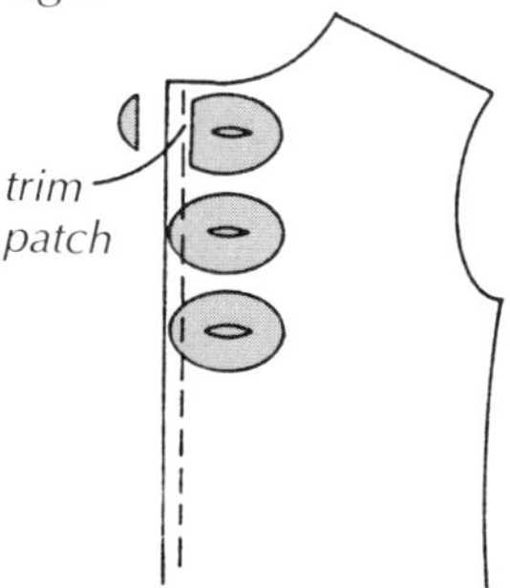

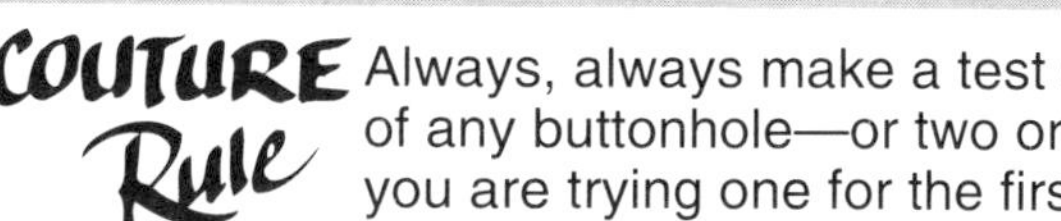

Always, always make a test sample of any buttonhole—or two or three if you are trying one for the first time.

The Spanish snap buttonhole method is **not** suitable for a pocket opening. If it is **longer than** $1\frac{1}{2}$" (3.8cm), it will gap! For a narrow-lipped pocket opening, use a hard-edge welt pocket. (See page 173.)

Triangular Buttonholes

lapel pocket

A triangular buttonhole can be used as a buttonhole or welt pocket. Triangular welt pockets using this buttonhole method on pants angling slightly toward center front can create the illusion of a smaller waist.

General Considerations for a Triangular Buttonhole

- The garment must be interfaced behind the buttonhole location. Baste sew-in interfacing in place or use a fusible as long as there is no show-through. Test first.
- It is fun to combine triangular buttonholes with a variety of button shapes. Because the button rides in the point of the buttonhole, the buttonhole can be made larger than needed to create a dramatic effect.

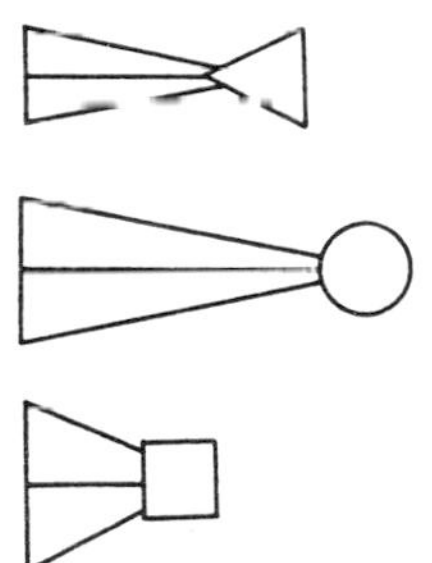

- Triangular buttonholes are particularly effective when the triangle is cut from a contrasting color or from a different fabric than the garment itself. Triangular buttonholes with lips made from a firm flat fabric are fine in fluffy fabrics, tweeds and other textures unsuitable for standard buttonholes.
- The patch for the lips of a triangular buttonhole can be interfaced to stiffen or stabilize the fabric.
- As with any buttonhole be sure to make a sample first.

Steps for Making a Triangular Buttonhole

1. Chalk mark buttonhole placement lines on **wrong side of garment**. Buttonhole will start 1/8″ (.3cm) past center front line. Mark center front and buttonhole width lines. Thread trace all markings to right side of garment. Width lines need to continue several inches into the body of the garment to be seen.

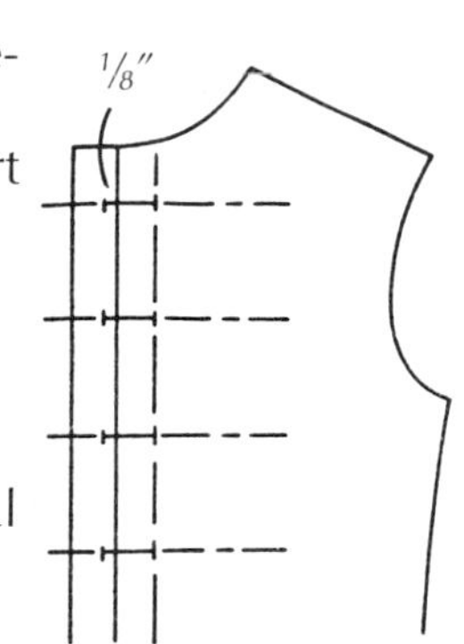

2. Cut sizeable fabric patch approximately 4″ × 6″ (10 × 15cm) for a 1″ to 1½″ (2.5 to 3.8cm) buttonhole. Cut patch fabric so that the cross grain goes through the center of the buttonhole.

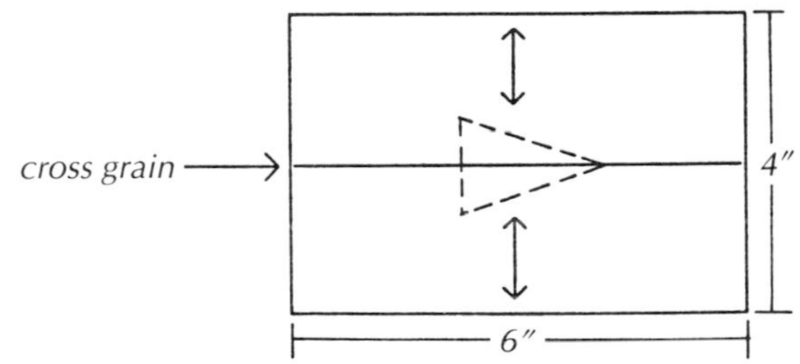

Note: It never hurts to cut a large patch, as excess can be cut away after the buttonhole is complete. If the patch is too small, the lips won't fill the buttonhole completely.

3. Place patch on garment front, right sides together, and pin or baste to keep flat and secure. Chalk center front and width line across all **patches**.

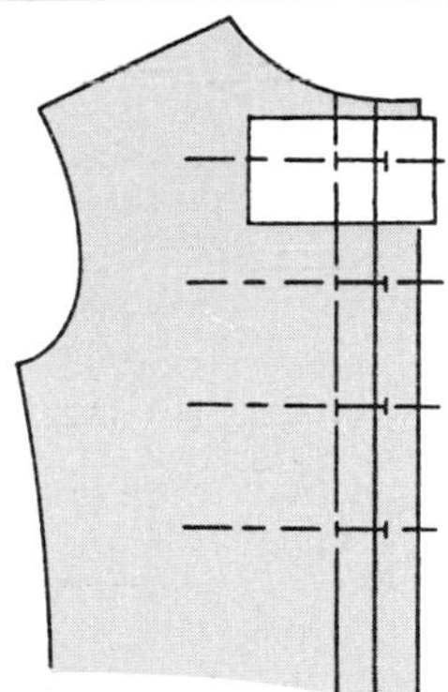

4. Draw triangle on the patch with sharp chalk and ruler. Be precise. Allow lines to cross at each point of the triangle for absolute accuracy.

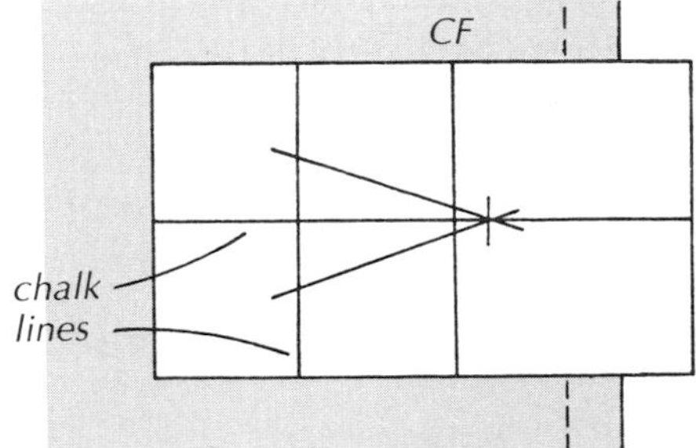

5. Beginning at middle of one leg of the triangle rather than in a corner, machine stitch using 20 stitches per inch. Take two stitches across each point rather than pivoting right at the point.

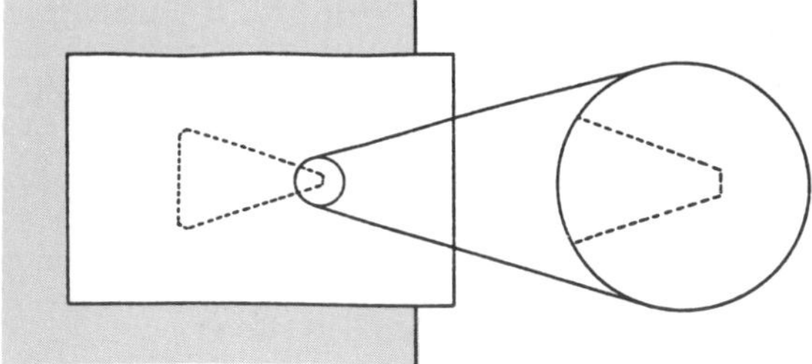

6. Meld threads.

7. To create the hole through which to turn the buttonhole, cut through **center** of triangle and into each corner, cutting through patch, interfacing and garment. Be sure to accurately cut down center of triangle as these will become the two lips.

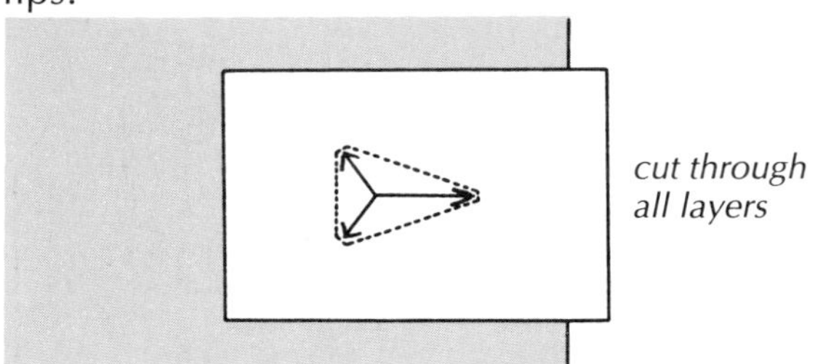

8. Make three slashes through the **patch only**, cutting from the outer edge of the patch to within 1/8″ of the corners of the stitched triangle.

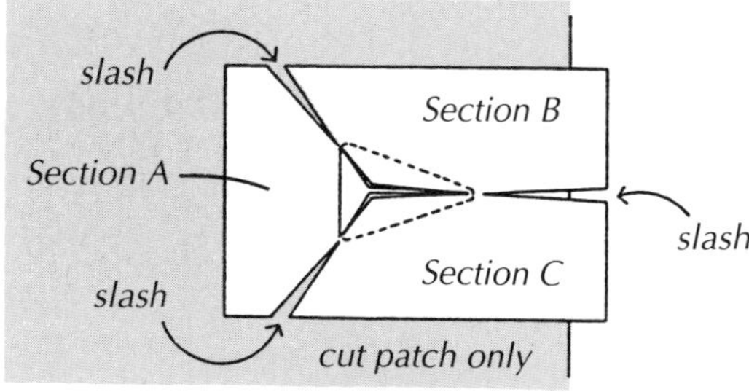

9. Pull section A through cut in triangle to wrong side and press hard with edge of iron so that no patch fabric shows through to the right side. Use edge of clapper to flatten.

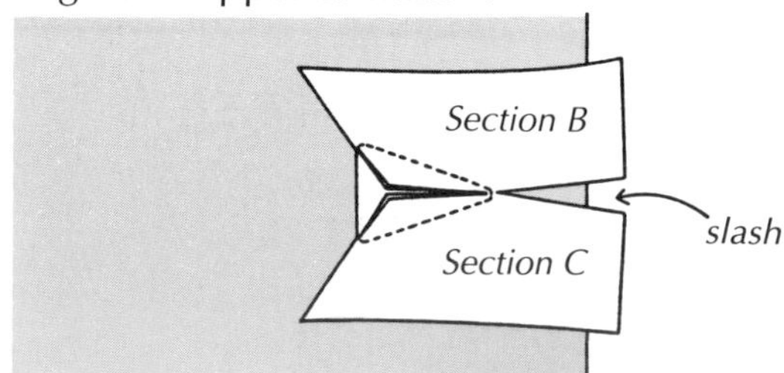

10. From the **right side**, press sections B and C toward center of buttonhole, then pull through to inside. Wrap patch fabric around the two lip edges in the center of buttonhole. Press from wrong side, checking right side to be sure lips are even and no puckers occur.

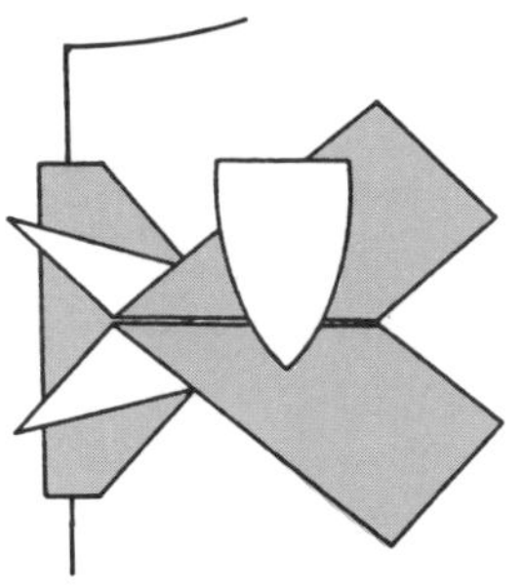

Note: If a little "blurp" or pucker appears in any of the three points, you have not cut all the way to the point, (step #7 above). At this stage it is easy to return patch to the outside again and clip closer to the points.

11. On the inside, turn the garment back on itself to expose the small triangular tab under section A. Using a zipper foot, stitch tab to patch, stitching through all layers to permanently anchor patch in place.

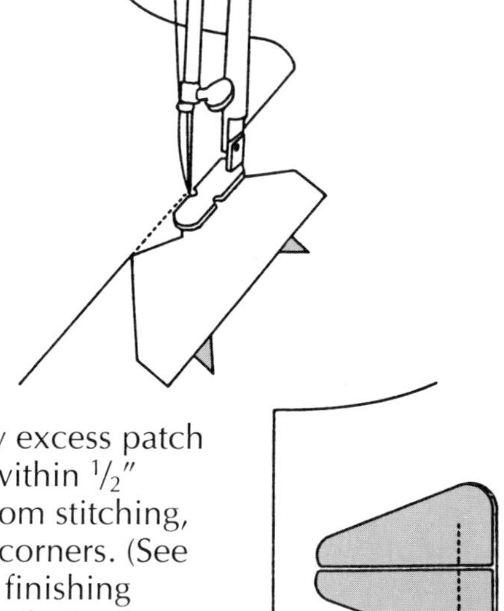

12. Trim away excess patch fabric to within 1/2″ (1.3cm) from stitching, rounding corners. (See below for finishing opening in facing.)

13. Repeat for remaining buttonholes.

The back of a triangular buttonhole can be a slit or it can be exactly the same size and shape as the buttonhole, making a mirror image. This is particularly effective on lapels where it is likely to be seen from both sides. See page 192 for facing a buttonhole.

Create a Pocket Pouch for Triangular Welt Pockets

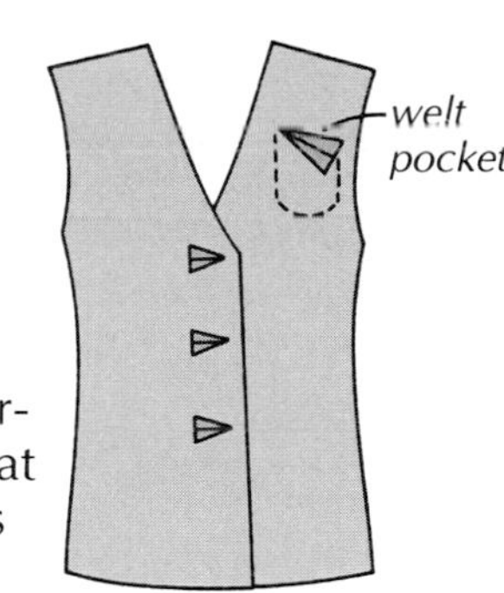

The secret to a pocket pouch for a triangular welt pocket is to keep the grain of the pouch the same as the garment grainline, no matter what angle on which the triangle is placed.

Use a rectangle of fashion fabric sewn to lining for the piece that would show through the pocket. The second piece can be all lining.

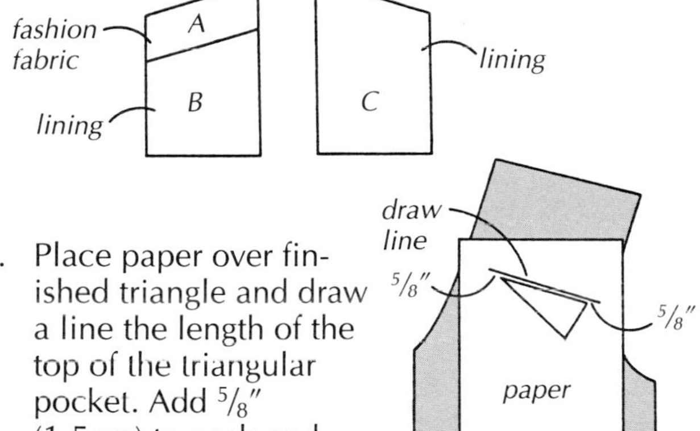

1. Place paper over finished triangle and draw a line the length of the top of the triangular pocket. Add 5/8" (1.5cm) to each end.

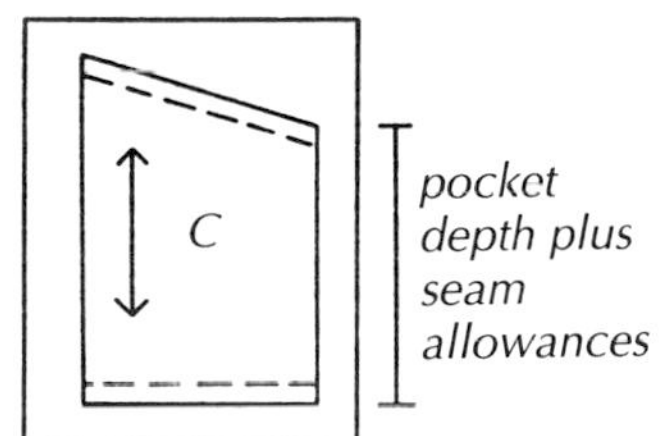

2. Extend side lines along straight of grain to desired depth of pocket. Connect the bottom with a cross-grain line. Add a 5/8" (1.5cm) seam allowance top and bottom.

3. Cut lining C to this shape.

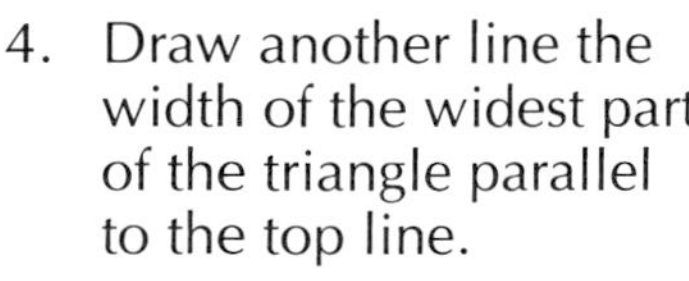

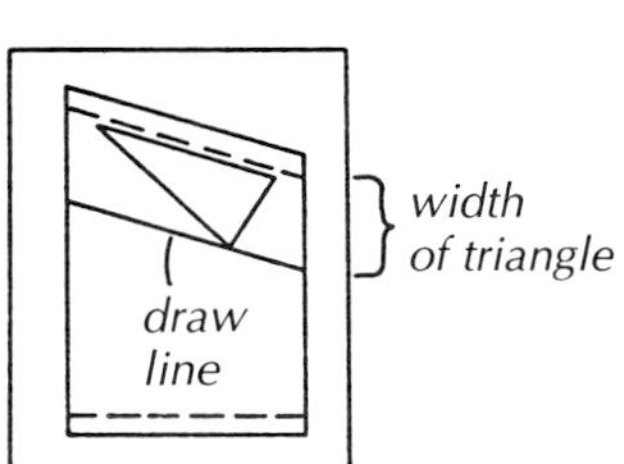

4. Draw another line the width of the widest part of the triangle parallel to the top line.

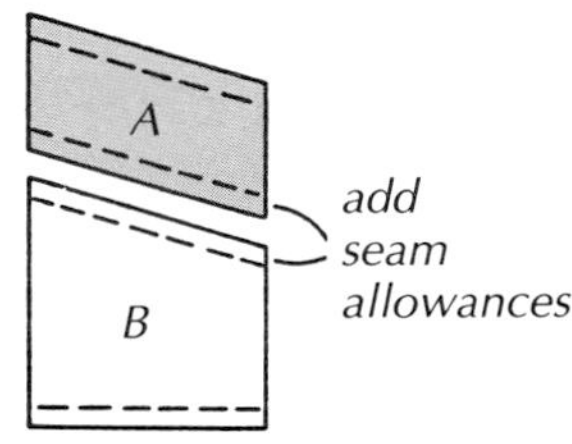

5. Cut on this line and add seam allowances to piece A (to be cut from fashion fabric) and B to be cut from lining.

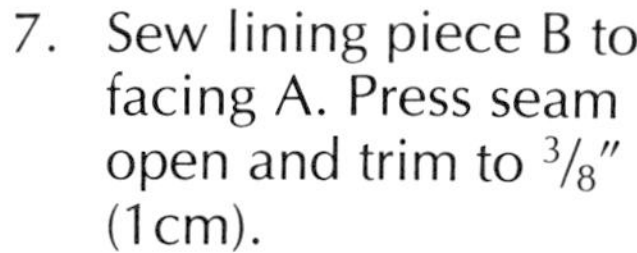

6. Cut facing A from fashion fabric and cut B from lining.

A
B
trim to 3/8"

7. Sew lining piece B to facing A. Press seam open and trim to 3/8" (1cm).

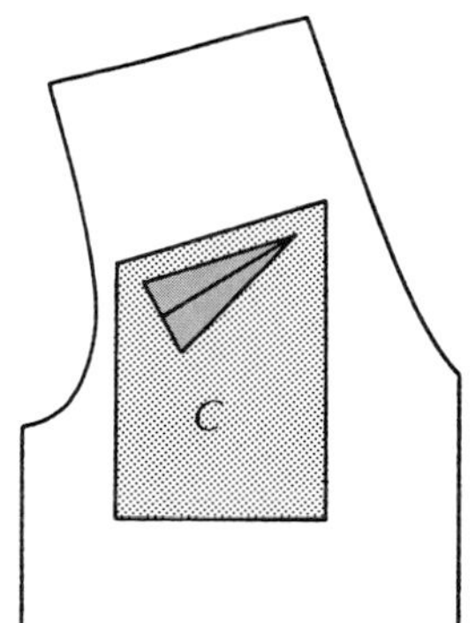

8. Using the method for finishing buttonholes on page 192, lay lining piece C on back of buttonhole as if it were a facing. Follow steps 2-11 on page 192.

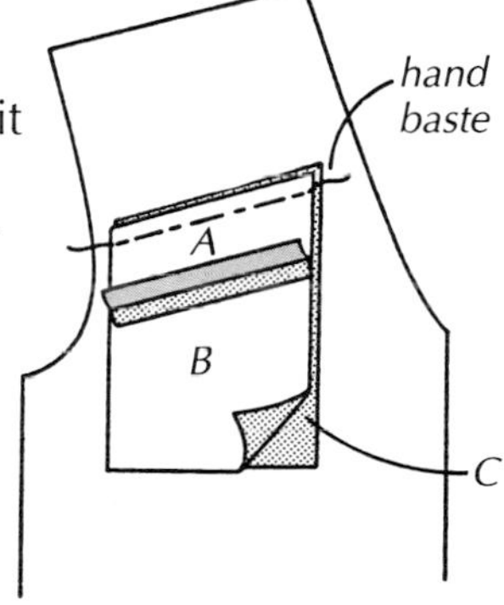

9. Place lining/facing unit AB on top of lining piece C, right sides together. Hand baste to upper welt of triangle through all layers.

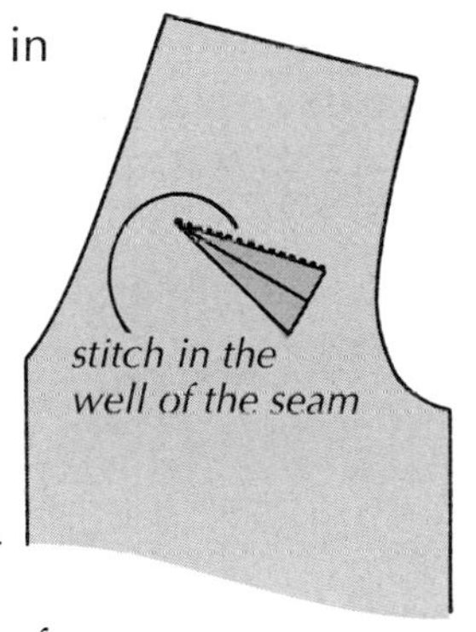

10. From right side, stitch in the well of the seam along top of triangle using 20 stitches per inch (8 stitches per centimeter).

11. From wrong side, machine stitch around three remaining sides of pocket pouch, rounding corners. Press to meld stitches.

12. Grade seams, 1/2" (1.3cm) for the one to the outside and 3/8" (1cm) on the one to the inside.

stitches from well of seam
machine stitch around sides and bottom

How to Finish the Facing for Bound Buttonholes

After making bound buttonholes, finish the facing as follows:

1. Apply facing, press and turn to wrong side of garment.

2. Pin a piece of silk organza, cut on the same grain as the facing, to the full length of the facing piece and cross baste it to the right side of the **facing only**, above and below each buttonhole location.

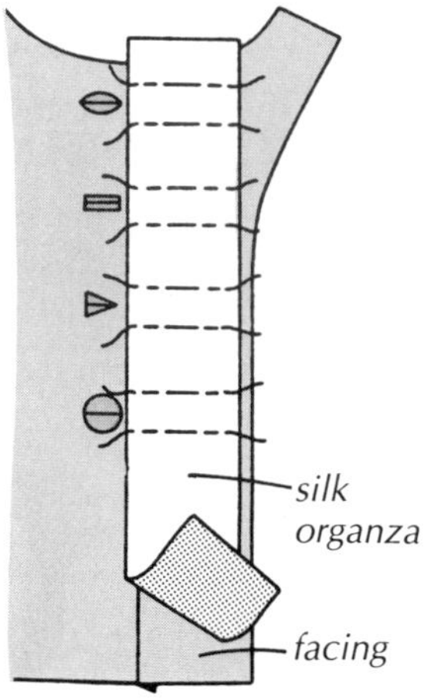

silk organza

facing

3. Place garment on grainboard, facing side down.

4. From the garment side stab pins through all layers to outline the buttonhole shape.

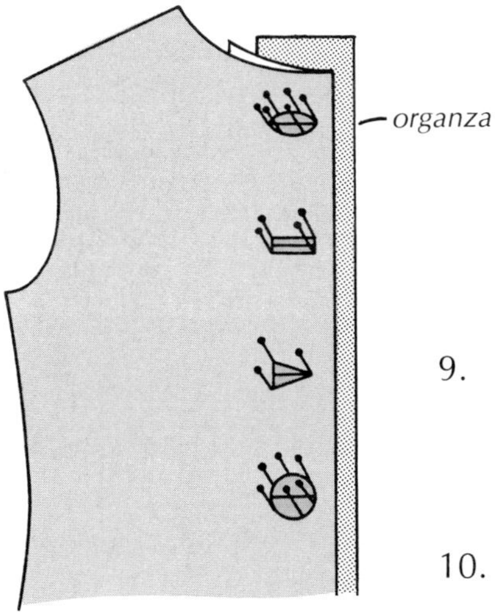

organza

Note: With a Spanish snap buttonhole you have the choice of making a football-shaped opening exactly like the buttonhole or a rectangle shape, which is easier to do and recommended for heavier fabrics. Both shapes are acceptable.

5. **Carefully** turn work to facing side and mark the outline of shape, connecting points where pin is showing. Use a pencil to mark the exact shape. (A sharp lead pencil gives a clear, very fine line on white organza. Use chalk on dark organza.) Remove pins. Open out facing.

6. Machine stitch outline of shape through facing and organza using 20 stitches per inch (8 stitches per centimeter).

7. Slash through organza and facing as shown.

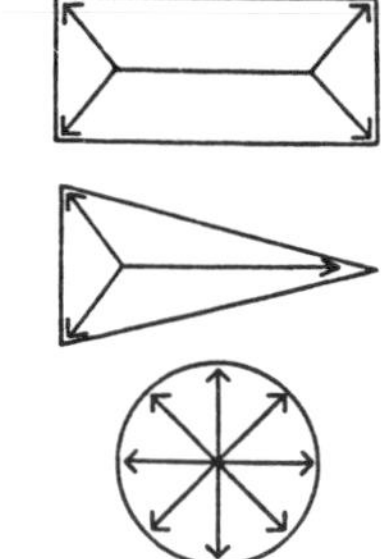

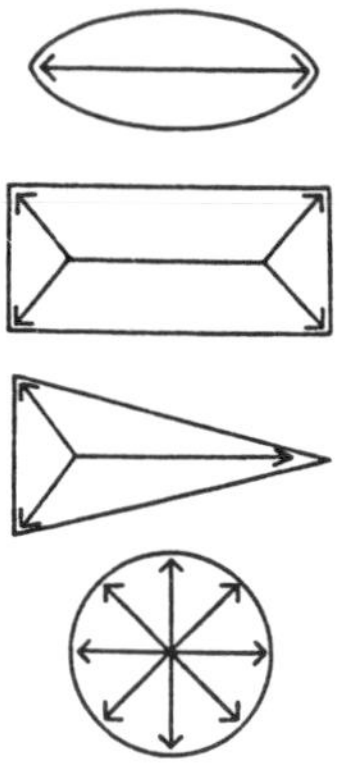

8. Remove cross basting. Cut away organza between the buttonholes.

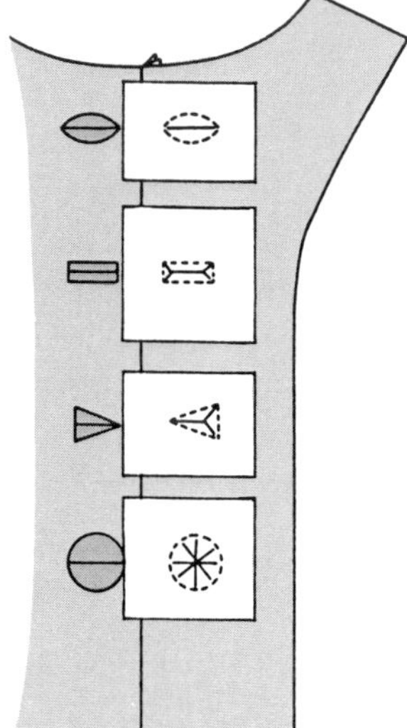

9. Turn organza patches to wrong side of facing and press **hard**. There should now be a faced opening for each buttonhole in the facing. Cut away excess organza leaving $1/2$" (1.3cm) on all sides.

10. Match opening in facing to the back of buttonhole and pin in place.

11. Slip stitch opening edges around back of buttonhole using small concealed stitches.

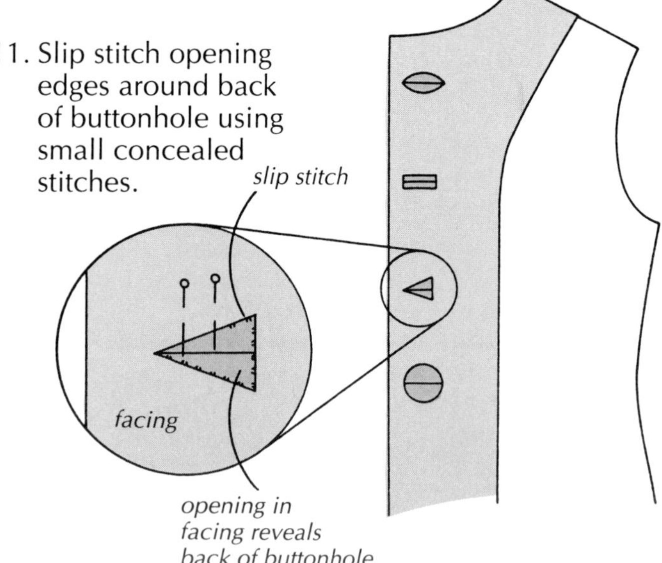

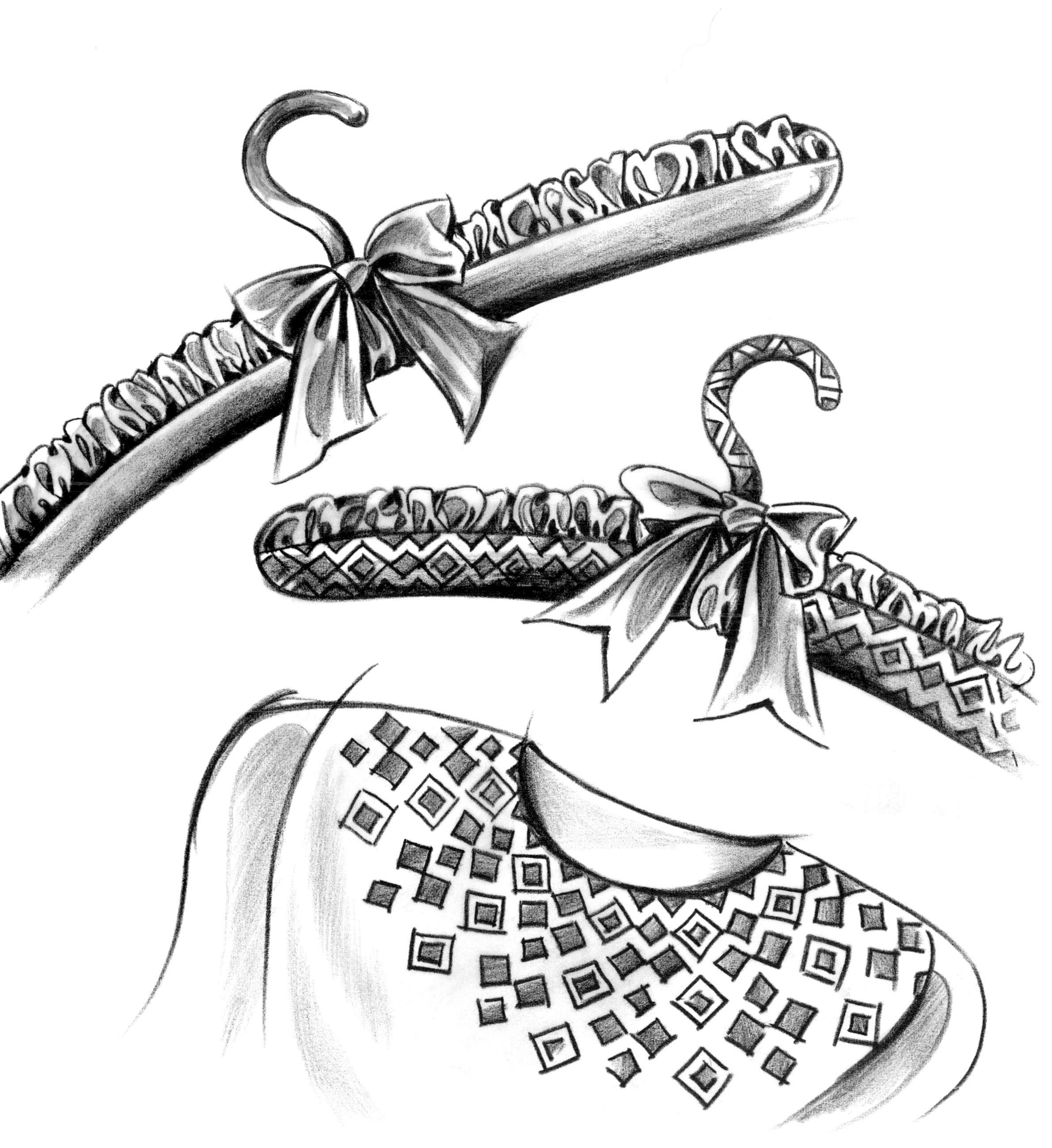

CHAPTER 24

Elegant Padded Hangers

Beautiful clothes should be hung on padded hangers to provide support and retain shoulder shape. Each hanger requires only ¼ yard of fabric. It's easy to cut a hanger of fashion fabric every time you make a garment. Hangers can be made of cotton, silk or wool. A natural fiber is best. You might also like to choose a fabric that coordinates with your bedroom color scheme. Scraps are also fun to use.

Materials Needed for Padded Hanger

* ¼ yard fashion fabric—wool, cotton, or silk
* 2 pieces polyester batting, 9″×14″ (23×35.5cm) and 1″ (2.5cm) thick
* Cotton or polyester quilt batting is preferred, as it is loftier than polyester fleece.
* 1 pair nylon stockings (old)
* 1 wooden hanger (easily purchased at dime stores)
* 1 yard ½″-wide (1.3cm) ribbon
* Hard paper, like a file folder, for making pattern

Make a Pattern You Can Use Over and Over

1. Cut a rectangle 3½″ × 21½″ (9cm × 54.8cm) (A) and another 3½″ × 10¼″ (9cm × 26.1cm) (B) out of heavy paper like a file folder. This size includes ⅝″ (1.5cm) seam allowances.
2. Round the edges at one end.
3. Indicate fold line ½″ (1.3cm) from squared off end.
4. Indicate grain lines. Pattern may be placed on crosswise or lengthwise grains. Bias is beautiful, but takes a bit more fabric.

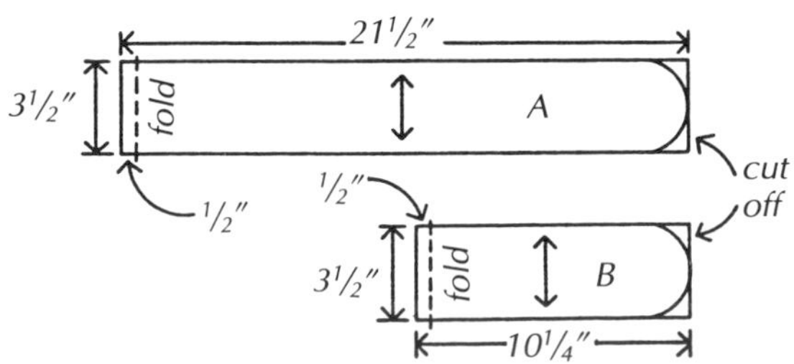

Padded Hanger Instructions

1. From fashion fabric cut two of each pattern piece A + B for one hanger.
2. Turn under ½″ (1.3cm) at squared off edges and press.
3. Make two rows of ease stitching on pieces A, placing one row ⅝″ (1.5cm) from the cut edge and the second ⅜″ (1cm) from the cut edge. Stitch on right side of fabric so bobbin thread is on the wrong side of the fabric.

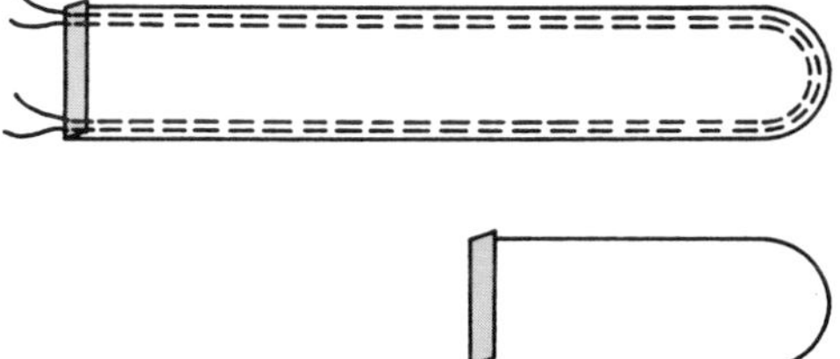

4. Pull up bobbin threads to gather until piece A matches the size of piece B. Tie off threads. Adjust gathers evenly on back side so gathers are at right angles to the stitching line. Be sure there are plenty of gathers at curved end.

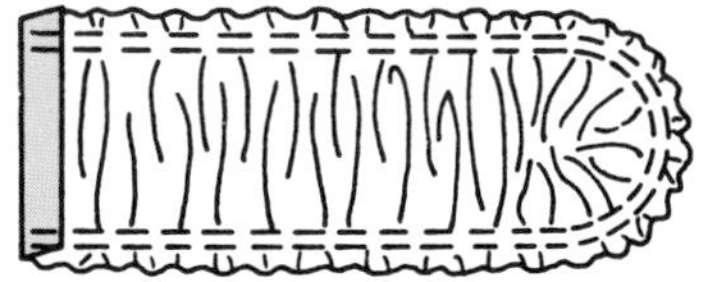

5. Pin gathered piece A right sides together with piece B.
6. Stitch ⅝″ (1.5cm) from cut edge, one thread away from original gathering line, on the two long sides and the curved end, leaving the folded end open.
7. Do not press and do not trim seam allowance. It is needed to give the hanger a puffy look.

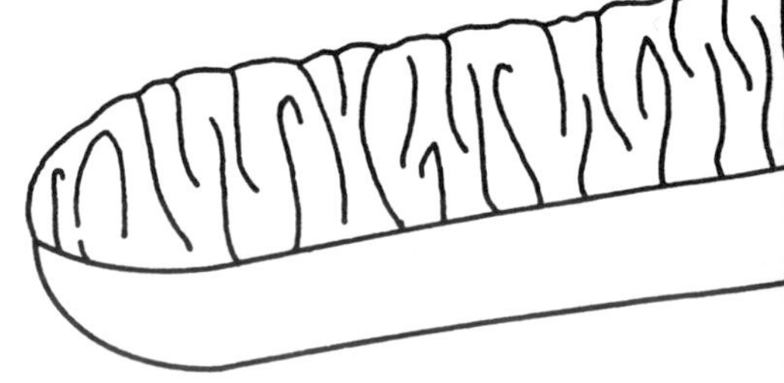

8. Turn right side out.

9. Cut two pieces of batting each approximately 9″ × 14″ (23 × 35.5cm). Depending on the thickness of the batting, you may want to use two layers for each half of the hanger.

10. Tightly roll batting over each half of the hanger, folding over the end of the hanger every once in a while. It is important to have plenty of batting at the end of the hanger so hanger won't poke through and damage clothing.

11. Nylon stockings (old hosiery) make a perfect cover to hold batting in place. Cut stocking at ankle, insert hanger into foot and pull stocking **tightly.** This will compress batting, which will expand once the hanger is covered.

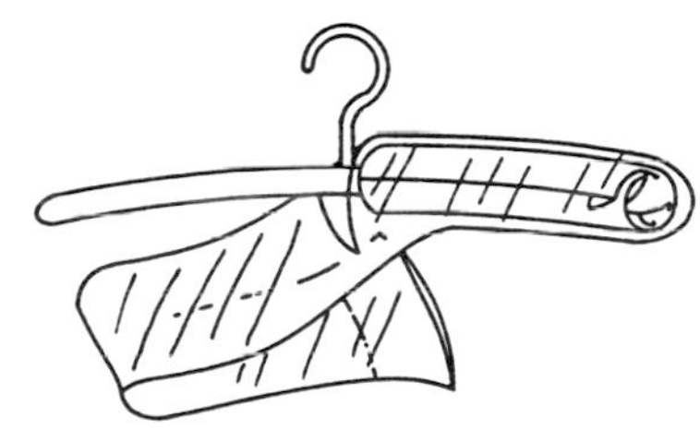

12. Insert each end of the hanger into the fashion fabric cover. Be sure gathered section is on top.

13. Once in, excess batting and stocking may appear near hook. Do NOT cut off—simply stuff into cover with bamboo pointer or table knife.

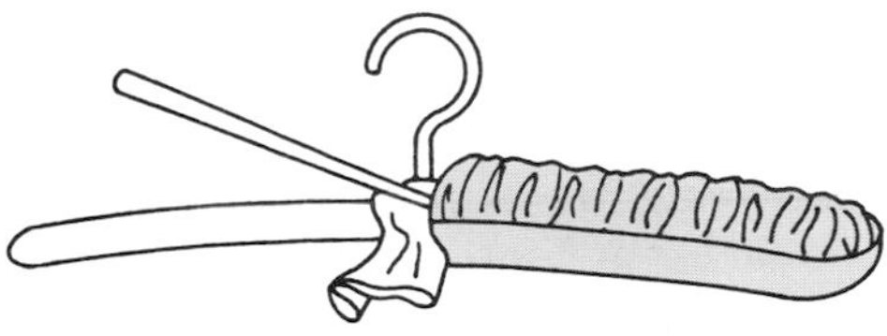

14. To cover the hanger hook, cut a bias strip $1\frac{1}{2}$″ × 7″ (3.8 × 18cm). Fold in half lengthwise, right sides together, and stitch $\frac{3}{8}$″ (1cm) from cut edge on one short end and long side. Turn. Do not press.

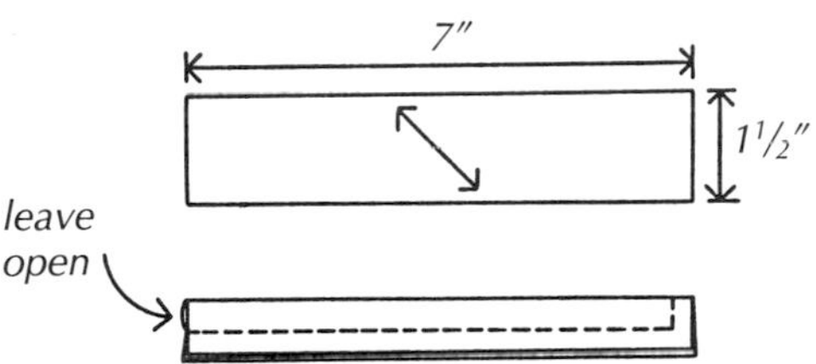

15. Slide bias tube over hanger hook and imbed end into covers. Whip stitch centers together. There's no need to be too neat here as it will be covered with ribbon.

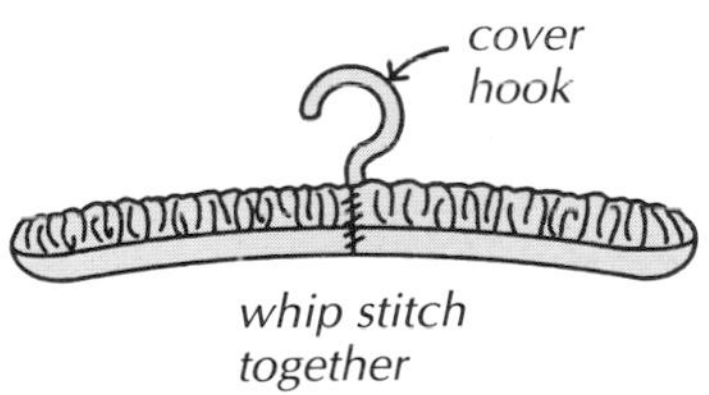

16. Loop $\frac{1}{2}$″-wide (1.3cm) satin ribbon around hook. Bring left strand around to back on right side, right strand around to back on left side. Bring both ends around to front and tie in a bow.

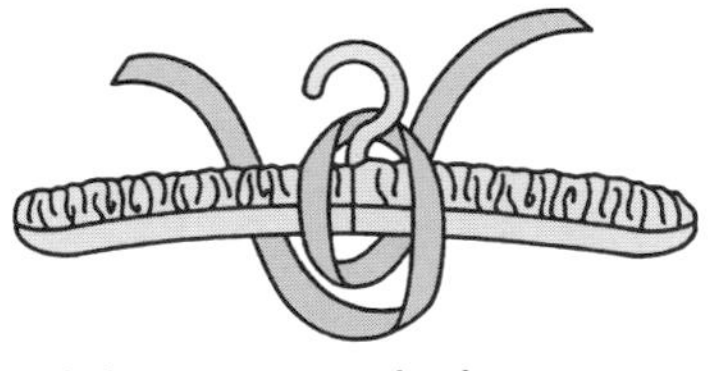

For scented hangers a little potpourri can be sprinkled into the covers before inserting the hanger. Do not use perfume as it may stain the hanger and damage clothes.

In a hurry? Cover inexpensive padded hangers with your fabric, adding a thin layer of batting to make them puffier.

Epilogue

Today as I finish writing this book, I feel as if I am having an out-of-body experience as my life flashes in front of me. You see, I cannot remember when sewing or learning to sew was not a part of my life.

I remember when my Aunt Mamie said, "If you'll go downtown (25¢ on the bus) and ask Mr. Garr (Garr's Fabrics, Providence, Rhode Island) he'll help you pick out some material. Wasn't she trusting? I was 8 years old. We picked out green cotton for a sundress and white pique for a bolero. Mamie supervised, but her philosophy was never to sew a stitch so that with great confidence and sense of accomplishment I could say "I made it myself" and I did. It was a wonderful outfit and I wore it out.

Then there was the polar bear evening gown. In high school it seemed appropriate at the time to become instantly sophisticated. I chose a designer pattern with a surplice bodice and slim wrap long skirt and made it in white faille. It was dramatic on the hanger but on me it added 20 lbs. and I looked like a prop for Dr. Zhivago. Needless to say I never wore it. But it was my first experience with the reality that the design and my body had to be compatible first—sewing came second.

I made my sister, Polly, a prom dress. I had seen a taffeta print with matching chiffon to go over it. Polly wanted only taffeta, so I made it that way. Strapless with a double circle skirt. Days before the dance she decided the chiffon overskirt would be grand. So, sure enough, I took it apart, added the skirt and made a firm commitment I would never go into an alteration business. To all of you who do alterations—a star for your crown and my admiration for your patience.

When I was living in Detroit, Mamie and I made a 9′ × 12′ wool felt rug for my new apartment. We took an $8^1/_2$″ × 11″ inch piece of paper and drew the greatest design. Once we translated it to 9′ × 12′—that sliver of black turned into a 15 inch piece that looked like a snake slithering across the rug. And so I learned copying by the grid method. The rug was 3-4 layers of 100% wool felt—an idea I saw in Family Circle. I used it as a rug for years; later, as a wall hanging.

Here's a funny story. I took the rug to be dry cleaned (circa 1969) and they said $60.00. Home I came with the rug. The next day I went back with the same item and said, "Can you clean this bedspread?" "Sure," they said, "$7.50."

I remember when I worked for Girls Scouts of USA and travelled with my featherweight Singer. I was in St. Louis at the Sheraton Hotel. Down the freight elevator in the alley was a dry cleaner with all sorts of steam presses. In a weekend (morning, noon, night) I made a cashmere winter coat. The best work I had ever done, with only 50 trips down that elevator to use the presses at the dry cleaners. Don't we wish we could have that equipment at home?

And then sitting on the porch of a little hall in Glen Haven, Colorado, at Ann Hyde's Haute Couture Summer School—I began to wonder if my sewing should be my career. Was my passion taking me in a new direction? Ann inspired me to look at couture, to expand my horizons and to test my hand at duplicating the best. I was so excited that I could do what the couturiers did and here was a teacher that could show me how. I wrote a letter to the Denver Post to tell them they had a national treasure in their midst and did they know Ann Hyde. Those warm feelings of wonderment come back to me now.

During that week at Ann Hyde's I met a student, Iva Bradley, from Fort Saskatchewan, Alberta, Canada. Who would know that in 1991, she would come to our booth at the In Stitches Show in Vancouver, British Columbia? What was I doing now? she asked. Just what I was thinking about on that porch in Glen Haven.

When I came to California to open The Fabric Carr in Los Altos, I took a class with Sandy Nager Erickson on "The Bias." She had researched Madame Vionnet and the more contemporary work of Charles Kleibacher and was sharing it with all who would come. To Sandy, I give a special thank you for exposing all of us in Northern California to the bias—its life and its rewards. Little did I know at the time that years later I would be asked to participate in Sewing by Satellite (AHSCA) and who would also be teaching but Charles Kleibacher. It was a treasured day for me.

On a trip back to Rhode Island to my cousin's 25th wedding anniversary, I needed a fancy dress. Very few of my family had seen me since I opened my fabric store and sewing school. I wanted a prosperity dress. Mary Margaret, a modern couturier, and I teamed up. I designed and she masterfully executed a black chiffon with satin and gold stripe dress. She would surely tell you of the hours it took to perfect the miles of double bias ruffles that fluttered around the neck and down the back, and of her innovation of the remarkable undergarment. (You can see it on page 19.) It's the kind of dress that never asks the question "How are you doing?" The answer is revealed in the dress.

My field is couture. Oh, you know what that means—structure, hand stitching, shaping, attitude and beautiful fabric. There was the day that my friend Rena Shaefer and I were invited to go to Africa and camp in the bush for six weeks. Does this sound like couture? Ann Person to the rescue. Stretch 'N Sew—14 pairs of pants each, 28 T-shirts (14 long sleeve, 14 short sleeve). All this was created in about ten days of sewing—pure magic! Comfortable, wearable and fun clothes with matching tote bags. Thank you, Ann.

One night at Lewa Downs in Kenya (you may have seen it in *Out of Africa*, or have been there), we were sitting looking out over the valley—adorned in pinwale corduroy pants and cotton T-shirts, sipping champagne from Baccarat crystal glasses. That's couture on safari.

The year before I did have a real chance to do couture sewing. Rena and I were invited to travel in Europe over Christmas/New Year's and attend many formal parties. I made a grey crepe dress with a jacket that had chiffon ruffles on all edges. After 100" using 10-to-1 gathering, I had 1,000 inches (8 feet) of bias ruffles. I couldn't keep them straight. So I tacked them to the baseboard of the sewing room. It worked fine. A new sewing tool had been discovered. I used ostrich feathers on the edge of a silver lam and velvet cape. Some of these dresses are shown in this book. Nine suitcases later, we were off on the trip of a lifetime.

As you know now, my aunt, Mamie, taught me to sew and my Aunt Ruth, the artist, also sewed. In 1982, after I had opened my fabric store and sewing school, I offered, as one of our services, the fitting of a basic muslin to be used as a sloper. Both my aunts wrote to say how much they wished I could make one for them. I went to West Virginia and in my Aunt Ruth's living room I fitted them—how my life had come full circle—I was fitting my Aunt Mamie—wow! She taught me well!

I am in California now teaching sewing, and part of the self-named Northern California Group. What is it that makes this area abound with sewing instructors, learning opportunities and just plain sewing excitement? Interaction and sharing is part of the wonder. No sewing book I would ever write or will write can be complete without a salute to my contemporaries. A thank you for being there whether it's a question about thread, what needle, who sells purple polka dot shoulder pads or "Can I talk to you—I've had a tough day."

You may recognize some of these names, some you may not. But I hope you'll meet each some day. They are very special people and I thank them all for keeping sewing alive and sharing each and every technique, idea and just plain "I bet we can."

To these special people—Sandra Betzina, Candice Bushnell, Ronda Chaney, Lois Erickson, Sandy Nager Ericson, Gale Grigg Hazen, Claire Shaeffer, Marcy Tilton and Ginny Winter—I'm glad I know you.

And then one day Pati Palmer called. All of a sudden my sewing time became writing time. It's hard to wear the printed page—but sewing books can be treasured as much as clothes. Pati's attention to detail, her clear focus and her lasting devotion to perfection is evidenced here. To Pati—my great admiration and appreciation for her spirit and all her contributions to sewing around the world.

To all the students of The Fabric Carr—those near and those far away that are wearing beautiful clothes and who continue to feed their passion for fine sewing, a heartfelt thank you for letting me be a part of your life. To those of you who often wished I would write a book—your wish has come true.

Roberta C. Carr

Photo by Stan Taylor

About the Contributors...

Here are The New Couturiers. These are contemporary, busy women who give sewing a priority in their lives and whose efforts you see photographed in this book.

Cynthia Berry is a supervisor at a major fabric chain's local store near her home in Hudson, Iowa. Having sewn since she was 7 years old, she has developed expertise in men's and women's tailoring and sewing Ultrasuede®. She is married and has three children and five grandchildren.

Luanne Carson learned to sew from her mother at a young age and never stopped! She has been a home economics teacher and owner of a full-service sewing store with classes, dressmaking, fabrics and notions. Now she is a free-lance consultant and writer of educational materials. Married to a pilot, Luanne also travels extensively, but calls Boulder Creek, California, home.

Ronda Chaney, it seems, is always educating about sewing. Her profession is administrator and chairman of the Fashion & Consumer Arts Department, specializing in textiles and clothing, at Canada College in Redwood City, Calif. But she also instructs at sewing schools in the San Francisco Bay Area—The Sewing Workshop, The Sewing Place and The Fabric Carr—and she lectures for the American Sewing Guild (ASG) and the Professional Association of Custom Clothiers (PACC). Her work has been published in "Update" newsletters, the Singer Sewing Reference Library and a quarterly publication by the Fashion Institute of Technology. Ronda also serves as a consultant to help develop fashion production programs in her community and to establish private businesses in the clothing field. She is married with two sons.

Karen Dutch started sewing at age 7, and won the "Make It Yourself with Wool" contest at the (Washington) state level when she was only 14. Today she still finds time to sew despite her active career and family life. She is a storage products consultant for a major computer company and travels extensively. She lives with her husband and child in San Jose, Calif.

Barbara Frohman's life has been an exciting combination of fashion and interior design-related work, volunteering in her community, and serving the Church through music, drama and art. In the late '70s, she founded and directed the "Pulpiteers," a troupe of teenage students who shared their faith through puppetry, mime, clowning and drama. She recently served as president of the auxiliary to the local chapter of the Society for Crippled Children and Adults, and currently serves on the local board of the Easter Seal Society. And she designs interiors and clothing in her own firm, Barbara B. Frohman, Fabrications. Married with four children, Barbara resides in Hillsborough, Calif.

Janet Ghilarducci, according to Bobbie Carr, is a "master dressmaker in the highest tradition of the couture." Her home-based business, Ghilarducci Designs, already cele-brated its 10th anniversary. Janet lives with her husband and three young sons in Palo Alto, California.

Patricia Hagen is a professional dressmaker and the national administrator of PACC. Having been a charter member and newsletter editor of the Oregon chapter of PACC, she has been a vital force in managing its growth. Married with one child, she lives in Portland, Oregon, where she also volunteers for 4-H and her child's school.

Lenore Hofmann is short in stature, but long on talent. Only 4' 11" tall, Lenore started sewing at the age of 5 even though she couldn't reach the treadle sewing machine pedals—so she had her sister work the pedals! Today the native Californian is a teacher, accountant, home management executive, volunteer and avid tennis player. She and her husband, who reside in Los Gatos, Calif., have two sons in college.

Nelda Jones is a master at her hobbies of couture sewing, embroidery and gardening. As a world traveler and lecturer, she studies peoples, customs, cultures, dress, architecture, home kitchens and native food. Having been to 103 countries to date, Nelda believes, "If we all learned how everyone lived and thought, there would be peace around the world." Married with two children, she resides in San Jose, Calif.

Marla Kazell moved from her native Wisconsin after college to become a sample seamstress in the research and development department at Stretch & Sew in Eugene, Ore. Now she has been a couture dressmaker for 13 years and resides in the Portland area. An active member of PACC from its start, Marla was instrumental in the development of PACC on a national scale. Presently, she is the group's chairperson of member relations and editor of the national newsletter.

Joy Lempert didn't begin sewing until she was 18, but says she has constructed more than 500 garments using couture techniques. Though her occupation is owner of a wholesale cookie bakery and distributorship, her education and honors indicate her artistic bent. She has college degrees in fine art and industrial design, and earned an Alexander medal for her one-woman art show in New York's Metropolitan Museum of Art. She also presented 75 garments in a gallery show—a retrospective from 1952-1986—at The Fabric Carr. Married with three children, Joy lives in Los Altos, Calif.

Ruth Ann Loney taught herself to sew in high school, and didn't have any formal training for many years. But she's always enjoyed "anything creative," especially gardening, decorating, party planning—and sewing. A property manager by occupation, Ruth Ann lives in La Selva Beach, Calif., where she is married and has two children.

Paula Marineau is a designer of one-of-a-kind fabric art masterpieces that most frequently take the form of coats worn by sophisticated women around the world. She has been an entrant in The Fairfield Show in Houston, Texas, and The Oregon School of Arts & Crafts' Designed to Wear Show. Her talents often take the form of volunteer activity as when she was wardrobe coordinator for The Queen's Court of The Portland Rose Festival, designing and making eleven ball gowns. For the opening night of Theatre de la Mode, Paula coordinated the dressing of forty-four 28" dolls that served as table decorations and were auctioned to raise funds. Paula and her husband have three children and live in Portland, Oregon.

Mary Margaret is a designer, but don't assume that means just clothing design. Indeed, she lists her occupation as designer of haute couture, of computer software and of financial services. She's a woman of discipline with a universal attitude for perfection and meticulous eye for detail. She lives in Santa Cruz, Calif.

Carolyn Meyerhoffer has a long-standing interest in design. She is the former owner of Atelier, a boutique specializing in custom wearable art, and now she is a bridal consultant for a major fabric store. She makes her home in Woodside, Calif.

Nedra Michalek has relocated often for her husband's career, and that has allowed her varied work experiences in the fashion-sewing arena. She has been a tailor for Brooks Brothers in Tulsa, Okla.; for Frederick & Nelson in Olympia, Wash. (where she won a corporate award for outstanding customer service); a tailor and alterations manager for Nordstrom in Alaska, Washington and Oregon; and a seamstress for Fiandaca, an American couture designer in Boston. Today she is a couture dressmaker in Fresno, Calif., where she lives with her husband and child.

Marcia Noulles has sewn for herself and her two children for as long as she can remember. But just two years ago, at the age of 68, she became a professional dressmaker. She is active in the Tulsa, Okla., chapters of the American Sewing Guild and PACC. Her special expertise is making faux-fur coats, and she loves to travel, cook and play bridge. She also has five grandchildren.

Mary Oliveri is a woman of society who loves beautiful clothes. She gives great detail to wardrobe planning and accessory selection. Working closely with her dressmaker, she chooses beautiful fabrics, offers input about designs and expects the finest results. Her other special interest is gardening. Married with two children, Mary lives in Santa Cruz.

Mary Ann Speith, PhD, is a research geophysicist by profession. But she also enjoys exploring different weaving techniques on 4- and 8-harness looms. Weaving mostly cloth for use in garments, she works with multiple fibers in warps and wefts, including yarns, mohair, and leather and fabric strips. She and her husband have two children and reside in Altadena, Calif.

Jean Sutherland still sews everything on a Singer treadle machine which is the same age as she (70). In fact, she says the secret to her perfect topstitching is this "antique" machine. She has taught adult "homemaking," and is presently staff assistant to the research and development arm of an electric utility. Her home is in Palo Alto, Calif.

Vicki Swalko has a three-fold career as a dressmaker, sewing teacher and assistant to an art-to-wear designer. As a member of PACC, she was a major force on the committee that wrote the technical manual for PACC chapters across the country. She is currently vice chair of finance for the national organization and president of the Oregon chapter. She is also an active volunteer in support of her three children's activities and serves as VP-finance in her husband's business. They make their home in Portland, Oregon.

Joan Venturi has been sewing for 43 years, including the six years she and her husband camped on their property while they built their own house "from scratch." Lack of electricity didn't stop her she used a treadle machine. Today, the native Californian is head of the home decorating department for a major fabric store in San Mateo, Calif. She and her husband of 30 years have two daughters and live in Atherton, California.

Garment Credits

Page 17: Outfit designed and constructed by Barbara Frohman.

Page 18: Ribbon jacket designed and constructed by Barbara Frohman; dress designed and constructed by Roberta Carr.

Page 19: Silk chiffon dress and underslip designed by Roberta Carr and Mary Margaret. Constructed by Mary Margaret. Bubble skirt dress designed and constructed by Karen Dutch.

Page 20: Gold and black gown designed and constructed by Roberta Carr; cranberry silk taffeta and velvet dress designed and constructed by Joy Lempert.

Page 21: (upper left) Jacket designed and constructed by Rhonda Chaney; (upper right) ribbon fabric from a dress designed and constructed by Roberta Carr; (lower left) Alaskine dress designed and constructed by Roberta Carr; (lower right) shawl from the collection of Mary Oliveri designed and constructed by Mary Margaret, tassel designed by Roberta Carr.

Page 22: (upper left) Silk taffeta dress designed and constructed by Joy Lempert, rose designed and constructed by Sherry Merrill; (upper right) velvet coat constructed by Roberta Carr, braid by Christine Tharmstrom; (lower left) dress with sleeves of Dior roses designed and constructed by Barbara Frohman; (lower right) culottes and pantaloons constructed by Roberta Carr.

Page 23: Military dress designed by Roberta Carr and constructed by Patricia Hagen; white wool top and black jacket designed and constructed by Roberta Carr.

Page 24: Both designed and constructed by Roberta Carr.

Page 25: Tunic (Burda pattern 4865) and pants (Burda pattern 6068) constructed by Roberta Carr and Nedra Michalek, pant insert designed by Roberta Carr; wool crepe dress designed by Roberta Carr, constructed by Roberta Carr and Nedra Michalek.

Page 26: Cotton rose dress from the collection of Mary Oliveri designed and sewn by Mary Margaret.

Page 27: Cotton dress at left designed and constructed by Joy Lempert: at right, in the same fabric, a different treatment designed and constructed by Barbara Frohman.

Page 28: Leather trench coat and Cabretta suit are Burda patterns constructed by Joy Lempert.

Page 29: Houndstooth coat and culottes (Burda pattern #5016) constructed by Ronda Chaney.

Page 30: (upper left) silk crepe de chine dress constructed by LuAnne Carson; (upper right) silk & wool suit (a commercial pattern) constructed by Vicki Swalko; (lower left) mohair coat from the collection of Ruth Ann Loney is hand woven, designed and constructed by Mary Ann Speith; (lower right) ostrich feather shawl from the collection of Mary Oliveri is constructed by Mary Margaret.

Page 31: Wool doubleknit dress designed and constructed by Jean Sutherland; unlined coat (Burda pattern #4713) constructed by Joy Lempert.

Page 32: Dress (a Burda pattern) fabric concept and boa designed by Roberta Carr, constructed by Nedra Michalek.

Page 98: "Butterfly" dress (Vogue pattern #2185) constructed by Barbara Frohman.

Page 99: Lycra dress designed and constructed by Barbara Frohman.

Page 100: (upper left) Dinner suit (Burda pattern #5049) constructed by Vicki Swalko: (upper right) cocktail dress (a Burda pattern) constructed by Vicki Swalko during the San Francisco earthquake!; (lower left) summer dress (a commercial pattern) constructed by Nelda Jones; (lower right) winter dress (a commercial pattern) constructed by Vicki Swalko.

Page 101: Both dresses are Burda patterns. The dress at left was constructed by Barbara Frohman and the one at the right by Roberta Carr.

Page 102: Wool plaid pleated skirt designed and constructed by Barbara Frohman; black and white stripe is a copy of ready-to-wear constructed by Jean Sutherland.

Page 103: "Prosperity" dress (a Burda pattern) fabric concept and construction by Mary Ann Speith; belt designed by Carolyn Tanner Designs, Inc., Atlanta, GA.

Page 104: Bomber jacket (a Burda pattern) constructed by Roberta Carr and Nedra Michalek. Top (Stretch & Sew) and pants (Burda) designed and constructed by Roberta Carr. Yellow jacket and blouse designed and constructed by Marcia Noulles.

Page 105: Art jacket (Burda) concept and construction by Barbara Frohman.

Page 106: Bomber jackets from a Burda patterns. Top bomber jacket concept and construction by Marla Kazell; bottom jackets constructed by Joan Venturi.

Page 107: Silk T-shirt and pants constructed by Roberta Carr; blouse and bomber jacket (a Burda pattern) constructed by Cynthia Berry; pink jacket constructed by Roberta Carr and Nedra Michalek.

Page 108: (upper left) Beaded dress (Burda pattern #4728) constructed by Vicki Swalko; (upper right) shawl designed by Roberta Carr and constructed by Nedra Michalek; (lower left) Dior rose constructed by Roberta Carr; (lower right) fabric flower constructed by Marla Kazell.

Page 109: Wool and silk dress (a Vogue pattern) constructed by Roberta Carr.

Page 110: (upper left) scalloped edge dress, (upper right) ribbon sleeves, and (lower right) strapped cap sleeve all designed and constructed by Roberta Carr; (lower left) heart-shaped sleeve designed by Roberta Carr and constructed by Janet Ghilarducci.

Page 111: (upper left) polka dot cuff constructed by Joy Lempert; (upper right) topstitched wool cuff constructed by Roberta Carr (lower right) pieced sleeve constructed by Jean Sutherland; (lower left) piped cuff constructed by Roberta Carr.

Page 112: Circular pocket designed and constructed by Paula Marineau; triangular buttonholes designed and constructed by Marla Kazell; silk chiffon fabric from the collection of Mary Oliveri; navy and silver chiffon brocade constructed by Ruth Ann Loney; black & white cotton blouse designed and constructed by Lenore Hofmann, skirt by Joy Lempert; silver & white brocade jacket constructed by Roberta Carr, matching blouse by Pat Hagen. Buttons from Roberta Carr collection.

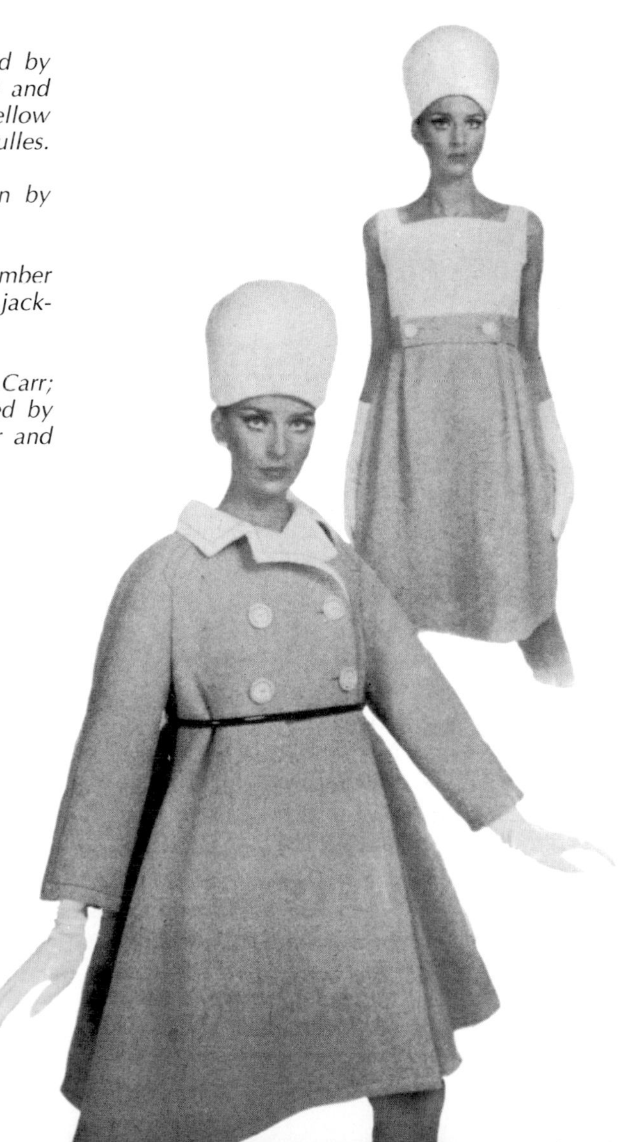

*A glimpse of the past—
a Fabiani design
from 1967.*

A Word About Metric by Pati Palmer, Publisher

I have decided it is high time a sewing book published in the United states incorporate metric. Actually, we should just **be** metric like most of the world. Well, the **Couture** book is our first effort and not an easy one.

Fortunately, I had an Australian, Nicki Young from Melbourne, attend our 4-day Sewing Vacations during the book edit. She offered to do the conversions for us and recommended a simple practical method of **rounding off to the nearest half centimeter.** That sounded sensible.

Then I began the final edit and it bothered me that using this simple method was different than pattern companies' chosen metric equivalent. Since I design patterns and write guidesheets, I decided to use the more accurate 6mm for 1/4″.

Well then, another Australian, Jude Ewen from Perth, came to stay with me and said that visually going from 6mm to 1cm is confusing because at a glance 6 is larger than 1.

Again, major discussions. Our final decision was to use the less simplistic, more accurate rounded-off method used by the pattern companies. Here is their chart:

The conversions from the large chart below appear in parenthesis after the Imperial inches measurements throught the book. Occasionally, we have simplified the rounding if quality would not be affected.

For those of you who want it to be simpler, use Nicki's. The point is, it doesn't matter as long as you are consistent throughout. Here is her chart:

Nicki's Approximate Conversions

1/8″	= .3cm	1 1/2″ =	4cm
1/4″	= .5cm	2″ =	5cm
3/8″	= 1cm	2 1/2″ =	6cm
1/2″	= 1cm	3″ =	8cm
5/8″	= 1.5cm	4″ =	10cm
3/4″	= 2cm	5″ =	13cm
7/8″	= 2cm	6″ =	15cm
1″	= 2.5cm	10″ =	25cm

For purists, and complete accuracy, we have printed a metric ruler on the side of this page.

After this experience, I'd recommend America just go metric—forget conversions!

Pattern Company Conversions

slightly rounded for your convenience

inches	centimeters	inches	centimeters	inches	centimeters
1/8	.3	7	18	29	73.5
1/4	.6	8	20.5	30	76
3/8	1	9	23	31	78.5
1/2	1.3	10	25.5	32	81.5
5/8	1.5	11	28	33	84
3/4	2	12	30.5	34	86.5
7/8	2.2	13	33	35	89
1	2.5	14	35.5	36	91.5
1 1/4	3.2	15	38	37	94
1 1/2	3.8	16	40.5	38	96.5
1 3/4	4.5	17	43	39	99
2	5	18	46	40	102
2 1/2	6.3	19	48.5	41	104
3	7.5	20	51	42	107
3 1/2	9	21	53.5	43	109
4	10	22	56	44	112
4 1/2	11.5	23	58.5	45	115
5	12.5	24	61	46	117
5 1/2	14	25	63.5	47	120
6	15	26	66	48	122
		27	68.5	49	125
		28	71	50	127

Metric conversion chart courtesy of The McCall Pattern Company

Couture Index

Bold numbers indicate photos.

PROJECT: ______________________________ Date: ____________

Design Idea: ______________________________ Date Completed: ____________

______________________________ Pattern Co.: ____________

______________________________ Pattern #: ____________

______________________________ Size: ____________

Sketch of garment
(or snapshot of finished garment)

Fabric Content & Care:

____

____

____

____

fabric swatch(es)

Notions:

____

____

Construction Notes:

____

____

____

From the time you have an inspiration, to the time, sometimes years later, that you go back to make an alteration or need your memory refreshed on fabric care, keeping a record of a project will save headaches. Cover up this paragraph, make a supply of photocopies on cardstock, and get organized!

Videos by Roberta C. Carr

Couture Techniques for Fine Tailoring

Here's what you've been asking for—TAILORING! The decisions , the judgements, the skills, and the criteria for each. Couture techniques for shaping a lapel, collars and pockets are demonstrated in a clear and easy manner. You'll learn the grid method of pad stitching, when and where to use fusible interfacing, as well as the inner shaping created by tailor and shoulder pads. Be inspired. From fabric to a finished jacket or coat—you'll be ready to sew! *120 minutes, $34.95*

Casual Couture

Casual clothes and a sportwear wardrobe can have a couture attitude. It starts with wonderful fabrics combined in unusual ways. Practical details such as pockets can be unique with large zippers inserted in a welt pocket. In this video you'll see piping and binding, ribbing, trim, decorative linings and design ideas to match your casual lifestyle and your couture taste. *60 minutes, $24.95*

Couture Techniques for Fine Sewing

This 90 minute video gives a variety of couture techniques, many that are not available in sewing books. Techniques include bias binding—how to do it, shaping process and a variety of uses. Many tailoring techniques with demonstrations of how to apply for the professional look. Sleeves, the various types, shaping a sleeve cap, a 2-piece sleeve and the application of each technique. Many beautiful examples of fashion ideas. There is also a demonstration of the use of a variety of sewing tools. *90 minutes, $34.95*

Couture Techniques for Sewing Pants

Easy-to-follow methods for perfect pants are demonstrated in this 90 minutes video. Starting with paper pattern preparation, you see the following: fabric preparation, underlining, slash pockets (that don't gap), shrinking and pressing for fit, easy fly front zipper, seam finishes, linings, and how to sew leather pants. Between each section you'll see beautiful pants outfits and fashion ideas. *90 minutes, $34.95*

Couture Techniques: Dressing for Special Occasions

Whatever you're sewing, using couture techniques will make it more wonderful. The emphasis here is on eveningwear with beautiful clothes to inspire you. However, each technique demonstrated can be used throughout your sewing. You'll learn to interface hems, work with beaded fabric, make spectacular flowers with fabric or ribbon, and you'll love the 5-minute dress and other super fashion ideas. *90 minutes, $34.95*

Couture Techniques—Designer Details

The most frequent concept seen in Couture Clothes is that of circles. Whether it is circular ruffles or a circle skirt, the possibilities are limitless. This video covers circles in depth—for necklines, cuffs, or at a hem. You'll be a designer whether you use commercial patterns or draft them yourself. Also demonstrated are French seams, military applique and piping as a real designer touch. Triangle bound buttonholes are easy. As is true with all Roberta Carr's videos—pause and enjoy—design ideas throughout and beautiful clothes. *90 minutes, $34.95*

Basic Burda—Achieving the Perfect Fit

You've been asking for it—here it is—a video describing how to use Burda patterns. European sizing, fitting the patterns, cutting and marking, the perfect pant. Everything you need to use these fabulous patterns. *60 minutes, $24.95*

To order, or for more information, contact:

The Fabric Carr
Box 32120
San Jose, CA 95152
(408) 929-1651

First Class Workshops

Roberta Carr offers a series of 12 workshops yearly, called **The Fabric Carr Sew Week.** Each session covers a separate couture topic, such as art-to-wear, designer details/decorative touches, or pattern drafting/design. Sew Week is held in the cozy environment of Roberta Carr's home in San Jose, California, with fabulous food prepared by her partner, Rena Shaefer. Meals *and* lodging are included. Each session is limited to five participants—which allows for lots of personalized attention and freedom to pursue your own special interests. For information and schedules, call or write:

The Fabric Carr
Box 32120
San Jose, CA 95152
(408) 929-1651

Palmer/Pletsch Workshops are also offered on a variety of topics, including *Pant Fit, Fit, Tailoring, Creative Serging, Wardrobe Planning, Knitting Machines, Ultrasuede,* and a special *Sewing Update* session. Workshops are held at the new Palmer/Pletsch International Training Center near the Portland, Oregon, airport. **Teacher training sessions** are also available on each topic. They include hair styling, make-up and publicity photo session, up to 300 slides and script, camera-ready workbook handouts and publicity flyer, the manual **How to Be A Great Teacher**, and practice teaching sessions. For information and schedules call or write:

Palmer/Pletsch Publishing
P.O. Box 12046
Portland, OR 97212-0046
(503) 294-0696
9-1 pm Pacific Time

Additional Products

These easy-to-use, information-filled sewing how-to books, manuals and videos can be found in local fabric stores or ordered through Palmer/Pletsch Publishing (see address on next page).

BOOKS

☐ **How to be a Great Teacher,** *Marcy Miller, 8½" x 11", 128 pages, $39.95 (or included in the Palmer/Pletsch Teacher Training)* If you want to be in the BUSINESS of teaching sewing, read this book which compiles 20 years of experience of Palmer/Pletsch, plus Miller's innovative ideas. Chapters include: Appearance and Image; Getting Started; The Lesson Plan; Class Formats; Location; Marketing, Promotion & Advertising; Pricing; Teaching Techniques; and Continuing Education—Where to Find It.

☐ **Couture—The Art of Fine Sewing,** *by Roberta C. Carr, 8½" x 11", 208 pgs., softcover, $29.95* How-to's of couture techniques and secrets, brought to life with illustrations and dozens of garments photographed in full color.

☐ **The Serger Idea Book—A Collection of Inspiring Ideas from Palmer/Pletsch,** *8½" x 11", 160 pgs., $18.95* Color photos and how-to's on inspiring and fashionable ideas from the Extraordinary to the Practical.

☐ **Creative Serging for the Home—And Other Quick Decorating Ideas,** *by Lynette Ranney Black and Linda Wisner. 8½" x 11", 160 pgs., $18.95* Color photos and how-to's to help you transform your home into the place you want it to be.

☐ **Sewing With Sergers—The Complete Handbook for Overlock Sewing,** *Revised Edition, by Pati Palmer and Gail Brown, 128 pgs., $8.95* Learn easy threading tips, stitch types, rolled edging and flat-locking on your serger.

☐ **Creative Serging—The Complete Handbook for Decorative Overlock Sewing,** *by Pati Palmer, Gail Brown and Sue Green, 128 pgs. $6.95* In-depth information and creative uses of your serger.

☐ **Creative Serging Illustrated,** *by Pati Palmer, Gail Brown and Sue Green, 160 pgs., $14.95* Same content as Creative Serging PLUS color photography.

☐ **Sew to Success!—How to Make Money in a Home-Based Sewing Business,** *by Kathleen Spike, 128 pgs., $10.95* Learn how to establish your market, set policies and procedures, price your talents and more!

☐ **Mother Pletsch's Painless Sewing,** *Revised Edition, by Pati Palmer and Susan Pletsch, 128 pgs., $6.95* The most uncomplicated sewing book of the century! Filled with sewing tips on how to sew FAST!

☐ **Sewing Ultrasuede® Brand Fabrics—Ultrasuede®, Facile®, Caress™, Ultraleather™,** *by Marta Alto, Pati Palmer and Barbara Weiland. 8½" x 11", 128 pgs., $16.95* Inspiring color photo section, plus the newest techniques to master these luxurious fabrics.

☐ **Sensational Silk—A Handbook for Sewing Silk and Silk-like Fabrics,** *by Gail Brown, 128 pgs., $6.95* Complete guide for sewing with silkies from selection to perfection in sewing.

☐ **Pants For Any Body,** *Revised Edition, by Pati Palmer and Susan Pletsch, 128 pgs., $6.95* Learn to fit pants with clear step-by-step problem and solution illustrations.

☐ **Easy, Easier, Easiest Tailoring,** *Revised Edition, by Pati Palmer and Susan Pletsch, 128 pgs., $6.95* Learn 4 different tailoring methods, easy fit tips, and timesaving machine lining.

☐ **Clothes Sense—Straight Talk About Wardrobe Planning,** *by Barbara Weiland and Leslie Wood, 128 pgs., $6.95* Learn to define your personal style and when to sew or buy.

☐ **Sew a Beautiful Wedding,** *by Gail Brown and Karen Dillon, 128 pgs., $6.95* Bridal how-to's on choosing the most flattering style to sewing with specialty fabrics.

☐ **Decorating with Fabric: An Idea Book,** *by Judy Lindahl, 128 pgs., $6.95* Learn to cover walls, create canopies, valances, pillows, lamp shades, and more!

☐ **The Shade Book,** *Revised Edition, by Judy Lindahl, 152 pgs., $9.95* Learn six major shade types, variations, trimmings, hardware, hemming, care, and upkeep.

☐ **Original Roo (The Purple Kangaroo),** *by Bob Benz, 48 pgs., $5.95* A whimsical children's story about a kangaroo's adventures and how she saves the day with sewing.

A New Collection for Children's Sewing:

☐ **My First Sewing Book,** *by Winky Cherry, 8½" x 8½", 40 pages + kit, $10.95* Yes! Five year olds can learn to sew and love it with author Winky Cherry's book on hand sewing. Written in rhyme, it has large line art in two colors and comes complete with a kit for making two birds. Read the book to 5-7 year old children first, then instantly help them sew up a bird.

☐ **Teaching Children to Sew Manual and Video,** *$39.95* The **Teaching Manual** tells you exactly how to teach young children, including preparing the environment, workshop space, class control, and the importance of incorporating other life skills along with the sewing. In the **Video**, see Winky Cherry teach six 6-8-year olds how to sew in a true-life classroom setting. Watch how she introduces herself and explains the rules and shows them how to sew. Then, see close-ups of a child sewing the project in double-time. This part could be shown to your students. Finally, Winky gives you a tour of a classroom set up in an ideal fashion. She also talks about the tools, patterns and sewing supplies you will need. 1 hour.

☐ **Teacher's Starter Kit.** *$49.95* The refillable kit includes these hard-to-find items—a retail value of $73: 50 wool felt pieces in assorted colors (9 x 12"), 6 colors crochet thread on balls, 2 thread snips, 2 packs needles with large eyes, 2 pin cushions, 12 pre-cut birds, and printed patterns for shapes.

More children's titles are in the development stages. Watch for them!

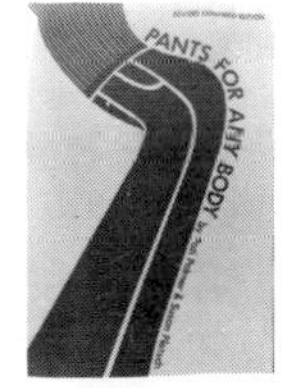

Also available spiralbound—$3.00 additional for large books, $2.00 for small.

VIDEOS

According to Robbie Fanning, author and critic, "The most professional of all the (video) tapes we've seen is Pati Palmer's *Sewing Today the Time Saving Way.* This tape should serve as the standard of excellence in the field." Following that standard, we have produced 6 more videos since Time Saving! *Videos are $29.95 each.*

☐ **Sewing Today the Time Saving Way,** 45 minutes featuring Lynn Raasch & Karen Dillon sharing tips and techniques to make sewing fun, fast and trouble free.

☐ **Sewing to Success,** 45 minutes featuring Kathleen Spike who presents a wealth of information on how to achieve financial freedom working in your home as a professional dressmaker.

☐ **Sewing With Sergers — Basics,** 1hour featuring Marta Alto & Pati Palmer on tensions, stitch types and their uses, serging circles, turning corners, gathering and much more.

☐ **Sewing With Sergers—Advanced,** 1 hour featuring Marta Alto & Pati Palmer on indepth how-to's for rolled edging & flatlocking as well as garment details.

☐ **Creative Serging,** 1 hour featuring Marta Alto & Pati Palmer on how to use decorative threads, yarns and ribbons on your serger. PLUS: fashion shots!

☐ **Creative Serging II,** 1 hour featuring Marta Alto & Pati Palmer showing more creative ideas, including in-depth creative rolled edge.

☐ **Sewing Ultrasuede Brand Fabrics—Ultrasuede, Facile, Caress, Ultraleather,** 1 hour featuring Marta Alto and Pati Palmer with clear, step-by-step sewing demonstrations and fashion show.

☐ **Creative Home Decorating Ideas: Sewing Projects for the Home,** 1hour featuring Lynette Ranney Black showing creative, easy ideas for windows, walls, tables and more. Companion to *Creative Serging fo the Home.*

An additional video from Palmer/Pletsch is available on **Teaching Children to Sew**, as par of a training package described on the previous page. For information about Roberta Carr's videos see page 205.

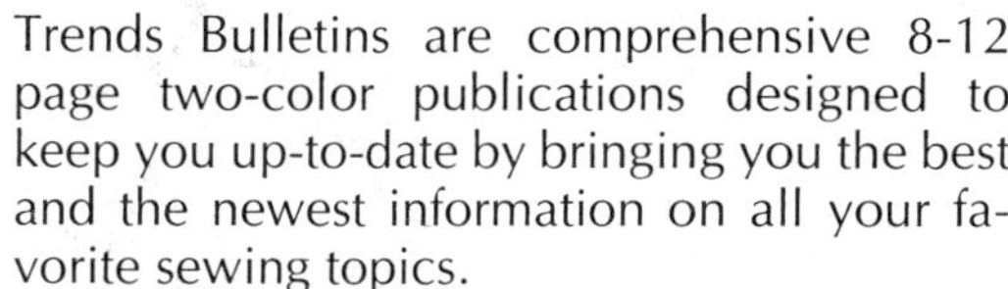

TRENDS BULLETINS

Trends Bulletins are comprehensive 8-12 page two-color publications designed to keep you up-to-date by bringing you the best and the newest information on all your favorite sewing topics.

☐ **The Newest in Sewing Room Design,** by Lynette Ranney Black. This is the handbook for designing a sewing room covering, proper sewing and pressing heights, layout styles, lighting and more! *$3.50*

☐ **The Newest in Ultrasuede Brand Fabrics,** by Marta Alto & Ann Price, gives pattern selection guidance, layout, cutting, and sewing of the new Facile, Caress and Ultraleather. *$3.50*

☐ **Trends in Decorative Threads fo the Serger,** by Ann Price, gives the mos up-to-the-minute information on decorativ threads including how and where to us them. $3.50

☐ **Knitting Machines—An Introduction,** by Terri Burns, presents the basics o machine knitting, including stitch patterns explanation of single and double bed machines, and a step-by-step guide to makin your purchasing decision. *$3.95*

☐ **Interfacings,** *by Ann Price, sorts out a the recent changes, presenting a* clear pictur of the interfacings available today and hov best to make use of them. *$3.95*

Palmer/Pletsch also carries hard-to-find and unique notions including Perfect Sew Wash-Away Fabric Stabilizer, Decor 6 Rayon thread and Henckels scissors. Check your local fabric store or contact Palmer/Pletsch Publishing, P.O. Box 12046, Portland, OR 97212-0046. (503) 274-0687 or 1-800-728-3784.